The Texas Heritage

The Texas Heritage

FOURTH EDITION

Ben Procter &
Archie P. McDonald,
Editors

Harlan Davidson, Inc.
Wheeling, Illinois 60090-6000

Library of Congress Cataloging-in-Publication Data

The Texas heritage / Ben Procter & Archie P. McDonald, editors.—4th ed.
      p. cm.
    Includes bibliographical references (p.) and index.
    0-88295-994-8 (alk. paper)
    1. Texas—History. I. Procter, Ben H. II. McDonald, Archie P.

    F386.5.T48 2003
    976.4—dc21
                                                    2002155119

Cover photograph: The Alamo by Sally C. Hoffman
Cover design: DePinto Graphic Design

List of Contributors

Félix D. Almaráz, Jr., is Professor of History at The University of Texas at San Antonio and a former President of the Texas State Historical Association. He is the author of *Knight without Armor: Carlos Eduardo Castañeda, 1896–1958* and numerous journal essays on the history of the Spanish culture in the Americas.

Alwyn Barr is Professor of History at Texas Tech University, Lubbock. He is a former President of the Texas State Historical Association and the author of *Reconstruction to Reform* and *Black Texans: A History of African Americans in Texas, 1528–1995.*

Mark Daniel Barringer is Assistant Professor of History at Stephen F. Austin State University, Nacogdoches, and Associate Editor of the *East Texas Historical Journal.*

Norman D. Brown is Barbara White Stewart Centennial Professor in Texas History at The University of Texas at Austin. He is the author of *Hood, Bonnet, and Little Brown Jug: Texas Politics, 1921–1928.*

Robert A. Calvert, deceased, was Professor of History at Texas A&M University, where he taught Texas history for more than twenty-five years. He was a former President of the Texas State Historical Association as well as a Fellow and Honorary Life Member of that organization. He was the coauthor of *The History of Texas.*

Michael Collins is Professor of History and Dean of the College of Liberal Arts at Midwestern State University, Wichita Falls. He is the author of *That Damned Cowboy: Theodore Roosevelt and the American West, 1883–1898* and the coeditor of *Profiles in Power: Twentieth-Century Texans in Washington.*

Arnoldo De León holds the C. J. "Red" Davidson Endowed Professorship at Angelo State University, San Angelo, Texas. He has written extensively on Mexican-American history and is coauthor of *The History of Texas,* with Robert A. Calvert.

George N. Green is Professor of History at The University of Texas at Arlington. He is President of the Texas State Historical Association, 2003–2004. He specializes in the history of Texas labor and politics, and he is the author of *The Establishment in Texas.*

Kenneth E. Hendrickson, Jr., is Chair of the Department of History at Midwestern State University, Wichita Falls, and Hardin Distinguished Professor of American History. He is a former President of Phi Alpha Theta, the East Texas Historical Association, and the Texas Oral History Association. His numerous books and essays on Texas history include *The Chief Executives of Texas.* He is coeditor of *Profiles in Power: Twentieth-Century Texans in Washington.*

Linda S. Hudson is Professor of History at East Texas Baptist University, Marshall, and a former President of the East Texas Historical Association. She is the author of *Mistress of Manifest Destiny: A Biography of Jane McManus Storm Cazneau, 1807–1878.*

Archie P. McDonald is Regent's Professor of History at Stephen F. Austin State University, Nacogdoches, a former President of the Texas State Historical Association, and Director of the East Texas Historical Association. He is coeditor of *The Texas Heritage.*

James W. Pohl is Professor of History at Southwest Texas State University, San Marcos, a former Director of the Texas State Historical Association, and the author of monographs and articles on military and sports history.

Ben Procter is Professor Emeritus of History at Texas Christian University, Fort Worth, and a former President of the Texas State Historical Association. He is the author of *Not Without Honor* and other works on Texas history. He is coeditor of *The Texas Heritage.*

Stanley Siegel is Professor Emeritus of History at The University of Houston. He is the author of works dealing with the history of the Republic of Texas.

Donald R. Walker is an Associate Professor of History at Texas Tech University, Lubbock. His publications include several articles and two books, *Penology for Profit: A History of the Texas Prison System, 1867–1912* and *A Texas Frontier Mercantile: The History of Gibbs Brothers and Company, Huntsville, 1841–1940.*

Eddie Weller is Professor of History, Social Sciences Department Chair, and Honors Program Director at San Jacinto College, South. He is the author of *Joe T. Robinson: Always a Loyal Democrat.*

Table of Contents

Introduction

THE FIRST EDITION OF *THE TEXAS HERITAGE* appeared in 1980 under the Forum Press imprint. Over the next few years Texas history received concentrated study, much of it spurred by the statewide extravaganza of the Sesquicentennial in 1986. This 150th anniversary of Texas independence generated a higher level of interest in the history of the state. Among other changes this prompted was the acquisition of *The Texas Heritage* by Harlan Davidson, Inc.

For nearly two decades the contributors have enjoyed a close relationship with publisher Andrew Davidson. He reminds us when time and new directions in Texas history necessitate a revision of the text. Sometimes this has resulted in minor alterations to existing articles as well as wholesale revisions, but through three subsequent editions it also has produced entirely new articles that offer new insight into Texas's old story. This edition includes four such articles prepared by Mark Daniel Barringer, Donald R. Walker, Linda S. Hudson, and Eddie Weller.

"Across the ages men and women have endeavored to discover— or rediscover—their past." Thus began the first edition of this collection of essays, and this fourth edition is testimony to the verity of that statement. Texas itself is an excellent example of change and renewal. All students in grades four and seven in Texas public schools receive instruction in their state's history; unfortunately these experiences are as varied as the enthusiasm of the teachers involved. Often students emerge from these early classes in Texas history with bitter memories of tedious assignments and compulsory study. Usually, then, many Texans do not begin to appreciate their heritage until later in life. Happily, this interest truly develops for some when attending colleges and universities, where Texas history often is one of the most popular course offerings. Others do not develop a similar interest until even later in life, once they finally have the leisure to learn more about Texas. This book is intended for all groups.

What a rich heritage Texans have! Throughout the state are vestiges of an American-Indian culture influenced strongly by that of the Spanish peoples who came to inhabit the land. Upon their arrival, Anglo Americans imposed their own customs and instructions upon the peoples they met in Texas, and for a time they all but eliminated the Spanish/Mexican culture. But life in Texas never stops—especially in light of continuing migration of people from Mexico and the infusion of still new peoples from European and African cultures—so that the heritage of Texas, a state under many flags, is unique among the nation's fifty states.

At times, Texas histories have not reflected this uniqueness, at least not in an interesting manner. Consequently the editors consult with instructors who teach Texas history in universities, colleges, and community colleges to help determine the topics that a vibrant and balanced history of the state should include. The chapters that follow reflect a consensus of these consultations. The editors select only authors who have written Texas history extensively and who have years of experience teaching a course in the subject at their respective institutions.

The Texas Heritage, Fourth Edition, contains eighteen chapters. The first eleven tell the state's story chronologically, from Native-American prehistory to the present. The remaining chapters address specific topics such as Mexican Americans, the civil rights movement, women's history, the cattle frontier, the oil and gas industry, Texas Rangers, and an old favorite, sports in Texas. This edition introduces for the first time a number of maps, an appendix—Texas governors from Spanish administration to the present and U.S. Senators from Texas—and a comprehensive subject index, enhancing the book and facilitating its use.

Our book has many potential users. Some instructors may choose to use *The Texas Heritage* as a reader to enrich all standard survey texts. Others may choose to use it as a core text, its length and affordability leaving room in student itineraries and budgets for an array of supplementary material. Finally, and unlike many other academic books, *The Texas Heritage* can easily be read and enjoyed by anyone wishing to know more about the Lone Star State.

The editors wish to thank Andrew J. Davidson for his suggestions, confidence in our work, and keen editorial eye, each of the contributors for lending their expertise to the project, and, most of all, the many Texans who hold the old, old story dear, yet find it always fresh and challenging.

Ben Procter
Archie P. McDonald

The Texas Heritage

Satanta, or White Bear, one of the most formidable nineteenth-century Texas Indians, commanded the respect of his Kiowa people as well as that of the Texans who feared him. *Courtesy of the East Texas Research Center, Stephen F. Austin State University.*

CHAPTER ONE

American Indians in Texas

Mark Daniel Barringer

THE PREHISTORIC ERA IN TEXAS ENDED IN
November 1528. That month, little more than thirty-six years after
Christopher Columbus landed in the Bahamas and pronounced New
World inhabitants "Indians," storms wrecked a Spanish ship near
present-day Galveston Island. Of the 242 men on board, only a
handful survived. Those hardy souls, famed Spaniard Alvar Núñez
Cabeza de Vaca and the African Estevanico among them, lived for
nearly six years among the Indian people of the Texas coast, probably as slaves. Eluding their captors, four of the castaways crossed
Texas on foot, eventually reaching Culiacán in western Mexico. Accounts of their ordeal, which included descriptions of the indigenous people of Texas, spread throughout New Spain and later Europe. From that time on, the story of the American Indians in Texas
has been tied inextricably to those of the Spanish, French, Mexican, and American people who vied with them for control of the
land.

This frontier odyssey, however, hardly marked the beginning
of Texas history. Indeed, some of the earliest evidence of human
habitation on the North American continent has been unearthed
inside the present-day boundaries of the state. While archaeologists rarely agree on specific time frames, most who have studied
early occupants of the Americas have concluded that migrants from
Asia crossed the Bering Land Bridge, possibly in addition to a number of sea-borne immigrants from across the Pacific, as early as
forty thousand years ago. Known collectively as Paleo Indians, these
first inhabitants moved south and east from Alaska and left evidence of their existence throughout the Americas. In North Texas's
Denton County, near the city of Lewisville, archaeologists have
uncovered artifacts that may be as many twenty-five to thirty-five
thousand years old. This site, part of an ancient cultural complex

known as Llano, produced the oldest evidence of human occupation in the state. Another prehistoric settlement, this one excavated at Yellowhouse Draw, just north of Lubbock, contains artifacts radiocarbon dated at more than ten thousand years of age. And near Plainview, in Hale County, a similar find places inhabitants in the South Plains equally as long. The latter sites both contain evidence of a culture known as Folsom, a successor to the Llano culture named for the small town in New Mexico where the distinctive spear points that distinguished it from earlier cultures were discovered first. Other Llano and Folsom sites lie scattered throughout West Texas, evidence that Paleo Indians made Texas their home for many thousands of years.

Paleo Indians, whether members of the Llano, Folsom, or other cultural groups, shared many characteristics. All of them were nomadic hunters who lived together in small groups and followed the migrations of large game animals. Llano people specialized in hunting a now long-extinct species of elephant that occupied the South Plains, while later Folsom people depended upon a species of giant bison, the extinct ancestors of today's bison, commonly known as buffalo. All Paleo Indians utilized rudimentary stone tools and weapons; the well-known Clovis spear point, fashioned from flint or similar material, has provided tell-tale archaeological evidence of the Llano culture as definitively as the longer, fluted Folsom point distinguished the later inhabitants. Paleo Indians used spears almost exclusively when hunting, although some enhanced those simple weapons with *atlatls* (spear-throwers). Cooperation played a key role in Paleo Indian hunting. Periodically, Folsom people formed larger than usual groups to surround and kill many bison at one time. While Paleo Indians depended on large animals such as bison for many of their survival needs, they regularly pursued smaller game as well. Recently archaeologists have uncovered evidence that Paleo Indians likely spent more time gathering edible berries and plants and digging roots than previously believed, although none of them practiced any form of agriculture.

About 8000 B.C., Paleo Indian culture evolved into a more advanced Archaic culture. Although Archaic Indians initially remained nomadic, evidence has suggested that they consumed a good deal more plant matter than did Paleo people. The Archaic peoples' stone tools, more elaborate and numerous than those of Paleo groups, included such items as mortars and pestles as well as flint-tipped arrows for use in rudimentary bows. While early Archaic people lived in small bands organized around kinship, as had Paleo Indians, subsequent groups grew larger, reflecting Archaic peoples' ability to utilize available resources more efficiently. Perhaps most important, some Archaic Indians eventually adopted agriculture, which transformed Native culture more completely than any other single factor. By the end of the Archaic period, roughly 1000 B.C., indigenous civilizations stood poised on the brink of great change.

Major cultural advances during the Archaic period led to what many scholars call the Golden Age of American prehistory, from 1000 B.C. to about A.D. 1250. Based principally on the successful cultivation of the so-called trinity of Indian food crops—maize (corn), beans, and squash—agriculture allowed some Indian peoples to live together in larger numbers than ever before and to develop complex social and economic structures. Several times over the course of the Golden Age, this new degree of permanence and stability fostered the rise of vast cultural empires in North America. The mound-building Adena and Hopewell cultures, centered in the Ohio River valley as early as 1000 B.C., gave way to the more geographically expansive Mississippian culture about A.D. 700. Its members spread the practice of mound building from the Great Lakes to the Gulf of Mexico. Meanwhile, in what is now the American Southwest, Mogollon, Hohokam, and Anasazi—known collectively as Pueblo peoples—used various forms of irrigation to produce dependable food supplies, which in turn allowed them to establish large population centers and extend their political and cultural influence regionally. All of these Golden Age civilizations reached into the current boundaries of Texas, but none dominated there. Instead, Texas became an interchange of Indian cultures, a land where various groups met, interacted, and negotiated coexistence. Such negotiations began thousands of years ago, when the fringes of each Golden Age culture breached the boundaries of Texas, and continued for centuries as new groups—both indigenous and foreign—arrived to stake their claim.

Throughout the Archaic period and the later Golden Age, Indians living in Texas shared little in the phenomenal cultural advances of the great civilizations of the era. Shortly after the end of the Golden Age (circa A.D. 1250), when the great indigenous empires in North America fractured and Indian people dispersed into tribes, the lifestyles of Texas Indians became differentiated into several recognizable archetypes. Some groups utilized agricultural technology, where the landscape allowed; others lived much as their ancestors had for centuries as nomadic or semi-nomadic hunter-gatherers. Hundreds of different groups probably lived within the boundaries of the state, but cataloguing all indigenous cultures has been an undertaking best left to ethnographers.

W. W. Newcomb, Jr., in his authoritative study *The Indians of Texas: From Prehistoric to Modern Times* (1961), organized early occupants of Texas into four cultural divisions. Newcomb's main groupings—Western Gulf, Pueblo, Southeastern Mound-building (also know as Mississippian), and Transitional—include the majority of indigenous Texans as they existed before a series of cataclysmic invasions by Indians from other parts of North America as well as Europeans, beginning with the arrival in 1528 of Cabeza de Vaca.

Each of the four major groups of Texas Indians was associated with a distinctive physical environment, the cultural characteristics of each group shaped by its responses to and utilization of the landscape. Cultural geography, or the ways in which people live in a given place, is tied closely to physical geography, or the climate, soil composition, topography, vegetation, and other factors that shape a region. Few examples illustrate this relationship better than the history of Texas Indians. The diverse physical geography of the state, ranging from the humid forests of the eastern edge to the resource-rich marshlands along the Gulf Coast, from deserts averaging fewer than ten inches of precipitation per year to the green, limestone-spring lushness of the Hill Country, from dense eastern thickets to the foreboding emptiness of the High Plains, present a wealth of distinctive landscapes. As a result, few places boast such a rich diversity of Indian cultures.

The Coahuiltecans and the Karankawas, both members of the Western Gulf Culture, were among the most primitive of Texas Indians. The Coahuiltecans, who inhabited the arid, rolling plains and brush country of inland South Texas, perhaps lived the most difficult lives of any early inhabitants. Agriculture in such a region was possible only with irrigation, and the Coahuiltecans possessed no such expertise. Nor did they manage to domesticate animals except dogs, which they used as beasts of burden. They hunted the few large game animals of the region—deer, antelope, javelina, and the occasional buffalo—but their diet consisted mainly of plants like cacti, mesquite beans, berries, and nuts, supplemented with small game they could capture such as rabbits, rodents, reptiles, birds, and insects. Digging sticks and bows-and-arrows were their principal tools and weapons. Like all such hunter-gatherers, Coahuiltecans spent so much of their time supplying basic needs that they developed little social, political, or religious organization. The primary social unit was a family typically consisting of a married couple as well as their sons, daughters-in-law, and unmarried daughters. Families rarely exceeded twelve or fifteen persons. Because this system of organization traced kinship through fathers, it is know as patrilineal. During harvest seasons, several families sometimes congregated into bands, but even then the carrying capacity of the land—the number of people who could exist on available resources—limited the maximum number of people composing a band to fifty. The Coahuiltecans' lifestyle never fostered the rise of an elite priestly class. Instead, religion remained personal, animistic, and polytheistic.

Karankawa Indians, the other Western Gulf Culture group in Texas, hunted and gathered closer to the shore, mainly along the Gulf Coast prairies and marshes. Karankawas fashioned small dugout canoes, which they used to roam the coast to hunt many of the same food sources on which the Coahuiltecans depended. They further enjoyed the rich marine life their environment offered, including nutritious fare such as mussels, oysters, turtles, fish, and waterfowl. Although the family functioned as the basic social unit, the Karankawas frequently lived in groups as large as thirty or forty persons. In these small communities, labor was divided by sex; women performed most camp chores while men hunted and fished. Karankawas were the first Texas Indians encountered by Europeans, and early tales of tall, tattooed, cannibalistic warriors with pierced nipples and lower lips have flavored subsequent perceptions of these coastal residents. While no doubt physically striking—evidence has suggested that they were, in fact, tall, and that the men at least decorated their bodies lavishly—and practitioners of ritualistic forms of cannibalism (as were many indigenous peoples), Karankawas likely lived mostly quiet lives of subsistence before European contact.

In West Texas, from present-day El Paso to the Big Bend region of the Rio Grande, lived the mysterious Jumanos, Indians representative of the Pueblo grouping. Scholars still struggle to understand their culture. The term *Jumano* itself, applied by early Spanish chroniclers to all Indians who painted or tattooed their bodies, has contributed to the confusion. Recently it has been used to refer to two distinct groups of Trans-Pecos people. One, an offshoot of the Pueblo culture of New Mexico, utilized rudimentary flood irrigation techniques to support the production of maize, beans, and squash. These people lived semi-sedentary lives in small villages of freestanding adobe houses, quite unlike the multistory cliff dwellings associated with Golden Age New Mexican Pueblos. The

Jumanos' social structure, more complex than that of the Western Gulf peoples, featured chiefs as heads of village. The second group known as Jumanos were nomadic hunters who roamed the Chisos and Davis Mountains and the adjacent plains in search of buffalo and other game. They lived in small bands organized around family units and regularly traveled to the Rio Grande villages to trade. Whatever their relation, if any, both Jumano groups disappeared from Texas sometime in the eighteenth century, victims of European-borne diseases, Spanish slave-raiding expeditions, incursions by Apache bands from the North, and droughts that devastated their farming villages.

The Caddoan, Southeastern mound-building peoples, of East Texas have provided a different example of indigenous life. They altered their lush environment extensively and created some of the most sophisticated societies in Indian Texas. Although known commonly as Caddos, the people who inhabited East Texas were members of a confederacy called Hasinai, itself part of a larger mound-building culture that included groups in Louisiana (Natchitoches) as well as Arkansas and eastern Oklahoma (Cadohadacho). The Caddos achieved a level of cultural development far surpassing that of other Texas Indians. They were skilled agriculturalists who grew two crops of maize per year, in addition to squash, pumpkins, sunflowers, and five or six varieties of beans on lands they cleared of trees and brush with controlled fires. Combined with the abundant plant and animal resources of the Piney Woods—bears, deer, some buffalo on the western edge of their range, and a variety of edible roots, nuts, berries, and seeds—domestic crops supplied the Caddos with sufficient food for them to devote much time to the development of complex social, political, and religious structures.

Due to extensive archaeological work done in the twentieth century, the Caddos are among the best known of indigenous Texans. Caddo history began about A.D. 800, the dawning marked by the rise of large ceremonial centers along the Red River and its tributaries as part of the general growth of the Mississippian culture. This Golden Age occupation of East Texas peaked about A.D. 1200. Civic and religious leaders, called *caciques* (chiefs) by the Spaniards, administered the centers and oversaw the construction of the mounds. The productivity of Caddo agriculture allowed for the formation of specialized political and religious classes. It also enabled the development of extensive trade networks, bringing such exotic goods as Great Lakes copper and Rocky Mountain obsidian to Caddo villages. By the time Spanish explorers arrived in East Texas in 1541, Caddos largely had abandoned the ceremonial centers in favor of smaller villages and scattered farmsteads. Although organized around kinship patterns, even the smaller villages included priests, bureaucrats, and artisans such as potters and weavers. Job specialization was another outgrowth of productive agriculture. The Hasinai confederacy of East Texas included dozens of villages and thousands of people housed in conical, grass-covered dwellings utilized by all Caddoan Indians.

Finally, Transitional cultures that bridged gaps between two distinct ways of life were represented by the Tonkawa people of Central Texas. Living on the Edwards Plateau and in the Brazos River bottoms to the east, the Tonkawas were the southernmost extension of the pre-horse Plains culture. Like the Western Gulf people, they painted and tattooed their bodies and lived without benefit of agriculture. Tonkawas ate buffalo, rabbits, rodents, snakes, fish, and various plant foods. They were a nomadic, clan-based people who—although not located in the heart of buffalo country— relied on buffalo extensively for food and clothing, much like the Plains tribes farther north. Indeed, access to buffalo was the major factor that differentiated Tonkawas from the slightly more primitive Karankawas and Coahuiltecans. After the Spanish introduced horses into the Americas, Tonkawas, like true Plains Indians, changed their lifestyles, becoming more mobile and more dependent on the buffalo for subsistence. By the start of the eighteenth century, other Indians were crowding the Tonkawas out of their traditional range, making it impossible for them to adopt fully the horse-and-buffalo culture so characteristic of nineteenth-century Indian life on the Great Plains.

The adventures of Cabeza de Vaca, Estevanico, and their companions between 1528 and 1536 initiated a long period of European exploration and settlement of Texas. In 1541, Francisco Vásquez de Coronado led a party of nearly four hundred Spaniards and one thousand Mexican Indians across the Texas Panhandle. Searching for legendary cities made of gold, Coronado traversed the lands both north and south of the Canadian River. It was he who named that flat, high plains country *Llano Estacado* (Staked Plains). Coronado encountered few Native people while in Texas, only scattered bands he called Querechos, likely nomadic Apaches. Traveling from Arizona to Kansas, Coronado eventually decided that the cities of gold did not exist and returned to Mexico. About the same time, in 1542, Luis de Moscoso de Alvarado guided a party of Spanish conquistadors into East Texas. These men, survivors of the De Soto expedition—which had begun in Florida and lost its leader after continual conflict with Indians east of the Mississippi River—were desperately seeking a way home. Coming into conflict with the Hasinai Caddos of East Texas, Moscoso and his men fought a running battle all the way to the Trinity River before deciding to retreat to the Mississippi, float downstream to the Gulf of Mexico, and sail for Mexico. Once back in New Spain, both Moscoso and Coronado reported to Spanish authorities that Texas was largely a barren land peopled with hostile Indians—hardly worth the trouble it would take to settle it. Therefore, except for the establishment of isolated missions near present-day Juarez in 1659 and one at Corpus Christi de la Isleta near El Paso in the 1680s, Spanish incursions into Texas halted until French explorer René Robert Cavalier, the Sieur de La Salle, arrived on the Gulf Coast to claim Texas for France in the 1684. Although La Salle's nascent colony foundered in the face of fierce Karankawa resistance, the French claims to Texas had alarmed Spanish officials. Now they moved pointedly to establish more missions among the Hasinai, who by this time had become favorably disposed to contact with Europeans and the trade goods that they could provide. A new Spanish mission went up at San Francisco de los Tejas, in present-day Houston County. And shortly after the turn of the eighteenth century, another half dozen missions stood between the Neches and Red Rivers.

At this point, two factors played pivotal, if not tragic, roles in transforming the lives of Indians in Texas. The first, the spread of Old World diseases, had a devastating impact on Native populations. The second, the introduction of the horse, brought different Indian tribes to prominence, created enormous pressures on certain others, and generally helped fuel a monumental conflict between European and indigenous peoples.

Having lived in relative isolation from the rest of the world for thousands of years, American Indians had little or no natural immunity to European diseases; soon after first contact, epidemics of measles, smallpox, and other illnesses ravaged Native communities. Jumano settlements along the Rio Concho and Rio Grande were hit hard in the years following Spanish settlement at Isleta and Juarez. Combined with Spanish slave-raiding expeditions to the Trans-Pecos to gather laborers for silver mines in northern Mexico, the impact of the illnesses on these indigenous people was fatal. Jumanos were essentially gone from Texas by the beginning of the nineteenth century; the surviving few joined the New Mexico

Pueblos of the upper Rio Grande or were absorbed into Apache bands. Likewise, most Coahuiltecans died quickly after contact with Spanish missionaries and soldiers. The Karankawas managed to survive as an identifiable group into the first years of the nineteenth century. The Hasinai confederacy of East Texas also was debilitated by epidemics brought by Spanish missionaries and French traders who settled among the Caddos early in the eighteenth century. These peaceful, agricultural people also found themselves at the center of dozens of territorial battles during the eighteenth and nineteenth centuries, as Spanish, French, American, and Indian interlopers all attempted to take control of the rich East Texas lands. Up in the Hill Country, Tonkawas were spared the worst effects of the epidemics, but their population also declined.

Meanwhile, the introduction of the horse led to the development of what most consider typical "Texas" Indian culture during the seventeenth and eighteenth centuries. Some Native groups usually thought of as Texan, however, were relative latecomers to the area. The Wichitas, for example, migrated southward from Kansas into North Texas in the face of pressure from the Sioux and the Pawnees; similarly the Kiowas, forced from their home in the Black Hills of Dakota Territory by the westward expansion of the Sioux, arrived in West Texas during the eighteenth century. But of all the immigrant tribes to Texas, the Apaches and Comanches, both of whom typified the success of Plains Indians in adapting their lifestyles into horse cultures, had the greatest impact.

Little is known about the origins of Apaches, who likely arrived on the southern Great Plains circa 1350. Living much like other nomadic Indians in the region, the Apaches traveled in small, family-centered bands in pursuit of buffalo, antelope, javelinas, and other game and planted small gardens to supplement their resources. Apaches acquired horses before 1650, possibly the descendants of animals lost by the Coronado and Moscoso expeditions or, perhaps, by trading with the Rio Grande Pueblo people. In any case, the newly mounted Apaches moved in force into West Texas soon after 1700. Depending increasingly on buffalo for all their needs, the Apaches—usually categorized as Mescalero, Lipan, Chiricahua, White Mountain, or another tribal group, all of whom shared linguistic or other cultural characteristics—took control of much of West Texas.

It was the Comanches, however, who became, in the words of one prominent historian, the "Lords of the South Plains." A Shoshonean people of the Great Basin region of Nevada, Utah, and

Idaho who moved south and acquired horses sometime around the mid-seventeenth century, the Comanches had mastered the horse like no others, before or since. By 1705 they appeared in New Mexico; and by 1750 they had completed their conquest of the South Plains from the Arkansas River to the Rio Grande. As the feared Comanches moved south, they forced most of the Apaches westward into New Mexico and Arizona, with the exception of the Lipan Apaches, who remained in far southwestern Texas. Highly mobile and ruthless as warriors, the Comanches created an effective barrier to Spanish, Mexican, and later American expansion into West Texas for more than a hundred years.

One of the most mythologized groups in Texas history, the Comanches came to control the lands south of the Red River and west of the Cross Timbers to the mountains of New Mexico. Although they had perfected the horse-and-buffalo culture of the Great Plains tribes, from the mid-eighteenth century on, the Comanches were quintessentially Texan Indians, sharing few characteristics with Plains tribes such as the Sioux, Cheyenne, or Arapaho. Never a tribe in any real political sense, Comanches instead traveled in bands rarely numbering more than a few dozen persons, with tribal sub-designations that included groups such as the Quahadis and Penatekas. Armed with short bows and arrows, they lived almost entirely off the southern bison herd: their dwellings buffalo-hide tepees bound with sinews; their few tools fashioned from the bones of buffalo; and their clothing buffalo hides and fur. Their reputation for savagery was unequalled and well-deserved; and few words instilled more terror in early Spanish settlers in Texas than "*los Comanches.*" In many ways a primitive people without the complex social structures of more sedentary agricultural Indians, Comanches nevertheless challenged all who wished to possess Texas west of the Trinity River.

Spanish-Indian relations during the eighteenth century were complex. Missions designed to Christianize and civilize Native people, such as those established on the Rio Grande in the 1580s, in East Texas during the 1680s, and around San Antonio early in the 1700s, both aided and weakened different Indian tribes. The Jumanos who congregated in the West Texas missions were naturally more susceptible to epidemics than those who remained in small, nomadic bands. Yet the missions provided shelter for the sedentary Jumanos in the face of the Apache onslaught. Many Tonkawas and Wichitas also adopted mission life when faced with Apache or Comanche threats after 1760. In East Texas, the Caddos regularly found themselves caught between Spanish missionaries and French traders. Ultimately, most Caddoans preferred access to French trade goods over life among the missionaries. Indeed, many of the East Texas missions had been abandoned before 1750.

Apaches, Kiowas, and Comanches resisted Spanish hegemony most successfully. These nomadic tribes remained uninterested in adopting a sedentary mission existence, preferring instead to raid Spanish settlements for horses and slaves. During the first half of the eighteenth century, Spanish expeditions into *Apachería*, as the land north and west of San Antonio was known, failed to pacify the plains tribes. But by the 1740s many Apaches, especially the Lipans, were having a difficult time defending themselves against Comanche interlopers and, for the first time, seemed interested in an alliance with Spain.

When several Lipan warriors came to San Antonio to request a mission in their lands in 1745, Spain balked. Then, in 1757, Colonel Diego Ortiz Parilla, together with one hundred soldiers and six Franciscan friars, founded the San Sabá Presidio and Mission San Sabá de la Santa Cruz on the San Saba River, in the heart of Apachería. Some Lipans took up residence in the mission complex, but few of them proved able or willing to trade permanently their nomadic lives of hunting and making war for those of sedentary mission farmers. In February 1758 small parties of Comanches, Wichitas, and Tonkawas launched a series of raids on the mission, killing most of the community's livestock. In March, nearly two thousand Indians attacked the mission, killing seventeen mission Apaches and eight Spaniards, including all but one of the priests, before briefly laying siege to the presidio.

The next year, Ortiz Parilla led about six hundred soldiers deeper into Apachería seeking revenge. Upon arriving at a large Wichita village later named Spanish Fort, he and his men encountered nearly six thousand well-armed Wichitas and Comanches entrenched behind a moat and a wooden stockade. The Indians flew a French flag, doubtless an indication of the source of their firearms and ammunition. While horses had come to the Plains Indians from the Spanish to the south, firearms arrived in the region via French Traders. These traders, traveling along the shores of the Great Lakes and their tributaries, had long ago established a relationship with the Wichitas, who in turn traded guns to the Comanches. In a four-hour battle, the Indians routed Parilla's hopelessly outmatched attack force. The Comanches and their temporary allies had proved more than equal to Spanish military might, and these tribes held firmly to their lands on the plains of Texas throughout the Spanish colonial era.

During the early years of the nineteenth century, the Native landscape of Texas changed yet again. Mexico's independence from Spain in 1821 and the formation of a constitutional republic in 1824 accelerated the transformation. Immigration policies of the Mexican government included actively recruiting American citizens to colonize Texas. The arrival of Stephen F. Austin and his settlers to the lands between the Colorado and Brazos Rivers early in the 1820s created immediate conflict between the newcomers and the Karankawas. By 1827, repeated clashes between Anglo settlers and Indians in Austin's colony, as well as in the colonies founded by the *empresarios* Martín DeLeón and Green DeWitt, led the Mexican government to move against the "Cronks," as they were known to Anglo immigrants. After defeating the Indians in several military engagements, Mexican officials in Texas signed a treaty with the remaining bands of Karankawas in 1827, but the peace was illusory. Armed conflict between the Karankawas and settlers continued in the years following Texas Independence from Mexico. In 1840 Republic of Texas President Mirabeau B. Lamar pronounced the Karankawas "too few to be formidable." Those that had survived fled to Tamaulipas, Mexico, before returning to settle into small villages along the Rio Grande late in the 1840s. Conflict between Anglos and Karankawas resumed, however, and a final militia assault on the Indian villages in 1858 completed the extinction of this once imposing tribe. Similarly, the dwindling population of Tonkawas had been expelled from the *empresario* lands late in the 1820s. The remnants of this once large tribe wandered for years before being settled on a reservation along the upper Brazos River in 1854.

Meanwhile, pressures from American settlers in the eastern United States pushed new groups of Indians west into Texas, including Cherokees, Kickapoos, Coushattas, Delawares, and Shawnees, all of whom settled along the Sabine River and in the woodlands of East Texas. At the time, most Anglo settlers in Texas resided too far south and east to clash regularly with the Comanches. One notable exception took place in May 1836, while most Texans were caught up in the excitement of their recent victory over Mexico. A raiding party of Comanches attacked Parker's Fort, in Limestone County, and carried off Mrs. Rachel Plummer and nine-year-old Cynthia Ann Parker, both destined to become famous Indian captives. Soon thereafter, the westward push of American settlers created almost constant tension with the Comanches, the only Indian people left in Texas who posed a serious threat to frontier expansion.

Soon after the formation of the Republic of Texas in 1836, controversy developed over Indian lands and Indian policy. Contradictory ideas about how to treat Indians proved one of the most divisive issues between Sam Houston and Mirabeau B. Lamar, the leading political figures of the Republic. Houston was conciliatory toward Native peoples, while Lamar was unabashedly hostile to most Indians. In the early days of the Republic, relations between Indians and other Texans remained calm. That changed after Lamar succeeded Houston as president. In 1839 Lamar ordered attacks on Comanche bands along the upper Colorado River in an attempt to push the frontier westward. He also reversed Houston's peace policy toward the Cherokees and the other recent Indian immigrants in East Texas—a policy that had proven wise during the fight for independence.

In July, Lamar used a rumored alliance between Mexico and Chief Duwali of the Cherokees (whom the Texans called Chief Bowles) to order the Cherokees and other recent Indian immigrants off the rich agricultural lands of East Texas. When the Indians refused to surrender their lands, Lamar sent five hundred men of the Texas Army commanded by Kelsey H. Douglass to remove them forcibly. On July 15 and 16, at the Battle of the Neches, west of present-day Tyler, the Texans defeated the Cherokees and their Kickapoo allies, killed Duwali, and chased the survivors across the Red River into Indian Territory. Lamar presided over a renewed period of conflict with the Hasinai people as well, which led to their removal to reservations in West Texas and, eventually, to Indian Territory, or Oklahoma.

The violence that marked Lamar's presidency culminated in two famous encounters between Texans and Comanches in 1840. In March, sixty-five Comanche men, women, and children came to San Antonio seeking peace. Most of them were Penateka Comanches whose lands were being threatened both by the Texans and by Cheyennes and Arapahos moving in from farther north. Texas officials demanded that the Penatekas return all their white captives, abandon their Central Texas lands, and promise not to interfere with white settlements. When the Indians showed up to the negotiations in San Antonio with only a few captives, authorities demanded that the Penatekas bring others as well. But the remaining captives were held by other Comanche bands who had little interest in giving them up. Negotiations broke down; the Penatekas and other Comanches became hostages in the Council House, where the talks had been conducted. When they tried to escape, Texas soldiers killed most of the Indians waiting in the courtyard of the Council House. Thirty Penateka warriors died, along with five women and children. Twenty-seven others remained for a short time as hostages while the Texans tried to engineer a trade for other Comanche prisoners, but these Indians soon escaped. The so-called Council House Fight convinced Comanches that Texans could not be trusted, and initiated several months of brutal Penateka raids on Texas settlements.

All summer, Comanche attacks along the Guadalupe River terrorized Texans. The Indians killed settlers, stole horses, and burned homes and fields of crops. Linnville, a small Guadalupe Valley settlement, was destroyed, as were several other small communities. In August, an army of Texas volunteers led by General Felix Huston, accompanied by a small group of Texas Rangers under Ben McCulloch, confronted the Comanches at Plum Creek, near present-day Seguin. In a brief fight the Texas forces defeated the Comanches decisively, thus ending months of terror for Texas families and pushing the Indians westward. From then on, the struggle between Texans and Comanches occurred on the frontier, far from populated areas.

In 1843 Sam Houston, who had reclaimed the presidency of the republic from Lamar, renegotiated peaceful settlements with various tribes. The Treaty of Bird's Fort, concluded in September of that year, ending conflict with the Hasinai Caddos, Delawares, Shawnees, and Wichitas. Trying to replicate this success, Houston appointed several commissioners to negotiate with other tribes, including a few Comanche bands, at Tehuacana Creek in October of 1844. The resulting agreement called for a permanent dividing line between Indian lands and Texas settlements, cessation of hostilities, and exclusive trade agreements between the Republic of Texas and the tribes. The treaty proved ineffective, however, when the boundary separating Texans from Indian hunting lands became little more than an imaginary border. Texas settlers pushed westward relentlessly, the desire for land overwhelming both the legal agreements made with the Indians and the possibility of hostile Natives. For their part, the Indians regularly raided frontier farmsteads and settlements throughout the remaining months before the annexation of Texas by the United States in 1845.

Following annexation, the U.S. government assumed responsibility for Indian policy in Texas—with mixed results. The federally appointed Indian agent in the state, Robert S. Neighbors, proved to be a skilled and efficient advocate for peace, but American settlers pushing into West Texas made further conflict with the nomadic and far-ranging Comanches and Kiowas inevitable. In 1849 the United States Army established a line of forts, stretching northward from the Rio Grande to Fort Worth on the Clear Fork of the Trinity, to protect the western line of settlement from Indian raids. Meanwhile, Texans pressured the government for a permanent agreement with the Indians of the region. In 1854, at the behest of the Texas legislature, two federal Indian reservations were created on state land in West Texas. One, located on the upper Brazos, was for the remnant populations of Delawares, Shawnees, Tonkawas, and Caddos who had been essentially homeless for years. The other, on the Clear Fork, was for the Comanches—that is, for those few bands who agreed to come on to it. That same year, another Indian reservation was created in East Texas for Alabama and Coushatta Indians who had migrated from Alabama and Louisiana and had proven friendly to Texans during the independence battles.

Back in West Texas, despite the best efforts of Neighbors to keep the Indians on the reservations, Comanche raiding parties continually left to hunt or conduct raids on frontier settlements. Other Comanches stayed off the reservation altogether, refusing even to pretend to be interested in peace if it required them to abandon their traditional nomadic lifestyles. But little room remained for these small bands of Natives, and the buffalo upon which they depended were becoming scarce as well. Nevertheless, they refused Texan demands that they move to the reservation, so in 1858 Texas governor Hardin R. Runnels assigned Texas Ranger Captain John S. "Rip" Ford to solve the "Indian problem." Ford, along with fellow Ranger and future governor Lawrence Sullivan "Sul" Ross, pursued bands of Comanches and their allies across the Red River into Indian Territory, where the renegades felt safe. There, however, the Rangers, more mobile, better-armed, and more adept at guerilla tactics than the regular army units stationed in the Texas frontier forts, inflicted irreparable damage on Comanche morale and populations, killing warriors and terrorizing women and children. By this time, pressure from Ford, Ross, and other Texans in no mood to distinguish between peaceful tribes and those resisting reservation life forced the federal government to dissolve the Texas reser-

vations. In 1859, Neighbors quietly escorted the residents of the Brazos River reservation north to new lands in Indian Territory. By the start of the Civil War, the only Indians left in West Texas were those most staunchly resistant to frontier expansion.

After the war, peace seemed possible on the southern plains. In 1867 most of the region's tribes—including many Comanches and Kiowas—signed the Treaty of Medicine Lodge Creek in Kansas. In it, the tribes promised to live on reservations in Indian Territory in return for government rations of food and supplies. But federal officials failed to deliver the full allotment of supplies on a regular basis, if at all. By 1868 small bands of Indians, well mounted and heavily armed, left the reservations to hunt buffalo and raid settlements. Troops stationed at frontier forts found it impossible to catch these fast-moving parties. In November 1868, General of the Army William T. Sherman ordered the commencement of U.S. Cavalry attacks on the Indians' winter camps, comprising women, children, and elderly as well as warriors, hoping to catch them off guard and in a weakened condition. This was a form of "total" war that Sherman and his primary field officer in the West, General Philip Sheridan, had waged during the Civil War. In short, he reasoned that such measures would convince the Indians that they had no choice but to return to the reservation. After Colonel George A. Custer destroyed a Cheyenne and Arapaho camp on the Washita River in Indian Territory, Sheridan rounded up scattered bands of Kiowas and Comanches and took them to the Fort Sill reservation. Again, not all of the promised rations were forthcoming. In 1869, the newly elected President Ulysses S. Grant initiated a "peace policy" toward the Indians, appointing Quakers as Indian Agents on the theory that Quaker pacifism would defuse the tense situation in the West. Iowa farmer Lawrie Tatum, one such Quaker agent, reported to Fort Sill to implement the policy. He soon discovered, however, that the Indians living there would not be deterred from raiding into Texas.

The final chapter in the story of Texas Indians in the nineteenth century played out in the decade following the Civil War. Both Quanah Parker, a Comanche chief, and Satanta, the White Bear of the Kiowas, were pivotal characters. Those Comanches and Kiowas still living on the reservation at Fort Sill were regularly taunted by Parker, the son of Cynthia Ann Parker, a white woman who had been kidnapped by the Indians as a girl in 1836, and the great Comanche war chief Peta Nocona. Parker and his renegade band of Quahadi Comanches frequently visited the reservation and tormented the residents, calling the young men cowards and "squaws" and urging them to join him in resisting the indignities of reservation life. Between 1868 and 1871 Satanta was himself a resident of the Fort Sill reservation, having been taken hostage by Custer and held until many Kiowas agreed to abandon their traditional ways of life.

By 1870, conditions on the reservation had deteriorated, and the simmering distrust that characterized relationships between Indians and government officials erupted into open conflict. With rations short yet again, small bands of Comanche and Kiowa warriors began slipping off the reservation and across the Red River, stealing horses and weapons from Texas ranches and farms, then retreating back to the safety of Fort Sill, onto which troops were forbidden to follow them. Quanah Parker and his Quahadis were among the most recalcitrant of the Indians, but dozens of other bands also wreaked havoc along the Red River frontier.

The situation continued to worsen. In 1871 Satanta, along with fellow Kiowa leader Big Tree and several others, left the reservation for Texas and attacked a wagon train at Salt Creek, near Jacksboro, killing several men. General Sherman, who had come west to observe the situation personally, ordered the Kiowa chiefs arrested. Some escaped; others died trying to do so. Big Tree and Satanta, however, were tried, convicted, and sentenced to hang for the killings at Salt Creek. Retaliatory raids by Kiowas convinced authorities to commute the sentences to life in prison. In 1873 authorities released the two men on their promise to remain on the reservation. Raids into Texas continued, however, and Sherman again ordered the arrest of Satanta. The old Kiowa chieftain was imprisoned in Huntsville, Texas, until 1876, when he took his own life rather than remain incarcerated. For their parts, Big Tree and other Kiowa leaders, along with chiefs of the reservation Comanches, renounced renegade tactics and promised to abide by earlier agreements.

Neither promises nor renunciations stopped the raids. The Oklahoma reservations continued to serve as havens for hostile Comanche and Kiowa raiders, and tensions escalated as buffalo hunters moved onto lands west of the reservations, land previously promised to the Indians as their exclusive hunting grounds. In July 1874, a combined force of seven hundred Quahadi Comanches, Kiowas, Arapahos, and Cheyennes attacked a group of twenty-eight buffalo hunters at the small Texas Panhandle settlement of Adobe Walls. The Indians failed to overrun the hunters, however, and in frustration engaged in a new round of depredations along the frontier from Texas to Kansas. Finally, the continual skirmishes between Indians and American settlers exploded into open warfare—the Red River War. Now Sherman launched a major federal offensive designed to end the "Indian problem" once and for all. He ordered Colonels Nelson A. Miles and Ranald S. MacKenzie to clear the buffalo-hunting lands between the Cimarron and Red Rivers of Indians. Between August and December 1874, Miles forced renegade bands back to their reservations. The most devastating blow to the Indian holdouts came in September, when MacKenzie surprised a large encampment of Comanches, Kiowas, and Cheyennes in Palo Duro Canyon. In the engagement, federal troops killed only three Indians but burned four hundred lodges and captured nearly fifteen hundred Indian ponies, shooting most of the animals to prevent their recapture. Without their horses the Plains Indians were virtually helpless. Throughout the winter of 1874–75, starving Indians straggled into reservation agencies. The last to surrender was none other than Quanah Parker, who led his Quahadis to an Oklahoma agency in April 1875.

By the end of the nineteenth century, Texas was as devoid of Indians as any place in the United States. That does not mean, however, that none remained. Like American Indians throughout the United States between the 1890s and 1960s, Texas Indians—those on the last remaining reservation in Polk County and others—suffered from vacillating government policies, racial discrimination, and economic deprivation while trying to acclimate themselves to mainstream American life. Non-reservation Indians typically lacked even a formal identity, as being an Indian in the eyes of the law required formal recognition of tribal standing by the federal government. Without such recognition, government programs and services including healthcare, education, and economic assistance remained unavailable. The Alabamas and Coushattas themselves lost federal recognition as a tribe in 1954, even though most tribal members lived on the Polk County reservation. Their status was restored, however, and they have recovered and flourished in comparison with many Indians on reservations around the country.

Other Texas Indians have more recently gained federal tribal recognition as well. In 1968, President Lyndon Johnson signed a bill recognizing the Tiguas, descendants of a puebloan people along the Rio Grande. The Tiguas subsequently established a reservation at Ysleta del Sur, near El Paso. In 1983 Texas Kickapoos, whose ancestors had fled to Mexico in the mid-nineteenth century, received federal recognition and founded a reservation on a land grant south of Eagle Pass.

During the last decades of the twentieth century, renewed interest in Native cultures has contributed to the growth of tourism on reservations and new economic opportunities for tribal members. The 2000 U.S. Census reported Texas's Indian population at 118,362, about 0.6 percent of the state total. All three of Texas's federally recognized tribes have experimented with casino gambling to improve economic conditions on their reservations. State authorities, however, disputed Indian gaming rights on the Tigua and the Alabama-Coushatta reservations, and as of 2002 the casinos on both sites had been closed, their future uncertain. Unlike the Alabama-Coushattas and the Tiguas, who remain under partial state authority, the Kickapoos enjoy sovereign nation status, and their Lucky Eagle Casino, which generated more than $4 million annually in profits for the eight hundred tribal members, contributed immensely to the tribal welfare. Despite the ongoing disputes over casino gambling and state jurisdiction over Indian tribes, as the twenty-first century began, Indians in Texas, like Indians elsewhere in the United States, stood on the brink of a cultural and economic rebirth.

Suggested Reading

Calloway, Colin G. *First Peoples: A Documentary Survey of American Indian History.* Boston: Bedford/St. Martins, 1999.

Carter, Cecile Elkins. *Caddo Indians: Where We Come From.* Norman: University of Oklahoma Press, 1995.

Fehrenbach, T. R. *Comanches: The Destruction of a People.* New York: Da Capo Press, 1994.

Foster, Morris W. *Being Comanche: A Social History of an American Indian Community.* Tucson: University of Arizona Press, 1991.

Hooks, Jonathan B. *The Alabama-Coushatta Indians.* College Station: Texas A&M University Press, 1997.

Johnson, Bobby H. *The Coushatta People.* Phoenix: Indian Tribal Series, 1976.

Newcomb, W. W. Jr. *The Indians of Texas: From Prehistoric to Modern Times.* Austin: University of Texas Press, 1961.

Noyes, Stanley. *Los Comanches: The Horse People, 1751–1845.* Albuquerque: University of New Mexico Press, 1993.

Richardson, Rupert N. *The Comanche Barrier to South Plains Settlement.* Glendale, CA: The Arthur H. Clark Company, 1933.

Smith, F. Todd. *The Caddos, the Wichitas, and the United States, 1846–1901.* College Station: Texas A&M University Press, 1996.

Wallace, Ernest, and E. Adamson Hoebel. *The Comanches: Lords of the South Plains.* Norman: University of Oklahoma Press, 1952.

Winfrey, Dorman, and James M. Day, eds. *The Indian Papers of Texas and the Southwest, 1825–1916.* 5 vols. Austin: Texas State Historical Association, 1966.

Illustration by José Cisneros. *From the private collection of Félix and Dolores Almaráz.*

CHAPTER TWO

Spain's Cultural Legacy in Texas

Félix D. Almaráz, Jr.

IN MIDSUMMER OF 1821 MILITARY AND
civilian leaders in San Antonio de Béxar formally inaugurated Mexican independence in Texas, bringing to a close a three-hundred-year history of colonial rule. Although sovereignty passed from Hispanic orientation to Mexican direction in the first quarter of the nineteenth century, the roots of Spain's cultural legacy remained deeply embedded in Texas. Whereas Spanish explorers made initial contact with Texas in the sixteenth century, not until other Europeans later challenged Iberian hegemony in North America did the Spaniards resolve to claim the region in tangible ways. The results of Hispanic colonial efforts contributed significantly to the cultural heritage in Texas.

Following Christopher Columbus's encounter with the New World for the crown of Castile, the successful conquest of Mexico by Hernán Cortés in 1521 motivated contemporary Spaniards to attempt comparable accomplishments in adjacent areas. Near the time of Cortés's adventure with the Aztecs was Alonso Alvarez de Pineda's maritime exploration of the coastal arc of the Gulf of Mexico, part of which included the future province of Texas. Although the reconnaissance did not result in permanent occupation, two subsequent naval expeditions by Diego de Camargo and Francisco de Garay reinforced Spain's claim to the region.

Notwithstanding the physical contacts of the mariners with the Texas coastline, it was Alvar Núñez Cabeza de Vaca and three companions who compelled Hispano officials to take cognizance of the northern lands of New Spain. As a member of the ill-starred expedition of Pánfilo de Narváez into Florida in 1527, Cabeza de Vaca was one of several hundred castaways who survived a tropical hurricane in the Gulf of Mexico. Marooned on a coastal island east of the mouth of the Brazos River, the ravages of winter, illness, and hunger reduced the number of castaways until only four remained to endure several years of captivity by nomadic Texas Natives. Thinking quickly, Cabeza de Vaca posed as a "medicine man." Using his acquired skills of the healing arts, he managed to improve his standing among the Indians and keep his companions (one of whom was Estevanico the Moor) together. In 1536, the Spanish captives escaped and, after surviving many hardships, they meandered across mountains and deserts until they arrived at the remote community of Culiacán, whence Spanish soldiers escorted them the rest of the way to Mexico City. To a newly appointed royal official, Viceroy Antonio de Mendoza, Cabeza de Vaca submitted a report of their odyssey in the wilderness that contained stories of fabled cities of gold in the North. Later published in Spain as *Relación*, his comprehensive report, together with Fray Marcos de Niza's exploratory confirmation of the existence of the Seven Cities of Cíbola, aroused considerable public interest in the mystery of the northern lands.

Francisco Vásquez de Coronado's renowned pageant in the wilderness, from 1540 to 1542, marked the end of a generation of aggressive conquest in North America. His expedition, and that of Hernando de Soto from the southeast, touched the outer margins of Texas. Of the two *entradas*, the one led by Vásquez de Coronado left a more lasting imprint upon the cultural geography of the region. Traveling through the present-day Panhandle in search of a mythical Gran Quivira, a rich Indian province in the high-grass plains, the Spanish explorers encountered the twofold problem of navigating in a vast terrestrial flatness and the gripping isolation of the prairie. They responded to the difficult challenge of finding their way back to field headquarters by marking their route with scrub-brush stakes as directional reference points. In light of the outstanding elevated nature of the terrain, they named the region *El Llano Destacado*. (Later versions of the name appeared without the initial consonant, leaving only the misnomer *Estacado*.) Of more significance in terms of the cultural geography was their discovery of the *barrancas* (ravines) of Palo Duro Canyon, where they celebrated their survival on the plains with a prayerful liturgy and a bountiful meal of roasted wild game. Vásquez de Coronado failed to achieve the material objectives of the magnificent expedition that he led. Still, the documents the chroniclers compiled, particularly the records of Pedro de Castañeda that described the geography of the area and its native inhabitants, constituted an important information source for the succeeding generation of explorers moving into Texas and the Spanish borderlands.

The conclusion of the expeditions by Vásquez de Coronado and Hernando de Soto coincided with the promulgation of the New Laws of 1543, issued as a human-rights edict by the crown to correct abuses perpetrated against the Indian peoples of New Spain. A practical effect of the legislation was a temporary halt to colonial expansion in the direction of Texas. As the sixteenth century passed midpoint, the authority of the crown supplanted the personal leadership of conquistadores, whose daring exploits had formerly given them power. Assuming dominant roles in the emerging frontier society were miners, ranchers, merchants, farmers, missionaries, and soldiers. Gradually, sometimes sporadically because of silver discoveries, these new frontiersmen extended the line of settlement northward to the Rio Grande. By the end of the sixteenth century, Juan de Oñate, leading a major colonizing expedition of four hundred soldiers, missionaries, and settlers, including 270 women and children and more than seven thousand head of livestock, performed the customary act of possession, mandated by Spanish law, at El Paso del Norte as a prerequisite to the permanent occupation of New Mexico. Remarkably, on April 20, 1598, twenty-three years before the Pilgrims landed at Plymouth Rock, these Spanish pioneers celebrated the first recorded Thanksgiving at a remote corner of Texas over which the United States eventually extended its jurisdiction. Farther south, below the Big Bend of the Rio Grande, military and civilian colonists during the last quarter of the sixteenth century secured the province of Nuevo León, with its capital at Monterrey. Later they penetrated the neighboring territory, which the Natives called Coahuila. In these two northern provinces of New Spain, the frontier institutions of the *misión* (mission) and the *presidio* (garrisoned fort) became standardized means of colonial expansion.

In the latter decades of the seventeenth century the union of state and church, as exemplified by the interdependence of missionaries and presidial soldiers on frontier duty, rested on a solid foundation known as the *patronato real* (royal patronage), which had originated in 1508, when Pope Julian II outlined the special relationship of the church of Rome and the crown of Spain in the Iberian Peninsula and in the New World colonies. As the sixteenth century yielded to the seventeenth, the monarchs of Spain interpreted the royal patronage to mean that the crown would oversee and promote the spread of Christianity and, at the same time, assume responsibility for the maintenance of the church. In turn, the church would endorse the aims of the state from the pulpit and permit political intervention in ecclesiastical affairs. Hence, in the conquest, exploration, and colonization of Spanish North America, the patronato real enabled the state to use the colonial clergy in the secular expansion of the Spanish empire.

In the vanguard of New Spain's northern push to the Lower Rio Grande region were Franciscan missionaries. Members of this order, founded in 1210 by Francis of Assisi, drew inspiration from Matthew's biblical allusion (from the beginning) to the "least of the brethren." Calling themselves Friars Minor, the Franciscans voluntarily directed their ministry to the lower classes of society. Allowing the members individual choice of their spiritual vocation, the Franciscans established three orders (priests and lay brothers, nuns, and laity) to foster the memory and ideal of their founder. In the seventeenth century, members of the First Order of Friars Minor (OFM) entered the missionary frontier of northeastern New Spain. Their clothing consisted of bluish gray habits and cowls, tied with a white cord. To remind them of their station in life, the Franciscan community's constitutions prohibited the friars from riding horses (although mules and donkeys were permissible).

To understand the Franciscan missionary effort in Texas one must have some knowledge of the purposes and goals of the Apostolic College of Santa Cruz de Querétaro, and its spin-off institution, Nuestra Señora de Guadalupe de Zacatecas. Founded in 1683 and located in Querétaro, about 150 miles northwest of Mexico City, Santa Cruz de Querétaro was the model for a series of similar colleges for training missionaries for frontier service. Based on strict religious discipline, the curriculum included ethnology, Indian dialects, anthropology, moral theology, mission administration, herbal medicine, rudiments of architecture, and the art of preaching. When the collegians completed training, administrators selected missionaries of strong mind and physical stamina for assignment to distant posts.

As originally conceived in medieval Europe, a "mission" was essentially an activity; it was definitely not a building in a given location. In colonial New Spain, as frontiersmen extended the boundaries of territorial occupation and settlement, missionaries in the field found themselves distantly removed from major cities and towns. By the end of the seventeenth century, as the frontier encompassed vast stretches of terrain, a mission (including a church proper and a complex of ancillary buildings) became a highly visible material presence as well as a spiritual center.

As the eighteenth century unfolded, the Spaniards standardized the method of converting Indians to Christianity and to royal
fidelity. The process began with the founding of a mission for Natives, whom the Spaniards presumed to be deficient in formal religion. Ideally, within twenty years (equivalent to one generation)
the methodology progressed through several stages—congregation,
conversion, doctrinal instruction, and preparish. Advancement to
the final stage signified the passage from transient mission to permanent parish and *pueblo* (town) under the care of the diocesan
clergy. For the Indian converts who witnessed the secularization
of a mission, the designation of parish denoted a change of their
social status from wards of the state to *gente de razón* (rational beings) with law-living habits and civic responsibilities. Although the
ideal tenure of a mission was twenty years, the uncertainties of
frontier experience, as the Texas story demonstrated, frequently
delayed the schedule of secularization.

Closely related to the mission as an institution of frontier control was the presidio. Emanating from Old World origins of the Roman *praesidium*, which denoted a group of soldiers assigned to guard
an exposed line of defense in Iberia, the institution evolved in New
Spain in the sixteenth century from the military necessity of se-
curing the central corridor, a vast, semiarid tableland north of
Mexico City, bounded by the Sierra Madre Oriental and the Sierra
Madre Occidental. At times borrowing defensive measures from
the ingenuity of miners or ranchers who constructed *casafuertes*
(fortified houses), the presidial cavalry units became permanent
garrisons along the *camino real* (royal road) that penetrated the
wilderness. By the seventeenth century both the presidio and the
mission were time-tested institutions with moderate degrees of
success.

For nearly 135 years after the conclusion of Vásquez de
Coronado's expedition, Spanish authorities ignored the province of
Texas. Content merely to claim the region as part of Spain's far-
flung empire, they kept Texas outside the zone of immediate concern, the central corridor, which abounded with mines, ranches,
presidios, towns, and capital cities. In 1675, as frontiersmen pushed
the line of settlement into the interior of Coahuila, presidial soldiers and Franciscan missionaries conducted the first reported expedition into Texas via the eastern corridor adjacent to the Gulf of
Mexico. The Bosque-Lários expedition traveled as far as present-
day Del Rio and Uvalde to determine the advisability of future mis-

sions for the Natives identified as Coahuiltecans. Before constructive measures based on the recommendations of the Bosque-Lários
expedition could be implemented, an unexpected external event
on the Texas coast forced Spanish attention away from the middle
Rio Grande frontier.

In 1685, René Robert Cavalier, the Sieur de La Salle, suddenly
appeared on the Texas coast, where he attempted colonization; this
sent reverberations from Mexico City to the northern province of
Coahuila. Captain Alonso De León, first governor of Coahuila, led
several expeditions in search of French interlopers in order to evict
them from Spanish dominions. At the same time maritime patrols
searched the coastal waters with similar objectives. The significance
of De León's expeditions stemmed not so much from the eventual
discovery of the charred ruins of La Salle's colony but in his introduction of the mission process in the humid forests of East Texas.
In 1690, Governor De León founded Mission San Francisco de los
Tejas, staffed by religious personnel from Santa Cruz de Querétaro.
Throughout the final decade of the seventeenth century, government authorities concentrated on bolstering the missionary frontier of East Texas, hoping to create a bulwark against potential aggression by French intruders in the Mississippi Valley.

To offset foreign encroachment, state officials helped Franciscan
leaders expand their missionary work in the Piney Woods among
Indians of the Hasinai Confederation. Before the decade ended,
however, officials in New Spain became convinced that French aggression had subsided, and the state decreased its level of support
for frontier missions. Without the benefit of public assistance, the
Franciscans evaluated their situation as untenable and terminated
operations in East Texas. The line of the frontier receded to the Rio
Grande.

At the beginning of the eighteenth century, the focal point of
New Spain's interior defense shifted from the humid forests of East
Texas to the semiarid wilderness of Coahuila. Adjacent to the west
bank of the Rio Grande, the Spaniards established a strategic out-
post of empire, consisting of three Franciscan missions and a royal
presidio, which collectively became known as San Juan Bautista.
Using the riverside settlement as an avenue of approach to Texas,
Spanish presidials and missionaries reinstated the colonial effort
in the distant eastern forests during the first fifteen years of the
new century. Among the transported material provisions were sizable herds of livestock (cattle and horses, primarily, but also mules
and donkeys), herds of sheep and goats, farm implements, grain
seeds, military stores, and church supplies, all of which contrib-

uted to the transplanting of a dominant culture among the Native tribal groups. Moreover, the growth and development of San Juan Bautista safeguarded the Rio Grande as a resource center and lifeline to Texas.

In the second decade of the eighteenth century Hispano-Franco rivalry in the Red River Valley renewed tensions, prompting officials in Coahuila and other seats of power in New Spain to expand the colonial enterprise on the northern frontier. Toward this end, Zacatecan missionaries joined their Querétaran brethren in the conversion of the Indians. To reinforce the defense posture in Texas, church and state authorities approved an innovative proposal submitted by a Querétaran friar at the Rio Grande. In 1717, Fray Antonio Olivares convinced viceregal bureaucrats that by suppressing one of the Rio Grande missions it would be possible to transfer its material and human resources to the San Antonio River. Thus, on May 1, 1718, Father Olivares founded Mission San Antonio de Valero, with adequate military protection offered by the subsequent establishment on May 5 of Presidio San Antonio de Béxar. These two institutions, representing the dual relationship of state and church, became the genesis of a modern metropolis and a lasting tribute to the foresight and tenacity of a Franciscan missionary.

As the fledgling colonial settlement along the banks of the San Antonio River struggled for survival in its formative years, Hispano-Franco rivalry on the province's eastern border flared into hostility in 1719. Forced to abandon the missionary field in the East Texas woodlands, the Spanish refugees sought shelter at San Antonio. Inclined to apply strong countermeasures, viceregal authorities in 1720 dispatched the Marqués de Aguayo, of Coahuila, along with impressive reinforcements in material and manpower, to secure the province of Texas for the Spanish empire.

Aguayo's expedition did establish Spain's claim to Texas for the remainder of the colonial period. At the conclusion of his Texas assignment, the Marqués had left in his wake ten missions (including San José y San Miguel de Aguayo in San Antonio, administered by Zacatecan friars), four presidios, numerous soldier-settlers, dedicated missionaries among the Indian cultures, and vast herds of livestock. From these nuclei the Hispanic culture flourished in Texas's pioneer outposts.

Downshifts in international conflict, coupled with retrenchment policies in colonial administration, prompted Spain to mandate major readjustments in Texas during the 1730s. The suppression of Presidio Dolores in East Texas, which had provided some security to Querétaran missions in the area, compelled the Franciscans to seek permission to transfer three of their spiritual centers to the relative safety of the San Antonio River area. Thus, in 1731 the Franciscans relocated Nuestra Señora de la Purísima Concepción de Acuña, San Juan Capistrano (formerly San José de los Nazonis), and San Francisco de la Espada (the latter continuing its tenure as the first mission founded in Texas). The presence of five Franciscan missions, safeguarded by an adjacent presidio, plus the arrival in 1731 of civilian families from the Canary Islands, who established a municipal government, solidified the colonial enterprise along the San Antonio River. Although the human demands upon limited natural resources frequently resulted in complaints filed either with the gubernatorial office or the town council, the positive interdependence of Spanish frontier folk upon one another usually outweighed the negative aspects of community living. In the 1740s minor expansion occurred on the fringes of the province, generally in the form of new mission establishments or transfer of operations to more environmentally suitable sites.

Beginning at midcentury, José de Escandón founded his renowned colonia of Nuevo Santander in the Nueces-Rio Grande basin. Technically, Nuevo Santander was not within the traditional boundaries of Texas. For years frontiersmen recognized the Nueces River as the southwestern line of demarcation for Texas. Other acknowledged boundaries were the Gulf of Mexico in the south; the Sabine River on the east; and a jagged, irregular line sweeping in an arc from the Medina River in the center to the Red River in the north. Notwithstanding the vague definition of the southwestern riverine boundary, the colonial achievements of José de Escandón complemented the Spanish Texas record of progress, especially in the livestock industry.

With the founding of towns and ranches in the lower Rio Grande Valley, a pastoral enterprise thrived in the grassland south of the Nueces. The *ranchos* of the Franciscan missions and of military and civilian colonists in both riverside clusters—San Antonio and its environs and Nuevo Santander—extended in a haphazard checkerboard pattern over the landscape. On such a vast range, fences were impractical, and shared traditional values and ranching techniques inherited from Spain rendered them unnecessary. The *Mesta* system of old Spain, a guild for the protection of the interests of sheep raisers, underwent modification in central Mexico to meet the heavy demands of widespread livestock production. The new rules of the Mesta required Texas *rancheros* to conduct semiannual *rodeos* (roundups) of cattle and horses in order to determine ownership of the animals. Whenever necessary, a *juez de campo* (field judge) representing municipal government adjudicated disputes and recorded marks and brands used by individual ranchers in a public registry. Often the design of the brand reflected the artistic and material values of the owners. Notwithstanding the rigor and danger of ranch work, the Spanish pioneers introduced the technology and vocabulary for the management of cattle on horseback over vast stretches of land. In the nineteenth and twentieth centuries the range industry expanded significantly into northern pastures, but the origins of the modern livestock management business remained in South Texas, where the *vaqueros* (cowboys) left reminders of their work in place-name geography.

Throughout most of the first half of the eighteenth century, intercolonial rivalries in North America continued to affect frontier communities in Spanish Texas. At the conclusion of the French and Indian War (called the Seven Years' War in Europe), peace negotiators in Paris in 1763 redesigned the configuration of North American colonial possessions at midcontinent to reflect the elimination of France as a contender. With the Mississippi as a dividing line, England received all territory east of the river (except New Orleans), and Spain, in compensation for losses elsewhere, acquired title to lands west of the demarcation (including the Crescent City). The acquisition of such extensive territory motivated Spanish officials in Madrid and Mexico City to assign fact-finding survey teams to inspect the condition of towns, presidios, missions, and roads in the northern borderlands of New Spain and to recommend reforms in frontier administration. Accompanied by a small entourage of cartographers, army engineers, scribes, and accountants, between 1767 and 1768 the Marqués de Rubí critically evaluated the zone of defense in Texas from the Nueces to the Sabine and beyond. As a result of Rubí's findings, culminating in the promulgation of the Royal Regulations of 1772, several important changes occurred in Texas.

Since the fear of French aggression on the eastern border was no longer a factor, Spanish authorities reduced the level of military preparedness in the Piney Woods and transferred the provincial capital to San Antonio de Béxar. With the closing of the few Franciscan missions remaining in East Texas, frontier officials adopted Rubí's recommendation for removing Hispanic colonists in the vicinity of the Presidio of Los Adaes and resettling them on vacant lands near Mission San Antonio de Valero. Reacting to the arbitrary relocation, Gil Antonio Ybarbo emerged as the leader of the uprooted families that became known as *Los Adaesanos*. Meanwhile, as settlers from East Texas temporarily resided in San Antonio, the Franciscan friars of Querétaro, after careful deliberation, in 1772 willingly relinquished control of their missions to their coreligionists from Zacatecas and withdrew to new frontiers in Sonora and Arizona, thus creating a shortage in personnel to instruct the Indian converts. The following year, independent of the friars' decisions, Ybarbo initiated a series of petitions to government officials asking permission to lead the settlers back to their former homes in East Texas. Impressed by Ybarbo's persuasive arguments, in 1774 Hispanic executives allowed Los Adaesanos to return northeast as far as Santo Tomás Crossing on the Trinidad River, where they founded the town of Bucareli, named in honor of the incumbent viceroy of New Spain. Five years later, Ybarbo and the settlers abandoned Bucareli and migrated farther into the Piney Woods to reconstruct the community of Nacogdoches.

In the last half of the eighteenth century the success of the livestock industry ironically contributed to the economic decline of the Franciscan missions. Following the implementation of administrative reform, which culminated in the establishment of a new office to oversee New Spain's defense, the Commandancy General of the Interior Provinces, Teodoro de Croix, the first commandant-general of the *Provincias Internas*, conducted an extensive inspection of Spanish outposts. The vast herds of cattle and horses, many of which roamed wild and unbranded (*mesteñas*), attracted Croix's acute attention as potential sources of revenue. The tax that he imposed on mesteñas, requiring all those who wished to hunt, brand, or slaughter the formerly unclaimed animals to purchase a license, struck hard at the economic foundation of the Texas missions, which was one reason the friars of Querétaro volunteered for other assignments in the borderlands, leaving the field entirely to the Franciscans of Zacatecas. Hence, Croix's decree of 1779 forced the Zacatecans, in light of their shrinking assets, to reevaluate their missionary commitment.

In the 1790s a lack of replacement personnel to assign to missionary establishments at various locations pressured the Franciscans in Texas to consider recommendations for secularization. The process by which the missions changed status from transitory spiritual centers to permanent parishes and pueblos began in April 1793, with the inventory of the temporal property and its distribution to the Christianized Natives of San Antonio de Valero. In the summer of 1794 the course of secularization continued at the adjacent riverside missions and extended into the frontier. Three missions near the Gulf Coast—Nuestra Señora del Espíritu Santo, N.S. del Rosario, and N.S. del Refugio—received exemption from the secularization mandate. In the wake of Croix's decree, the Zacatecan Franciscans voluntarily remained in Texas to instruct the new parishioners in civic responsibilities and to operate the coastal missions. In effect, the uninterrupted performance of the friars signified that only partial secularization had been achieved.

At the beginning of the nineteenth century, the province of Texas constituted a neglected frontier that Spain vigorously defended in periods of crisis and ignored during interludes of peace. The three principal centers of population were San Antonio de Béxar (capital of the province), La Bahía del Espíritu Santo, and Nacogdoches. The Louisiana Purchase (1803) precipitated an arms buildup at the Sabine River border in 1805 that Hispanic and American soldiers counterbalanced with a Neutral Ground agreement. Admittedly, the creation of a free zone (over which neither Spain nor the United States exercised jurisdiction) temporarily prevented an outbreak of border warfare, but soon lawless elements took advantage of the unpoliced terrain to infiltrate the Neutral Ground in search of plunder.

In the insurrection against Spanish authority launched by Father Miguel Hidalgo on September 16, 1810, Texas became a battlefield upon which advocates of independence and proponents of royalism collided. In 1811, a revolutionary movement led by Captain Juan Bautista de Las Casas overturned royalist control in Texas. Within a few weeks a counterrevolution rallied around the guidance of Juan Manuel Zambrano, a subdeacon of San Fernando Church. This movement promptly restored Hispanic power and earned for San Antonio de Béxar the civic distinction of *ciudad* (city). In the meantime, a band of Spanish Texans, including the provincial governor, captured Father Hidalgo and his chief lieutenants at the Wells of Baján in Coahuila. Hidalgo's execution momentarily halted the insurrection, but soon other followers assumed the mantle of revolutionary leadership.

During the War of 1812, between the United States and England, American filibusters migrated into the Neutral Ground to join Mexican insurgents in adventurous expeditions against Spanish Texas. Notable among the filibustering groups was the Gutiérrez-Magee expedition, which invaded Texas in 1812. After surviving a winter siege at La Bahía, the filibusters attacked San Antonio in the spring, capturing Governor Manuel de Salcedo and his military staff. The subsequent assassination of the Spaniards promptly aroused military officials in Mexico City to dispatch a sizable punitive expedition to Texas. At the Battle of the Medina River (August 18, 1813), General Joaquín de Arredondo's royalist forces won a decisive victory over the filibusters and reestablished Hispanic authority in Texas for the remaining years of the colonial era.

In the final years of Spanish Texas, frontier officials maintained a holding action against the continual threat of rebellion. In 1821 Governor Antonio Martínez persuaded the town council of San Antonio de Béxar to participate in the inauguration of Mexican independence. Thus, on July 23, civilian and military leaders celebrated the transition of authority from Spanish to Mexican control.

The transfer of allegiance from Spanish to Mexican rule occurred in an orderly manner in Texas. At the outset of Mexican nationhood much of the governmental machinery survived the initial shock. Alterations in the political structure appeared as Mexico experimented with the innovative philosophy of federalism. Culturally, however, the legacy of Spain remained intertwined in the fabric of society. Foremost was the Spanish language, which lingered as the principal medium of oral and written expression for literature, law, and popular communication. Next, through the vehicle of Hispanic evangelization, Christianity continued as a dominant value in the lives of the Mexican people. In Texas and elsewhere, the missions stood as symbols of the commingling of cultures, the fusion of Native American folkways with the Spanish traditions. In other ways, such as in geography and cartography, the Hispanic influence is clear. Every major river in Texas bears a Spanish name, (even in cases where translation into English resulted in new forms, such as the Sabine and the Trinity). Throughout much of Central and South Texas, the landscape absorbed the Hispanic heritage in a multitude of place-name geography. As a cultural extension, Texas architecture has borrowed several characteristics—arches, decorative ironwork, patios, spacious rooms, and tiled floors—from early Spanish designs.

As a fountainhead of culture, Spain bequeathed numerous living traditions to the New World. Along the border and into the hinterland, folklore in the form of *dichos* (witty proverbs) and *cuentos* (stories) penetrated the consciousness of society even to the present time. Likewise, Spanish legal concepts found a receptive environment in Texas. The Catholic sovereigns of Spain, Isabel and Ferdinand, proclaimed that property acquired by a husband and wife in turbulent warfare (in their case the Spanish *guerreros'* last campaign against the Moors) deserved to be enjoyed in the tranquility of the household. This concept constituted the genesis of the homestead tradition in law that Mexico transmitted to Texas and, in turn, the Lone Star Republic conveyed to the states in the Midwest. Spain also codified and exported overseas the concepts of property rights for women, adoption of orphaned children and their designation as rightful heirs, and state ownership of subsoil resources. In the distribution of land grants, Spanish officials frequently described the award in terms of *haciendas* or *leguas* (4,428 acres), *labores* (177 acres), and *varas* (33¹/₃ inches), remnants of which can be found in deed records filed in many county courthouses in Texas.

Among the obvious aspects of a living heritage were folk dances, music, and foodstuffs, but with respect to cuisine, what Texas received actually originated in the northern frontier. Less prominent but still observed in Spanish-dominant communities were the churchyard dramas that Franciscan missionaries introduced to the Indian converts—*Las Posadas* and *Los Pastores*—to celebrate the advent of Christmas and the New Year.

In the wide sweep from Corpus Christi to El Paso, including the interior cultural oases of Austin, San Angelo, and San Antonio, the heritage of Spain (and by extension, Mexico) received recognition in street names, plazas, bridges, roads, and buildings. Not to be overlooked, the Spaniards left an indelible mark of their presence in the environment with the names they ascribed to bushes and brush (*carrizo, cenizo, chaparral,* and *retama*), to cacti (*biznaga, maguey, nopal,* and *tuna*), to flowers (*azulejo, girasol, manzanilla,* and *pita*), and especially to trees (*álamo, huisache, mesquite, nogal, palo blanco, roble,* and *sabino*).

Notwithstanding the significance of the material culture Spain bequeathed to the New World, the descendants of Hispanic pioneers have inherited the responsibility of preserving the living legacy of their heroic ancestors who immigrated to Texas. In the aftermath of the *quinto centenario*, the 1992 observance of Columbus's encounter with the West Indies, the heirs of *Hispanidad* should look for colorful swatches of the Texas saga to weave into the larger American fabric of many peoples, one nation.

Suggested Reading

Almaráz, Jr., Felix D. *Governor Antonio Martínez and Mexican Independence in Texas: An Orderly Transition.* San Antonio: Bexar County Historical Commission, 1997.

——. *Tragic Cavalier: Governor Manuel Salcedo of Texas, 1808–1813.* Revised edition, College Station: Texas A&M University Press, 1991.

——. *The San Antonio Missions and Their System of Land Tenure.* Austin: University of Texas Press, 1989.

——. "Texas Governor Manuel Salcedo and the Court-Martial of Padre Miguel Hidalgo, 1810–1811," in *Southwestern Historical Quarterly* 99 (April 1996), 435–464.

Bolton, Herbert Eugene. *Texas in the Middle Eighteenth Century.* New York: Russell & Russell, Inc., 1962.

Castañeda, Carlos E. *Our Catholic Heritage in Texas, 1519–1936.* 7 vols. Austin: Von Boeckmann-Jones, 1936–1958.

Chipman, Donald E. *Spanish Texas, 1519–1821.* Austin: University of Texas Press, 1992.

——, and Harriet Denise Joseph. *Notable Men and Women of Spanish Texas.* Austin: University of Texas Press, 1999.

Cruz, Gilbert R. *Let There Be Towns: Spanish Municipal Origins in the American Southwest, 1610–1810.* College Station: Texas A&M University Press, 1988.

De la Teja, Jesús F. *San Antonio de Béxar: A Community on New Spain's Northern Frontier.* Albuquerque: University of New Mexico Press, 1995.

Faulk, Odie B. *The Last Years of Spanish Texas, 1778–1821.* The Hague: Mouton & Co., 1964.

Foster, William C. *Spanish Expeditions into Texas, 1689–1768.* Austin: University of Texas Press, 1995.

Jackson, Jack. *Los Mesteños: Spanish Ranching in Texas, 1721–1821.* College Station: Texas A&M University Press, 1986.

——, ed., and William C. Foster, annotator. *Imaginary Kingdom: Texas as Seen by the Rivera and Rubí Expeditions, 1727–1767.* Austin: Texas State Historical Association, 1995.

Leutenegger, Benedict, and Marion A. Habig, editor. *Nothingness Itself: Selected Writings of Ven. Fr. Antonio Margil, 1690–1724.* Chicago: Franciscan Herald Press, 1976.

Simons, Helen, and Cathryn A. Hoyt, eds. *Hispanic Texas: A Historical Guide.* Austin: University of Texas Press, 1992.

Weddle, Robert S. *San Juan Bautista: Gateway to Spanish Texas.* Austin: University of Texas Press, 1968.

——. *Wilderness Manhunt: The Spanish Search for La Salle.* Austin: University of Texas Press, 1973.

Stephen F. Austin. *Courtesy of the Prints and Photographs Collection, The Center for American History, The University of Texas at Austin, #CN 01436.*

CHAPTER THREE

Anglo-American Arrival in Texas

Archie P. McDonald

"WESTWARD I GO FREE!" IN THESE FEELING words, Henry David Thoreau summed up the spirit of nineteenth-century America. This spirit—the restless, ceaseless, unquenchable desire to move west, to find a fresh start, to seize opportunity, to forget mistakes (or have others forget them), to build a nation, to manifest an individual expression or a dream even yet unformed, or just to have something to do—is part of all the reasons for moving west. And each American invader's matrix of reasons was unique. Thoreau, and America, rejected the human and geographic restraints that barred the other points of the compass and looked to the West because there the restraints were at last invisible or imperceptible to expectation's star-filled eyes.

These restraints were real enough, for hostile Indians, dust, aridity, extremes of heat and cold, poisonous snakes and plants, and sheer space were all factors of reality, and even hope and faith were not always sufficient to overcome them. Ignorance of the impediments, as many migrating Americans found out, did not provide a reprieve, but each barrier could be overcome by persistence; so in a cumulative victory, the invader became a new breed, an American. And some Americans became Texans.

The Texan-American or "super-American" experience, as some have called it, is but an extension of the general American frontier process. The process in Texas faced a slightly different factor: the presence of a well-established, if somewhat weak, preexisting society. Here the frontier provided the familiar battle with nature, but it also involved Spanish—and then Mexican—society, a scattered French influence, and the most capable and determined Indians yet encountered. Some Americans were aware of the differences that this circumstance would make, but they did not realize how fiercely the Spaniards and then the Mexicans would contest them for the land. One invader does not easily give way to a successor.

Most Spaniards, it is sometimes said, came to Texas and the rest of the New World pursuing the alliterative formula of "gold, glory, and gospel." For many Americans, this impetus might be better expressed as "running from" or "running to" with the appropriate object being supplied by the individual invader. Herein lay a great difference in the settlement methods of the two cultures.

Except for the Los Adaes settlers in East Texas and Escandon's settlers along the Rio Grande, nearly all Spaniards who had come to Texas since 1528 had done so by accident or fate, in which case they quickly left. Few remained for an entire generation to plant permanent homes or businesses, and none did so because the government wished for them to do so, save the Canary Island settlers at San Antonio. The Spanish society in Texas, as it did everywhere in the colonies, reflected the government's desire to discover even more precious metals, to reduce the Indians to a manageable and tolerable status, and to squeeze some kind of produce from the land. But most of all, the Spanish wanted to prevent other peoples from taking the land from them.

On the other hand, the Americans reflected the diffusions and confusions of their British parenthood. Their plantations appeared helter-skelter and diverse, sometimes reflecting, but just as often differing from, the homeland. Unlike the Spanish orthodoxy in religion and ethnic compulsion, English colonies in America produced seemingly infinite varieties of faiths and government forms. Political, social, and economic institutions developed amid bitter hardships, often without notice or concern, and sometimes in spite of that concern, for a British policy seeking to discourage a particular trade might only encourage it by making that business more profitable in the smuggling trade.

The Anglo-European frontierspeople, who started out on the Atlantic coast, thus metamorphized into Americans. They had faced down challenges to their presence in North America from Indians, the Dutch and the French, and the environment; and, by the beginning of the nineteenth century, they appeared ready to take on the Spaniards, whose claims lay in their westering path. Like a giant arrow pointed southwestward from the Atlantic seaboard, this new breed ricochetted along the Great Lakes, followed the river valleys of the continent's interior, and sped through lands once Indian or French, directly confronting the Spanish holdings north of the Rio Grande.

The Spaniards could, of course, see the trouble coming. Ever since the Frenchman La Salle had threatened their authority in Texas in 1684–85, Spanish jealousy flamed each time a new French or Anglo-American presence appeared.

By all rights, the Spaniards should have enjoyed a period of calm following the conclusion of the Seven Years' War. By the Peace of Paris, 1763, Spain reaped the reward of about half of France's North American holdings for fighting on the winning side in this first truly international conflict. The treaty not only eliminated the French as a Mississippi Valley neighbor, but it also placed the English, who received the remainder of French holdings, as a distant neighbor. The two powers bordered on the Mississippi River, but Anglo settlement still lay mostly east of the Appalachian Mountains, while Spanish settlement, scattered in small clusters in Texas, almost stopped at the Rio Grande, nearly a thousand miles away from the Mississippi River.

This distance should have provided adequate insulation for both nations, but it failed to do so. For one thing, the Anglo-American migration kept moving past the Appalachian line. By 1790, some 277,000 Anglos already had made homes in the regions west of the Mississippi River. And after 1783 they no longer represented the British, a familiar opponent, but thereafter became agents of a new, energetic, aggressive nation; they already had determined on a "Manifest Destiny" for themselves, several generations before the phrase had been coined.

And things changed within Spain as well. In 1800, as a result of the Napoleonic disturbances in Europe, France forced Spain to return its North American holdings lost in 1763. This transfer increased American concern in this theater, because the French were much more threatening to trading interests along the Mississippi. Efforts to purchase the port city of New Orleans to protect American backcountry trade resulted instead in the startling purchase of all of the Louisiana Territory in 1803. This acquisition produced a giant step westward toward the boundary between the United States and the Spanish territory in the Southwest, but seemingly neither power knew exactly just how big a step.

The Jefferson administration preferred to believe that the Louisiana Territory extended south to the Rio Grande, but it probably would have accepted the Brazos River as the borderline and been thankful for it. The Spaniards, of course, thought the line was surely much farther east, holding out for the Arroyo Hondo, a tributary of the Red River. The conflict was not settled until 1819, and in the meanwhile the Americans, sometimes covertly and sometimes openly, encouraged their citizens to penetrate the disputed land. Most required little encouragement—they were ready to move west.

After nearly 250 years of controlling Texas, Spain, particularly through the government of New Spain, should have been holding that territory in a firmer control. It defended Florida, the Gulf coastal rim, and the New Mexican territory adequately. Texas eluded the Spaniards, if not their grasp, because of the French, or the Indians, or perhaps because of their own lack of attention. New Spain's seven-million-person population more than doubled that of the infant United States; its mineral wealth, within the limits of contemporary technology, exceeded that of the Americans; and its society shone with a sophistication that greatly eclipsed that of the cruder Americans. But its strength was more apparent than real. When the house was shaken by turmoil in Spain itself, republicans emerged in New Spain to turn that land into Mexico, and the contagious disease of republicanism swept away all mainland Spanish colonies within twenty-five years.

Under such conditions the Americans helped themselves by occupying Spanish territory at every opportunity. And sometimes the Spanish helped them. For example, in 1776, Don Francisco Bouligny, who commanded upper Louisiana, known as Missouri, proposed the admission of Americans to his territory. This suggestion recognized the fact that ethnic solidarity already had been lost in that area by the presence of so many French people who lived along the Mississippi from St. Louis all the way down to New Orleans. These French had come under Spanish control by the Peace of Paris, but Bouligny knew they would never consider themselves Spanish.

So, he suggested, why not bring Americans into New Spain and turn them into Spanish vassals with the promise of abundant and inexpensive land? They would need only to swear allegiance to the Spanish government and become Roman Catholics. Governor José de Gálvez, Bouligny's superior, agreed even to the point of winking at the religious requirements because of his own affiliation with Freemasonry. Both officials were motivated by their official charge to develop the country economically and to hold the line against the British, and then later against the Americans. They thought that they would be more likely to succeed by encouraging Americans to become Spaniards than by attempting to keep the Anglos out.

The American movement for independence provided a steady stream of takers for this scheme, including those who refused to participate in the Revolutionary War, loyalists, and, finally, the veterans, all of whom were looking for land and a new start. The Spaniards accepted them all, helping some find land in the Amite River area. During the period of the Articles of Confederation in the young United States, Gálvez's successor, Esteban Miró, even authorized Spanish agents to solicit more American settlers.

A significant change in the method of settlement occurred in the 1790s when Colonel William Morgan of New Jersey obtained the first empresarial grant given to an American by the Spanish government. Through this arrangement, Morgan obtained a large block of land in the southeast section of Missouri that he could offer to Americans for settlement under the same conditions of political and religious affiliation as the previous settlers. Morgan received total authority and total responsibility; as far as the Spanish officials were concerned, he would be the only one with whom they dealt. Morgan soon disappointed them by permitting a somewhat more democratic arrangement within his colony: he allowed his colonists to elect him as their representative to the Spanish.

Still, the idea seemed to work. One who observed that it did was Moses Austin, himself a migrant to the upper regions of Missouri. He would later remember Morgan's example when he wanted to settle families in Texas. But such methods, called a "Conspiracy" in American history, failed to hold the land for the Spanish because the United States proved too strong and because the apparently potent Spanish empire collapsed from its own weakness. America's strength lay in its still flexible institutions; Spanish steadfastness, in the same area, resulted in their downfall. So the Americans came. And, after the retrocession of the border area to the French—and, in turn, its sale to the United States—they came uninvited.

The term *filibuster* is often used to identify such men as Philip Nolan, Aaron Burr, Augustus Magee, and James Long, the best known of the type. It refers to a type of adventurer who commandeered land for personal gain, but who seemed also to bear a quasi-governmental status. Inevitably when such men proclaimed their empires, they seemed to help their parent government, and their empires seemed destined to come under the control of the parental government.

The first important filibuster, Philip Nolan, came to Texas several times beginning in the 1790s. He captured horses in the Central Texas plains, then trailed them to the Mississippi River country to sell them to the Americans. Nolan's activities were known to the Spanish authorities, who even tolerated them awhile. But when

Spanish agents reported that Nolan spent too much time with American frontier military commander General James Wilkinson, that he even visited Thomas Jefferson, they became alarmed. So Governor Juan Bautista de Elguezabal ordered Nolan's arrest. Nolan resisted and was killed in a fight. His ears were sent to the governor as proof of his death. The survivors in Nolan's party were taken to the Stone Fort at Nacogdoches for a brief period, then moved to Mexico under guard. They languished in prison for an extended period while their case was ignored, finally learning that their penalty for trespass would be decimation—one in ten would be killed and the remainder would receive ten years imprisonment at hard labor. Only nine had survived. When men threw dice for the lowest number, Ephraim Blackburn lost.

Another filibuster, Peter Ellis Bean, became a true survivor. The revolutionary General José María Morelos was causing the Spanish government much trouble then, so Bean convinced his captors to allow him to fight with them against the revolutionaries. As soon as he was released from prison, Bean defected to Morelos and convinced the general to send him to New Orleans for military supplies. Bean did send the supplies, but he did not return with them. Later, however, he returned to Mexico and became an officer in both the Spanish and Mexican services.

Aaron Burr, United States presidential and New York gubernatorial hopeful and unhappy Vice President under Thomas Jefferson, also added tension to the border area. Following his falling out with Jefferson, Burr spent a great deal of time with Wilkinson. Burr's intentions are difficult to determine because Wilkinson accused Burr of treason in 1805 before his plans really developed. Wilkinson claimed that Burr intended to take part of Louisiana or Mississippi for a personal empire. Burr was known to have enlisted men and stored military supplies for some kind of adventure, but at his trial in 1806 he was acquitted because of the narrow interpretation of what constituted treason by Chief Justice John Marshall. Much later, following the successful Texas revolution from Mexico, Burr claimed that his intentions had been to do something of the kind in Texas during the Spanish regime.

Meanwhile, many law-abiding Americans made their way onto Spanish lands. In 1804 a census indicated that sixty-eight foreigners lived in Nacogdoches. Many of these were Americans who had not bothered to take out Spanish citizenship, although some had done so. James Dill, originally from Pennsylvania, moved there in

1793 to trade with the Indians; later he became *alcalde* (mayor). William Barr and Peter Samuel Davenport also operated a mercantile trade in Nacogdoches. Edward Quick acquired property on the site of present San Augustine in 1801. Other Anglo settlements were located on the Ouachita and Red Rivers.

The Spanish doubted the sincerity of such invaders as William Dunbar and George Hunter, who explored the Arkansas country in 1804–05, and of Dr. Peter Custis, who came to the Red River country with an expedition from Fort Adams early in 1806. When the party attempted to open trade negotiations with the Coushatta Indians, some of the Natives informed Spanish authorities of the Americans' presence. A Spanish patrol under Francisco Viana located the party and chased them from Texas.

Such activities as those of Nolan and Burr caused tensions to rise between the Spanish and American military commanders within the disputed territory, and sometimes the American commander, James Wilkinson, deliberately encouraged such tension. He often has been accused of being a double-agent, a man who lined his own pockets from both sides by alternately creating or calming the international tension. Serving his American bosses, Wilkinson in 1807 dispatched a force under Zebulon Pike to scout the Arkansas River country.

After following the river for several hundred miles, Pike turned southward toward Santa Fe, where he and his troops were captured by Spanish troops. Unlike Nolan's men, Pike's uniformed soldiers could claim that they were lost, so the Spaniards accepted this charitable interpretation and treated Pike's men to a tour of Mexico on their way back to the United States. Pike's report, complete with maps smuggled out in the linings of his coat and in gun barrels, revealed that the Spanish society's glitter really masked weakness, and that their territory could be taken easily. However, his characterization of the Far West as a "great desert" also sapped American interest in taking the land, even holding up its settlement after it became United States territory.

In November 1806, Wilkinson met with Colonel Simon de Herrera, this time both of them on a mission to dampen tensions over the disputed territory. The resulting agreement created a Neutral Ground between the Sabine River and the Arroyo Hondo. Both sides pledged to prevent clashes by not patrolling the area or permitting settlement there. Neither, however, could prevent individuals from moving into the area, where a total lack of military or other law enforcement provided a haven for the lawless of both societies. Each side occasionally sent expeditions into the Neutral Ground on justified policing missions.

Lieutenant Augustus Magee led one such mission. He did his work well and, in the course of his duties, learned much about the territory and the people. Later, when he became disgruntled over his failure to receive promotion to captain, Magee fell in with a Spaniard-turned-Mexican nationalist named José Bernardo Gutiérrez de Lara. Gutiérrez had come to American territory as an agent of the revolutionary Father Hidalgo, who published his *grito* (cry) for Mexican independence in 1810. In San Antonio an insurgent party overthrew the government authorities, but Juan Zambrano led a counterrevolutionary movement there which restored royalist authority and separated Gutiérrez, then in Louisiana, from Hidalgo. In 1811 the priest was captured and later executed at Chihuahua City.

Gutiérrez had come to the United States to find help for Hidalgo among the Americans; now he looked to them to fight for him in an effort to regain his lands and perhaps add to his holdings. Gutiérrez visited with Dr. John Sibley at Natchitoches; eventually he even visited Washington and Philadelphia, seeking to arouse American interest in moving onto Spanish territory. He hoped the immigrant settlers would do the fighting while he reconstructed an independent government in Texas. The U.S. government would not do this for him, of course, but many private citizens showed interest, some even offering him money and supplies, others their services. Gutiérrez returned to New Orleans where he met with William Shaler, a consular officer, who put him in touch with Magee at Natchitoches. Shaler was probably the one who persuaded Magee to join with Gutiérrez in a scheme to invade Texas in June 1812.

The Gutiérrez-Magee partnership was shaky from the first. Magee led the military forces, called the Army of the North, with the rank of colonel; Gutiérrez proposed the civilian government that they hoped to establish. Magee recruited among old Neutral Ground enemies who were willing to participate on promises of a $40 a month salary and large land settlements from the new government. In August the several-hundred-strong army of this pretender republic crossed the Sabine River and easily took Nacogdoches from a small Spanish garrison; the civilians offered no resistance at all. Many joined with Magee; others cooperated, although some later correctly claimed that they had had little choice. After taking Nacogdoches, Magee commanded more than eight hundred men. He posted his green flag on the Stone House and used the building as a headquarters. There, type was set for the first newspaper to be published in Texas, the *Gaceta de Texas*, or *Texas Gazette,* by a Philadelphia printer named A. Mower who accompanied the expedition. The newspaper was little more than a propaganda sheet for the political movement, but it made journalistic history in Texas.

In was also in Nacogdoches that the partners proclaimed Texas free from Spain on April 6, 1813, the first such declaration of independence in Texas. Afterwards, Gutiérrez began asserting more control. He persuaded Magee to move on to La Bahía, or Goliad, where 1,500 Spanish troops were stationed under Jose Antonio Saucedo. Magee flanked the Spanish garrison, captured their position, then released the men. Saucedo and his men moved briefly to San Antonio, then returned with reinforcements to besiege the Army of the North, which had stalled on the rich supplies of the Spanish. Magee's mental and physical condition may have deteriorated during this delay—Gutiérrez later claimed that Magee committed suicide—and he died there. Samuel Kemper, a competent officer, assumed command. When the Spaniards attempted to attack shortly after Magee's death, Kemper's command defeated them. He then pursued the retreating Spanish soldiers to San Antonio, where he destroyed the last stronghold of royal forces in Texas.

Gutiérrez demanded full control of the venture in San Antonio. His new republic, it seemed, would have little place for Kemper and the few honorable men in the command who had come for free land. So Kemper resigned and returned to Louisiana, only to be replaced briefly by Reuben Ross. When a new Spanish force under Ignacia Elizondo arrived, Ross advised against a fight, so Gutiérrez replaced him with Henry Perry, a daredevil adventurer who would fight anything. Perry defeated Elizondo in an action known as the Battle of the Alazan. Then José Alvarez de Toledo arrived from Natchitoches after conferring with Shaler, and intimidated Gutiérrez into surrendering the civilian authority in the, as yet, unestablished republic. Now commanded by Perry and Toledo, a true cutthroat element reigned in a venture that had begun with higher, if no more legal, motives.

Gutiérrez wisely left before a more potent Spanish force under General José Joaquín de Arredondo arrived. Arredondo drew Perry into battle at the Medina River in the summer of 1813, where he killed nearly all of the Americans who remained to fight. Many fled back to East Texas and Louisiana. Arredondo moved on to San

Antonio, where he arrested and killed everyone who had cooperated with the Americans, and he threatened the same for those at La Bahía and Nacogdoches. The latter community's citizens, Americans as well as Spaniards, vanished. One of Arredondo's cadet officers, Antonio López de Santa Anna, learned from his Spanish general a lesson that he later attempted to employ in 1836 during the Texas Revolution: the best way to end trouble with trespassers was to kill them.

The Gutiérrez-Magee expedition and its dreams of empire in an independent Texas proved a failure. But it encouraged the hopes of many who still longed for an independent Mexico and an independent Texas, and many of its participants returned later to make both a reality.

Individual Americans continued to make their way to Spanish lands in Texas following the failure of Magee, but the next major filibustering expedition came after the United States had renounced all claims to the lands beyond the Sabine River by the Adams-Onís Treaty of 1819. These negotiations resulted from an invasion of Spanish Florida in 1817 by Tennessee militia commander Andrew Jackson, who was pursuing renegade Indians. For years, Florida's Indians had raided American settlements, then hastily retreated to the protection of the Spanish territory. Jackson ignored the boundary and pursued these Indians until he fought them. And, without civilian trial, he also hanged two British subjects whom he accused of stirring up the Indians.

An international incident resulted which placed both the Spanish and the British government in opposition to the United States. Secretary of State John Quincy Adams advocated, and President James Monroe accepted, a tough policy toward these nations: they told the British to keep their agents out of Florida, and the Spaniards to police their Indians or the United States would do whatever was necessary to preserve its own interests. The British chose to drop the matter to protect their growing friendship with the United States in other areas, and the Spanish reluctantly but finally admitted that they could not control Florida.

In negotiations between Adams and Spanish minister Luis de Onís, the two nations agreed to the cession of Florida to the United States in return for $7 million, giving the latter country not only the peninsula itself but, for the first time, control of the Gulf Coast all the way to Spanish territory in Texas. Also the Adams-Onís Treaty attempted to settle the boundary between the two nations in Texas "permanently." The boundary line ran along the west bank of the Sabine River to the 32nd parallel, then directly north to the Red River and along its bank to the 100th meridian, then up that line to the Arkansas River headwaters, then due north to the 42nd parallel, and along that line to the Pacific Ocean. In the northern regions this agreement simply ignored preexisting British, American, and Russian claims. And in the lower regions, the treaty angered southern Americans who coveted the lands beyond the Sabine River as expansion territory for their agricultural economy and lifestyle, including African slavery.

Protest meetings raged through the South, but especially along the Mississippi line. At Natchez, Dr. James Long received the endorsement of one such meeting to lead an expedition into Texas to declare it independent and therefore available for southern American cultural and political expansion, despite the treaty with Spain. Offers to help Long came in, including one from Gutiérrez.

Dr. Long led an expedition of about 120 men across the Sabine River to Nacogdoches in June 1819. Within a short time, he occupied the Stone Fort, proclaimed Texas independent, and recruited another two hundred men. Long then traveled to Galveston to confer with the pirate Jean Lafitte, whom he hoped to enlist in the scheme to make Texas free. Lafitte already operated as freely as he wanted in the Gulf waters on a live-and-let-live basis with the Spanish government, so he refused. Without Lafitte's help, and lacking sufficient supplies, Long returned via Nacogdoches to Mississippi, then moved on to New Orleans, where he conferred with Mexican liberals seeking someone to fight the Spaniards for them. One José Félix Trespalacios helped Long plan an invasion of Texas at Bolivar, a coastal point just to the east of Galveston, which would guarantee a supply line.

Long's second expedition arrived at Point Bolivar in April 1820, with a large force and his young bride, Jane, and her servant girl, Kian. Long and Trespalacios soon parted, and Long took a small force to capture La Bahía. He succeeded at first, but soon a larger Spanish army arrived and captured Long, who was then taken to Mexico and executed. Jane Long decided to remain at Bolivar after the remaining "Patriot" army, as Long's men were called, returned to New Orleans. She and her slave wintered there, surviving on fish and what other seafood they could obtain, and using a cannon to keep curious Karankawa Indians from coming near them. When Jane Long learned of her husband's fate, she rode horseback to

Mexico in an effort to have his murderers punished. Unsuccessful in the attempt, she returned to Mississippi but eventually resettled in Texas. Jane Long became known as the Mother of Texas.

The pirate Lafitte, though not a true filibuster, was but one of several others who came to Texas in the twilight of Spanish control. For example, Louis-Michel Aury, a French naval officer and later privateer, prowled the Gulf until he and New Orleans associates established a rebel port at Galveston. José Manuel de Herrera, a Mexican rebel, had also settled at Galveston and proclaimed the island an independent republic in 1816. Francisco Xavier Mina also operated in and out of Texas during these years until captured and executed in 1817.

As long as they remained in authority, Spanish officials continued to repulse such invaders, but their day drew quickly to a close after the disposal of Long's last expedition. Spain's hold over all of Mexico was weakened by persistent nationalist movements—such as that of the padre Hidalgo—and because of the Napoleonic disturbances in Europe, especially those within Spain itself after Napoleon forced his brother upon the Spanish as their king. The Spanish-Mexican clergy, large landowners, and other vested interests feared the reforms and changes that the new order might require. The revolution resurfaced and smoldered under the leadership of José María Morelos and Vicente Guerrero.

By the end of the Napoleonic Era in Europe, it appeared that the restored Spanish monarchy under King Ferdinand VII might regain sufficient strength to hold onto New Spain. Viceroy Juan Ruíz Apodaca in 1819 even reported that no additional troops would be required to do the job. But further liberal changes that Ferdinand accepted under a liberal constitution alarmed conservatives in New Spain, who then determined that only independence could sustain their way of life and secure their hold on the church and land ownership.

So upper classes joined in support of a new leader, Augustín de Iturbide. In concert with the near-liberal Guerrero, Iturbide issued the Plan of Iguala in February 1821, proclaiming Mexico free from Spain. The new leaders planned for a Catholic nation, racial equality, and secured land titles. In August the last viceroy, Juan O'Donoju, recognized the independence of Mexico with Iturbide as chief executive. Thereafter, the administration of Texas affairs, although remaining somewhat confused, would come exclusively from Mexico. Soon thereafter a new stream of American invaders arrived to make those affairs more troublesome for the Mexican nation than they ever had been for the Spanish.

Land hunger, not easily satisfied at U.S. prices and terms, drew hundreds of settlers to Texas when the lands were opened to settlement by the new Mexican government under a revitalized empresarial system. Moses Austin and his son, Stephen Fuller Austin, led the way. Although settlements on the Red River at Pecan Point and Jonesborough preceded the Austins' activity, they were then regarded as a part of the Arkansas Territory.

Moses Austin followed the line of the frontier all his life. Born in Connecticut, he joined his brother in business in Philadelphia and later in Virginia, operating mercantile establishments and then engaging in lead mining. Austin moved to the Missouri territory in 1798 while the Spaniards still controlled it. He established the village of Potosi and again followed the mining and mercantile trades. His son, Stephen, born in Virginia and educated in Kentucky, worked with his father in the Missouri enterprises. He also served in the militia and the territory legislature before being appointed a territorial judge.

The Panic of 1819 eliminated the Austins' financial resources, especially following the failure of the Bank of St. Louis, in which they had invested heavily to bolster the sagging local economy. Stephen Austin then left for New Orleans to study law, perhaps hoping to make his way in that profession; but Moses Austin remembered the experience of William Morgan and looked to Spanish Texas for the solution to his financial problems. He traveled to San Antonio to request permission from Governor Antonio María Martínez, the last Spanish governor of Texas, to establish a colony of three hundred families in Texas. Martínez turned Austin down until an old friend from Missouri, the Barón de Bastrop, vouched for Austin's good record and former Spanish citizenship. Martínez then agreed to the venture, which also received endorsement by a board of supervisors of the provincial deputation at Monterrey. Moses Austin died soon after returning to Louisiana, but the project was assumed, as a death-bed promise, by Stephen Austin. He had taken little interest in his father's scheme until then; afterward, it became an obsession.

Austin visited San Antonio in the summer of 1821 to confirm the inheritance of his father's commission. Martínez recognized Austin's rights and told him to explore the country and to locate his colony. News of the venture reached Natchitoches before Austin returned there, and he found more than one hundred letters from interested parties. Austin's New Orleans law teacher, partner, and friend, Joseph Hawkins, helped him purchase the schooner *Lively* to ferry supplies. Austin dispatched it with eighteen settlers for a rendezvous at the mouth of the Colorado River.

Austin returned to Texas by an overland route to find the first settler, Andrew Robinson, already at the Brazos River. Shortly afterward, Robert and Joseph Kuykendahl, Daniel Gilliland, Thomas Boatright, and Jared E. Groce, the latter with a train of fifty wagons and ninety slaves, arrived. They established plantations and started settlements. Austin went to the mouth of the Colorado to meet the *Lively*, but it was not there; he moved to the Brazos and learned that the vessel had arrived sometime earlier and, despairing of meeting Austin, had returned to New Orleans. This incident only began his troubles.

Visiting San Antonio, Austin learned from Martínez that the Mexican government would not recognize his grant because it had been approved by the Spanish. He traveled to Monterrey and eventually to Mexico City to see what he could do about the situation, leaving Josiah Bell in charge of the colony. Austin spent more than a year unraveling the complexities of Mexican politics. Iturbide assumed power by the action of a close-knit junta. He dismissed the Congress, but not before it had passed the General Colonization Law of January 4, 1823, which authorized Austin's colony. Iturbide agreed to Austin's scheme as well. But in March, Iturbide was forced to abdicate. A new Congress approved Austin's claim again, then voided the Colonization Law, making his the only land grant issued under its provisions.

Austin was made totally responsible to the government for his colonists: they had to be or become Roman Catholic, be hard working, and be able to present certificates of good conduct from their former places of residence. Finally, in August 1823, with the Barón de Bastrop as the government's land agent, Austin began to issue land titles to his settlers. By the summer of 1824, he had issued 272 titles, with twenty-five remaining titles of his original grant being issued in the late 1820s, making a total of 297 grants. This group of grantees is known as "The Old Three Hundred."

Austin selected the site of his colony well. The Brazos and Colorado Rivers, the two most navigable streams in Texas, cut his lands into three approximately equal segments. In addition, his land was freer from timber than the area to the east, thus requiring less labor for clearing; yet it received more rainfall than the land to the west. The Indians in his area, mostly Karankawas, occasionally posed problems, but they were easier to deal with than were the Comanches or the Apaches. By law, each colonial family received one *labor*, 177 acres, of land if they farmed, and one *sitio*, a square league or 4,428 acres, if they were ranchers. On such terms, most testified that they were ranchers. Few ever paid Austin his agent's fee of twelve-and-a-half cents per acre; some could not because cash remained a scarce commodity in colonial Texas, and some refused to do so because they figured that the nearly forty thousand acres he had received from the government made him rich enough. In cash, however, Austin remained poor for the remainder of his life.

The Mexican Congress enacted another general colonization law in 1824. This legislation turned over to the state governments the administration of all land alienation to settlers and colonization policies. It provided, however, that the state laws conform to general constitutional provisions, that foreigners should not settle near the coast or international boundaries, and that all who received land become Mexican citizens. Another act passed on May 7, 1824, combined Texas and Coahuila as one state until Texas's population grew to sufficient size to justify reseparation.

Thus the state legislature, meeting at Saltillo, had charge of land affairs in Texas. The Coahuila-Texas Colonization Law, passed in 1825, broadened the empresarial system. Land could be obtained by individuals, but if settlers worked through an empresario, they also received that officer's assistance in settlement and representation. An empresario's contract lasted six years. He received compensation by means of a fee paid by the settler, and by personal land grants from the government. Between 1825 and the revocation of this system by the Law of April 6, 1830, the Mexican government issued some twenty-five empresarial contracts. Under the program, Austin obtained a contract to settle five hundred additional families on his original lands, another in 1827 to settle one hundred families on the Colorado River immediately to the north of his original grant, and yet another grant in 1828 to settle three hundred families in an area between the Lavaca and San Jacinto Rivers. On his four grants Stephen F. Austin settled 1,200 families, with a population exceeding four thousand persons.

In 1825 Green DeWitt received a grant to settle 400 families between the Lavaca and Guadalupe Rivers, and Gonzales became his principal town. Toward the coast from De Witt, Martín de León obtained a grant, and, because of Indian problems in 1826, many of DeWitt's people moved downriver to de León's lands. Arthur Wavell received a grant along the Red River in the northeast corner of Texas, although his associate Ben Milam actually located the settlers there. In South Texas, grants were obtained by James Power and James Hewetson and by John McMullen and James McGloin, who attempted to attract direct European immigration. But they settled few families.

The most troublesome contract was East Texas. Haden Edwards obtained lands with Nacogdoches as the capital, but because his grant contained settlers with grants dating from early Spanish occupation, he experienced difficulty in proving out claims. This difficulty ultimately resulted in a brief and unsuccessful declaration of independence for a Fredonia Republic in 1826, but even Austin helped Mexican authorities put down the Edwards revolt. Edwards's lands were given in three grants to David G. Burnet, Joseph Vehlein, and Lorenzo de Zavala, who turned their lands over to a land speculation company called the Galveston Bay and Texas Land Company to solicit settlers in the United States. Finally, Drs. John Charles Beales and James Grant, physicians, obtained a contract to settle European immigrants between the Rio Grande and the Nueces, but they had little success.

The scramble for land grants also brewed conflict amongst the Anglos themselves. In the middle 1820s, Sterling Robertson had obtained a grant just north of Austin's original grant. Robertson really represented the Texas Association of Nashville, a land speculation company. Before the Law of April 6, 1830, became effective, Samuel May Williams, in partnership with Austin, sought to obtain Robertson's land to settle some eight hundred families. The Mexican governor first forfeited Robertson's colony and gave it to Austin and Williams, but then reversed the ruling and returned it to Robertson when he showed that he had already settled more than one hundred families on the land. Austin and Williams later regained the land after 1830. Bitterness between the families lingered for decades.

Life in this colonial period can be characterized as isolated. Austin's capital, San Felipe de Austin, remained the largest Anglo center. It was second only to San Antonio in total population, but it could not be called a real town. A few log structures in the middle of nowhere is a better description. Yet settlers came to his colony, attracted by the inexpensive land. Some walked; some rode horseback with their goods in saddlebags; some trudged beside wagons laden with supplies, seeds, and hopes for the future; others came by coastal vessels from New Orleans.

Jared Groce's wealth was unique among Austin's colonists. Most were poor, even by American standards of the time; they lacked capital, cash, and credit. Shelter posed a constant problem. The one-room cabin was the dominant domicile, made of logs if available, and of anything else that was handy such as rocks, stones, or mud-on-stakes. As settlers became established, some built second adjacent cabins bonded by a common roof, in the southern American style. Such breezeway or dog-run houses became common in Texas. Furnishings could only be called functional; homemade was in vogue. Cross sections of logs became chairs and tables; bamboo reeds were fashioned as forks or carved into spoons; corn husks or moss became mattress ticking; gourds were used as dippers or drinking vessels.

Food in its natural state abounded in small and large animals and fishes; in season, berries or nuts were plentiful; bees provided honey as a food sweetener and preservative; and in time, field crops and gardens supplemented such fare from the hunting and the fishing trips. In addition, hunting also provided clothing, for deer hides could be fashioned by frontierspeople into very suitable wearing apparel that lasted almost indefinitely.

Because of their restricted, monotonous diets, early Texans did not enjoy good health. Even when their communities became established, their food remained seasonal: that is, they had plenty of green foods in the warmer months and few in the winter because their only method of preserving meats or vegetables was by drying or salting. If a physician's care was available for injury or sickness, it might be worse than none at all since anyone could advertise himself as a doctor. And even the best so-called doctors sometimes prescribed dubious treatments such as laxatives to cure diarrhea, and bleeding to relieve a variety of problems. Furthermore, none of them had learned of bacteria or viruses.

In matters of faith, all had "officially" agreed to worship as Roman Catholics. Father Michael Muldoon, allegedly an alcoholic priest banished to Texas to serve the Americans, performed baptisms without much catechism, and most Texans continued as either nonbelievers or Protestants of some kind. As early as 1832 Samuel Doak McMahon operated a Methodist Sunday School in East Texas, and William Stevenson wandered East Texas preaching from a Methodist pulpit. Baptists Joseph E. Bays and Thomas J.

Pilgrim preached in their own ways with relative freedom, and Cumberland Presbyterian Sumner Bacon did the same.

Colonial Texas had no formal system of education, although a public school had existed in San Antonio for a time under the Spanish, and Nacogdoches, San Augustine, and Jonesborough also had schools. Usually sons learned from their fathers how to earn a living and daughters learned from their mothers how to keep house. Most immigrants were functionally literate: a boast that many of their children could not make.

Farming and trading were colonial Texas's chief enterprises. Sugar cane was grown along the rivers, especially the Brazos, while some cotton was also cultivated. Corn, used to feed livestock and people alike, also grew here. Primitive trade centers existed in most empresarial grants, and those at San Felipe and Nacogdoches could be called "developed." No banks or credit institutions existed to help expansion, and a chronic lack of cash reduced most exchanges to barter. Most Texans remained dependent on trade from the United States for staples.

Colonialism in Texas offered the settlers a hard life, but one that promised much in the future. For the moment, these last invaders remained guests in a land where the hosts first welcomed them, then grew fearful of their growing numbers. But these invaders had come to stay, no matter what.

Suggested Reading

Almaráz, Jr., Félix D. *Tragic Cavalier: Governor Manuel Salcedo of Texas, 1808–1813.* Revised edition, College Station: Texas A&M University Press, 1991.

Bannon, John Francis. *The Spanish Borderlands Frontier, 1513–1821.* New York: Holt, Rinehart, and Winston, Inc., 1970.

Barker, Eugene Campbell. *The Life of Stephen F. Austin.* Austin and London: University of Texas Press, 1969; copyright 1926 by Lamar and Barton.

Billington, Ray Allen. *Westward Expansion.* New York: Macmillan Company, 1949.

Hackett, Charles Wilson. *Pichardo's Treatise on the Limits of Louisiana and Texas, Vol. I–III.* Austin: University of Texas Press, 1931.

Jones, Jr., Oakah L. *Los Paisanos.* Norman: University of Oklahoma Press, 1979.

McDonald, Archie P. *Texas: All Hail The Mighty State.* Austin: Eakin Press, 1983. Material in this chapter is drawn from this publication.

Perrige, Lynn I. *The American Southwest.* New York: Holt, Rinehart and Winston, Inc., 1971.

Vigness, David. *The Revolutionary Decades, 1810–1836,* in Seymour V. Conner, *The Saga of Texas Series.* Austin: Steck-Vaughn, Co., 1965.

Wallace, Ernest, and David M. Vigness. *Documents of Texas History, Vol. I.* Lubbock: Texas Tech Press, 1960.

Wortham, Louis J. *A History of Texas, Vol. I.* Fort Worth, Texas: Wortham-Molyneaux Company, 1924.

Yoakum, Henderson. *History of Texas.* Austin: Facsimile Reproduction by the Steck Company; copyright 1855 by Redfield of New York.

The Battle of San Jacinto by H. A. McArdle. *Courtesy of the Archives Division, Texas State Library, photo by Eric Beggs.*

CHAPTER FOUR

Texas Independence

Archie P. McDonald

THE QUEST FOR TEXAS INDEPENDENCE began long before actual trouble erupted between Anglos, living in northern Mexico, and the central government. The longing for independence of mind and action rolled along with American pioneers as they made their way westward. These frontiering people rarely thought about independence in the limited sense of political arrangement, but they lived it in the constant struggle to survive. The doers among them became their heroes, the best at this or that skill useful in a tense situation or in daily labors. Feelings of self-worth and individuality developed, as well as a curious dependence-independence dichotomy. On the one hand the American frontiersman thought government ought to leave him alone and not interfere in his actions; on the other, he believed his government should stand ready to lend a hand if the load proved too heavy. Above all, he participated in the decision process, almost from the beginning of English colonial existence, and the roots of his participatory democracy stretched eastward across the Atlantic and backward in time to the evolutionary development of English parliamentary government.

But not all of the Anglos' cultural baggage shown with glory. Along the way Americans had also picked up African slavery, a lack of respect for Indian ownership or occupancy of lands they themselves desired, and a general intolerance for peoples who differed from them in nationality, religion, political system, or attitude.

Time, land-hunger, the constant need to grow, and perhaps plain cussedness brought the American frontiersmen westward. The Atlantic coastal plantation, bow-like, fixed its arrow of Southern-oriented American migrants on a southwestward course through Kentucky, Tennessee, Mississippi, and Arkansas or Louisiana. Settlement of the Old Southwest, the Louisiana Purchase, and the Adams-Onís treaty punctuated their progress. Indians, trees, animals, and miles of wilderness surrendered to their expansion, to their growing consciousness as Americans.

Then they reached Texas. Here other Europeans already ruled. Other customs of land acquisition, governmental traditions, religious practices, and language more or less prevailed. Here Spaniards-become-Mexicans remained few, but their regulations loomed as formidable obstacles to the Anglos. Few as they were, the Anglos soon outnumbered those whose claim to rule they eventually came to recognize only as first, not best. So the contest began. Americans, coming from a liberal tradition defined in a Declaration of Independence that spoke of "right," and consecrated in a Constitution that placed "power" in the functions of a limited government, came to a land where "right" and "power" drew their definition from authority and centralization. Even though the Americans changed their locations and homes or even seemed willing for a time to change their religion and nationality, they were unprepared for the kind of changes they saw in the revolving government of Mexico after 1830.

Americans felt that change ought to come from a liberal, yet conservative force, which allowed them at least the illusion that their rules and arrangements sprang from individual participation. The more they saw of the Mexican system, the more they disliked its tendency to become conservative, and at the same time radical. That is, its changes of direction came suddenly and mostly moved power into very few hands.

Many of the early Anglo population found the initial migration easy because Mexico's Constitution of 1824 established as pure a state's rights government as ever existed. Americans came from the tradition that produced Thomas Jefferson's theory of interposition and would produce John C. Calhoun's concept of concurrent majority and nullification, both statements of local, or state's rights. Such ideas made Mexican Texas seem worthy of the price of admission. But the Mexican Texas that developed in less than a decade, one that their increasing numbers helped produce, eventually became unacceptable to the Anglos. While the majority of Anglos probably would have endured, even prospered, under the most centralized and perhaps hostile conditions, the continual renewal of liberalism by the arrival of newer Americans—especially after the first stages of resistance developed—pushed the American presence into full revolt.

Some might date the beginning of the Texas revolution from the arrival of the first Americans in the region, and in a sense that thesis is defensible. Although many American immigrants followed Stephen F. Austin's lead in an attempt at full compliance with Mexican requirements, their obvious differences from the Mexican people and their institutions made disagreement inevitable. Disagreements bred of such differences in time become clashes. However, most of the new arrivals from the United States did make the effort to Mexicanize, at least in their outward appearance and activities.

The first serious misunderstanding came at Nacogdoches. By the terms of the Constitution of 1824, land alienation became a function of the Mexican states. The Coahuila state legislature's land policy, passed in 1825, provided for the awarding of empresarial grants to individuals who, in turn, sponsored others to receive specific tracts of land. Haden Edwards secured such a tract, in what is now eastern Texas, which proved troublesome because it already contained a significant population of Spaniards, some Mexicans, and many Indians. The colonization law required him to honor prior claims, but Edwards had difficulty in identifying those who had them. He posted a notice in Nacogdoches stating that all who could prove legitimate claims to their land do so or risk having it confiscated and made available to new settlers. Although only one case of reselling such land occurred, the excitement Edward's policy produced was considerable.

Austin's colonization proceeded more smoothly, partially because he wisely selected vacant land. He urged Edwards to move slowly and to avoid trouble, but, even as tensions mounted in eastern Texas, Edwards posted a second notice, which also caused tempers to flare. In addition, he became embroiled in an election dispute in which his son-in-law, Chichester Chaplin, opposed Samuel Norris. These two represented the newcomers versus the old settlers, and the lines were drawn. Chaplin claimed victory in the election, but Norris protested to the authorities in San Antonio, who sustained him. Despairing that he would ever achieve a peaceful settlement, in 1826 Edwards and his brother Benjamin proclaimed the Fredonia Republic as an independent state. Its promise of "independence, liberty, and justice" remained unfilled, but it did have one interesting feature. A red-and-white flag symbolized the Republic's proposed union of Indian and Anglo settlers, with each promised approximately half the territory claimed. Edwards needed Indian help to resist the anticipated Mexican suppression, and the Indians wanted their claims to their lands guaranteed, an offer not forthcoming from the current government. The whole affair ran its course quickly; the faithful were but a few Anglos, and when an armed Mexican force received orders to go to Nacogdoches, the Fredonians quickly disbursed. The Indian leaders were put to death by their own people, and the Edwards brothers fled to the United States for safety. The only permanent result of the episode was the alarming of some Mexican leaders that other Americans might harbor similar intentions.

Almost simultaneously in Mexico City a minister from the United States, Joel Poinsett, unwittingly contributed to this distrust of Americans by offering to buy portions of eastern Texas. The offer mostly courted western American votes for President John Quincy Adams, and probably was not a serious one on the part of the United States. But it worried some Mexicans, especially after Poinsett also meddled in internal political disputes in an attempt to further his cause. Perhaps he did not understand the game. Anyway, such leaders as Lucas Aláman, José María Tornel, and Manuel Mier y Terán, among others, persuaded President Vicente Guerrero to issue a decree in 1829 outlawing slavery in Mexico. Since Texas was the only Mexican state comprising slave owners, the point was obvious.

Anglo Texans found ways to avoid the enforcement of the decree, but they soon faced a more serious problem. On April 6, 1830, the central government reclaimed authority in land alienation from the states. One article of the enabling legislation forbade further American colonization in Texas, and another prohibited the importation of slaves by those settlers already there. In addition: more Mexicans would be sent to colonize Texas, even if they came from prisons; customs, long neglected, would be collected; trade with the United States was forbidden; and governmental investigators would visit Texas more frequently to monitor the situation. Most of these measures seemed calculated to handle an emergency; however, such an emergency really did not exist, at least not until the law precipitated it. Mexican concern for the growing American population was understandable. The Mexicans were cast in the role of laborers instead of employers in their own land. Understandably, their pride suffered.

So far, most Americans had shown few signs of unhappiness with the existing regime. Now they worried about losing another, more needed (or so they thought) labor supply; they showed irritation at the collection of customs and the loss of favored and familiar trade routes; and they resented the forced introduction of convict settlers and "spies." In short, their pride also suffered. Austin secured exemption for his lands, and lack of enforcement might have spared the rest. But the damage was done. In less than a decade, the American-Mexican arrangement in Texas wore thin, and full revolt lay on the horizon.

The causes of the rebellion were many, but mostly they related to major differences between the two cultures—and to the opportunism of a few. Americans in Texas, at least after they took charge of their own area, assumed that the Mexican government would leave them to themselves. Thus a kind of "salutary neglect" existed, and the Anglos bristled at the government's efforts to end it. The customs exemption enjoyed since 1824 was due to end, but they did not want it to end. The redirected trade to Mexico might have proved beneficial, but they were reluctant to alter established and familiar practices. One requirement of their legal immigration had been a good reputation, so Anglos resented the idea of convict migration. Finally, the quick turn-around in Mexican politics baffled them. They watched as, in rapid succession, Vicente Guerrero lost an election to Gómez Pedraza, refused to relinquish his office, and suffered execution by Anastasio Bustamente. Then, Gómez Pedraza was placed in the office that he had legally won by military force, not by the normal political processes.

In short, Americans failed to understand the political struggle in Mexico. On one hand the centralists feared U.S. intentions in the Southwest and regarded Anglo presence in Texas, perhaps innocently but nonetheless accurately, as the first wave of an American takeover. On the other hand the decentralists or state's righters, no less than the Americans in Texas, wished power to remain localized, and strangely found themselves on the same side as the Americans in the opening stages of the Texas movement. Ultimately the centralists won, and, in the winning, Mexicans came together in their attitudes on Americans. At the bottom of the Texas trouble, one fact remained: the Americans could not understand why the Mexicans feared them or would not let them have their own way in a land they so obviously dominated. For their part, Mexican authorities came to mistrust the Americans completely and failed to share their feelings of Anglo righteousness. In the end a kind of racial as well as political repugnance developed.

Trouble boiled in the wake of Anglo reaction to the Law of April 6, 1830. The attempts to collect customs started it, much as it had the American Revolution fifty-five years earlier. The stationing of customs officers at the mouth of some Texas rivers, and locating troops at Nacogdoches under José de las Piedras, at Velasco under Domingo de Ugartechea, and especially at Anahuac under John Davis Bradburn, provided the explosive element. Arguments soon raged. Importers and sea captains resented the difficulty of obtaining clearance papers; arriving settlers resented detention and the fact that the centralist military officials would not allow them to obtain land, despite the fact that state officials seemed willing to give it to them. Perhaps they expected too much of fellow American immigrant Bradburn, who commanded the Mexican troops at Anahuac, where the first spark of revolution came. Before the summer of 1832 had ended, the conflagration had spread to many other parts of Texas.

Bradburn tentatively reopened the rivers in response to the protest over their closure, but the situation remained tense. He arrested some of the more vocal protectors, but soon released them. Then, in May 1832, a series of events led to a crisis. Following an embarrassing incident involving slaves who belonged to a man from Louisiana, who challenged Bradburn's authority to retain his human property, Bradburn ordered the arrest of attorney William B. Travis, who represented the slave owner. Travis's partner, Patrick Jack, protested, so Bradburn's men arrested him as well. Jack's brother William spread the word that the two were being held, and men gathered from the American camp. Bradburn, already hated by the Anglos for having arrested Francisco Madero, a state officer who tried to establish a community at Liberty. In the central versus states' rights argument, Bradburn was a centralist who sought to enforce the Law of April 6, 1830, which, as noted, forbade further land grants to Anglos.

Now the Americans decided to get their kind out of prison. They gathered at Turtle Bayou, where they drafted resolutions pledging loyalty to the legitimate government under the Constitution of 1824 but also affirmed their determination to thwart the illegal arrests. That done, John Austin took some men to Velasco to fetch a cannon they thought they might need.

Soon thereafter a showdown between the opposing sides occurred. Following the American capture of a Mexican patrol, the Anglos offered to swap hostages. Bradburn agreed, but he got them to release his men first, then refused to free Travis and Jack. Only the arrival of Piedras from Nacogdoches restored calm. Piedras, who outranked Bradburn, solved the problem by firing Bradburn and releasing Travis and Jack. The Americans rejoiced, but they mistook their man: Piedras was not their friend. Upon returning to Nacogdoches, he determined to avoid a similar situation by ordering the Anglos in his district to surrender their arms. They did indeed bring their guns to town, but the result was a two-day battle that ended in Piedras's defeat. Meanwhile, John Austin had acquired his cannon, but in order to get it up to Turtle Bayou he had to fight his way past Ugartechea.

These three military incidents marked the beginning of actual fighting in the movement for Texas independence, but few would have viewed them as the beginning of a revolution. Many Americans thought of their actions as being in line with the activities of other states' righters. Meanwhile, the leader of the states' rights movement (and revolution) in Mexico, Antonio López de Santa Anna, sent José Antonio Mexia to find out what was going on in Texas. Stephen F. Austin convinced Mexia that the Anglo's activities merely supported their own, and that Americans remained loyal to Mexico.

The next action came at San Felipe de Austin when the council there called for a convention to meet in October 1832 to draft resolutions to the government. Austin presided. The resolutions seemed reasonable to the Americans, who asked for: a renewal of land grants; more units of local self-government; exemption from customs collection for three more years; and a militia for defense against the Indians. They also requested a separate statehood within the Mexican government. In turn, the government's reaction was to remind them of their lack of authority to hold such a meeting. A short circuit in communication thus occurred. To the Americans, theirs was an orderly petition; to the government, it was an unauthorized and extraordinary act. Further, many regarded the request for separate statehood as the revelation of a revolutionary plot. Rebuffed, the Americans tried again in January 1833. This time a somewhat more militant spirit prevailed, as was evidenced by the election of William Wharton and not Austin to preside, since the latter was the traditional leader of the Anglo community. Still, the requests differed little from the prior set, except this time they framed a constitution. To the Americans, who drew on their experience in the United States, this action was the way to gain admission to the union; to many Mexicans, it represented the next step in revolution.

Austin carried the message to Mexico City. But as the days dragged into months and still no decision on the Anglo's request came, he grew anxious. One reason for the delay was that Antonio

López de Santa Anna, who had been elected president in 1833, was away from the capital. Santa Anna left the government in charge of his vice president, Gómez Farias, who was too busy to worry about Austin. His own reforms in the areas of land ownership, the church, and the army more than occupied his time. Austin did effect a working relationship with Lorenzo de Zavala in the Congress, but at his last audience with Farias he told the acting president that he might as well recognize the Texans' bid for separate statehood because it practically already existed. Candor looked more like a threat to Farias. In a pique, Austin wrote the civil authorities in San Antonio to go ahead and organize a separate state. But his letter found its way back to the central authorities without his knowing it, and later caused him grave difficulties.

Just before leaving Mexico City, Austin spoke with Santa Anna, who had returned to reassume control. The meeting ended cordially with Santa Anna giving Austin nearly everything for which he had asked except separate statehood, which was refused on the reasonable grounds that Texas lacked sufficient population to justify it. And one thing more: the president told Austin that troops would be sent to Texas to protect the citizens from Indians. If this action was a cat-and-mouse game, Austin apparently had no clue as to what awaited him. He traveled as far north as Saltillo, where he was arrested and returned to Mexico City. For the next year and a half he remained in prison.

Austin's arrest hushed Anglo political activity in Texas. Fearing for his safety, the previously vocal groups became so silent that in time Austin came to wonder if they had forgotten him. Spencer Jack and Peter Grayson finally traveled to Mexico City to plead Austin's cause, and at least for the final months of his "arrest" he had the freedom of the city. Austin never received a formal list of charges, never appeared in court, and in the end was released on grounds of general amnesty. He finally quitted Mexico in July 1835, and traveled home via New Orleans.

In Texas, 1835 proved to be a significant year. In January the customs collectors came again. At Anahuac, Captain Antonio Tenorio commanded a small garrison to assist in the collection. In June, a group headed by J. B. Miller secretly met and agreed to support William B. Travis and a band of followers in driving Tenorio from the small coastal town. Travis succeeded easily, but the act offended the authorities and frightened settlers who desired only peace. Expecting a hero's welcome, Travis and his men found themselves in disgrace, branded outlaws by General Martin Perfecto de

Cos, the new military commander of Texas, and worse, saw Tenorio greeted as the honored guest at a party in Brazoria. But Cos pushed too hard. He called for the arrest of Travis and the others, and the result was the organization of committees of correspondence and the laying of plans for resistance.

In August a meeting at Columbia called for a Consultation of all Texans to gather in October to devise ways to secure peace on constitutional terms if possible and, if not, to plan for war. Roughly, the country people constituted a peace element, and the town dwellers, especially representing many new immigrants from the United States who had arrived too late to receive bona fide land titles, made up the war group. Austin returned to find this situation, and his attitude had changed. No longer was he *"Éstevan."* Once again thoroughly American, he told a crowd at San Felipe that "war is our only resource."

While Texans still struggled with preparations for the Consultation, a new crisis developed at Gonzales. Now the rhythm of the revolution was seen: crisis, reaction, crisis.

It began in October, when Cos urged Ugartechea to take possession of a cannon at Gonzales, which had been permitted there for Indian defense. When the small Mexican force arrived, Alcalde Andrew Ponton refused to surrender it. Others buried the cannon while he delayed. Later, when Captain Francisco Castañeda returned with a force of two hundred men to take the cannon, Anglos under the persuasions of John Moore dug up the cannon, painted a homemade flag that read "Come and Take It," and made ready for war. The Americans fired first, and when Castañeda asked why, he was invited to join them if he claimed to be a republican, or to fight. He simply withdrew. Now several hundred men arrived at Gonzales to defend a principle and a cannon that already had been defended. Austin arrived also, and despite his lack of military training, quickly became the recognized leader. Rumors of Cos's imminent arrival in San Antonio made that city the obvious destination of this group of Americans in search of action. While the Consultation deliberated, the so-called "Army of the People" lay siege to San Antonio.

At the same time, the Consultation at San Felipe finally proceeded, this after nearly three weeks spent fretting over a quorum. On November 7 they pledged loyalty to the Constitution of 1824 and announced their opposition to the usurper Santa Anna. They asked for aid from Mexican liberals and hoped for help from the United States. They passed an instrument known as the Organic Law, which fashioned a provisional government for Texas until the issue was decided with Santa Anna. Henry Smith of Brazoria became governor and James Robinson of Nacogdoches the lieutenant governor. Sam Houston became commander of the army. They also named a council to balance the executive leadership. The results were disastrous. Smith and the council quarreled, the council named Robinson to replace Smith; there was no money, and Houston had difficulty finding enough men to compose an army.

The force at San Antonio lost the leadership of Stephen F. Austin when he, Branch T. Archer, and William Wharton were named as agents to the United States and dispatched to seek aid. Edward Burleson succeeded Austin in command. Ben Milam finally led three hundred or so men into San Antonio early in December. After a five-day action ending on the 10th, the Texans captured the city despite the death of Milam. Now led by Francis Johnson, this force wanted to march southward to plunder Matamoros. The council agreed, but it wanted James Fannin, who had assembled a force of newly arrived Americans near Goliad, to lead it. Smith wanted Sam Houston to lead the expedition, and, at one point, James Bowie was asked to lead it. The debate resulted in nothing more than a waste of time and supplies, for none of the three agreed and Johnson ultimately led the force south.

Now Governor Smith succeeded in getting William B. Travis, who had been named commander of the cavalry by the Consultation and the Provisional Government, to take as many volunteers as he could muster to San Antonio to relieve Colonel James C. Neill who commanded there after the departure of Johnson. Travis arrived on February 3, 1836, and James Bowie came to San Antonio with one hundred volunteers. For most of February they readied to meet the army of Santa Anna, who was reportedly on his way north to clear Texas of its Anglo population. When not working under Green B. Jameson's direction to prepare their Alamo fortress, Travis and Bowie quarreled, welcomed the arrival of David Crockett, and finally worked out a joint command. Santa Anna and his force arrived on February 22, and a thirteen-day siege followed. On March 6, a Mexican assault carried over the walls of the compound and ended the lives of the 183 male defenders. Only a few women and a slave were spared. The dead bodies were heaped in piles and burned, and "Remember the Alamo" became a rallying cry for the Texans who reconvened at Gonzales. Travis had pled for assistance for days, but only the thirty-two-man population of Gonzales arrived before the Alamo's fall. Within a matter of days nearly four hundred men gathered at Gonzales, too late as usual. Sam Houston provided leadership for their next action.

While the drama at the Alamo played out, yet another Convention met at Washington-on-the-Brazos. This time no pledges of loyalty to an old order sounded. On March 2 they quickly adopted George Childress's draft of a Declaration of Independence, which was closely patterned on that of the United States in form and language. By March 16 they had also adopted a Constitution that created a unitary republic. It provided for a president, vice president, and a congress, and named David G. Burnet and Lorenzo de Zavala to hold the executive offices provisionally until formal elections determined an orderly succession. Thomas J. Rusk became secretary of war, and Houston was reconfirmed to command the army, if he could find one. He did so at Gonzales.

With troops arriving daily from the countryside and from the United States, Houston wisely delayed attacking Santa Anna at San Antonio. At first Houston hoped Fannin could come up from Goliad with his approximately four hundred men; then word came that this group had been captured and massacred by General José Urrea. In addition, most of Johnson's men, who had stopped short of Matamoros, were captured at San Patricio, and only a few of them had escaped. So Houston moved eastward at the head of the only remaining Texan military force. He stopped periodically to rest and to train his army, but mostly he moved away from danger. The civilian government moved even faster, all the way to Harrisburg. Houston's retreat, plus the news of the Alamo and Goliad, produced the unhappy "Runaway Scrape," as noncombatants fearing for their lives raced for the safety of the U.S. border. On April 20 the running stopped.

Santa Anna had divided his forces into several groups and scattered them in southern, central, and southeastern Texas. He personally commanded only about eight hundred men as he trailed Houston's force of about an equal number. On April 20 Houston's men made camp between Buffalo Bayou and the San Jacinto River, the water at their backs and a rolling prairie approximately two miles wide in front of them. The Mexican camp lay to the south toward a marsh area. After a brief skirmish late in the afternoon, the two forces sat watching each other. Santa Anna was waiting for reinforcements led by Cos, who arrived during the night and early the next morning. Still the two camps faced one another. After taking his only counsel-of-war of the campaign, Houston decided to attack in the afternoon. Miraculously, he caught the Mexican camp in almost total surprise. A brief, eighteen-minute action decided the battle and, ultimately, the fate of Texas. The Texans' revenge for the Alamo and Goliad, however, continued for some time. Two

Texans were killed, and seven of the thirty wounded later died. The Mexican forces suffered nearly 630 casualties, and more than 700 were captured, including Santa Anna.

Three weeks later Santa Anna agreed to the Treaty of Velasco, which recognized Texas independence and called for hostilities to cease. He ordered all Mexican troops in Texas, then under the command of General Vicente Filisola, to return to Mexico. Of course, the treaty was not valid, since Santa Anna had negotiated it as a captive. The Mexican Congress quickly denounced it. The war for Texas independence thus miraculously ended, but the struggle to maintain it had only begun.

Suggested Reading

Barker, Eugene C. *The Life of Stephen F. Austin, Founder of Texas, 1793–1836*. Nashville: Cokesbury Press, 1926; republished in paperback. Austin: University of Texas Press, 1969.

——. *Mexico and Texas, 1821–1835*. Dallas: P. O. Turner Company, 1928.

Binkley, William C. *The Texas Revolution*. Baton Rouge: Louisiana State University Press, 1962. Part of the Walter Lyowood Flemings Lectures.

Castañeda, Carlos E. *The Mexican Side of the Texan Revolution*. Dallas: Southwest Press, 1928.

De la Pena, José Enrique. *With Santa Anna in Texas: A Personal Narrative of the Revolution*. College Station: Texas A&M University Press, 1975.

Jenkins, John H., gen. ed. *The Papers of the Texas Revolution, 1835–36*. Austin: Presidial Press, 1973. Ten volumes.

Lack, Paul D. *The Texas Revolutionary Experience: A Political and Social History, 1835–1836*, 2nd ed. College Station: Texas A&M University Press, 1996.

Lord, Walter. *A Time to Stand*. New York: Harper & Row, 1961.

Vigness, David M. *The Revolutionary Decades*, 2nd vol. of *The Saga of Texas Series*. Austin Steck-Vaughn Company, 1965.

The Republic of Texas. *Map by Jane Domier.*

CHAPTER FIVE

The Republic of Texas

Stanley Siegel

On March 2, 1836, Texas proclaimed itself an independent nation. By that time all efforts at reconciliation with Santa Anna's Mexico had failed. A few weeks after the fighting began at Gonzales in October 1835, Texans sought only statehood within Mexico. However, the logic of events now compelled a statement of independence. In the midst of the Alamo campaign, freedom from Mexico was proclaimed. Relying on Thomas Jefferson, George Childress, the author of the Texas statement, compared Santa Anna to George III as a "tyrant" who must be overthrown. It was not the last time that Texans would see their own struggle through the prism of the American Revolution.

After they proclaimed independence, the delegates remained at Washington-on-the-Brazos to draft a constitution. Thomas Jefferson Rusk presided over a committee that soon had a document completed for review. Modeled closely after the United States Constitution, the Texas document also reflected the Mexican colonial experience. The Republic's constitution barred successive terms by the nation's president because its framers distrusted a strong chief executive. The powers of Congress and courts were also similar to the American experience. A bill of rights guaranteed freedom of speech, press, and religion. Slavery was sanctioned as a legal institution, and slaves could not be imported from anywhere outside the Republic except from the United States.

The first presidential race in the Republic of Texas took place in September 1836. Stephen F. Austin, Branch T. Archer, Henry Smith, and Sam Houston announced as candidates for the new nation's highest office. The "Hero of San Jacinto" emerged as the clear-cut winner, principally because of the prevailing belief that Houston's close friendship with United States President Andrew Jackson would insure annexation, but also because of the glory Houston won at

San Jacinto. Texans endorsed, in a straw ballot, union with the United States by a count of almost 98 percent. The Republic's constitution was formally ratified and Mirabeau B. Lamar was elected vice president. Politics in the early years of the Republic was a contest of personalities not of parties. Houston and Lamar, although yoked in the same administration, differed markedly on a number of major political questions, and each man attracted his own group of supporters.

During the brief period of Texas statehood (November 1835–March 1836) diplomatic recognition by the United States was sought for the first time. A trio of "executive agents," Stephen F. Austin, Branch T. Archer, and William Wharton, were sent to the United States to raise money and garner support for the Texas cause. After Houston was elected, he replaced the above team with Peter Grayson and James Collinsworth, both eyewitness veterans of San Jacinto. While they were in Washington, a resolution was introduced to recognize the independence of Texas, but it was opposed by northern antislavery interests. Since he did not wish to threaten Martin Van Buren's chances in the presidential election of 1836, President Jackson let the matter rest until after Van Buren won. On March 3, 1837, as the final act of his administration, Jackson extended diplomatic recognition to Texas. Shortly thereafter, Alcee La Branche was named as the first envoy from the United States to Texas.

Buoyed by the overwhelming Texas vote for annexation, President Houston moved to accomplish that purpose. However, President Van Buren and his secretary of state, John Forsyth, coldly rebuffed all such overtures. Engulfed by the financial panic of 1837, Van Buren had little time or patience for delicate diplomacy. All parties understood that the major barrier to the admission of Texas into the Union was the question of slavery. With black servitude a legal institution in the Republic, Texas incurred the ire of northern abolitionists. Almost ten years would pass before the annexation issue was finally resolved.

Another complex problem facing President Houston during his first term in office was the permanent location of the seat of government. Although the capital was located at various places during the Revolution, Houston was inaugurated at West Columbia, but that site was never intended as a permanent capital. After a number of cities submitted petitions, the Congress decided in favor of the new city of Houston, with the proviso that the capital remain there until 1840. Described by one resident as the "greatest sink of vice and dissipation" in modern times, even Sam Houston had little affection for his namesake city. However, his political following was based there, and from its inception the city was lauded as a potential rail and trading center.

While Houston reflected the popular will on the annexation and seat-of-government issues, his attitude toward the Cherokees did not. Houston had lived with the Cherokees in Tennessee several times. Styled "The Raven," Houston sought refuge with the tribe once again after the failure of his marriage, and his resignation from the governorship of Tennessee. In January 1836, Houston was one of three commissioners who signed the Cherokee treaty, which came before the Senate for ratification during his presidency. The treaty had pledged the Indians to remain neutral in the impending war between Mexico and Texas; in exchange, Houston and other negotiators had agreed to recognize the Cherokee title to lands claimed between the Nueces and Sabine Rivers after the war. The Cherokees kept their promise and spared the Texans from having to wage a two-front war. But the Congress rejected the treaty on the narrow grounds that it had been signed before independence and therefore was not binding. Actually, the Congress had no intention of surrendering such valuable land to the Indians. The issue would come up again in the politics of the Republic.

Because of the constitutional provision outlawing successive terms, Houston could not run again in 1838 for the presidency. After Peter Grayson, the candidate he sponsored, committed suicide, the Houston faction turned to James Collinsworth. Shortly thereafter, this former Chief Justice of the Texas Supreme Court jumped from a ship in Galveston harbor to his death. The bizarre campaign concluded with the election of Mirabeau B. Lamar, who probably would have won anyway. David G. Burnet, the president of the interim government during the revolution, was elected vice president.

Lamar spent his youth in Georgia. He edited a newspaper at Columbus and engaged in other businesses before migrating to Texas. He commanded the cavalry at San Jacinto and was singled out for his brave conduct by General Houston. Lamar was never at home in the rough and tumble of frontier politics; rather he was a sensitive man with talents that ran to poetry and literature. Although he had served as Houston's vice president from 1836 to 1838, the two officials often clashed bitterly. He staked out his future political opposition to Houston when he opposed the decision to spare Santa Anna's life after San Jacinto. Defeated on that question, Lamar became the spokesman of those who generally stood against Houston.

On the Indian question, Lamar and Houston differed most radically. Not only did Lamar refuse to approve the Cherokee treaty, but he also demanded increased appropriations to strengthen the defense against Indian attacks. Then, when Lamar was presented with irrefutable proof of Mexican intrigue among the Cherokees, he decided upon a course of rapid action. When talks broke down between the Republic and the Indians regarding the worth of their lands in East Texas, Lamar moved against them. As a result, the Cherokees and their Kickapoo allies were harried from the Republic and forced to seek asylum in the Indian Territory north of the Red River.

Repeated Comanche attacks against the cities of San Antonio and Austin forced Lamar to fashion a policy toward that tribe as well. However, he proceeded more cautiously with those fierce Indians. Negotiations were to take place at the Council House in San Antonio, but when the Comanches reneged on their promise to free a number of captives, fighting began. Successful Comanche raids on Victoria and Linville followed, until Lamar marshaled the full force of the republic's military power. Texas troops, aided by Tonkawa scouts, defeated the Comanches at the battle of Plum Creek, near Seguin, in August 1841. While the Apaches and Comanches continued to strike isolated farmhouses and carry off captives, Indian resistance to frontier settlement ended during the period of the republic.

By legislation passed in the first session of Congress, the capital was, as noted, supposed to remain in Houston until 1840. But from the onset of his administration, Lamar was determined to move it to another site. Seeking to build a political base in the West, Lamar objected to the city of Houston more on political than personal grounds. Again petitions were forthcoming from such places as San Antonio, Washington-on-the-Brazos, and others, but Lamar had his mind set on still another location. While on a hunting trip, he had visited the little village of Waterloo, located on the Colorado River. While hardly a propitious name for a seat of government, Waterloo and the surrounding area had a strong appeal for him because of the hilly terrain and general beauty. Renamed "Austin" in honor of the great colonizer, who had died in 1836, the capital was relocated to that site. Lamar's anti-Indian sentiments and efforts to develop a great network of railroads and turnpikes in that section of Texas were popular along the frontier. However, the matter of the permanent location of the capital still was not fully resolved.

Because he was adamantly opposed to annexation to the United States, Lamar sought peace with Mexico and continued independence for the Republic of Texas. During the course of his administration he dispatched three teams of envoys to Mexico City, none of which returned with an honorable peace. When the Mexican state of Yucatán declared its independence of Santa Anna, Lamar was quick to provide naval assistance. After all such strategies resulted in failure, he embarked on what was to prove the nadir of his presidency. Consistent with the Texas position of the "Rio Grande from source to mouth" as its boundary, Lamar issued a proclamation claiming that Santa Fe was within the limits of the Republic. If the citizens of the area did not accept Texas sovereignty willingly, Lamar threatened to "let the sword do its work."

Commanded by General Hugh McLeod and with a substantial number of volunteers from the United States, the ill-fated expedition departed from Austin on June 18, 1841. George Wilkins Kendall, editor of the *New Orleans Picayune* and a volunteer, wrote a classic account of what took place. Kendall's *Narrative of the Texan Santa Fe Expedition* conveys the sense of doom that soon affected the participants. Uncertain of the route and menaced by Apache raids, McLeod and company covered some 1,300 miles before reaching Santa Fe. There, they were disarmed by Mexican troops and forced to surrender. Some hope was held out that the American members of the party would be released, but ultimately all were started on a march to Mexico City. Many died along the way. Those who survived the trek were imprisoned in Perote Castle prison, outside Mexico City. It was not until after the War with Mexico (1846–1848) that some of these prisoners gained their liberty.

On the positive side, Lamar could claim two notable achievements in the area of domestic legislation. Justly revered as the "Father of Texas Education," he urged the Texas Congress to comply with the constitutional mandate that called for a "uniform system of free public education." The Education Bill of 1839 was piloted through the Congress by Augustus W. Cullen, whose Georgia roots and respect for education were similar to those of the president. This law granted three leagues of land to each county for the maintenance and support of public schools. The Congress also set aside fifty leagues of land for the "establishment of a University of the first class." Although it was to be situated in central Texas, nothing more was done until the 1880s, the War with Mexico and the Civil War taking precedence. Over the years, the state legislature also set aside lands in the Permian Basin of West Texas, the proceeds from which were to benefit a future state university. The fortuitous discovery of oil on those lands in 1923 proved to be a bonanza for The University of Texas and, to a lesser degree, Texas A&M University.

The enactment of the Homestead Act (1839) constituted Lamar's other major success. Anxious to facilitate emigration from the United States, particularly in the wake of the Panic of 1837, the law was designed to encourage agrarian colonists to settle in Texas. The statute provided that every head of a family could exempt from financial judgment or execution his homestead, basic household furnishings, and the "tools, apparatus, and books belonging to the trade or profession of any citizen." Reflecting the somewhat tolerant Spanish and Mexican attitudes toward indebtedness, the legislation was rooted early in Texas history. Its land alienation policy became the model for the federal Homestead Act (1862) and similar debtor laws in a number of states. With some minor adjustments, the law has remained in force in Texas to the present day.

The election of 1841 provided Sam Houston with an opportunity to return to the presidency. Ineligible to succeed himself, Lamar supported the candidacy of Vice President David G. Burnet. Because of a financial recession and the absence of a genuine peace with Mexico, Burnet's prospects for victory were slim. Once General Houston announced his candidacy, the result of the contest was a foregone conclusion. As a member of the Texas Congress from San Augustine, Houston had castigated Lamar's Cherokee and seat-of-government policies bitterly. Concentrating on those issues and emphasizing his desire to renew annexation talks with the United States, Houston won election with ease. At the same time, running independently of Houston, Edward Burleson was elected vice president.

Soon after he retook office, Houston announced that he would move the capital once more. He insisted that the archives and public papers of the government were not safe at Austin because of the danger posed by Mexican or Indian attack. Congress responded favorably by enacting two bills sanctioning removal of the records. One statute authorized the president to remove the archives to a safer place, and the other empowered both branches of Congress to select a site for a new capital.

On March 5, 1842, fifteen hundred Mexican soldiers commanded by General Rafael Vasquez entered San Antonio. They encountered no resistance. As if to underscore the danger to Austin, other Mexican troops temporarily occupied Goliad and Refugio. No casualties on either side and little destruction of property resulted from these actions. The obvious purpose of the raids was to base a claim to the Nueces River as the northern boundary of Mexico should annexation talks between Texas and the United States resume. The danger to Austin was real, and President Houston announced that the next session of Congress would be held in his namesake city.

After meeting in Houston for less than a month, Congress was told that it would next assemble at Washington-on-the-Brazos. Since he intended never to return to Austin, Houston ordered the removal of the government's official papers and records from that city. When carters left Austin with the archives they were fired upon by a group of local citizens and forced to surrender the archives. The inglorious "Archives War" reflected credit upon neither the president nor the townspeople of Austin. Ultimately the records remained at Austin, but President Houston continued to govern from Washington-on-the-Brazos.

On September 5, 1842, Mexican troops once again rode into San Antonio, this time led by General Adrian Woll. A proclamation stating that the "laws of Mexico" were operative in Béxar was read. As a further insult, three Texas congressmen were among the hostages Woll brought along on his retreat to the Rio Grande. Captain Jack Hays and Texas Ranger units gave chase, but to no avail. This second Mexican "invasion" within months caused President Houston a great deal of embarrassment. Although he understood that Santa Anna sought to influence the annexation talks being conducted in Washington, politics and emotion compelled a response in kind from Texans.

Houston activated two militia regiments and requested volunteers to gather at San Antonio for a campaign. General Alexander Somervell led the force, but from the beginning the volunteers were restless under Somervell's leadership. Laredo, on the Rio Grande, fell to the Texan force, but Somervell refused to approve a campaign on Mexican soil, citing insufficient supplies. Many of the volunteers then returned to their homes, but approximately five hundred of the men displayed enthusiasm for an invasion of Mexico. After electing Colonel William Fisher as their commander, this group crossed the Rio Grande at the little Mexican village of Mier.

The invading army's intelligence was faulty; a Mexican force had occupied Mier two days earlier. On Christmas Day 1842, a battle ensued, resulting in Fisher's surrender to General Pedro de Ampudia. With memories of the Alamo and Goliad fresh in his mind, Fisher secured a written pledge that the captives would be treated fairly and eventually exchanged. The terms of the agreement were violated and the prisoners set out on a forced march to Mexico City. At Saltillo, in northern Mexico, they attempted an escape. A few did gain their freedom, but many others died from lack of food and exposure. Ultimately 176 Texans were recaptured and returned to Saltillo.

Despite Santa Anna's insistence that all the Mier Expedition captives be executed, the governor of Coahuila amended the sentence to the execution of one man out of ten, with the remainder to be imprisoned. Of the 176 prisoners, seventeen had to forfeit their lives. What transpired next, the infamous "black bean" incident, is one of the most memorable events in Texas history. Seventeen black beans were placed in an earthen jar and mixed with 159 white beans. The prisoners were blindfolded and forced to draw beans from the jar, the officers choosing first. The bravery of the Texans was best summarized by the comments of one captive: "This beats gambling all to hell, boys." After all had picked from the jar, the seventeen who held the black beans were lined against a wall and shot. While the tragedy depicted Mexican callousness and brutality, it also revealed the military shortcomings of the Republic.

Now, when the situation in Texas appeared so desperate, interest in annexation resumed. The question had been dormant since 1837, when the first overtures from Texas had been rebuffed. Since that time the Republic had commenced diplomatic relations with England and France. Trading agreements with those countries had been signed, as well as with Belgium, the Netherlands, and some of the towns of the Hanseatic League. Still, it was obvious to all that admission into the Union as a state was the best solution for Texas.

Elected in 1840, the elderly and infirm William Henry Harrison served but one month in the U.S. presidency; this was the shortest tenure of any chief executive. He was succeeded by Vice President John Tyler, a southerner favorably disposed toward the annexation of Texas. Tyler named fellow Virginian Abel Upshur as secretary of state, following the resignation of Daniel Webster. Treaty negotiations between Upshur and Isaac Van Zandt, the Texas minister at Washington, were proceeding when Upshur was killed in a naval accident. After John C. Calhoun was appointed secretary of state, a treaty calling for the admission of Texas into the Union as a slave state was quickly prepared.

President Tyler submitted the treaty to the United States Senate with a message urging ratification. The timing was not good, and the treaty rapidly became embroiled in the presidential campaign of 1844. Henry Clay, the Whig candidate, attempted to straddle the issue by favoring annexation, but not at the risk of provoking a war with Mexico. And if Texas was annexed, he did not favor assuming responsibility for Texas's indebtedness. James K. Polk, the Democratic candidate for President, adopted a "Manifest Destiny" position campaigning for the "re-annexation of Texas and the reoccupation of Oregon." The slate was completed when James G. Birney, a former slaveholder turned abolitionist, captured the nomination of the Liberty party. This new group, a precursor of the Free Soil and Republican Parties, vehemently opposed the annexation of Texas as a slave state.

The treaty came to a vote in the Senate on June 8, 1844, after the nominating conventions but before the national elections in November. To the surprise of many in Congress, the measure was rejected by a tally of thirty-five opposed to sixteen for, far short of the two-thirds "present and voting" required for ratification. That the vote was split along sectional and party lines was apparent. Only one northern Democrat, Levi Woodbury of New Hampshire, joined fifteen fellow Democrats from southern states to vote for the treaty.

Rejected in the Senate, the treaty was only moribund, not completely dead. The final verdict awaited the results of the presidential election in the fall. In the interim, attention was focused upon a similar campaign in Texas. Once again barred from serving as chief executive, Houston backed the candidacy of his secretary of state, Dr. Anson Jones. Unable to interest either Lamar or Burnet to mount a challenge, the opposition pinned their hopes on General Edward Burleson. Formerly the vice president in the second Houston administration, Burleson had broken with "Old Sam" over the Mier disaster and was eager to make the race. Both Jones and Burleson endorsed annexation; basking in Houston's popularity, Jones was elected as the last president of the Republic.

At the age of forty-nine, James K. Polk was the youngest President to that time. With 170 electoral votes to Clay's 105 total, he was a decisive winner. Yet even though Liberty Party candidate Birney failed to capture a single state, he did lessen Polk's popular majority, making the race somewhat closer in that regard. If nothing else, the election demonstrated that Polk's expansion themes in Texas and Oregon were popular with the voters. However, the president-elect failed to sweep many Democratic congressional candidates into office "on his coattails." This meant that the composition of the United States Senate had changed very little. Since a treaty calling for the admission of Texas would most likely still fail, another solution had to be found.

Despite his lame-duck status, President Tyler continued to strive for annexation. In his final message to Congress, he raised the specter of an increased British naval presence in the Gulf of Mexico unless Texas was annexed quickly. Polk's statement that he had no objection to annexation taking place before his inaugural set off a flurry of activity in Congress. Following the sage advice of James Pinckney Henderson, the special minister from Texas in Washington, to assist in the deliberations, Texas solicited admission by "joint resolution" of Congress. Perfectly constitutional, this strategy required only a simple majority vote, but in both branches of the national legislature.

The Benton-Walker bill providing for the annexation of Texas contained the following provisions: (1) Texas would be admitted into the Union as a state, with all formalities and requirements satisfied by July 1, 1846; (2) all outstanding boundary questions would be "adjusted by the United States"; (3) Texas would retain title to its public lands, and apply the proceeds from the sale of such lands to the indebtedness of the Republic; (4) Texas would turn over its military and naval equipment to the United States; (5) with the consent of Texas, new states, not to exceed four in number, could be carved out of the original boundaries of the state, with the proviso that slavery be outlawed in any such state located north of 36°30' north latitude.

Stripped of formal terminology, the bill stipulated that the United States would place the boundary at the Rio Grande rather than the Nueces River. Also, there was an implication that if Texas ceded all or a portion of its public lands to the United States, the latter would assume responsibility for some portion of the Texas debt. Finally, the national debate over slavery, which had beset Congress since 1820, was reflected in the application of the Missouri Compromise line to the annexation resolution.

Few new arguments were heard in the final debate on the "Texas Question." Those who favored annexation spoke of the economic boon to the United States that would follow Texas statehood. They also insisted on the right of the South to have equal access to the territories and noted that the Missouri Compromise did not prohibit slavery in Texas. At the same time, those opposed insisted that war with Mexico must certainly follow annexation because of placing the boundary at the Rio Grande rather than the Nueces. They argued that such a conflict would be a "dishonorable war" since it would be waged to entrench slavery. On January 25, 1845, the House of Representatives approved the annexation bill, and on February 26 the Senate assented by a narrow margin. Then on March 3, 1845, just prior to Polk's inauguration, President Tyler signed the annexation bill. There remained only the affirmation of Texans to seal statehood.

Stirred by the prospect of the annexation of Texas to the United States, at the eleventh hour England and France sought to prevent it. Upon instructions from their respective foreign offices, Charles Elliot and Alphonse de Saligny, the British and French ministers to Texas, journeyed to Mexico City. Acting in concert, they met with Mexico's foreign secretary, Louis Cuevas, and signed a "Diplomatic Act." By its terms, Mexico offered to recognize Texas independence, with final boundaries to be determined by the mediation of London and Paris. Trade agreements would follow the settlement of limits. If the Republic accepted annexation to the United States, the Mexican proposal was inoperative. After ten years of neither peace with Mexico nor union with the United States, Texas must choose one or the other.

Following some deliberation and pressure exerted by the new U.S. minister to Texas, Andrew Jackson Donelson, President Anson Jones forwarded both offers to a specifically elected convention meeting at Austin. The American proposal of annexation was accepted with but one dissenting vote; the Mexican proposal was never put to an official vote. A committee was appointed to write a state constitution and that task was completed within two months. Earlier, President Jones had decreed that both the annexation resolution and the new state constitution must be approved by the people of Texas. Although some latent anti-annexation sentiment surfaced, both resolutions were ratified by wide margins. The last step was completed when President Polk certified "a republican form of government" to the United States Congress. He then signed the bill on December 29, 1845.

"The Republic of Texas is no more," remarked President Anson Jones as he personally pulled down the Lone Star emblem and raised the American flag in Austin on February 29, 1846. The celebration marked the inauguration of James Pinckney Henderson as the first governor of the state of Texas. It was said that Sam Houston and others wept as they witnessed the ceremony. A decade of independence and sovereignty thus came to an end. The Republic had constituted a glorious era in Texas history, but the onset of statehood presaged an even brighter future.

Suggested Reading

Barker, Eugene C. *The Life of Stephen F. Austin, Founder of Texas, 1793–1836: A Chapter in the Westward Movement of the Anglo-American People.* Austin: Texas State Historical Association, 1949.

Callcott, Willfrid Hardy. *Santa Anna: The Story of an Enigma Who Once Was Mexico.* Norman: University of Oklahoma Press, 1936.

Fehrenbach, T. R. *Lone Star: A History of Texas and the Texans.* New York: the Macmillan Company, 1968.

Friend, Llrena. *Sam Houston: The Great Designer.* Austin: University of Texas Press, 1954.

Haynes, Sam W. *Soldiers of Misfortune: The Somervell and Mier Expeditions.* Austin: University of Texas Press, 1990.

Hogan, William Ransom. *The Texas Republic: A Social and Economic History.* Norman: University of Oklahoma Press, 1946.

Jones, Anson. *Memoranda and Official Correspondence Relating to the Republic of Texas, Its History and Annexation Including a Brief Autobiography of the Author.* New York: D. Appelton & Company, 1859.

Meinig, D. W. *Imperial Texas: An Interpretative Essay in Cultural Geography.* Austin: University of Texas Press, 1969.

Pletcher, David. *Diplomacy of Annexation: Texas, Oregon, and the Mexican War.* Columbia: University of Missouri Press, 1973.

Reichstein, Andreas V. *Rise of the Lone Star: The Making of Texas.* College Station: Texas A&M University Press, 1989.

Siegel, Stanley E. *A Political History of the Texas Republic, 1836–1845.* Austin: University of Texas Press, 1956.

Smith, Justin H. *The Annexation of Texas.* New York: Barnes & Noble, Inc., 1941.

Struve, Walter. *Germans and Texans: Commerce, Migration, and Culture in the Days of the Lone Star Republic.* Austin: University of Texas Press, 1996.

Tijerina, Andrés. *Tejanos and Texas Under the Mexican Flag, 1821–1836.* College Station: Texas A&M University Press, 1994.

Cynthia Ann Parker and her daughter, Prairie Flower. *Courtesy of the Western History Collections, University of Oklahoma Archives.*

CHAPTER SIX

Statehood, 1845–1860

Michael L. Collins

THE BOUNDLESS MAGNIFICENCE OF THE LAND lay before them. Vast, immense, seemingly limitless, the timbers and prairies stretched to the horizon's infinity. From the Piney Woods along the Louisiana border to the southern spurs of the Great Stony Mountains, it was a sprawling land of legends, a barbaric new land of new beginnings that beckoned a pioneering people. Perhaps settler John Linn expressed it best when he observed that the fledgling Lone Star State loomed over the American Southwest like a "lusty young giant."

Little wonder that this country assumed, in the minds of American frontierspeople, almost mythical proportions. By 1845, Texas already held a mystique not unlike that of a religion. Rich in resources, abounding in opportunity, the region was rumored to be a veritable Garden of Eden, a pastoral paradise for yeomen farmers and their families. According to the Anglo-Texan Creation Myth, a man named Moses—Moses Austin—first pointed his people to the Promised Land. There they heeded the Old Testament command to be fruitful, to multiply, and to establish dominion over the earth. And they remained supremely confident in the faith that God Almighty had separated the light of Texas from the darkness of Mexico. To them, the Texas soil was sacred ground, sanctified by sacrifice, baptized in the blood of martyrs, enshrined in the memories of that American Thermopylae—the Alamo. In short, more than simply another state in the Union, Texas represented an idea and an ideal, indeed a state of mind.

Perhaps it was more than symbolic that the flag of the newest state bore a solitary star. After all, at the time of annexation, Texas stood unique among all the states. An independent nation for almost a decade, the Republic of Texas entered the Union without undergoing territorial status. Moreover, by the unprecedented terms of annexation, Texans reserved the option to divide into as many as five states. Even more significant, only Texas retained control of public lands within its boundaries, a fact made all the more important considering that fully two-thirds of the state remained unsettled and unexplored in 1845. To complicate matters for Texans, thousands of nomadic tribesmen, namely the fierce Comanches and elusive Kiowas, had been neither subdued nor removed as a barrier to settlement. Finally, no other state shared a 1,200-mile border with the Republic of Mexico.

The Rio Grande boundary had been a source of conflict since the days of the Texas Revolution. Now, with the annexation of Texas completed, that disputed boundary contributed to the rapid deterioration in United States–Mexican relations. Consequently, Texans had little time to enjoy their new status of statehood, for events soon hastened toward war. Following the failure of negotiations to resolve several troublesome issues, not the least of which was the border question, early in 1846 President James K. Polk dispatched General Zachary Taylor and a force of four thousand regulars to the South Texas coast, where they encamped near the mouth of the Nueces, not far from the squalid fishing village called Corpus Christi. After several weeks Polk ordered Taylor's command southward to establish a station on the north bank of the Rio Grande, a few miles from the mouth of the muddy Bravo at present-day Brownsville. Then, early in April, several border skirmishes occurred. Angry words and gunfire were exchanged across the river. Mexican President Mariano Paredes then did exactly what Polk had hoped he would. He asked the Congress of the Republic of Mexico to declare war on the United States, and he commanded General Pedro Ampudia to cross the river and attack Taylor's dragoons near Fort Brown. "American blood has been shed on American soil," President Polk cried.

The electrifying news of war with Mexico streaked across Texas like a lightning bolt. Nothing could have pleased most Texans more. All too vividly they remembered the Alamo and Goliad, and they would neither forget, nor would they forgive these and other Mexican atrocities—both real and imagined. Imbued with the spirit of Manifest Destiny, that simple faith in the superiority of Anglo-American institutions and ideals, they rushed to volunteer in what was considered a crusade to extend the dominion of democracy.

Texans found themselves on the front lines of the War with Mexico in more ways than one. By the thousands they enlisted during the opening days of the conflict. So many joined, in fact, that the state legislature declared Governor James Pinckney

Henderson (1846–1847) on furlough for the purpose of organizing a brigade of five thousand Texan volunteers. The first engagements of the war, at Resaca de la Palma on May 8, 1846, and at Palo Alto the following day, were fought north of the Rio Grande, a fact which did not go unnoticed in Texas. When the fighting began, Texans considered the war as the moral equivalent of Armageddon, and they proudly and eagerly took up arms in the name of Protestantism and patriotism. Ranger units mustered into service across the state were among the first volunteers to reach General Taylor. Almost immediately these Texan "spy companies" became the eyes and ears of the United States Army. Riding at the vanguard of American forces, at times ranging far in advance of regular units, these scouts spurred their mounts deep into the desert and mountainous regions of Mexico, reconnoitering enemy troop deployments and carrying vital intelligence to American commanders.

Dust-covered, tobacco-stained, and surly in appearance, these undisciplined Texas Rangers behaved more like a mob than a military force. But they could fight like demons possessed, as they proved at the Battle of Monterey in September 1846, and at Buena Vista five months later. On horseback, with six-shooters in hand, they served as the shock troops of the United States Army. Tragically, however, some Texans committed atrocities against Mexican civilians and thus earned the feared reputation as *"Los Diablos Tejanos"* (the Texas devils). The bitter legacy of the Texas Revolution and the War with Mexico poisoned racial relations in the Southwest for decades to follow.

So much of the lore of the Lone Star State has surrounded the mythic figure of the fearless Texas Ranger captain. And the War with Mexico produced larger-than-life heroes such as John Coffee "Jack" Hays, Ben McCulloch, Samuel Walker, and John Salmon "Rip" Ford. Anglo Texans lionized them as daring defenders of the borders, while Tejanos and Mexicans viewed them as devils on horseback. Whether patriots or pagans, heroic rangers or riders from hell, one thing is certain—the Texas Rangers who rode into the storms of the War with Mexico have remained as archetypes of both bravery and savagery. Even today the grimly determined Ranger, like his kinsman the cowboy, continues to symbolize the state's frontier heritage.

In 1850, Texas could be characterized as a frontier in every sense of the word. After traveling across the state, New England missionary Melinda Rankin observed, "a person coming into Texas, direct from the Northern States might, perhaps, be surprised upon seeing many places called towns. . . . He would probably, as has been frequently the case, inquire, 'Where is the town?'" Most "towns" in Texas during those days were little more than a few mud-chinked cabins and drafty clapboard buildings. Even in the largest of settlements, the comforts and amenities of civilization were in short supply, as were good manners and money. Noting the absence of currency, either paper scrip or specie, German immigrant Ferdinand Roemer commented: "Trading and bartering are more common in Texas than in any other part of the United States. A Texan is ready at any moment, even while traveling, to trade or sell anything he wears, whether it is a coat or shirt [on his back], if he can make an advantageous trade."

Most early Texans placed the highest premium on utilitarian skills, and the greatest virtue they recognized was physical strength. An education was something a young man or woman received behind a mule and plow. Schools were few, and so were churches. Only on occasion did the faithful gather to worship, and then usually irrespective of denomination, whenever a circuit-riding minister passed through the county carrying the Gospel in his saddlebags. In wagons, on horseback, even on foot, pioneer families would come from miles around to that frontier institution called the camp meeting revival. Most could relate to the lengthy sermonizing of Bible thumping fundamentalist preachers who spoke of the Old Testament God of judgment and of the laws of the prophets, which simply stated "an eye for an eye" and told of the ancient Israelites' sufferings while wandering in search of a wilderness Zion.

As with any frontier, Texas at midcentury was a society on the move. But as thousands of immigrants streamed into the state each month, they found cross-country travel slow at best, on occasion impossible. Melinda Rankin understated the case when she wrote of the primitive condition of transportation, "a great deal of remissness is observed in the . . . state upon the subject of internal improvements. Attention has not been paid hitherto to the improvement of roads." Frederick Law Olmstead, who embarked upon a saddle trip across the Southwest in 1853, could not have agreed more: "That Texas, with all . . . [its] capabilities and productions, lacks only the means of cheap and steady transportation, to become the richest and most attractive . . . [southern] state in the Union, is the very first and last reflection that forces itself upon the traveler." During his trek, Olmstead passed along roads that were little more than rude wagon ruts or hoof tracks. At times he and his companions found themselves guided by "indistinct paths and erroneous information." Maps seemed always inadequate, if not misleading, road signs nonexistent. Often the path ahead turned out to be choked with stumps, fallen tree trunks, thick underbrush, and menacing mudholes; a sudden cloudburst could transform the trail into a quagmire.

Then, inevitably, the greatest challenge awaited—fording rivers and streams. Olmstead described ferry crossings at numerous rivers and bayous as "costly and ill tended," while bridges seemed nowhere to be found. Of course, with the coming of heavy spring rains, most streams and creeks swelled beyond their banks, sometimes flooding miles of bottomlands. Under the circumstances the sight of immigrant families waiting for days, even weeks, along the rushing waters of the Trinity, Brazos, or Colorado Rivers became all too common. So were reports of drownings.

With overland travel and the freighting of commerce by wagon painfully slow and sometimes perilous, Texans depended heavily upon coastal and river traffic. Steamboats regularly churned through the channels of Galveston Bay and the Buffalo Bayou below the township of Houston. But the major rivers of East Texas could be navigated only for four or five months of the year, and even then for little more than thirty miles inland. Sandbars and snags of driftwood and debris clogged upstream waters, making them impassible. From the midsummer through winter, only small flatboats could float down the shallow Brazos and Colorado carrying bales of cotton, bushels of corn, and other produce to coastal ports such as Velasco (near present-day Freeport) and Indianola (near present-day Port Lavaca). Likewise, the Trinity could be navigated for limited distances only. The Red River alone provided Texans with a reliable inland waterway to channel commerce year-round, as evidenced by the rapid growth of one Marion County community into a major East Texas hub of trade. Nestled in the cypress swamps along Caddo Lake, and linked to the Red River and, therefore, to the great Mississippi, the town of Jefferson was destined to develop into a bustling center of commerce.

With travel difficult, most Texans learned to accept isolation as a fact of life. The United States Census for 1850 revealed that 96 percent of Texans lived in remote, rural areas. Not surprisingly, therefore, antebellum Texas could be best described as a state of farmers.

In his autobiography, James "Buck" Barry described life on a typical Texas farm as simple yet hard. The work hours were long, and the labor was tiresome and tedious. Barry noted the "drab, monotonous side of the daily life" on the farm "spent in a daily routine of ordinary duties." Whether plowing or planting, shucking corn or shoeing a horse, repairing a saddle and harness or tending to livestock, building a split-rail fence, or scalding and butchering a hog, the work never seemed to end. Chores such as cutting wood, drawing water, picking pecans, milking cows, and churning butter occupied many of the hours of young men and women. Texans had little time for such preferred activities as molding bullets, cleaning rifles, and hunting in the case of boys, or quilting, sewing, and cooking in the case of their sisters.

Life on the Texas frontier was especially lonely and wearisome for women. As chronicler Noah Smithwick remarked, Texas was "a heaven for men and horses, but hell for oxen and women." The ordeal of childbearing, the years of child rearing, and the exhausting burdens of caring for a family all took their toll. Women usually married young, bore children at an early age, and grew old before their time. Sickness and death seemed their constant companions on the frontier. After traveling from one homestead to another in 1853, Olmstead observed that Texas women appeared "far superior to their lords. They have, at least, the tender hearts and some of the gentle delicacy that your 'true Texan' lacks. They are overworked, however, as soon as married, and . . . [time] gives them thin faces, sallow complexions, and expressions either sad or sour."

Countless Texas women droned away the precious years of their youth surrounded by much misery and little luxury. Of course, the common dwelling of the day, the log cabin, offered few comforts and conveniences. Hand-hewn and mud-chinked, with a gabled clapboard roof and dirt floor, the typical farmhouse proved stifling hot in the summer, drafty and even frigid in the winter. In his journal, Olmstead described an overnight stay in one cabin in which he could recline in the loft and "look out . . . at the stars between the logs." During a trip through Texas, young Rutherford B. Hayes, the future president of the United States, recalled one stark house with walls so poorly constructed that you could "throw a cat through at random." Oftentimes the large size of families necessitated the construction of the familiar double log cabin, with two rooms separated by a breezeway or "dog trot," and a veranda extending the entire length of the structure. Almost inevitably, nearby stood the smokehouse where meats—when available—were cured.

The diet of pioneer Texans was every bit as monotonous as the drudgery of daily existence. Pork, potatoes, and corn provided the staples of most meals, while beans, squash, and other vegetables were usually served only in season. Not more than several times a year would beef appear on the family table, and such pleasures as sugar, flour, coffee, and salt could be obtained only at considerable cost from the nearest merchant, who might be a half-day's ride away. Fresh milk and butter also were luxuries not regularly available to many.

Regarding social life and entertainment, the frontier afforded little of either. As many early Texans like to muse, not much happened but morning, noon, and night. At times even inclement weather would be welcomed as a departure from the routine. An occasional wedding, house raising, funeral, or public hanging offered a break from the boredom of everyday existence. So did Sunday sermons and prayer meetings, which took on a social as well as spiritual significance.

Although news of the outside world was slow in coming, and printed materials were scarce, the typical Texan of the day assumed a more than passive interest in state and national politics. In fact, political candidates had little difficulty in attracting large crowds wherever they traveled, and for good reason. The brawling and gaudy nature of Texas politics and the ballyhoo of a campaign on the stump provided at least as much excitement as those traveling salvation shows called revivals. Both were diversions from an otherwise dreary life, both conducted with the same missionary zeal, and both drew throngs of the curious as well as the committed.

In Texas, politics generates an almost religious fervor. During the 1850s few public issues evoked more emotions than what Texans like to term the "Indian problem." In the first fifteen years of statehood, a striking divergence developed between the Texan and national view on many crucial issues, chief among them the questions of frontier defense and the Indian barrier. While federal officials sought to carry out a concentration policy designed to herd the plains tribes onto reservations, the average Texan resented this eastern-imposed program, preferring wars of extermination, or, at the least, Indian removal and relocation to distant and arid lands. To add to the confusion, although the United States Department of War shouldered the responsibility for protecting the Texas frontier, the state government controlled the disposition of unsettled public lands west of the line of settlement, which in 1850 ran roughly from present-day Gainesville near the Red River, west of Waco and Austin, to San Antonio, and then all the way to Laredo on the Rio Grande. Compounding the difficulty, the Indians never understood that the white men from Washington spoke with a different voice than those in Austin. For their part, many white Texans failed to grasp that a deal struck with the leader of one band might not be honored by that of another—even if both bands were technically part of the same tribe. The result was misunderstanding, feelings of betrayal, and a decade of brutal border warfare.

As early as 1846, and again in 1848, United States Indian commissioners negotiated treaties with the headmen of several Comanche bands during councils at Comanche Peak in present-day Hood County. In exchange for pledges to refrain from further attacks upon Texan settlements and homesteads, the Indian spokesmen were assured that their peoples could continue to hunt the bison herds, as they had for centuries, without fear of intervention by whites. But these arrangements proved impractical. For one thing, federal negotiators could not guarantee reservation land in Texas without the approval of state officials, and they could not prevent the continued westward advance of the farmer's frontier. Secondly, the buffalo knew no political boundaries, and neither did the Comanches. Even more significantly, Anglo Texans refused to acknowledge such agreements between the United States and loosely aligned bands of Native plains horsemen. They insisted that, under the terms of the ordinance of annexation, only the state of Texas could dictate policies affecting the unsettled public domain. Besides, they pointed out, United States Indian commissioners were badly mistaken in assuming that the Comanches would give up their customary ways of warfare and plunder so easily.

In response to Texan demands for increased border defense, the United States Department of War constructed a string of eight frontier forts in 1849. The northernmost of these outposts, Fort Worth, stood upon a bluff overlooking the Trinity River; the two southernmost, Fort Duncan and Fort McIntosh, commanded strategic positions on the lower Rio Grande. But this line of fortifications proved inadequate. Located too far apart and understaffed with small garrisons of dragoons, or horse- and mule-mounted infantrymen, these log stockades provided a static defense that was no match for the mobile and swift-riding Comanches, called by Captain George McClellan the "best light cavalry in the world." After seeing the slow-moving army bluecoats performing drill, one seasoned Texas Indian fighter supposedly remarked that the only way these dragoons could subdue the marauding Comanches would be to cause them to laugh themselves to death.

Frustrated and disillusioned about the failure of federal troops to defend the borders and either prevent depredations or at least punish the marauders, Texans soon demanded that an effective state Ranger force be reinstituted to deal with the problem. But the state legislature and Governor Peter H. Bell (1849–1853) believed that raising companies of mounted volunteers to patrol the frontier would be too costly. So, as historian Walter Prescott Webb noted, for several years the Texas Rangers remained "little more than a historical expression."

By 1854 the United States Department of War answered Texan indignation not with an aggressive policy of the sword, but with a reservation policy promising to bring peace to the Southern Plains. Secretary of War Jefferson Davis and state officials agreed to set aside sixty thousand acres of land on the upper Brazos River for two Indian reserves. Early that year Captain Randolph B. Marcy of the United States Army Topographical Engineers arrived in Texas to oversee the surveys. The Brazos River Reservation would be carved out of marginal lands west of present-day Graham for the sedentary Anadarkos, Wacos, and Tonkawas, while the Clear Fork Reservation would be laid out forty miles farther to the west for the more nomadic and warlike Penateka Comanches. To serve as supervising agent for these reserves, the Office of Indian Affairs selected Major Robert S. Neighbors.

A better man than Neighbors could not have been chosen for this post. A seasoned frontiersman and former Texas Ranger, Neighbors earned the respect and confidence of the Indians in his custody as well as both civilian and military officials. A large man in stature, he demonstrated courage and compassion during his struggles to protect more than one thousand reservation Indians. With fierce determination he fought the racial prejudices of white Texans who interfered with his administration of the agencies, and he worked tirelessly to overcome the incompetence and apathy of federal bureaucrats who burdened him with foolish regulations. When the Department of War failed to provide adequate food and provisions for half-starved Indians who were wards of the agencies, he encouraged the Natives to assemble peaceably in protest of such unconscionable neglect—an act which many whites interpreted as rebellion. Desperately he tried to persuade the young Indian men to remain on the reservation, although understandably more and more of them drifted away to hunt buffalo or to steal horses and cattle in order to survive. Faced with mounting frustrations and growing pressures, he nevertheless continued to defend the reservation experiment as a humane alternative to bloodshed.

In the end, Neighbors's work was in vain. In the summer of 1859, he received orders to close the unpopular reservations and escort their several hundred gaunt survivors under his protection to the Wichita Mountains in western Indian Territory. After leading them north of the Red River that September, he lamented in a letter to his wife: "I have this day crossed all of the Indians out of the heathen land . . . of the Philistines. If you want to have a full description of our exodus out of Texas—read the Bible where the children of Israel crossed the Red Sea . . . [only here] our enemies did not follow us." Soon thereafter, Neighbors—by now the hated symbol of federal Indian policies in Texas—returned to his headquarters at Fort Belknap, where he was shot in the back by an assassin. He was buried in an unmarked grave, probably in the post Indian cemetery.

During the administration of the Connecticut-born Governor Elisha M. Pease (1853–1857), the only thing lower than the morale of state Ranger forces was their state appropriation. But the coming of the new governor, Hardin R. Runnels (1857–1859), meant the reactivation of state volunteer units to defend the borders against "hostiles" who raided isolated homesteads and rode away with ponies, livestock, and sometimes captives, or merely their scalps. To restore the Rangers to respectability, Runnels appointed the legendary plainsman Captain John S. "Rip" Ford to organize and lead companies of mounted volunteers against the lords of the South Plains, the Comanches. What followed was a brutally effective campaign in which "Old Rip" and his Rangers pursued the raiders across the Red River into the sanctuary of Indian Territory, to the Wichita Mountains, and to the Canadian River in far western Oklahoma. On the morning of May 12, 1858, Ford ordered an attack upon a large Comanche encampment. During the remarkable, seven-hour battle that followed, the Texans shot and killed the venerable chief "Iron Jacket" and subsequently chased down and killed seventy-five of his warriors, while losing only two Rangers.

Despite such successes, Comanche raiding parties continued to trouble the plains for years; and each time Texas Rangers were called out to meet them. Ironically, while state volunteers were demonstrating their stealth in border warfare, a revamped Department of War placed units of mobile cavalry throughout the West. Among the best of these forces was the Second United States Cavalry, deployed on the Texas frontier along a line of newly constructed posts that included Fort Phantom Hill near present-day Abilene, Fort Chadbourn on the upper Colorado, Fort Mason in the Texas Hill Country, and Fort Clark on the Rio Grande below present-day Brackettville. During the 1850s, therefore, the Indian frontier in Texas became the proving ground for cavalry tactics that would revolutionize U.S. military strategy on the eve of the American Civil War. Just as important, the Lone Star State became the training ground for an entire generation of army officers who would gain valuable experience fighting Comanches on the borders—knowledge also employed on Civil War battlefields. The officer corps serving in the Second Cavalry in Texas during these critical years included such commanders as Captain John Bell Hood, later known as the "fighting general" of the South; Colonel Albert Sidney Johnston, the Texan destined to die at the Battle of Shiloh in 1862; and Colonel Robert E. Lee, the Virginian who would within a few years make his mark upon American history as the "Gray Fox" of the Confederacy.

Almost as successful as Ford's campaign on the Canadian was a sweeping offensive conducted by companies of the Second Cavalry in September 1858. Guided by a scouting party of state Rangers led by future governor Lawrence Sullivan "Sul" Ross, regulars under the command of Major Earl Van Dorn scoured the region north of the Red River, moving more than ninety miles in a rapid forced march to attack and overrun an unsuspecting Comanche village near the Wichita Mountains.

Employing a similar swift strike in December 1860, Captain Ross's company of Rangers and a platoon of U.S. troopers surprised the camp of the Comanche Chief Peta Nocona near the Pease River in present-day Foard County. On a cold and rainy winter morning the Texans and army regulars stormed through the Indian village in a blaze of gunfire, torching tepees, shooting men and terrorizing women and children as they attempted to flee.

During the chaos one young Ranger discovered a blue-eyed woman huddled under a blanket, clutching her infant daughter. Days later it was confirmed that this defiant Comanche, the wife of Peta Nocona known to her people as Naduah (meaning "Keeps Warm With Us") was actually a white woman who had been missing for more than twenty-four years. Taken captive as a child during an Indian raid in Limestone County in 1836, she had grown to adopt the Comanche ways and had long since lost most memories of her earlier life. Her name was Cynthia Ann Parker, and her story continues to haunt the Texas experience.

Returned soon to her white relatives, Naduah resisted their affections and tried on several occasions to escape back to her people on the prairies. After her daughter Topsannah, or "Prairie Flower," died, Cynthia Ann mourned in the manner of a Comanche mother, cutting off her hair and slashing her arms and breasts with a knife before grieving herself to death in 1870 at the home of her brother. Her legacy lived on, however, in the person of her son, who grew tall like the men of his mother's family but carried the blood of both races in his veins. Naduah had named the boy Quanah, or "Fragrance," and he became the last great war chief of the Comanches.

The legacy of Anglo-Indian warfare remains a part of the Texas heritage. The irrepressible martial spirit of Texans, their fixation with firearms, their steadfast faith in Anglo superiority, their lack of faith in a distant national government to solve their problems, and their acceptance of violence as a fact of life: all would long remain as vestiges of the Indian wars.

During the 1850s the frontier character of the state was evidenced in many ways. Thus antebellum Texas could be described as a society slowly emerging from the wilderness. While a pronounced anti-intellectualism existed among Texans of that generation, a trend that would continue through the decades, notable advances were made in the field of education. The Constitution of 1845 required that the Texas legislature reserve at least one-tenth of state revenues for a perpetual public school fund. In 1850, when Texas ceded claims to the upper Rio Grande country in exchange for $10 million in federal compensation, the state legislature set aside $2 million of those funds for a permanent public education endowment. This windfall, combined with the sale of public lands, provided a sustaining source of revenue for appropriations to support the free-school movement. Still, the need for a uniform system of textbook adoption as well as the challenge of recruiting qualified teachers remained a growing concern of those Texans who preached the importance of an enlightened populace. Institutions of higher learning likewise began to appear on the landscape of antebellum Texas. First among them was "Old Baylor," the Baptist college founded in Independence in 1845 and later moved to Waco; Austin College was established in Huntsville by the Presbyterian movement in 1849, which later relocated this school in the North Texas town of Sherman; and St. Mary's, a Catholic school, was organized in 1852 at San Antonio.

Texas society during the 1850s appeared to be more literate than that of most border states, not so much because of the state leaders' commitment to education, but because of the rapid immigration into the region from established states east of the Mississippi. Between 1850 and 1860 the population of Texas nearly tripled, from

212,592 to 604,215. One traveler in 1847 described that growing population as "composed to a great extent of the most degraded riff-raff, adventurers, gamblers, swindlers and murderers—the scum of all nations," while another chronicler three years later commented that Texans were a "heterogenous mass from . . . all ranks and conditions," most being desperately "in need of mental and moral improvements." Yet over the course of the next decade more farmers, craftsmen, teachers, ministers, physicians, attorneys, and other desired professionals arrived by the thousands.

The reasons for the migration were simple—cheap land and opportunity. In 1854 the state legislature reaffirmed the generous land policy established during the years of the Republic. A Preemption Act passed that year provided for the sale of 160-acre tracts of public land to homesteaders for as little as fifty cents an acre. Even the coveted bottomlands of the Trinity, Brazos, and Colorado Rivers rarely sold for more than $6 an acre, by any measure a bargain for immigrants looking for new lands and a new life.

In 1854 Governor Pease signed into law another bill that helped to prepare the way for growth and expansion. The act authorized the state to grant private railroad corporations sixteen sections of land (10,240 acres) for each mile of railway constructed within the state. Although at that time only one thirty-mile spur line existed in all of Texas—that from Harrisburg near the Buffalo Bayou to Richmond on the lower Brazos—almost four hundred additional miles of track would be laid before the Civil War. With the laying of rails and the coming of the locomotive, Texas now stood poised to enter the new age of steam and steel.

The railroad appeared as the harbinger of social change and economic progress. But not until the post–Civil War era would the railways dominate the landscape as well as the politics of Texas. For the time being, the fastest means of transportation across the state remained the Butterfield Overland Stage line which linked the Southwest to the Pacific Coast of California. The most popular methods of cross-country travel were on horseback or by ox-drawn wagon.

During the 1850s Texas not only experienced phenomenal growth, but the changing demographics of the state underscored its distinctive character. Unlike other southern states and border states, Texas was fast becoming a confluence of many cultures, as increased immigration from foreign nations—especially Germany, England, Ireland, France, and the Scandinavian countries—mixed with the established populace of Anglos, Hispanics, American Indians, and black Africans to produce a melting pot of peoples and races. While still far from urban, by 1860 Texas was beginning to assume a cosmopolitan appearance.

Nowhere was this more evident than in the seaport of Galveston. A bustling center of trade and a funnel for commerce on the Gulf Coast, the insular city of 7,300 inhabitants seemed alive with the constant hum of manufacturing and transport, as evidenced by warehouses filled with cotton, foundries and machine shops near the shores, and narrow streets thronged with markets and lined with banks, hotels, and barrooms; more important were the "witches of the waves," the ocean-going steamers and great clipper ships anchored in the harbor and prepared to set sail for distant ports in faraway lands. Thus Galveston emerged as the fulcrum of the Texas economy and a cultural center, according to Melinda Rankin, "refined . . . and equal to any other southern city."

Only San Antonio rivaled Galveston in size and importance in antebellum Texas. A vital depot of commerce nestled along the natural gardens and clear waters of the San Antonio River, the town stood as a reminder of Texas's storied past as well as a reflection of its future potential. Its dusty streets and plazas offered a picturesque panorama of adobe dwellings, modest white limestone stores, a few cantinas and boarding houses, and the ruins of old stone missions that were, in the words of Frederick Law Olmstead, "in different stages of decay." As Olmstead described the shrine of Texas independence, the Alamo, "it consists of a few irregular stuccoed buildings, huddled against the old church, in a large court surrounded by a rude wall." A makeshift arsenal for the U.S. Army quartermaster, the chapel appeared to be "a mere wreck of its former grandeur." Throughout San Antonio the atmosphere was leisurely though bustling in the daytime, always festive and filled with music after dark, a curious mixture of enterprise, serenity, and celebration. On the prairies surrounding the town, settlers raised cattle and sheep or cultivated corn, beans, and squash in fields watered by the aqueducts radiating from the river, which wound its way through the settlement. As the Civil War approached, historic San Antonio thus stood as a strategically located crossroads of commerce and cultures on the South Texas plains; boasting more than 8,200 inhabitants, the town was easily the largest in the entire state.

If the promise of progress and prosperity loomed ahead on the Texas horizon in 1860, so did danger. For a decade and more the explosive potential of the slavery issue threatened to splinter the Union and plunge the nation into war. The American people were polarizing into two hostile and equally uncompromising camps, and Texans were no exception. As early as 1856, the climate of violence seemed to spread across the country like a prairie fire, from the plains of "Bleeding Kansas" to the halls of Congress. The battle lines were drawn between militant abolitionists who demanded the immediate emancipation of all enslaved persons and southern firebrands who stridently defended slavery while openly threatening secession from the Union. The following year the United States Supreme Court further fueled the conflict by handing down its controversial decision in the Dred Scott Case. Southerners welcomed the majority opinion of Chief Justice Roger B. Taney that Congress has no constitutional right to restrict slavery from new territories and states in the West and that slaves could not enjoy the legal benefits of citizenship and thus "had no rights that any white man is bound to respect." The antislave voices of the North, abolitionist and free-soiler alike, reacted angrily to the decision, which appeared to them to preempt any possibility of purging the land of that "peculiar institution" by any means other than bloodshed.

Amidst this gathering storm in 1857 the people of Texas elected Trinity-River planter, slave owner, and secessionist Hardin R. Runnels as governor, rejecting the candidacy of unionist Sam Houston by a margin of 32,552 to 28,678. Two years later Houston and his supporters reversed the earlier results, as the Hero of San Jacinto defeated Governor Runnels by 33,375 votes to 27,500 votes, the outcome probably having more to do with the enormous stature of "Old Sam" than with his vow to head off the secessionists.

But newly elected Governor Houston (1859–1861) soon discovered his task to be virtually impossible, as events accelerated toward an appeal to arms. In October 1859, a thunderbolt struck a nation and a state already gripped by fear, hate, and suspicion. John Brown raided Harpers Ferry, Virginia, to seize the federal armory there, and his thwarted scheme to incite a general slave uprising throughout the South sounded an alarm heard as far away as Texas. Although the fanatical abolitionist was captured and executed for treason several weeks later, the incident ignited the emotions of Texans who lived in fear of a slave rebellion. Many wondered aloud if other John Browns might be lurking in the thickets, awaiting the opportunity to foment a slave uprising. The images of slaves poisoning their masters, running away, and slitting the throats of innocent whites led to the further radicalization of opinions in Texas and throughout the South. In the North, "Old Osawatomie" (Brown) might have become the martyred saint of abolitionism, but in the Lone Star State his ghost evoked the worst passions of a people no longer governed by reason.

Smoldering discontent over the New Mexico territorial cession of 1850, issues of Indian policy, frontier defense, and states' rights erupted anew and merged with the raging firestorm over slavery. The combustion occurred in 1860. That spring a citizens' committee in Palestine held a book-burning of presumably dangerous publications, chief among them Harriet Beecher Stowe's *Uncle Tom's Cabin*. Yankee merchant seamen were mobbed and beaten on the wharves of Galveston, while across the state shops owned by Northerners and known unionists were ransacked and torched. Then, in July, North Texas was engulfed in an inferno as a series of suspicious fires broke out in Gainesville, Pilot Point, Denton, McKinney, Waxahachie, and Fort Worth. In Dallas on Sunday, July 8, flames swept through the town's business district, reducing to ashes twenty-five residences and stores, including the three-story Dallas Hotel. Whether these conflagrations resulted from the deliberate acts of incendiaries or from the spontaneous combustion of a store of new phosphorus "prairie matches" has remained a matter of conjecture. But in the hysteria that followed, a vigilante court in Dallas singled out and arrested three slaves—Samuel Smith, Patrick Jennings, and Old Cato—accused them of attempted insurrection and arson, then hanged them without a trial. Less than two months later, a mob in Fort Worth lynched Northern Methodist minister Anthony Bewley, charging that the suspected abolitionist had made inflammatory statements intended to incite a slave rebellion.

The history of people and nations may not be told by statistics alone, but the United States Census of 1860 reveals several important facts about Texas. Fewer than 5 percent of Texans owned slaves, and less than 10 percent of those who did owned twenty or more bondspeople. Only 265 Texans listed themselves as plantation owners in that year. A closer study of the census shows that approximately 10 percent of slaveholders in the state owned more than half the 182,566 slaves listed on the rolls. While most slaves appeared to be field hands on plantations that produced cotton, sugar, and other cash crops, a significant minority worked as domestic servants, some even possessing valuable skills. Two inescapable conclusions emerge from a survey of this data: the labor system of slavery was a vitally important part of the Texas economy on the eve of the Civil War; and a small but influential class of wealthy planters stood to gain the most from its preservation.

No matter that some might argue that the conflict that followed was a "rich man's war." What mattered most was that the imminent struggle was to be every man's fight. Convinced that the North would not take up arms to preserve the Union, much less to free the black slaves, most Texans failed to see the coming of the unthinkably-horrible war. But not Governor Houston. As the presidential election of 1860 approached and tensions mounted, he continually warned that any movement for Southern independence would result in a war of disastrous dimensions. For this foresight his enemies scorned and cursed him as a coward and, worse, a traitor.

News of the November election results confirmed the worst fears of Southern firebrands from Virginia to Texas: the new Republican Party of the North and its standard bearer, Abraham Lincoln, had won on a free-soil platform calling for the restriction of slavery in new western territories and states. In the following days the President-elect pleaded with his countrymen to listen to the "better angels" of their nature. But the time had come, as Houston prophesied, when Texas and the nation would be hurled into the madness of total war, when the "demons of anarchy" would be unleashed. Or, as Noah Smithwick recalled: "the dogs of war were . . . turned loose, and the devil concealed in men unchained."

Suggested Reading

Barry, James B. *Buck Barry: Texas Ranger and Frontiersman*. Edited by James K. Greer. Lincoln: University of Nebraska Press, 1978.

Buenger, Walter. *Secession and the Union in Texas*. Austin: University of Texas Press, 1984.

Campbell, Randolph B. *An Empire for Slavery: The Peculiar Institution in Texas*. Baton Rouge: Louisiana State University Press, 1989.

De Cordova, Jacob. *Texas: Her Resources and Her Public Men*. Philadelphia: J. B. Lippincott and Co., 1858.

Ford, John Salmon. *Rip Ford's Texas*. Edited by Stephen B. Oates. Austin: University of Texas Press, 1963.

Jenkins, John Holland. *Recollections of Early Texas: The Memoirs of John Holland Jenkins*. Edited by John Holmes Jenkins III. Austin: University of Texas Press, 1958.

Linn, John. *Reminiscences of Fifty Years in Texas*. Austin: The Steck Company, 1935.

Olmstead, Frederick Law. *A Journey Through Texas: Or a Saddle Trip on the Southwestern Frontier*. Austin: University of Texas Press, 1978.

Rankin, Melinda. *Texas in 1850*. Waco: The Texian Press, 1966.

Roemer, Ferdinand. *Texas: With Particular Reference to German Immigration and the Physical Appearance of the Country*. San Antonio: Standard Printing Company, 1935.

Smithwick, Noah. *The Evolution of a State: Or Recollections of Old Texas Days*. Austin: The Steck Company, 1935.

Freed slaves celebrate Juneteenth, the day of emancipation in Texas. *Courtesy of The Austin History Center, Austin Public Library, PICA #05476.*

CHAPTER SEVEN

Change and Continuity in Texas during the Civil War and Reconstruction

Alwyn Barr

THE CIVIL WAR AND RECONSTRUCTION CAUSED revolutionary changes and stirred struggles between advocates of further change and supporters of continuity in Texas and throughout the South. The war crushed forever the idea that a state could break away from the United States legally and peacefully. Thus the nature of federal-state relations had been clarified in a way sharply different from the prewar views of most Texans. Slavery died with the Confederacy. This fundamental change produced other crucial developments in the economy and society of Texas and the South.

Some historians have argued that events within the Confederacy foreshadowed those changes, previously seen as imposed on the South from outside. Moreover, these historians have concluded that a far greater number of fundamental changes occurred or began within the Confederate states as a result of the Civil War. But what of Texas? Did this Southern frontier state feel the full impact of wartime change as did the older Confederate states located east of the Mississippi? Historians also have debated the amount of change brought by Reconstruction, and some have asserted that white Southerners' opposition to innovation proved successful in maintaining considerable continuity.

To recognize changes caused by the Civil War and Reconstruction, one must have a clear picture of antebellum Texas and the South. Politically, most Texans shared the prewar Southern inclination toward the states' rights philosophy. They did not oppose federal action uniformly, however, if it meant protection of slavery in the territories or the protection of frontier settlers against Indians. Yet the Texas secession convention did base its action on states' rights, with later affirmation from 75 percent of the state's voters. Texas delegates then committed the state to the Confederacy, whose constitution sharply limited the powers of its central government.

Texans, because of the war for independence from Mexico, had a more recent and vivid tradition of military revolution than other Southerners. The Texas military experience also emphasized volunteers rather than professional soldiers trained at military academies, although the state contained new schools such as Bastrop Military Institute. The Texas economy in 1860 remained even more agrarian than most states in a predominantly rural region. Slaveholders and planters did not dominate Texas society to the extent they did in some of the older states in the Deep South. But as slaveholders grew in numbers and in leadership positions during the 1850s, they became the ideal for a majority of their fellow Texans. Slavery received the support of most nonslaveholding Texans, as well as slaveholders, because it provided not only a system of controlled labor but also a means for social domination of black people, whom most whites in the nineteenth century considered to be inferior.

Texans shared in varying degrees other attitudes common to most Southerners. They seemed to be ardent individualists, who were influenced by their frontier existence. Their recent arrival in Texas, the last Southern frontier, seemed to stimulate a strong Lone Star nationalism, rather than to reduce the often-noted Southern sense of place. Southern Protestantism, with its emphasis on an evangelical style and individual salvation, dominated Texas religion, though the state contained a larger Catholic minority than most states of the Confederacy. Southern cultural romanticism in Texas more often took the form of tall tales about Davy Crockett than the reading of Sir Walter Scott novels. Women on some Texas plantations received the deferential treatment for which the South had become famous. Yet taming a frontier demanded even more time and labor of Texas women than was required in more settled states. Texans joined in the Southern commitment to a way of life based on a mixture of these traditions.

Among the Southern "fire-eaters" who raised the possibility of separation from the Union in the years before 1861, several Texans played prominent roles. While they sought a conservative goal, protection of the status quo in Texas and the South, they adopted the method of stirring revolutionary ferment. At every opportunity during the 1850s, Louis T. Wigfall opposed compromise with the North and defended the right of secession—views which led to his election as United States senator in 1859. In the late 1850s Texans organized numerous chapters of the Knights of the Golden Circle, which promoted secessionist sentiment and intimidated

Unionists into silence. When Governor Sam Houston refused to call the legislature or a convention to consider separation, Texas secessionists took revolutionary action by calling an unofficial convention to carry out their views.

After secession, the Confederate government, created by Texans and other Southerners, seemed firmly committed to states' rights in its constitution. On the state level, Governor Pendleton Murrah struggled with Confederate General John Bankhead Magruder over control of state militia members in 1864. State-national conflict also developed over the Confederate decision to impress cotton, slaves, weapons, horses, and supplies.

Several Texas newspapers defended Confederate actions and criticized state opposition on the ground that war necessities had forced a revolution in the philosophy and action of government. Moreover, Texans had expanded state government activities into several new areas or had greatly stimulated trends begun in the 1850s. The legislature and Governor Francis R. Lubbock created a state Military Board, which bought cotton to exchange for supplies to be sent to Texas troops. The board also established arsenals to manufacture cannons, rifles, and ammunition to defend the Lone Star State. The state prison converted mills in Huntsville to produce uniforms and blankets. Confederate shops in Texas manufactured medicine, shoes, harnesses, and utensils, while shipyards on the coast built and repaired blockade-runners. To control and expand transportation in a state with few railroads, the Confederacy built or impressed wagons. The Texas legislature offered state land in an unsuccessful effort to promote the construction of new railroads and factories. Unlike some Confederate states, Texas did not place limits on agricultural production. But late in 1863 the legislature authorized counties to prohibit distilleries as a means of preventing the conversion of needed food crops into liquid form. A state foundry in Austin manufactured plows to meet the needs of farmers. To pay for these increased government economic efforts, both the state and county governments issued paper money and bonds and raised taxes. Despite all of these efforts, supply never matched demand.

Government activities touched Texas society as well as its economy. The state government imported cotton cards, which were sold to counties for resale to families for making their own clothes. State legislators authorized $200,000 in 1863 to aid sick or destitute soldiers and offered cloth for their families. Counties joined the effort to assist soldiers and their dependents. For example, Smith

County devoted $4,749.50 to support the families of its military men. Confederate, state, and county governments supported hospitals for the wounded.

The necessities of war forced the Confederacy into less popular interventions in the lives of its people. In 1862 Louis T. Wigfall, champion of states' rights, proposed—and the Confederate Congress enacted—a military draft to keep its armies at full strength. The possibility of being conscripted led many men to volunteer while others accepted the call to serve without question. But others "took to the woods" rather than be forced into the army, and deserters joined them to form bands that held out against all authorities. Their reasons ranged from reluctance about secession to frustration over the exemption of planters from the draft. To control such resistance, especially in Unionist areas, the Confederate government declared martial law. A military court in San Antonio during 1862 left lasting bitterness by sending several men to jail or into Mexican exile.

Some aspects of Texans' military efforts seemed as innovative in style as did many government activities. The Confederacy did not adopt a full-scale revolutionary war with guerrilla tactics. Some historians have suggested, however, that Confederates, while adopting a defensive strategy, sought to surprise and defeat Union armies by taking the offensive on the battlefield or through cavalry raids. Texans defended their state at Sabine Pass in 1863 and at Mansfield, Louisiana, in 1864, but they played significant roles in carrying out offensives several times. Albert Sidney Johnston launched a surprise attack at Shiloh (in Tennessee) in 1862, which almost won a major victory for the Confederacy, but ultimately cost Johnston his life. Texas troops on cotton-clad river steamers recaptured Galveston in a surprise predawn attack on New Year's Day, 1863. John Bell Hood directed the ill-fated counterattacks around Atlanta and in Tennessee in 1864, though his defeats left his reputation in shambles. Tom Green won a reputation as a successful cavalry commander by slashing raids on Union camps or columns in Louisiana during 1863 and 1864. Texas cavalry regiments participated in successful raids east of the Mississippi with Nathan Bedford Forest and Joseph Wheeler. Others joined forays into New Mexico in 1862 and into Missouri throughout the war. Union forces never occupied any extensive portion of the Lone Star State, thus no Confederate guerrilla bands operated within its boundaries. But vigilantes seized and hanged several suspected Unionists in North Texas after unofficial trials, and Confederate troops tracked down and destroyed most of a German Unionist band in South Texas.

The Texas economy experienced some adjustments, though probably not as great as those experienced in other Confederate states. Most states behind Confederate lines reduced their production of staple crops, such as cotton and tobacco, and increased their production of food crops. These shifts reflected the greater need for food supplies, as well as the inability to sell tobacco and cotton, because planters and farmers found themselves increasingly cut off from Northern or foreign markets by the war and the Union blockade. Yet Texas, because of its border with Mexico, continued to produce cotton in large quantities for sale across the Rio Grande to Mexican and European buyers. The border trade also meant that Texans did not suffer from shortages of manufactured goods to the same extent as Confederates in states located east of the Mississippi. Nevertheless, Texans faced the need to develop substitutes for some unavailable items, fashioning cotton wicks for candles and homemade straw hats.

Texas urban areas remained smaller and less vulnerable to military attack or the impact of inflation than many cities elsewhere in the Confederacy, but most of them keenly experienced wartime changes. Galveston found its trade reduced by the blockade and fear of Union occupation, which took place briefly in the fall of 1862. Throughout most of the war it remained a garrison city. Alternately, Houston and especially San Antonio became active and growing centers for the new trade through Mexico. Along with Austin, they served as focal points of government and military activities. Meanwhile, speculation and inflation drove the prices of medicine and food up as much as 400 percent in some cases. Enraged by such drastic price increases, a mob formed in San Antonio in 1862 to seize the city market. Theft became more common in Texas cities, while vigilantes formed in San Antonio to enforce their own brand of order. Looting broke out in Houston, Austin, and other towns during the spring of 1865 as the state and Confederate governments began to collapse. Refugees from Galveston and other coastal towns, as well as from Arkansas, Louisiana, and Missouri, poured into Texas cities, which soon became crowded. Most towns provided some refugee assistance but such large numbers of dispossessed persons seeking housing, jobs, and schools for their children created tensions and left many newcomers feeling unwelcome.

War needs led to the establishment of new factories, which further stimulated urban growth in Texas. Tyler's citizens saw their community industrialize almost overnight with the construction of a new hat factory, tanneries, sawmills, wool-carding mills, a spinning-wheel factory, and a major salt works. Sixteen salt works operated in different locations across the state. Fourteen towns housed munitions factories, while eight supported tanneries, and four contained powder mills. The number of state-chartered manufacturing companies, primarily producing iron and textiles, jumped from six in 1861–62 to thirty-three in 1863–64.

Slavery, an aspect of the Texas economy and society, changed little at the beginning of the war, except for new laws tightening controls over bondsmen. But military needs and movements soon disrupted the peculiar institution in some regions. Refugees took their slaves with them as they fled to avoid Union armies. Confederate commanders impressed one-fourth of the slaves on plantations to construct earthworks for defense along the coast or to drive supply wagons. Poorly fed and clothed by Confederate officials, many of these laborers fell ill or died. Such disruptions opened the way for more escapes from slavery. Some runaways, usually young men without families, fled to Federal lines in Arkansas, the Indian Territory, Louisiana, or to ships along the Texas coast, while others made their way to Mexico. Urban bondsmen such as Dave, a slave of Galveston attorney William P. Ballinger, rebelled against the farm labor expected of them after their cosmopolitan masters became refugees. Dave and others escaped and returned to the more diverse town life to which they had become accustomed. Most slaves did not attempt to escape, however, because they had children or elderly family members who could not stand the hardships involved and because Union armies generally remained too distant to excite much hope of success. Those who continued to labor on farms and plantations often gained greater control of their day-to-day lives since they received less supervision with so many white men away in the Confederate army. Some slaves talked back to slaveholders more openly, while others resisted punishment. Still, slavery changed less and seemed further from collapse in Texas than in other Confederate states which were occupied or more frequently invaded by Union armies.

The wartime reactions of white Texans to slavery varied sharply. Near Tyler, whites executed a slave and arrested several others whom they suspected of plotting a slave revolt. Fearful citizens burned another slave to death for killing his owner. Despite continued enforcement of slave laws, wartime defeats stirred some white Texans to wonder if God refused to bless the Confederacy because of the treatment of slaves. Thus some changes in attitude appeared, such as a state constitutional amendment that allowed jury trials for slaves charged with serious offenses. Several Texas officers in the Army of Tennessee joined their division commander, General Patrick Cleburne, in urging the Confederacy to free individual slaves who would promise to serve as soldiers. In the Confederate Congress, Texas Senator W. S. Oldham introduced such a bill in February 1865, which passed in amended form the next month. Although the idea generated strong opposition from some Texas newspaper editors, it suggested growing diversity in racial attitudes under the pressure of wartime necessity.

The attractions of planter status in Texas faced other challenges during the Civil War. The military draft exerted a leveling influence on the aristocratic pretensions of some individuals. Urban unrest, military desertions, and opposition to government impressment of cattle and crops all reflected degrees of social democracy and reaction against a government led by the slaveholding class. Urban and industrial growth opened the eyes of some Texans to alternate paths of upward mobility during the postwar period.

Military service also proved to be a route to postwar prominence for many Texans. The colonels who first commanded cavalry and infantry regiments from Texas in 1861 and 1862 held their rank because of prewar leadership; they averaged between forty and fifty years of age. From among this group came such postwar politicians as Governor Oran M. Roberts and Senator Samuel Bell Maxey. But second and third colonels, generally younger men who became regimental commanders later in the war because they displayed leadership under fire, rose to postwar positions of leadership in greater numbers. From among them came Governor L. S. "Sul" Ross, Senator Roger Q. Mills, and congressmen David B. Culberson and G. W. "Wash" Jones. Other postwar governors came from even lesser Confederate ranks: Lieutenant Colonel John Ireland, Major Joseph D. Sayers, and Captain Richard Coke. Not one among them claimed former planter status.

Texas individualism and sense of place also suffered under the influences of war. While many soldiers asserted their individualism through desertion, even larger numbers accepted a degree of regimentation and the need for cooperation as they joined and remained members of military units during the war years. While some of those units served in Texas, a majority answered orders that sent them outside its boundaries. Walker's infantry division and several cavalry and infantry brigades served in adjoining Trans-Mississippi states. Ross's cavalry brigade, Granbury's infantry brigade, and other Texas units fought with the Army of Tennessee. Hood's infantry brigade became a famous command in the Army of Northern Virginia. While most of those men would return to a rural life after the war, they could never again be quite as provincial once they had seen Richmond, Memphis, and New Orleans, or had mingled with soldiers from the mountains of North Carolina, the tidewater of South Carolina, or the delta of Mississippi.

Religion retained its concern with individual sin, but war also forced Texas church members to grapple with collective sin and social needs. Denominations that once had focused their attention on sending missionaries to serve settlers on the frontier shifted their concern to soldiers in the Confederate armies. Virtually every church group provided chaplains to minister to Texas troops. These denominations also supplied soldiers with Bibles and religious literature. As the war went against the Confederacy in 1863–64, Christian Leagues were organized, while chaplains and ministers found great enthusiasm for revivals among both Texas troops and the civilian population of the state. The hope that God might recognize their increased virtue and come to the aid of their cause motivated many such efforts.

At home the churches exhibited increased social concern. The Christian Church at Tyler gathered its female members to produce clothing for soldiers, an example of widespread collective action. To meet the needs of the Confederate army for a hospital, Soule University, a Methodist institution located in Galveston, turned over its medical department for military use. Some local churches followed a similar course when the need arose. Catholic sisters turned the Ursuline Convent into a hospital and nursed the wounded after the battle at Galveston. The Texas Baptist Convention collected money especially to provide education for disabled soldiers and children who had lost their fathers in the war. Individual congregations provided assistance to refugees arriving in their communities from the coast or neighboring states.

Romanticism maintained its influence among some wealthier Texans and refugees into the state. The wives and daughters of planters continued to read romantic European literature, attend concerts, give private plays for friends, and generally limited their activities to the home and upper-class society. The young women of Eastern Texas Female College in Tyler held military drills similar to those by men their age. Yet for most, the war imposed new duties or opened new fields of opportunity. "I am still on the weary treadmill of work, work, work," complained Kate Stone, "our sewing seems endless." Other women set up spinning jennies and looms in their homes to produce not only clothing, but also tents, packs for carrying equipment, and blankets. In Houston, some women raised money to purchase material to carry out such efforts. Other women and children became industrial workers in munitions factories. Visits to hospitals to nurse and feed the wounded occupied some women, while others made bandages, or supplied other medical necessities. Eveline Storeham treated the patients left at home by her brother, a doctor who served in the medical corps of the Confederate army. To replace male teachers who entered military service, an increasing number of women assumed the direction of Texas schools, despite the grumbling of some male newspaper editors. Nacogdoches University kept its doors open only with the aid of female instructors.

For women who remained at home in rural areas, a variety of new tasks awaited them. In addition to raising children, cooking, sewing, and possibly directing household servants as they had before the war, they found themselves faced with actual farming or the overseeing of slave field hands. On the frontier, the daily routine might be interrupted by the necessity of fighting off an Indian raid. To maintain even their basic lifestyle, women sought out substitutes for goods no longer available as a result of the Union blockade. Thus, berries, moss, and minerals became the sources of dye for coloring cloth. The limits and frustrations of such an existence, when revealed to husbands or sons in the army, could cause desertions. Even the many who never spoke out about their problems could, late in the war, be "tired of the whole mess" and admit "victory no longer seemed important." The impact of wartime reality clearly dominated any lingering romanticism in the minds of most Texans.

The Confederate armies surrendered in 1865—the last one at Galveston in early June following a final skirmish at Palmito Ranch near Brownsville. Texans and Southerners then faced a period of transition without a clear sense of how much change would be expected of them. Since secession had failed, what would be the relationship between the federal and state governments? Since slavery had been abolished, what would be the new status of the freed people? Many former Confederates hoped to retain as much as possible of their antebellum lifestyle and dominant roles in society. Some hoped for greater economic diversity as well as recovery and rebuilding. Former Unionists hoped for recognition of their hardships as dissenters in the Confederacy, as well as greater opportunities for leadership in place of the defeated ex-Confederates.

Black Texans sought to translate their freedom into economic and educational opportunity, family stability, and the development of their own churches, all supported by equal civil and political rights. With both change and continuity as goals for different groups, conflict seemed sure to arise, as in the case of the state's economy.

Economic recovery and opportunity became chief priorities for most Texans. The war had brought destruction in areas along the coast, reduced investment capital when Confederate money became worthless, and ended slavery as a labor system for one-third of the state's population. Although the former slaves remained in the state and usually in the same counties as workers, former slaveholders had lost their once valuable property. Harrison County planters owned an average of $48,000 of property in 1860, but only $9,000 of property, mostly land, in 1870.

In search of continuity, white landowners convinced the state constitutional convention that met in 1866, as well as the next legislature led by former Confederates, to adopt a Black Code that contained apprenticeship, vagrancy, and contract laws to control black labor. Considerable violence occurred as another means of forcing blacks to work in patterns preferred by whites. In response to complaints by African Americans about these discriminatory actions, Congress extended the life of the Freedmen's Bureau to help blacks obtain fair contracts and to challenge inequitable state laws. The Bureau's efforts remained limited by a shortage of funds and agents. From this struggle eventually emerged the sharecropping system in which former slaves and some whites rented land from planters with whom they divided the crop. The new system allowed black Texans some autonomy because they farmed individual plots of land without constant supervision. A limited number of the tenant farmers saved money and bought land, although many others found themselves in sporadic or even permanent debt.

Despite wartime problems and the struggles over a new labor system, economic recovery and growth followed the end of the war. Cotton production in Texas, which had been 431,000 bales in 1859, fell to 350,000 bales in 1869 before reaching a new peak of 487,000 bales in 1873. In corn production, Texas advanced from seventeenth in the United States in 1860 to ninth by 1870. Ranching burst into postwar prominence when herds driven to Kansas railroads totaled 1.5 million head from 1867 to 1871. Manufacturing doubled from 983 establishments producing $6.5 million worth of goods in 1860, to 2,399 producers in 1870 who generated $11.5 million. Railroads also doubled from 307 miles of track in 1860 to 711 miles in 1870. These developments resulted in significant changes in the pattern of wealth and economic prominence. Planters fell from 65 percent of wealthy Texans with $100,000 or more of property in 1860 to 17 percent in 1870. Merchants among the wealthy had increased from 16 percent in 1860 to 40 percent by 1870. A new elite had arisen to share economic leadership.

As economic alterations influenced social status, other aspects of society also underwent important transformations, especially among African Americans. When freedom came in 1865, freedpeople immediately sought to stabilize their families. Large numbers of former slave couples formalized marriages that previously had been denied legal standing. Many sought family members from whom they had been separated. Some black women stayed home to raise children, something they had not been able to do under slavery.

Stronger families received support from the developing churches in the black community. Former slave members broke away from the limitations of white-dominated congregations to control their own services and to develop their own ministers and lay leaders. The new churches, usually Baptist or Methodist, often joined all-black denominations, such as the African Methodist Episcopal Church. The new congregations also became central institutions in the black community, as they provided social activities, developed future political leaders, and supported education.

Schools for black Texans appeared in most towns with the assistance of local black churches, Northern freedmen's aid societies, and the Freedmen's Bureau. About five thousand black students began to receive some instruction late in the 1860s through these efforts. Then, early in the 1870s, Republicans developed a state system of education which included about fifty thousand black students and even more white ones in schools segregated in practice though not by law. An expanded state system of education represented an area in which white Texans also experienced major social change.

While African Americans achieved several advances in their social status, some white Texans experienced changes in their lives. Many women continued to play more diverse societal roles after the Civil War because of the high percentage of men killed or disabled in the fighting. Some women operated farms or businesses, while others taught in schools or began to occupy government positions such as operating post offices.

Migration of women and men from other states, primarily in the South, and some immigration increased the state's population from 604,215 in 1860 to 818,479 in 1870. Towns grew even more rapidly, with Galveston advancing from 7,307 in 1860 to 13,818 in 1870 to rank first in the state. Important urban growth included San Antonio's increase from 8,235 to 12,256 people and Houston's expansion from 4,845 to 9,382 in the same period. In these towns, team sports such as baseball and permanent theaters joined older forms of recreation such as minstrels and traveling circuses. The organization of fraternal, cultural, and benevolent societies in the towns represented another change from the greater individualism and isolation of rural life. Yet fraternal groups such as the Masons quickly restored their prewar national connections after the conflict to provide some continuity as well as change. Despite population and urban growth, many Texans preserved a degree of social stability, especially in rural areas, with traditional forms of recreation such as hunting and horse racing.

While Texans and other Southerners pursued diverse social goals, they struggled over the degree of political change that should follow the Civil War. The leadership of former Confederates in 1865 and 1866 under President Andrew Johnson's plan of Reconstruction produced the Black Codes and seemed unable to control violence against freedmen and Unionists. To relieve those problems, Congress undertook a greater role in Reconstruction with the Freedmen's Bureau and the Civil Rights Act of 1866, followed in 1867 by legislation that required that blacks not be denied the right to vote. By 1870 Congress added constitutional amendments to protect civil and political rights.

Those changes led to the creation of the Texas Republican party, which included primarily former Unionists and African Americans. The party dominated the state constitutional convention in 1868–69 but split into two factions for the election of 1869 over economic, regional, and racial issues. With the support of most black voters, E. J. Davis won a close gubernatorial race. The Davis Republicans then sought to promote education, railroads, and frontier defense, while working to control violence. Their efforts stirred Democrats to criticize the development of centralized authority, the interracial State Police force, and the higher taxes necessary to fund schools and law enforcement. More violent responses to conflicting views included attacks on black and white Republicans—some by the Knights of the Rising Sun, a Texas version of the Ku Klux Klan, vigilante activities such as the Heel Flies of Bell County, a number of feuds such as the Sutton-Taylor conflict in DeWitt County, and the deadly acts of gunfighters like John Wesley Hardin.

Democrats' charges helped them win support from a majority of white Texans and regain political leadership in a series of elections from 1871 to 1874. Their victories led to the drafting of a new state constitution in 1876 that tried to revive some continuity with prewar Texas society and limit the changes caused by the Civil War and Reconstruction. Many of the transformations could not be undone.

While Texas remained a predominantly rural state after the Civil War and Reconstruction, many of its citizens had learned the value of industry and began to promote its development. Texas manufacturing establishments increased in number five times from 1870 to 1900. Business activity led to rapid urbanization as Texas cities generally doubled in size from 1860 to 1880, and again from 1880 to 1900. These industrial and urban trends produced a new elite that challenged the farmers and ranchers for economic and social leadership in Texas.

The patterns of rural life remained individualistic in many ways after the war. But wartime regimentation perhaps opened the way for acceptance in the 1870s and 1880s of organizations such as the Grange among farmers, the Knights of Labor, and professional groups such as the State Bar of Texas and the Texas State Teachers Association. Anglo Texans developed a segregated society after Reconstruction with limitations on black voting, but African Americans in Texas continued to defend their aspirations for equality through conventions and court cases that led to revived civil rights in the twentieth century.

The Civil War and Reconstruction caused fundamental changes in some aspects of Texas life. In others, Texans struggled over the degree of change they would accept and even retained some continuity from their antebellum society.

Suggested Reading

Anderson, John A., ed. *Brokenburn: The Journal of Kate Stone, 1861–1868*. Baton Rouge: Louisiana State University Press, 1955.

Barr, Alwyn. *Black Texans: A History of African Americans in Texas, 1528–1995*. Norman: University of Oklahoma Press, 1996.

Baum, Dale. *The Shattering of Texas Unionism: Politics in the Lone Star State during the Civil War Era*. Baton Rouge: Louisiana State University Press, 1998.

Betts, Vicki. *Smith County, Texas, in the Civil War*. Tyler: Smith County Historical Society, 1978.

Campbell, Randolph B. *Grass Roots Reconstruction in Texas, 1865–1880*. Baton Rouge: Louisiana State University Press, 1997.

Gallaway, B. P., ed. *Texas, the Dark Corner of the Confederacy: Contemporary Accounts of the Lone Star State in the Civil War*. Lincoln: University of Nebraska Press, 1994.

King, Alvy L. *Louis T. Wigfall, Southern Fire-Eater*. Baton Rouge: Louisiana State University Press, 1970.

McCaslin, Richard B. *Tainted Breeze: The Great Hanging at Gainesville, Texas, 1862*. Baton Rouge: Louisiana University Press, 1994.

Moneyhon, Carl H. *Republicanism in Reconstruction Texas*. Austin: University of Texas Press, 1980.

Smallwood, James. *Time of Hope, Time of Despair: Black Texans during Reconstruction*. Port Washington: Kennikat Press, 1981.

Thomas, Emory M. *The Confederacy as a Revolutionary Experience*. Englewood Cliffs, NJ: Prentice-Hall, 1971.

Wheeler, Kenneth W. *To Wear a City's Crown: The Beginnings of Urban Growth in Texas, 1836–1865*. Cambridge: Harvard University Press, 1968.

Winsor, Bill. *Texas in the Confederacy: Military Installations, Economy and People*. Hillsboro, TX: Hill Junior College Press, 1978.

Wooster, Ralph A., ed. *Lone Star Blue and Gray: Essays on Texas in the Civil War*. Austin: Texas State Historical Association, 1995.

——. *Texas and Texans in the Civil War*. Austin: Eakin Press, 1995.

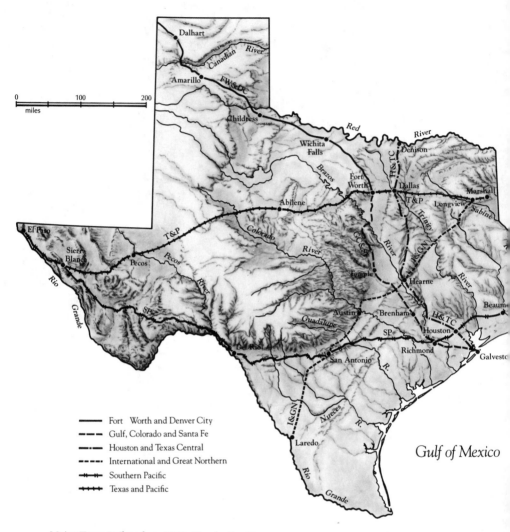

miles
0 100 200

Dalhart
Canadian River
Amarillo
FW&DC
Childress
Wichita Falls
Red River
Denison
H&TC
Dallas
Fort Worth
T&P
Marshall
Longview
Sabine
Abilene
Brazos
Trinity
El Paso
T&P
Colorado River
GC&SF
I&GN
River
Hearne
River
Sierra Blanca
Pecos
Pecos River
Temple
Beaumon
Rio Grande
SP
Austin
Brenham
H&TC
Guadalupe
SP
Houston
Del Rio
Richmond
Galvesto
San Antonio
R.
I&GN
Nueces
R.
Laredo
Gulf of Mexico
Rio Grande

———— Fort Worth and Denver City
– – – Gulf, Colorado and Santa Fe
–·–·– Houston and Texas Central
------ International and Great Northern
–x–x– Southern Pacific
+++++ Texas and Pacific

Major Texas Railroads to 1900. *Map by Jim Bier.*

CHAPTER EIGHT

Texas Transformed, 1874–1900

Donald R. Walker

THE HISTORY OF TEXAS IS THE STORY OF people, individuals with the desire and strength to effect positive change, even in the face of arduous circumstances. Texans of the late nineteenth century serve as an excellent illustration. Because they had been on the losing side in the Civil War, Texans also had recently lost social, economic, and political institutions with which they were familiar. Having chafed under the federally imposed policies known collectively as Reconstruction, many white Texans wished to retake control of state government from Radical Republicans and transplanted Northerners. Accordingly, they had to make adjustments in recognition of the changed circumstances, even as they tried to retain their valued traditions and forge a better, more prosperous, future. The tasks before them were monumental, and they were not resolved easily or quickly. This was especially so regarding race relations, for not until the middle decades of the twentieth century did African Americans in Texas make progress towards full integration into the larger society. In other vital areas, however, Texans persevered through adversity and approached the turn of the century with the realistic hope that a modern industrial commonwealth, one with opportunities available to all, lay within their reach.

The first task they undertook consisted of restructuring the state's politics to produce a system with which they felt more comfortable. Of key importance in their minds lay the questionable status of African Americans. Although no longer slaves, black Texans continued to exist in an inferior social and economic state as compared to whites. And over the last quarter of the nineteenth century, "Redeemer" Democratic politicians used every means available—legal, extralegal, and violent—to guarantee white supremacy.

With the inauguration as governor of the Conservative Democrat Richard Coke on January 15, 1874, Radical Republican rule—and with it Reconstruction—in Texas ended. For the next 104 years, Democrats controlled the state, successfully defeating all attempts to challenge their political dominance. Governor Coke and his immediate successors—Richard B. Hubbard, Oran M. Roberts, John Ireland, and Lawrence Sullivan Ross—governed in the firm belief that Texans wanted, and required, only a small, decentralized government. Indeed, they felt that state government should restrict itself to a limited number of priorities and not generate an excessive tax burden for the citizenry. As one of his earliest acts as the state's chief executive, Coke spoke of the need to remove all vestiges of Republican rule and restore to Texans the kind of government they preferred. Shortly thereafter, in August 1875, voters selected delegates to draw up a new state constitution. In mid-February 1876, they approved the new document by a margin of nearly three to one.

If Texans truly had desired a state government of limited size, as Coke asserted, the one created by the Constitution of 1876 should have met their every expectation. The new governing document reduced the terms of office for all elected officials, severely restricted the range of activities for both the executive and legislative branches, and made all judicial positions elective directly by the people. Additionally, the legislature could meet only once every two years and sessions were limited to just a few weeks. In short, the government the new constitution created appeared to harken back to the earliest days of statehood in the mid-1840s.

Despite the expectations of those who drafted the Constitution of 1876, Texas underwent several major transformations, yielding a society that anticipated the future rather than one that mourned the past. Indeed, during the last quarter of the nineteenth century, state government actually began to take a more active role in the regulation of business and the remedy of social ills. Moreover, the economy and society moved to a type of pre-industrial order in which the citizenry had a much greater choice of occupation, modern urban centers emerged, and all parts of the state were linked by an all-weather transportation system. With the foundation of a modern economy in place, the discovery of a great deposit of oil at Spindletop in 1901 enabled Texas to move quickly to become an industrialized and urbanized state, one that reached maturity in the middle of the twentieth century.

Among the more important developments of the period, the dramatic growth of the state's population was prominent. Much as it had throughout its history, Texas in the years after the Civil War attracted sizable numbers of immigrants. Most of the new residents came from the older states of the American South, the region that had endured the greatest amount of destruction during the war. All came to make a new start in a place that offered greater opportunities. Typical of those who relocated to Texas at the time was Martha Anne Otey, a young Mississippi schoolteacher, Confederate widow, and mother of two small children. She journeyed to Texas in 1867, seeking employment in one of the emerging towns in the state. In letters to her family in Mississippi, she described the countryside as she entered the state just to the north of Galveston:

> Only the real prospect can give you any idea of the beauty of this country. Miles and miles onward stretches the vast sea of living verdure, enameled with a thousand flowers of every shade, and covered with cattle grazing at leisure . . . so different from the broken hills and circumscribed lanes of our section of Mississippi.

Otey's vivid description of Texas persuaded her younger sister and other family members to leave their ancestral home and settle in Texas. Letters from other visitors and new arrivals prompted a similar reaction among loved ones left behind. The cumulative effect of all this favorable publicity helps explain, at least in part, the rapid population growth of the period. Between 1870 and 1900, the number of Texans more than tripled, increasing from slightly more than 800,000 to more than 3 million.

Most of the new arrivals were farmers seeking new lands and new opportunities away from the destruction and continuing economic deprivation in the older parts of the South. Texas gave promise of becoming a new agricultural empire, one in which hard work would surely bring financial success. Yet, as one of the more astute chroniclers of Texas during the late nineteenth century has pointed out, while significant changes occurred in Texas agriculture in the decades after the Civil War, success eluded many if not most Texas farmers.

During the late nineteenth century, agriculture in Texas moved from primarily subsistence farming, wherein a farmer produced a variety of crops to meet his immediate needs and enjoyed some measure of financial independence, to one that left him more vulnerable. The arrival of commercial agriculture witnessed the emergence of cotton as the principal crop, with cotton growers increasingly linked to the fluctuations of national and international prices and markets. In other words, many Texas farmers, like their counterparts across the South and Midwest, now lay dependent on economic forces beyond their control. In addition to cotton, production of all agricultural commodities steadily increased during the period but prices generally remained flat or declined. Seemingly, the harder the farmers worked, the less benefit they realized from their labor. Over time, farmers saw themselves as victims of a hostile economic system in which larger percentages of their income passed into the hands of suppliers, marketers, bankers, and assorted middlemen. Moreover, with the population swelling, land values increased dramatically, making it more difficult to acquire good farmland. These factors combined to produce greater farm indebtedness, increases in foreclosures on and sales of farms, and rising rates of farm tenancy and sharecropping. During the last two decades of the nineteenth century, the percentage of Texas farmers working land owned by others increased from 37.6 percent to 49.7 percent, well above national averages.

The straitened, at times desperate, circumstances in which farmers across the state found themselves, and their seeming inability to work their way into better times, led many to support various political and reform movements they hoped would bring them some relief. Many Texas farmers supported the Grange, the Greenback movement, and especially the more militant Farmers' Alliance, and the emergent People's party. Collectively, these groups called for an expanded role for government in such areas as currency reform, corporate regulation, and a greater expansion of democracy.

The National Grange of the Patrons of Husbandry, commonly referred to simply as "the Grange," had its origins in the months immediately following the end of the Civil War and sought to encourage farmers to act in unison to address their common problems. Strongest initially in several of the midwestern states, Grangers soon focused on the railroad companies and their political allies in state legislatures as the principal source of the misery of the agricultural sector. Using both the ballot and the lawsuit, Grangers sought to force the railroads into public accountability but met with limited success in the courts. Texas farmers established their first Grange chapter in 1873. The movement grew rapidly and by the late 1870s, Texas Grangers boasted a membership of approximately forty-five thousand, roughly one-fifth of the state's total electorate. Texas Grangers comprised almost half the membership at the constitutional convention and played major roles in fashioning most of those constitutional provisions that drastically curtailed the size of the Redeemer state government.

Although the Grange claimed a wide following in Texas, many divisions existed among agriculturalists that led some to move in widely divergent political directions. The more affluent farmers typically remained within the fold of the conservative Redeemer Democracy. The more financially hard-pressed farmers, however, needed immediate relief and searched beyond the Grange chapters and the Democratic party for a vehicle to express their political aspirations. In the mid-1870s, the first of almost five hundred Greenback clubs appeared in the state. Drawing their inspiration from a national organization of the same name, Texas Greenbackers opposed recently enacted federal policies that established specie (coins) as the nation's only legal tender. They wanted paper money (printed during the war) to remain in circulation and urged the printing of even more. To withdraw paper currency, Greenbackers argued, placed an unbearable burden on small farmers and working people, the debtor class already suffering from the national economic downturn and who had no readily available sources of credit. Greenbackers attempted to ally themselves with other political factions in the state but realized only limited success. Early in the 1880s, their strength began to wane as a more overtly political farmers group began to exert a profound influence on Texas politics.

At about the same time that the Greenbackers made their entrance into Texas, other groups of financially strapped farmers gathered in rural areas of Lampasas, Wise, and Parker Counties. These groups eventually brought forth a new organization, the Farmers' Alliance, which, although indigenous to Texas, spread throughout most of the farming regions of the nation. Alliance lodges in Texas eventually totaled some three thousand, all of which were devoted to improving the plight of the agricultural class through direct political action. In 1886, meeting in Cleburne, Texas, Alliance members served notice that they wanted change and planned to support only those elected officials who endorsed their program. What Alliance members may have lacked in wealth they more than made up for in numbers. After issuing what became known as the "Cleburne Demands," they promised to use the ballot box to "reward their friends and punish their enemies."

Late in the 1880s and into the 1890s, membership in the Alliance nationwide grew steadily, and a number of governors, legislators, and congressional representatives owed their election to Alliance support. In 1892, representatives from lodges throughout the United States met in Omaha, Nebraska, to decide what political position they should take relative to the presidential election of that year. Out of their deliberations came a new political party, the People's party, commonly called the "Populists," that would change American politics forever.

In their program, Populists sought to address the accumulated problems and frustrations that had been mounting throughout the previous quarter century. They came out in favor of government ownership of vital transportation and communications systems. They supported dramatic changes in the nation's currency base that would permit more money to enter circulation. They proposed innovative government assistance programs to provide direct aid to struggling farmers and generally help the agricultural sector yield a larger and more sustainable level of production. For the working-men, they endorsed restrictions on immigration and called for an end to the use of private police forces by companies seeking to punish strikers. The Populist party enjoyed considerable success in Texas as recruiters and speakers traveled the state seeking converts. The party had its own publications, its own list of preferred speakers, and, at the peak of its power, could command approximately one-third of the roughly 600,000 eligible voters in the state.

Although the Populists never elected a governor in Texas and never captured control of the state legislature, their impact can not be considered as nominal. The sustained nature of their complaints and the increasing stridency of their appeals ultimately influenced the leadership of the Democratic party to abandon its rigid adherence to the maintenance of a small, limited government and consider one that played a much larger role in the economy and society.

While the state's farmers struggled to overcome adversity and uncertainty in world markets, another branch of Texas agriculture demonstrated a rapid pattern of growth driven by healthy profits. After the Civil War, the open-range cattle industry and the trail drives to get the animals to markets generated considerable income for the state's ranchers. It was a new kind of business activity, one that stimulated other sectors of the state economy. Of equal importance, it brought forth the cowboy as the unique symbol, the icon, of Texas in the minds of people around the world. But the impact of ranching extended well beyond the creation of a romantic myth. The cowboy and the ranching industry carried with them none of the traces of the sectional resentments that had lingered after the Civil War. Ranching and life on the open range was neither Northern nor Southern in character. If anything, it was a unifying force that helped direct the nation's attention away from the deep divisions of the recent past and focus on a future that included expansion and development of the lands west of the Mississippi River.

A number of factors, including concern over the transmission of cattle diseases and increased use of barbed-wire fencing, combined to bring the days of the great trail drives to an end. Perhaps the principal agent in ending the drives was, ironically, the same that had helped initiate them: railroads. The goal of the earliest cattle drives had been to get the animals up to new railroad junctions on the Great Plains. By the mid-1880s, railroads had pushed deep into the Texas interior, eliminating the need to drive the cattle out of the state. Then, in the 1890s, a sprawling stockyard/packinghouse complex sprang up alongside the tracks of the Texas and Pacific Railway in Fort Worth, thus creating a major new industry for the state. The importance of railroads in establishing the meatpacking industry in Texas was duplicated in other areas of the state's economy and demonstrated the vital importance of effective transportation to the evolution of a modern state.

Arguably, the coming of the railroads did more to advance industrialization in Texas and hasten the process of urbanization than any other single event. Railroads not only brought technology to Texas, but they also brought skilled labor and more sophisticated labor specialization. In addition, they brought capital and finance, in the process fundamentally transforming the state. Railroads made travel possible year round and provided access to all areas of the state. Now, formerly small and migratory businesses were able to settle in one location, growing larger and realizing greater profits through the adoption of more efficient methods of operation and marketing.

In 1860, there were approximately 450 miles of railroad track in Texas, some 80 percent of it radiating from Houston into its surrounding agricultural and timber service areas. New rail construction halted during the Civil War, but after hostilities ceased in 1865 and Democrats returned to power in 1874, state leaders eagerly sought to induce the railroad companies to enter the state. The Constitution of 1876 made generous grants of state land to railroads for each mile of track laid, with the result that competing companies pushed their lines into the most remote areas. All told, the state gave railroad companies in excess of 32 million acres of its public lands, an area roughly equal in size to the state of Alabama. In addition, business and civic leaders in individual towns and cities, desperate to have a rail connection to ensure growth and prosperity, offered a variety of gifts and pledges to the companies to build the tracks to their towns. Among the bonuses typically offered to railroad companies were grants of right-of-way needed to build roadbeds, offers to build and maintain all depots and associated structures, and gifts of thousands of dollars in cash to help defray the cost of building the line. By 1900, the amount of operative track in Texas was nearly ten thousand miles, a phenomenal increase in the space of only four decades.

The principal lines in Texas included: the Texas and Pacific, which ran from Marshall to El Paso and on to San Diego, California; the Houston and Texas Central, which connected Galveston to Denison and on to points north; the Southern Pacific, which ran from Beaumont to El Paso and points east and west; the Gulf, Colorado, and Santa Fe, which stretched between Galveston and the Texas Panhandle; and the International and Great Northern, which connected Laredo with Northeast Texas and sites north. From these major trunk lines, an expansive network of shorter tap and tram lines was built to establish connections with adjacent cities and towns and into certain areas specializing in extractive industries such as mining and logging.

The financial impact of the railroad's arrival was immediate and substantial. The state treasury realized handsome profits from lease fees railroads paid for the labor of state prison inmates who cleared roadbeds and cut wood to fuel the locomotives. Construction companies of every sort saw immediate benefit, and the lumber industry could not have developed as rapidly as it did without the ability of the railroads to move heavy freight.

The dense stands of timber in eastern Texas had been harvested on a limited scale for as long as human beings had inhabited the area. But most of the cutting had been done sporadically and only to meet local needs. The early lumbering operations begun by Anglo Americans during the mid-nineteenth century brought slight increases in capacity but were limited in their production capabilities: they used human and animal power primarily and, in the absence of a dependable road system in the thick forests, had to remain small enough to be moved easily from one place to the next. It was not until the arrival of railroads after the Civil War that harvesting the forest on a commercial scale could proceed.

The individuals who brought the modern lumber industry to Texas and, in the process, demonstrated to others the enormous profits to be made therein were Henry J. Lutcher and G. Bedell Moore of Pennsylvania. After the end of the Civil War, these two Union Army veterans found timber stands in their part of western Pennsylvania rapidly approaching depletion. They visited Texas in the 1870s, found a wealth of virgin forests there, and decided to relocate. They built their mill, the first to incorporate the latest technology, in Orange near the mouth of the Sabine River. By locating their central operation along the lower banks of the river, they were able to harvest from forests both in eastern Texas and in western Louisiana. They logged along the upper Sabine and its tributaries then floated the logs downstream. Near the mill, a long boom stretched across the river caught the logs and funneled them into a holding pond. After they had removed all the trees accessible from the river, Lutcher and Moore built a railroad tram line into the forest to reach remote stands of timber.

Their success in the East Texas woods attracted the attention of others, one of whom went on to build the first million-dollar corporation in Texas and, for its time, the largest lumber company in the American South. John Henry Kirby hailed from Peachtree Village, a once-flourishing settlement located near Woodville in Southeast Texas. As a young man, he worked briefly as an employee of the Texas Senate, a position from which he could observe a great deal of the political and business activities taking place around the state. Recognizing the enormous financial potential of the lumber industry in Texas, Kirby allied himself with several wealthy investors from New England and established the Kirby Lumber Company, headquartered in Houston, in 1901. During its heyday, Kirby's company harvested trees from more than 800,000 acres, operated seventeen large mills, and employed more than seven thousand workers. It produced more than 300 million board feet of finished lumber annually and enjoyed earnings of some $40 million.

The wealth that flowed from the timber operations, coupled with the increase in personal mobility the railroads provided, enabled many Texans to travel and take advantage of a broader selection of occupational pursuits. Most of these appeared in urban areas, where much of the new wealth was concentrated. During the late nineteenth century Houston and Dallas, the largest cities in Texas today, emerged as major regional centers and positioned themselves to become metropolises of national importance.

Several important factors underlay the sustained growth of Houston and Dallas. Both benefited from a civic and business leadership committed to growth and economic diversity. Both had competitive urban centers nearby—Galveston for Houston and Fort Worth for Dallas—that simulated them to undertake ambitious, long-term plans to provide for continued dominance. And both cities launched aggressive campaigns to develop transportation infrastructure, especially dependable rail service, making rapid growth possible. By the end of the nineteenth century, San Antonio remained the largest city in Texas, with a population of 53,321, roughly double its 20,550 in 1880. During the same period, Dallas grew from 10,358 to 42,638 and Houston increased from 16,513 to 44,633, a growth rate almost fourfold in just twenty years. While the importance of railroads to the development of cities was obvious, as well as a source of great pride for urban residents, rural Texans and members of labor unions condemned the railroad companies as being guilty of a multitude of sins, including corporate arrogance and collusion in the fixing of prices at artificially high levels. Railroads, according to critics, operated with a complete disregard for the public interest or the safety of their workers and should be forced to change their ways. If necessary, the state should regulate the lines in order to serve the greater public good.

The push of railroads into the state also stimulated an increase in labor union membership and a growing assertion of workers' rights in several sectors of the state's economy. Labor activity in Texas during the period conformed closely to the actions of national federations. The more significant unions in Texas late in the nineteenth century included the Screwmen's Benevolent Association and the Noble Order of the Knights of Labor.

Composed of longshoremen on the Galveston docks, members of the Screwmen's Benevolent Association used giant screw jacks to pack as much cotton as possible into the holds of large ocean-going ships. The number of Screwmen grew substantially as cotton production increased in the years after 1865. The Association reached its peak of membership early in the 1890s but thereafter began a rapid decline, occasioned primarily by the introduction of automated cotton compressors on the wharves.

Formed in 1869, the Knights of Labor ultimately reached a national membership of more than 700,000 workers, some 30,000 of whom lived in Texas. The peak of the union came in 1886, the same year it mounted its largest and most sustained protest, the Great Southwest Strike. In mid-March, Knights struck several lines owned by railroad tycoon Jay Gould, demanding, among other things, regular paydays and improved working conditions. Considerable violence accompanied the strike, eventually forcing Governor John Ireland to call out the Texas Rangers to help quell the dispute. The strike ended early in May, with many of the strikers having lost their jobs to non-union workers. Throughout the remainder of the decade, the Knights slowly declined as a national labor organization.

With the failure of the strike against the powerful Gould interests and the steady collapse of the Knights, Texas workers entered a period of relative inactivity. Ultimately, the nature of labor organizations in the state changed dramatically with the emergence and growth of the American Federation of Labor (AFL) in the 1890s. Established late in the 1880s, the AFL sought to enlist only those workers deemed to have a specific, and therefore valuable, skill. The new union made no effort to organize the great mass of unskilled workers. The demands the AFL made of management usually were limited to calls for better pay and improved working conditions, especially for a shorter workday and workweek. AFL leadership in Texas generally refrained from intense political partisanship and generally avoided a directly confrontational approach to solving its problems. By 1900, the AFL membership in Texas stood at slightly less than 8,500, a number that would increase dramatically with the discoveries of Texas oil and the further industrialization of the state early in the twentieth century.

Additional pressure for state government to assume a more active role in society and undertake at least limited reforms arose from the efforts of certain officials who worked in various state agencies. These persons were aware of the problems confronting state government and worked from within to improve the system and effect meaningful change. One such individual, Thomas J. Goree, served as superintendent of the state prison system, a vitally important state agency. His labors in behalf of a number of reforms merit a close look for what they reveal of the ways in which competence in one's profession, coupled with sustained agitation and promotion in behalf of one's causes, can produce needed reform.

Goree, a native of Alabama, came to Texas early in the 1850s. He attended Baylor University, earned a law degree, and joined a law firm in Montgomery, Texas, a few months before the outbreak of the Civil War. He volunteered his services to the Confederacy and served throughout the conflict on the headquarters staff of

General James Longstreet, ultimately attaining the rank of captain. When the war ended, Goree returned to Texas but not directly to the practice of law, preferring instead to try his hand at managing his family's farms. Success as a farmer eluded him, however, and he soon joined a law firm in Huntsville. Goree now became active in Democratic party politics. He did not run for office himself but worked in behalf of the candidacy of others. He endured political exile along with other Democrats during the Republican years of Edmund J. Davis but re-emerged and re-established himself politically when the Democrats returned to power. In 1877, Governor Richard Hubbard appointed Goree the superintendent of the state prison—its offices located, at the time, inside the state prison in Huntsville—a position he held for fourteen years.

There is no question but that Goree received the appointment to the prison position in return for years of loyal service to the state Democratic party. It also helped that he had a distinguished record of military service in behalf of the "Lost Cause" and could call on a host of personal and political contacts he had made while serving as an aide to the prominent Confederate general. There was nothing in his background, education, training, or previous experience that would have given him insight on how to manage a prison. Yet once on the job he brought a quality of leadership to the institution not equaled until the state overhauled the prison system completely in the 1950s.

The principal explanation for Goree's success lay in his commitment to do his job well; he intended to treat it as more than a patronage plum. He studied the problems of prison administration. He observed how things were done in the more successful prisons in other parts of the nation, and he demonstrated a willingness to adopt innovative measures that might further the objectives of penitentiary incarceration. Finally, Goree used his influence and reputation among state leaders to secure legislative approval and funding for his ambitious and worthy projects.

During his tenure as superintendent Goree instituted a number of significant reforms. He established a prison school and library; he also segregated inmates as much as conditions would permit to keep the "incorrigibles" and other violent offenders away from the general prison population. A system of rewards, including reductions in the amount of time to be served, was established to encourage good behavior. Lastly, to administer to the moral needs of the inmates, Goree instituted mandatory weekly church services that lasted all day Sunday.

Two of the problems he addressed with particular persistence and enthusiasm, and brought to a successful resolution, had important consequences outside the prison walls. Goree expressed concern at the large number of inmates in the prison whose only crime was that they were mentally ill and could not function normally in society. Cities and counties without the facilities to provide even minimal custodial care for these individuals sent them to the state mental hospital in Austin. But this facility soon reached its maximum capacity, so, as a last resort, the mentally ill were sent to the state prison, where they could be controlled, fed, and housed. Goree observed that mental patients created a number of serious problems for the prison staff. Most of the handicapped persons could not carry out work assignments; they could not reside within the regular prison population, lest they become victims of aggressive acts; and they were unable to learn and obey prison rules and regulations, making them a constant source of disciplinary problems. Most important, there were no facilities or trained personnel in the prison who could provide the kind of specialized treatment such individuals needed. In Goree's mind, the state had an obligation to place mentally ill inmates in a facility in which they would receive proper medical treatment. After Goree importuned legislators in behalf of this problem for several years, in 1883 the state opened a branch of the Austin state hospital in Terrell, located east of Dallas. Six years later a third branch of the hospital opened in San Antonio.

A similar success attended another problem addressed by Goree as part of his work as prison superintendent. During the 1870s and 1880s, state courts commonly convicted youngsters no older than thirteen or fourteen years of age and sent them to the state prison. Once incarcerated, the young boys became victims of older, more hardened inmates. Those who managed to survive became hardened criminals themselves; in effect, they learned criminal ways and attitudes from the most knowledgeable and experienced of teachers. In Goree's view, the state should turn the young offenders away from pursuing a life of serious criminal behavior. They should serve their sentences in a separate institution, one in which prison staff would serve essentially as surrogate parents, giving the youngsters an education and the moral guidance necessary to become useful, productive citizens. His efforts came to fruition in 1889, when the state juvenile reformatory opened in Gatesville. It was the first state institution for juvenile offenders in the American South. In 1891 Goree retired from public service, spending most of his remaining years as an attorney for a land speculation and investment firm in Galveston.

Goree's considerable concern constituted only a small part of a growing awareness statewide that Texas's educational institutions were in need of sweeping reforms if they hoped to serve a society experiencing rapid change. Public education had not received much attention in Texas until the advent of the Radical Republicans late in the 1860s. The Republican leaders made provisions for an ambitious public school system centralized in Austin and directed by the state superintendent of public instruction. During Republican rule, legislators increased funding for public schools beyond anything the citizens previously had witnessed and school policy mandated that the institutions teach both white and black students.

With the return of the Democrats in 1874, and the approval of the new state constitution in 1876, elected officials attempted to revert to the pre–Civil War traditions that had held education to be a private matter, only of concern to heads of individual families. Indeed, state support for education remained extremely precarious and unpredictable throughout the remainder of the nineteenth century. The nadir came in 1879, when Governor Oran M. Roberts vetoed the school appropriation bill in the name of financial exigency.

Throughout these especially lean years, several enlightened individuals in the few private schools and academies in the state continued to push for an expanded public school system with greater government involvement. They realized some success in 1884, when the legislature rewrote the public school laws, thus paving the way for a state public school system that, eventually, would serve the needs of all. The new law made provision for an elected state education superintendent and placed local schools under the control of county judges. Individual counties could establish school taxing districts to raise funds for the local school, and youngsters between the ages of eight and sixteen years were required to attend classes. Regrettably, legislators did not make adequate provision for funding or for enforcing the new law, so local schools in Texas generally lagged far behind those in other parts of the nation. In the cities, where one generally found a more educated and informed population, citizens demonstrated a willingness to tax themselves to pay for better neighborhood schools. In the rural areas little changed until well after the turn of the century.

In the area of higher education, however, Texas made much better progress in the post–Civil War years. Thanks primarily to federal government incentives, the state established the foundations for a network of public universities that would serve the needs of the citizenry well into the future. Although funding problems remained near insurmountable for the first few decades of their existence, the state colleges and universities were, by the turn of the twentieth century, institutions of which Texans could justifiably be proud.

The Morrill Act, passed by the United States Congress in 1862, made gifts of land, or money, available to the individual states for the establishment of a public university. These institutions would later become known as the "land grant schools" and receive generous federal support to sustain their growth. Texas established its land grant school, Texas Agricultural and Mechanical College, in 1876, making A&M the oldest public university in the state. Three years later the legislature established a branch of A&M in Prairie View to provide limited educational opportunities for black Texans. In that same year, and with the generous support of philanthropic organizations outside the state, Texas opened its first "normal institute" for the training of public school teachers in Huntsville, naming it after the town's most illustrious former resident, Sam Houston. The University of Texas, envisioned in the Constitution of 1876 as "a university of the first class," received legislative approval in 1881 and began accepting its first students in 1883. Further constitutional mandates reserved for the University of Texas and A&M exclusive rights to the proceeds from the use of large blocks of the state's public lands. Since then, income from those lands—especially after great reserves of oil were discovered under some of them—has made the two institutions the wealthiest in the state.

Further advances in higher education came with the establishment of some twenty additional institutions. Many of these began as private schools but changed to public status after local citizens committed themselves to find the money to operate them. Among the more enduring of these institutions are: Blinn College, founded in 1883 as Methodist academy and later becoming the first county-owned junior college in Texas; Texas A&M/Commerce, formerly East Texas State University; Tarleton State University in Stephenville; the University of North Texas in Denton; Howard Payne in Brownwood; St. Edward's in Austin; Texas Lutheran in Seguin; Southwestern Adventist in Waxahatchie; and Texas Weslyan in Fort Worth. The expansion of the system of higher education resulted in larger numbers of Texans studying at the college level and a larger number of college graduates in the workplace, but, per capita, college attendance in Texas in 1900 remained much smaller relative to other parts of the nation.

Very near the end of the nineteenth century, an individual who seemed to be the progressive spirit personified rose to prominence on a pledge to bring further reform to Texas. His name was James Stephen Hogg. In 1891 the state inaugurated the charismatic, 6 foot three inch, three-hundred-pound Hogg as governor. Over the course of his two terms as the state's chief executive he initiated significant reforms and exerted a political dominance over Texas not seen since the years of Sam Houston.

In addition to his considerable political talent and personal charm, Jim Hogg owns the distinction of having been the first Texas governor to have been born in the state. He was also the first governor since 1865 who had not served in the Civil War. A resident of Wood County in the northeastern corner of the state, Hogg, who made a living as a journalist and an attorney, was an effective stump speaker who captivated audiences. After holding several local elective offices, in 1886 Hogg made his first run for a statewide race, that for attorney general. This was, as noted, the same year in which members of the Texas Farmers' Alliance laid out the "Cleburne Demands" at their state meeting. Among the reforms the farmers wanted to see enacted into law, each of which they prefaced with "We demand!", were: (1) government regulation of railroads; (2) a revision of the banking system; (3) the creation of an interstate commerce commission; (4) government recognition of labor unions; and (5) legislation to prevent speculating in land and agricultural futures. A friend to the farmers, Hogg campaigned on several of these issues and easily gained election to the first of two terms as the state's chief law enforcement officer.

As his most able biographer, Robert Cotner, has pointed out, Hogg grew up at a time of great turmoil and change in Texas and had lived and worked among the agricultural classes that had suffered the prolonged financial distress that accompanied the shift to commercial agriculture. He saw, perhaps more clearly than did other politicians, that government had a vital role to play in maintaining stability in the economy, and he was prepared to institute such governmental oversight. During his two terms as attorney general, he directed a statewide campaign to force insurance companies to adhere to state law, especially in the matter of honoring claims filed by Texas policyholders. Those companies, some forty in number, that would not comply with the law, he drove from the state. He also played an instrumental role in the drafting of Texas's first antitrust law, passed in 1889, which levied heavy penalties against corporations that colluded to fix prices or engaged in any activity designed to restrict trade. Finally, he spoke often of the need for additional state action to regulate railroad activity in Texas. By 1890, Hogg had emerged as the leader of the reform forces in the state, and he campaigned for governor that year in support of a constitutional amendment, also on the ballot, to create a state railroad commission. Hogg became governor and the amendment gained approval.

As the state's chief executive, Hogg fulfilled his promises to the voters and used the agencies of state government to correct what he and his supporters believed were long-standing abuses. Significant legislation passed during his administration included, in addition to the establishment of the Railroad Commission, the Alien Land Law (1891) which forced alien property owners to dispose of their holdings in Texas within six years; the Stock and Bond Law (1893) which gave the Railroad Commission the power to oversee the issuance of stocks and bonds by railroad companies in order to guarantee the validity of the issues; and the Perpetuities and Corporations Land Law (1893) which forced corporations to divest themselves of unused real estate holdings in Texas within fifteen years. Hogg also supported increases in funding for higher education, a limited set of prison reforms, and restrictions on the amount of indebtedness Texas cities and counties could incur. Hogg retired from public service at the conclusion of his second term with his record as the most reform-minded governor in the state's history clearly established. In the last years of his life, he amassed a large personal fortune in the Texas oil boom of the early twentieth century.

Hogg's successor, Charles A. Culberson, must be considered a reform governor as well, but his style was much less assertive and confrontational than that of Hogg and the causes he supported generated less controversy. Culberson oversaw a strengthening of the powers given to the Railroad Commission and endorsed tougher antitrust regulations, all the while using the veto to limit public spending.

Much of the Culberson administration bore the stamp of Edward M. House, an extremely capable private businessman who took an interest in state politics during the Hogg administration and, over time, managed to exert a great deal of influence in the process of selecting Democratic candidates to run for major offices in the state. House's wealth came from a sizable inheritance he received while still in his early twenties. He made a number of shrewd investments on his own, but he apparently tired of simply making money. His interest in politics likely arose from his personal concern over the financial instability that might develop should some of the more radical political reformers of the time gain the upper hand. Alwyn Barr, in his landmark study of the period, *Reconstruction to Reform: Texas Politics, 1876–1906,* has described House as an individual who "approached politics on a personal rather than ideological level, with great calculation and deliberation." House preferred to remain in the shadows of the political world rather than run for office himself, and he favored "limited regulations which created business stability and reduced demands for further reforms."

House's influence in Texas politics remained preeminent until the election reforms of the early twentieth century, which established the primary election as the means for choosing political candidates. House went on to the national stage, becoming a close friend and confidant of President Woodrow Wilson.

Symbolically, in Texas the nineteenth century ended on January 10, 1901, the day on which oil in deposits larger than any previously known was discovered at a place called Spindletop, located south of Beaumont. During the first decades of the twentieth century, oil transformed the state every bit as dramatically as had railroads during the final decades of the nineteenth century. Texas became wealthy and more highly industrialized as it, along with the rest of the nation, underpinned its economy and major industries on the availability of relatively inexpensive petroleum.

Texas of the early twentieth century differed substantially from the Texas of 1874, and the people who had persevered through the difficulties of the post-Reconstruction period could content themselves with the realization that they had laid the foundation that enabled Texas to become one of the most powerful and influential states in the Union.

Suggested Readings

Barr, Alwyn. *Reconstruction to Reform: Texas Politics, 1876–1906.* Austin: University of Texas Press, 1971.

Cotner, Robert. *James Stephen Hogg.* Austin: University of Texas Press, 1959.

Jordan, Terry. *Trails to Texas: Southern Roots of Western Cattle Ranching.* Lincoln and London: University of Nebraska Press, 1981.

Maxwell, Robert S. and Robert D. Baker. *Sawdust Empire: The Texas Lumber Industry, 1830–1940.* College Station: Texas A&M University Press, 1983.

McMath, Robert C., Jr. *Populist Vanguard: A History of the Southern Farmer's Alliance.* New York: W. W. Norton and Company, Inc., 1977.

Miller, Char and Heywood T. Sanders, eds. *Urban Texas: Politics and Development.* College Station: Texas A&M University Press, 1990.

Procter, Ben. *Not Without Honor: The Life of John H. Reagan.* Austin: University of Texas Press, 1962.

Reed, S. G. *A History of Texas Railroads and of Transportation Conditions Under Spain and Mexico and the Republic and the State.* Houston: The St. Clair Publishing Company, 1941.

Rice, Lawrence. *The Negro in Texas, 1874–1900.* Baton Rouge: Louisiana State University Press, 1971.

Spratt, John S. *The Road to Spindletop: Economic Change in Texas, 1875–1901.* Dallas: Southern Methodist University Press, 1955.

Walker, Donald R. *Penology for Profit: A History of the Texas Prison System, 1867–1912.* College Station: Texas A&M University Press, 1987.

Governor Pat M. Neff of Texas. *Courtesy of the Prints and Photographs Collection, The Center for American History, The University of Texas at Austin, #CN 00413.*

CHAPTER NINE

Progressivism in Texas

Norman D. Brown

FOLLOWING THE DEFEAT OF POPULISM IN THE presidential election of 1896, demands for political, economic, and social change rumbled beneath the surface until they produced a broad-gauged reform effort known as the progressive movement after 1900. "Progressivism" was an extremely complex phenomenon that defies description. It was not an integrated or unified quest for reform; rather, it encompassed a wide variety of objectives and interest groups. It embraced political reform. Progressives wanted to eliminate the "unholy alliance" between Gilded Age bosses and Robber Barons by granting the people a more direct voice in government. To that end they favored the direct primary, the direct election of United States Senators, the initiative and the referendum, and, in some cases, woman suffrage. To check monopolistic business practices, Progressives sought to extend state and federal control over large corporations. They hoped to make government more efficient and to improve the lives of the underprivileged through slum clearance, reduction of working hours, the restriction of child labor, unemployment insurance, and prison reform. Prohibition offered an example of reforming zeal channeled into a drive for moral righteousness and cultural conformity. Prohibitionists were able to equate saloons and the "liquor traffic" with the trusts and "special interests."

Southern progressivism, like its northern and western counterparts, was essentially urban and middle class in nature; it lacked Populism's agrarian radical edge. Historian Dewey W. Grantham notes in *The Life and Death of the Solid South* (1988) that "for all their talk of democracy, morality, and social uplift, southern progressives were cautious reformers, led by middle-class and professional men and women who were generally amenable both to the limits imposed by the centers of power in their states and to the restraints of regional values and traditions. Unlike the third-party radicals of the 1890's, the progressives contributed to the white consensus on the race question and did not make the mistake of bolting the Democratic party."

After 1896 the Populists disappeared as a viable party in Texas, leaving the Democrats in undisputed control of state politics. Populism's failure dampened the desire for class politics. Law formalized the one-party system that history and custom created, as Democrats moved to substitute the direct primary for the convention as the means of nominating candidates. The primary generally was associated with the movement against "machine politics" in the South. The Terrell Election Law of 1905, replacing a measure enacted in 1903, made a statewide nominating primary mandatory for all parties whose vote in a general election exceeded 100,000; only the Democrats had the requisite numbers. Participation in the primary required the payment of a poll tax and the signing of a party loyalty pledge. These stipulations removed many African Americans, Mexicans, and poor whites from the political process. "The real purpose of the political leaders who supported the poll tax amendment and the enactment of the Terrell election law," the *Dallas Morning News* asserted in 1905, "was to disfranchise poor people, or else to compel them to pay large poll taxes to lighten taxes on property." Gradual development of the white primary further lessened the chances for black men to take part. Texas Republicans could offer little resistance. An irritated Republican noted in 1912: "The primary election law was placed upon the statutes of this State with a view of perpetuating the Democratic hierarchy, and so effectual has been its operation that, today, a nomination in the Democratic primaries is tantamount to election."

Some imperfections remained in the election laws. In 1907, the legislature mandated that a candidate who received the most votes would be the nominee. In 1913, a second primary was required if no candidate received a majority of votes cast in a United States Senate race and, in 1918, the second primary law was extended to state and district races. The two candidates receiving the highest number of votes were to oppose each other in a runoff.

Southern progressive leaders were as sectional in their appeal for mass support as were the Populists of the 1890s. They envisaged the enemy as "foreign" interests in the Northeast, which, through railroads, insurance companies, oil companies, public utilities, and banks, were in conspiracy against the small businessman. Texas officeholders tended to be neo-Populists in some degree, and for many years any Yankee company was fair game. Stringent anti-trust laws were passed in Texas in 1889 and 1903, and crusading attorneys general successfully prosecuted a number of violators. Indeed, the Texas antitrust policy was more severe than that of the federal government.

The most famous Texas antitrust case involved the Waters-Pierce Oil Company, a Missouri-based corporation with Standard Oil affiliations. In 1897, Texas Attorney General Martin M. Crane brought suit for violations of the Texas antitrust act. A verdict canceling the firm's permit to do business inside the state was upheld by the United States Supreme Court in 1900. Then, claiming that it had reorganized and severed all ties with Standard Oil, the company secured new Texas and Missouri licenses, although not without the objections of such Texans as former governor Jim Hogg, who questioned the sincerity of Waters-Pierce officials. When it was later revealed that Standard Oil still controlled the company, Texas Attorney General R. V. Davidson obtained a trial judgment for ouster and penalties of $1,623,900. When higher-court rulings affirmed the decision, the Waters-Pierce Company paid a fine of $1,808,483.30, the largest collected by the state to that time, and the firm's Texas properties were sold at auction.

Meanwhile, the Waters-Pierce case provoked a political controversy known as "Baileyism." While a successful candidate for the United States Senate in 1900, the colorful five-term congressman and minority leader of the House of Representatives, Joseph Weldon Bailey, had ignored the possible conflict of interest and urged Governor Joseph Sayers and the state attorney general to allow Waters-Pierce to return to Texas. Although he did not receive a fee for this service, Bailey was employed by oilman Henry Clay Pierce as company counsel in other matters. Furthermore, in 1900 Bailey had borrowed $3,300 from Pierce who, unknown to the Senator, placed the note on the company records.

When investigations in 1905 and 1906 revealed the relationship between Bailey and Pierce, the state divided into angry camps of pro- and anti-Bailey men. Although Bailey ran unopposed and won reelection in the preferential Democratic primary of 1906, critics argued that the legislature should ignore the results of the primary and refuse to return Bailey to the Senate. Bailey, in response, contended that the whole affair was a conspiracy to deprive the nation of his great services; he swore he was going to "drive into the Gulf of Mexico" all the "peanut politicians" who had spoken out against him. When asked about the possibility of being replaced, Bailey said that a successor would fall so short of filling the seat that he would "rattle around like a mustard seed in a gourd."

Although the Texas legislature reelected Bailey to the Senate in January 1907, by a vote of 108 to 39, and he won control of the state delegation to the Democratic National Convention in 1908 as a test of his popularity with the people, differences still rankled. No doubt the controversy would have flared again in 1913 if Bailey had not voluntarily retired to private life. For nearly thirty years after 1900 (Bailey died in 1929), Texas voters were inclined to judge the qualifications of all candidates for public office on the basis of whether the aspirant favored or opposed Joseph Weldon Bailey. In 1922, Congressman Sam Rayburn briefly thought of running for the United States Senate, but, after weighing various factors, decided to remain in the House. In a statewide contest he believed he would be handicapped by his identification with Bailey. It was his curse, Rayburn lamented, that of "all the men in Texas who followed his flag in his black hour that I am the only one who today holds an office. I am truly the last of the Mohicans."

A similar situation existed in the fight over the prohibition of alcohol. Texans likewise measured all candidates for public office on the basis of whether they were "wets" or "drys." Following the defeat in 1887 of a statewide prohibition amendment to the state constitution by a margin of nearly two to one, the prohibition drive in Texas temporarily slowed; and it was not until the Progressive Era that the drys regained their enthusiasm. They succeeded in adding many dry counties to their list in North Texas through local-option elections, but they met with little success in the southern part of the state where the wets had sufficient strength, especially among Germans and Mexicans, to defeat them. In 1907, the Anti-Saloon League entered Texas. To meet this challenge, the powerful Texas Brewers Association raised more than $2 million between 1902 and 1911 by assessing members. Prohibition became the all-absorbing political issue in Texas because it spoke directly to most of the perceived social problems. There were in effect two Democratic parties in Texas, one prohibitionist and the other antiprohibitionist, within the same formal party structure. Progressive Democrats were usually dry; and conservative, old-line Democrats were wet, although the match was not perfect. In 1911, after an exciting contest, another statewide prohibition measure failed, this time by only 6,297 votes. The drys kept up the struggle, but made little progress for the next four years.

For eight years, 1899–1907, during the gubernatorial administrations of two elderly ex-Confederates, Joseph Sayers and S. W. T. Lanham, Texas had a conservative government and relatively little political excitement. Other topics, such as the Spanish-American War and the Galveston Hurricane of 1900, diverted public attention. The end of the period of political torpor came in 1906, as Baileyism divided the voters and prohibition created a strong interest in politics. A definite swing away from conservatism to progressivism was apparent in the gubernatorial contest in 1906, which was won by a lawyer from Palestine, Thomas M. Campbell, a dry who was regarded as the most progressive of the candidates. He energetically promoted tax reform, insurance regulation, improvements in education, additional laws protecting labor, and a number of other reforms. Supporting his efforts were: the State Federation of Labor, which met for the first time in 1898; the Farmers' Union, which organized in 1902 and by 1906 claimed 100,000 members; and the Texas Federation of Women's Clubs, with five thousand members. The latter group worked hard on behalf of better schools, pure food and drug laws, improved legal rights for women, and more public libraries.

Tax reform, begun under Lanham, continued in the Campbell years. Most important was the 1907 "full rendition law," which attempted to tax the intangible assets of corporations; it required that property be rendered for taxation at its "reasonable cash market value." The law nearly doubled the value of assets on the state's tax rolls, but it also provoked protests from corporation interests and landowning farmers. Campbell won a reputation for economy by vetoing some $1.7 million from the appropriation bill in 1909, but his critics claimed that most of the money had been marked for needed improvements. He also made a fruitless effort to get the legislature to impose a state income tax. He did get a light inheritance tax; it provoked a trickle of revenue and a flood of criticism.

Regulation of insurance companies was a signal accomplishment. Comprehensive codes for life, health, accident, home, and fire insurance were adopted. The Robertson Insurance Law of 1907 required companies to invest at least 75 percent of the funds drawn from Texans in Texas real estate and securities. James H. Robertson, the sponsor of the legislation, said that his purpose was "to stop the long continued practice of taking from Texas money belonging to Texas people, and hoarding it in New York to be there used by officials of the great insurance companies." Upon failing to defeat the bill, twenty-one insurance companies withdrew from Texas, arguing that the new law was unjust and unfair. Some of those companies returned after the state commissioner of insurance and banking modified some of the regulations. Others continued to work for the repeal or modification of the law, but it stayed in effect until 1963.

In a related area, Texas established in 1909 an insurance program protecting funds deposited in state banks. For a number of years the plan worked well, but numerous bank failures early in the 1920s put a heavy strain on the system; it was abolished in 1927. Not until the establishment of the Federal Deposit Insurance Corporation in 1933 was there similar national legislation.

A number of other progressive measures were adopted. In 1907, a new law strengthened antitrust restrictions; several others improved conditions for workers; and the legislature created a state medical board and a state board of health. It also established a department of agriculture, a state library, and a historical commission. Improvements also came in education, particularly in the area of financing. Campbell approved a law giving towns with populations of two thousand or more greater power to regulate utilities; and laws were passed restricting free passes by railroads, promoting pure food, and prohibiting nepotism in state government. There were laws against lobbying and several for road improvements. Prison reform, long overdue, began during Campbell's administration, and that of his successor, Oscar B. Colquitt. Colquitt, who publicized prison-system abuses during his campaign in 1910, such as the "bull bat whipping strap," found that the more obvious ones had been eliminated by the time he took office. In September 1910, the legislature voted to end convict leasing by 1914 and adopted other reforms. Although whipping was continued, its use was restricted.

Colquitt, a political "wet," was more conservative than Campbell and assuredly was not a crusader (except for prison reform); but his administration was not without progressive achievements. Additional prison reforms were adopted, a hospital for tuberculosis patients was established, and a training school for delinquent girls was founded. Laws also regulated child labor, promoted workplace safety, limited the hours of women workers, and allowed counties to establish poor farms for indigents. Most important was a workmen's law requiring that persons employed in most industries be insured against work-related accidents and setting forth rules for compensation in such cases.

Texas progressives felt especially close to President Woodrow Wilson. In the Democratic National Convention of 1912, the steadfast support of the "Immortal Forty" Texas Wilson delegates was of immense importance in overcoming the almost insurmountable odds against his nomination under the party's two-thirds rule. As a result of their support, two Texans—Albert Sidney Burleson of Austin as postmaster general and David F. Houston, a former president of both The University of Texas and Texas A&M University, as secretary of agriculture—became members of President Wilson's cabinet. They were joined by a third Texan in the summer of 1914 when Thomas Watt Gregory of Austin was appointed attorney general. Colonel Edward M. House of Texas, a superb backroom politician, became Wilson's closest advisor and his roving ambassador to Europe. Texas congressmen cast vital votes for New Freedom legislation, and Senator Morris Sheppard of Texas sponsored the prohibition amendment to the United States Constitution.

The dominant figure in Texas politics from 1914 to 1934 was James E. Ferguson. In 1914, Ferguson, a Temple banker and successful farmer and stock-raiser, jumped into the governor's race on his own initiative. He adopted a style of speaking that mixed bad grammar, folksy stories, sarcasm, and slander in about equal proportions and appealed to the rural voter. "He swayed them like the storm sways the slender pines, and voted them in droves and platoons," an admirer wrote. "He spoke the language of the corn rows and the vernacular of the country stores." Edmund Travis, an Austin newspaper editor, said that Ferguson "purposely played ignorant to win the rural vote." By 1911, nearly 52 percent of the state's farmers were tenants. "Farmer Jim," as Ferguson labeled himself, earned the votes and loyalty of the white tenant farmers, "the boys at the forks of the creek," by promising to secure passage of a law to limit the landlord's share of the crops to one-fourth of the cotton and one-third of the grain when the tenant provided everything but the land.

Ferguson's opponent, Colonel Thomas H. Ball, was a seasoned prohibition leader, but Ferguson made Ball's membership in the Houston Club a major issue, demanding to know why Ball, if he neither drank nor gambled as he claimed, did not resign from a club where liquor was served and card games were played for money. Ferguson, who consistently opposed prohibition, promised, if elected, to veto any bill that had anything to do with the liquor question, no matter from what source it came. "I will strike it where the chicken got the axe." He beat the "durned high toned" Ball by

45,504 votes in the Democratic primary and buried his obscure Republican opponent in the general election.

Once in office, Ferguson persuaded the legislature to pass a law regulating rents, but a state court struck down the seldom-enforced measure in 1921. He had stressed his commitment to rural education in his campaign speeches. The legislature responded by passing a mild compulsory attendance law. Rural schools received a special $1 million appropriation, and funding for The University of Texas was also increased. Ferguson wanted the Robertson Insurance Law amended to give tax breaks to national companies that resumed business in the state; but local bankers, indigenous insurance companies, and progressives opposed the change, which died in the Senate, handing the governor his only legislative defeat.

Ferguson retained the support of the farmers and easily won reelection in 1916. Meanwhile, he had become involved in a controversy with The University of Texas. In June 1917, he vetoed virtually the university's entire appropriation because the Board of Regents had ignored his suggestions regarding the selection of a new university president and had refused to dismiss faculty members whom the governor found objectionable. "It does seem that a lot of people have gone hogwild on the subject of higher education," he remarked. He complained that the university was "an institution of fads and fancies" where fraternities dominated. "If the University cannot be maintained as a democratic University, then we ought to have no University," Ferguson told a group of regents in his office.

Ferguson's veto forged a powerful coalition of former students of the university led by Will C. Hogg, prohibitionists, and woman suffragists seeking his removal from office. In August 1917, the Texas House of Representatives voted twenty-one articles of impeachment, and the Senate convicted him on ten counts. Five charges related to unlawful use of state funds; two involved loans he received, one from his bank in excess of the legal 30 percent limit and one in the amount of $156,500 from parties later identified as Texas brewers; and three concerned his relations with the Board of Regents of The University of Texas. The Senate verdict removed Ferguson from office and made him ineligible "to hold any office of honor, trust or profit under the State of Texas." His chief counsel, William Hanger, predicted: "Fergusonism will be an issue in the politics of Texas every year there is an election held until Jim Ferguson dies." And so it proved.

Ferguson immediately began a campaign for "vindication." With his friends still in control of the Democratic Executive Committee, he was allowed to run for governor in 1918 against William P. Hobby, who as lieutenant governor had succeeded him in 1917. Hobby, whom Ferguson derided as a "political accident," had the support of the progressive-prohibitionist wing of the party. Ferguson was crushed in the primary, by a vote of 461,479 to 217,012. As a result of the disclosure that the German-American Alliance had been "interested" in Ferguson's gubernatorial race in 1914, as well as of Ferguson's mysterious $156,500 loan, the Hobby organization successfully linked him to the German Empire in World War I; the United States had entered the conflict in April 1917. "I don't know where that $156,000 came from and Jim won't tell," former state attorney general Martin M. Crane declared in a Houston speech. "But if he got it from the brewers, it may have originally come from the Kaiser, for I say to you that the breweries and the German-Mexican Alliance were practically the same thing."

Prohibition had become a patriotic issue, a measure with which to help win the war. The antiprohibition cause was discredited because of Ferguson's impeachment and the support the wets had received from German brewers and German Americans, whose loyalty the public questioned. A state law, effective on April 15, 1918, forbade the sale of liquor within ten miles of any place where troops were quartered. In January 1920, the Eighteenth Amendment to the United States Constitution made the prohibition of alcohol national policy. The Texas legislature ratified the amendment, and on May 24, 1919, Texas voters ratified a prohibition amendment to the state constitution by a vote of 188,982 to 130,907. The drys seemed to have won their fight, but it soon became apparent that many citizens did not intend to abide by the law. The tenuousness of the dry victory was nowhere more evident than in the South, a major prohibition stronghold and a major producer of illicit whiskey. Nevertheless, the spirit of reform stayed alive.

Under the leadership of the Texas Equal Suffrage Association, the wartime era saw the triumph of the woman suffrage movement. In a special session in 1918, the legislature adopted a law permitting women to vote in all primary elections. That same year, several women won election to posts in local government and Annie Webb Blanton won the race for state superintendent of public instruction. On May 24, 1919, voters turned down by 25,120 votes a state constitutional amendment granting woman suffrage and specifying that aliens would have to be naturalized fully before being allowed to vote; since it was not a primary, Texas women had not been permitted to vote on the issue. Nevertheless, the cause soon triumphed anyway, inasmuch as the decision was made nationally. In June 1919, a special session of the Texas legislature ratified the Nineteenth Amendment (granting women the right to vote) to the United States Constitution, Texas being the ninth state in the union and the first in the South to give its approval. The amendment took effect on August 26, 1920.

The list of suffrage leaders in Texas included Minnie Fisher Cunningham, Jane Y. McCallum, Jessie Daniel Ames, and the aforementioned Annie Webb Blanton. With the vote secured, these women set an example for other women by working hard in politics. Indeed, in the 1920s, a coalition of women's groups known as the "Petticoat Lobby" (or Joint Legislative Council) became one of the most successful public-interest lobbying groups in Texas history. The organization backed legislation dealing with education, prison reform, prohibition enforcement, maternal and child health, the abolition of child labor, and other social reforms.

With the disintegration of the Wilson coalition and the Republican triumph in 1920, it seemed for a time as if progressivism had departed the national scene; but the decade of the 1920s was not bereft of progressive reform. Nor did progressivism disappear from the South, although in that region it was transformed through an emphasis upon certain of its tendencies and the distortion of others. One of southern progressivism's surviving strains expressed itself in prohibition enforcement, the antievolution crusade, and the revived Ku Klux Klan's efforts to protect traditional moral standards and cultural values. "The Ku Klux Klan in Texas is made up almost wholly of misled and misguided good people who are on the moral side of moral questions and on the progressive side of economic questions," Wilsonian leader Thomas B. Love of Dallas explained to columnist Mark Sullivan in 1922. "They are almost wholly of the class of people who carried Texas for Woodrow Wilson in 1912. They have been organized in a large number of counties on the anti-Catholic issue. There is little prejudice against the Jews, and the negro question has little or nothing to do with it. My opinion is that it is the sort of thing that 'dances only one set.' I think it will pass away within the next two years."

As a post–World War I crime wave hit Texas, the Klan, which appeared in the state late in 1920, declared that it stood for "law and order" (as it understood the term) and against corrupt officialdom. It undertook a campaign of intimidation and violence aimed mostly at bootleggers, gamblers, adulterers, wifebeaters, and other moral offenders. From 1922 to 1924, the Klan was the paramount issue in Texas politics, electing sheriffs, attorneys, judges, and legislators; and in 1922 it won one of the most important Klan victories in the nation—the election of Earle B. Mayfield, an admitted Klansman, to the United States Senate.

Another strain of southern progressivism in the 1920s was what historian George B. Tindall termed "business progressivism" in *The Emergence of the New South, 1913-1945* (1967). This neo-Bourbon political philosophy, manifested in a sequence of governors, emphasized the old progressive themes of public service and efficiency; it was broad enough to include administrative reorganization, tax reforms, good roads, better schools, and expanded health services; but it did not embrace any comprehensive challenge to conservative ideas in the area of capital-labor relations. The South lagged in supporting broad social programs, such as state protection for women and children in industry and workmen's compensation laws.

Two business progressive governors of Texas were Pat M. Neff (1921–1925) and Dan Moody (1927–1931). Governor Miriam A. Ferguson, who served one term during this period (1925–1927), as a proxy for her husband, Jim, offered a "plebian" contrast to the business progressive administrations of Neff and Moody.

In 1920, Neff, a Waco lawyer and former Speaker of the Texas House of Representatives (1903–1905) defeated one of Texas's political powers, former United States Senator Joseph W. Bailey, in the Democratic runoff primary by more than 79,000 votes. Bailey denounced labor unions, prohibition, woman suffrage, the League of Nations, the Wilson administration, socialism, monopoly, class legislation, and class domination. Neff, with his proposal to "make Texas the best place in the world to live," had the support of most of the anti-Bailey leaders of the 1906–1913 period, all of the prohibitionist leaders, most of the newly enfranchised women, and most of the Wilsonian progressives. He easily won the general election and was reelected in 1922. Neff's defeat of Bailey was hailed as a final victory, in the words of a Texas journalist, "for the achievements of the Wilson administration, prohibition and equal suffrage, the rule of right in this land of ours and for honest and progressive government conducted by honest and progressive men."

In his inaugural address on January 18, 1921, Neff struck a confident note. "Not only is Texas a land of opportunity, but ours is a day of opportunity," he told his audience. "Let no one throw himself across the track to block the train of progress. Obstructionists never win battles. It is the progressive, dynamic leader that counts. You, gentlemen of the Legislature, are privileged to be the spokesmen of a progressive and a forward-looking people."

In frequent messages to the Thirty-seventh and Thirty-eighth legislatures, Neff advocated the abolishment or consolidation of all unnecessary state boards and bureaus, more effective law enforcement, prison-system reforms, better labor conditions, improvements in rural schools and vocational education, improvement of the state highway system, new laws to attract industry, a better public health program, water conservation, and a constitutional convention. He recommended that the legislature raise gross receipts and corporate franchise taxes; enact a state income-tax law designed to reach even those with little or no physical property to be taxed; and levy at least a 5 percent severance tax on oil, natural gas, sulphur, quicksilver, and all other minerals produced in Texas.

The legislators took little action on the governor's progressive program. Although some offices were eliminated or consolidated, the legislature refused to modify greatly the organization of the state administration; no constitutional convention met; and there were no fundamental changes in the state tax system. Relocation and centralization of the prison system were considered but rejected. Neff thought the chief cause of the worst crime wave in Texas history was the suspended-sentence law and he asked for its repeal—again, to no avail.

Neff was an active Baptist and an enthusiastic advocate of prohibition. He asked the legislature to empower the attorney general to utilize *quo warranto* proceedings to remove local peace officers who refused to enforce prohibition. The legislature responded with a weak bill that permitted a district judge to remove a county officer for certain causes, but not for intoxication if it resulted from drinking liquor prescribed by a licensed physician. Some changes were made in the Dean Prohibition Law to make enforcement easier. Neff sent the Texas Rangers to San Antonio to stop the illegal liquor traffic and other law violations. In 1922, he used the military for approximately two months in Limestone and Freestone Counties to quell the lawlessness that accompanied the oil boom in Mexia. In 1937, historian Ralph W. Steen wrote of Neff: "Perhaps the most severe criticism which can be leveled at his administration is that in his zeal for the enforcement of the prohibition laws he seemed to forget other matters of great importance to the state."

In July 1922, when trouble developed in Houston, Denison, and other labor centers between striking railroad employees and workers who replaced them, Neff sent Rangers to Denison to preserve order; on July 25, he proclaimed martial law and ordered the national guard to the city. Rangers were also sent to Sherman,

Childress, and a number of other Texas cities, which also were placed under the state's open-port law. The governor announced that as long as the men of Texas could "pull a trigger," strikers would not obstruct the wheels of transportation; he maintained that the railroad employees had a right to strike, but not to interfere with other people who wanted to work. Organized labor objected vigorously to Neff's "interference"; and in the election of 1922 The Farm-Labor Union, the State Federation of Labor, and the Railway Brotherhoods endorsed Fred S. Rogers of Brenham for governor.

Relations between Neff and the legislature were never cordial or close. He adopted a rather lofty attitude towards the lawmakers, and he had no spokespersons or contacts on the floor of either the House or the Senate. T. Whitfield Davidson, lieutenant governor in Neff's second term, did not believe that he had an obligation to sponsor or push the governor's program in the state senate. Neff ran into difficulties with the legislature on money matters; therefore, during his two terms a total of five special sessions were necessary to pass appropriation bills.

A breach between the governor and the legislature also occurred because Neff granted few pardons, and none for prisoners represented by attorneys. Feeling former governors' free use of the clemency power had "helped to weaken the arm of the law in Texas," Neff disbanded the Board of Pardons and made his own investigation of every pardon he granted. Unwilling to temper justice with mercy, he issued only 92 pardons and 107 conditional pardons during his four years in office. However, Neff believed that there was some honor among convicts, so he established an honor farm where 150 men worked and slept without guards or locks. The farm was abandoned by the Ferguson administration after forty-five prisoners escaped from the facility in 1925.

Despite Neff's difficulties with the legislature, during his administration lawmakers did pass a number of measures he favored. They voted the largest appropriation for rural schools to that time, provided funds for vocational education, voted $1.3 million to enlarge The University of Texas campus, established Texas Technological College in West Texas and South Texas State Teachers College at Kingsville, provided building and operating funds for Stephen F. Austin State Teachers College at Nacogdoches, legalized the formation of cooperative farm marketing associations, authorized the creation of water and irrigation districts, authorized the licensing and supervision of maternity homes, created a tubercular hospital at Kerrville for ex-soldiers, authorized the establishment of city hospitals, and created a board to regulate the licensing of optometrists.

Neff strongly favored good roads. During his administration, the highway commission was reorganized, a gasoline tax of one cent per gallon was levied for the benefit of highway and public school funds, license fees for motor vehicles were increased, and a proposed constitutional amendment authorizing the state to take over the construction, operation, and maintenance of a state highway system was ratified by the legislature.

Neff also deserves credit for the beginning of the state parks system. Texas kept its public lands upon entering the Union, but later sold or gave away practically all of it. Indeed, the state did not own even one park for camping or recreational purposes. On May 1, 1923, Neff sent a message to the legislature recommending the creation of a nonsalaried state parks committee, with the duty of soliciting donations of parcels of land of any size suitable for use as a public park. Neff was ever a purveyor of colorful phrases, but he rose to new heights when challenging the legislators to come face to face with the automobile age and provide scenic beauty spots for the people "to go 'back to nature,' where the bees hum, the birds sing, the brooks ripple, the breezes blow and the flowers bloom."

Somewhat reluctantly, the legislature went along with the request, although an effort was made later to repeal the parks board bill. During his last year in office, Neff traveled nine thousand miles and made 110 speeches in behalf of state parks. In 1925 he was able to report that the parks board had received more than fifty tracts of land from private donors.

Neff was a crusader and a visionary, but his accomplishments in office fell far short of his expectations and hopes. "Early in my administration I discovered that it was impossible to do the things that I had dreamed I would do," he wrote shortly after leaving Austin. "Many things hindered. Numberless contending and opposing forces had to be reckoned with. Frequently a Governor is helpless to do the things that, as a matter of fact, should be done. At times he feels that about all he can do is to write proclamations that no one reads, and give advice that no one heeds."

Mrs. Miriam A. Ferguson succeeded Neff as governor. In the gubernatorial race in 1924, she ran as a proxy candidate in place of her husband, James E. Ferguson, whose impeachment conviction in 1917 had, as noted, barred him from running for a state office. Mrs. Ferguson based her campaign in part on her husband's vindication and in part on opposition to the Ku Klux Klan, who openly backed her challenger, Judge Felix D. Robertson of Dallas. "Ma"

Ferguson prevailed by a margin of 97,732 votes in the Democratic primary runoff. In the general election, Ferguson led her Republican opponent, George C. Butte, the former dean of The University of Texas Law School, by more than 127,000 votes. However, in this election thousands of rock-ribbed Democrats voted Republican for the first time rather than help return "Farmer Jim" to the executive mansion. These developments signaled the passing of the Klan as a dominant force in Texas politics. The following year the legislature made it unlawful for any secret society to allow its members to wear masks or disguises in public.

During Miriam Ferguson's administration reform took a holiday. "The Fergusons were elected by rustics," noted political scientist V. O. Key, Jr., in *Southern Politics in State and Nation* (1949). "As has often been true of southern governors with vivid personal appeal, they produced little in the way of governmental action to justify the support." The legislative session of 1925 passed almost no bills of outstanding public interest. Mrs. Ferguson's two years in office were marked by behind-the-scenes domination by her husband, favoritism in the granting of highway contracts to firms that advertised in the *Ferguson Forum*, the influence of Jim Ferguson over the state textbook commission, and an extremely liberal pardon policy. Indeed, the governor granted 1,318 pardons and 829 conditional pardons. In the murky world of statute books, there may well have been no illegality, but the Fergusons were guilty of a flagrant abuse of the ethical standards of public office.

In 1926 Mrs. Ferguson sought reelection but was defeated in the runoff primary by Attorney General Dan Moody, who reminded voters of Jim Ferguson's impeachment and promised to rid the state of "Fergusonism." In an effort to use the Klan issue as in 1924, the Fergusons attempted to link Moody with the "Invisible Empire." Jim Ferguson charged that "Moody's campaign was daddied in the evoluted monkey end of the Baptist church and boosted by the Ku Klux Klan and supported by the big oil companies opposed to the gasoline tax." However, since Moody, while district attorney from 1922 to 1925, had successfully prosecuted Klansmen in a Williamson County flogging case, the accusation fell flat. Moody went on to win the general election by 200,000 votes. In 1928, he was elected to a second term, receiving a large majority in the first primary over Louis J. Wardlaw, the Ferguson candidate, and two other opponents.

At thirty-three, Moody was the youngest man ever elected governor of Texas. Like Neff, he was more progressive than the legislators with whom he worked. Moody proposed a scientific tax system, judicial reform, a civil-service law, a unified accounting system for all state departments, warehouse and marketing systems for Texas agriculture, laws against indiscriminate pardoning of criminals, a system of correlated state highways and adequate revenues for the Texas Highway Department, government regulation of public utilities and motor transportation companies, election law reform, the amendment of Texas's libel law, concentration and modernization of the prison system, liberal state aid for public schools, the coordination of the state's universities and colleges to eliminate needless duplication, and the further development of Texas ports. Wrote Ralph W. Steen in 1937: "The Moody recommendations were in keeping with the best thought in political economy, and if adopted would have replaced the present government with a more modern government."

How did this ambitious "Moody program" fare? The legislators reacted negatively to most of his recommendations, and few of the major organizational changes he proposed were adopted. A state auditor's office was established, but civil service was turned down and the prison system was reorganized only partially. The ingrained opposition of state officials to change in the status quo had a tremendous influence on the legislature, whose members had a natural hesitancy to deal with the complex problem completely. And the voters rejected necessary constitutional amendments. But the greatest obstacle proved to be the argument that administrative reorganization would concentrate too much power in the governor's hands.

Business progressivism in Texas had little to offer African Americans and Mexican Americans. A law passed during the Neff administration barring blacks from Democratic party primaries was declared unconstitutional by the United States Supreme Court in *Nixon* v. *Herndon* (1927). The Fortieth Legislature responded by giving political parties authority to determine their own membership, provided that no one should be excluded because of former political party affiliations or views. There was much criticism of the corrupt South Texas machines, such as Archie Parr's organization in Duval County, but no serious attempt was made to break up the power that rested on the economic and political exploitation of the Mexican Americans.

Moody's record as governor was more noteworthy for its administrative than for its legislative endeavors. He reversed the Ferguson's liberal pardon policies and reformed the Texas Highway Department, two areas that had been the subject of much criticism during the previous administration. His demand that the Highway Department operate above the slightest suspicion of financial irregularities, his appointment of Ross Sterling (Chairman), Cone Johnson, and W. R. Ely to the Highway Commission, and the selection of Gibb Gilchrist as state highway engineer, laid the foundation for the department's "remarkable record of rectitude" in the years that followed. When Moody left office in January 1931, the *Dallas Morning News* noted that his record fitted well into the circumstances of his first election: "His candidacy for Governor was not a response to the call for great legislative enterprise needing a leader. . . . His candidacy was primarily, and almost exclusively, a pledge to rescue public services from the grievous state into which they had been brought by maladministration."

During his four years in office Moody had two regular legislative sessions, called six special sessions (five during his second term), vetoed fifteen bills during the sessions, and used the postadjournment veto 102 times—a record which earned him the title of "Veto Governor of Texas." Only one of his vetoes was overridden. Some Moody supporters attributed his difficulties with the legislature to the animosity of political rivals such as Jim Ferguson, State Senator Thomas B. Love, Texas's "dry messiah," and Lieutenant Governor Barry Miller, who hoped to succeed Moody. "I saw how Tom Love and Barry Miller acted with the rest of them just like a bunch of Monkeys," one indignant visitor to the Senate chamber wrote Moody. "Old man Jim Fergeson [sic] was sitting in the back tickled to death because the Senate would not do anything."

Moody's failure to mediate successfully the bitter fight between Al Smith and anti-Smith Democrats in Texas in the presidential election of 1928 left both factions dissatisfied with his leadership, and it embittered his relations with the Forty-first Legislature. "All the time the Legislature was in session, a crazy 'wild' group, and Dan sweating so hard to put over constructive measures," Mrs. Moody noted in her diary on May 25, 1929. "Reactions were deadly to the recent Smith-Hoover fight, with Dan the 'goat,' both sides." Jim Ferguson was "still working his hate" at the Capitol.

A "conspiracy" theory does not by itself explain the failure of Moody's program, since during his first six months in office, when his popularity was highest, and the only organized opposition to him was a small Ferguson clique in the Senate, his program was still rejected. According to the *Houston Chronicle*, it "was a bit too advanced for the legislators, especially on the subject of civil service. . . . Some of his friends opposed some of his measures and supported others."

Part of the explanation for the failure of Neff and Moody to win the support of their legislatures must be sought in the mental attitudes of Texas lawmakers and of the voters who sent them to Austin. While Texas had undergone marked changes in its economy and population distribution, it remained unchanged psychologically—its characteristic habit of thought was still rural. Besides the Texans who lived on farms, a large portion of the city and town population had rural origins and antecedents. A Texas magazine editor of the period, Peter Molyneaux, gave the following definition of the term *rural*: "In general it is a habit of thought to which almost anything which transcends a purely agricultural form of society is in some degree alien. In its most narrow form the rural habit of thought is a neighborhood habit of thought, prescribed in its outlook by the interests and horizons of a rural countryside."

Little wonder, then, that when financially strapped rural voters participated directly in the legislative process through referenda on proposed amendments to the state constitution, they turned down proposals for the general welfare if no apparent local benefit would result. This was true even if each amendment involved the expenditure of a relatively small amount of money. For example, in 1927 rural voters decisively defeated two constitutional amendments which would have raised the salaries of the governor and the legislators and increased the number of judges on the state supreme court from three to nine. A resident of a small town gave as one of the reasons for the rural vote against the amendments the fact that the big cities favored them. "The boys at the forks of the creek," he wrote in a letter to a newspaper, "see the cities becoming big and wealthy, commercial and financial interests merging for their own benefit . . . and they doubt the disinterestedness of their political friends and register their disapproval of anything they sponsor . . . on the theory that no good thing can come out of Nazareth."

This same rural habit of thought among lawmakers, almost untouched by the economic changes going on all around them, put roadblocks in the path of the business progressive reforms advocated by Neff and Moody which would have increased state expenditures but which did not address the farmer's most urgent problems. A look at those districts from which the nay-voting representatives hailed shows a pattern of rural counties and small towns.

In addition, the lobbyists representing the state's oil and gas, sulphur, and lumber companies throttled severance- or income-tax proposals. The powerful utilities lobby blocked bills supported by Moody to create a utilities commission with rate-fixing powers in the Forty-first Legislature. Texas did not establish such a body until 1975. No wonder, then, that when Dr. John C. Granbery wrote to Moody to commend his message to the legislature in 1929, the governor replied pessimistically: "Some parts of it, as you would imagine, have not met with any great amount of enthusiasm at the hands of the Legislature, and likely will not be enacted into law. I believe the time will come when some of these matters will be enacted into law. I have sometimes felt that our attitude in Texas is a little too reactionary and that we were not ready to accept progressive measures which worked successfully in other states."

Business progressivism, which had coincided with the boom years of the 1920s, waned following the stock market crash in 1929 and the Great Depression that followed. Its tenets did not play well in hard times. In Texas, state pensions for the elderly and other relief measures became the dominant political issue in the 1930s.

On the national scene in the 1920s, Texas was a pivotal state in the transitional struggle between the prohibitionist, native-stock, Protestant, southern and western wing of the Democratic Party, and its urban, wet, new-immigrant, northeastern faction. "Romantic in history, powerful in Democratic politics, Texas provides more interest for those watching political developments than almost any other State in the South," editorialized the *New York Times* in April 1928. "Ever since 'the Immortal Forty,' under the unit rule, stood by Woodrow Wilson at Baltimore until the nomination was won, an importance attaches to the Texas delegation out of proportion to the size of its vote or the State's geographical and industrial significance."

Thomas B. Love was the manager of the Wilson movement in Texas in 1911–12 and helped direct dry progressives in the reform battles of the next decade. From 1917 to 1920 he served as assistant secretary of the Department of the Treasury under Wilson's son-in-law, William Gibbs McAdoo. One of McAdoo's staunchest backers for the presidency, Love, aided by other old Wilsonians such as Marshall Hicks and Cato Sells, twice secured Texas's forty convention votes for him. These men and their followers regarded McAdoo as the heir of the Wilson legacy. When the Klan entered Texas politics, Love accepted its support for McAdoo. In the presidential primary, in May 1924, the Klan helped the McAdoo forces defeat both

Senator Oscar B. Underwood of Alabama, who had the backing of most of Texas's wet leaders, and Governor Pat Neff, who wanted to send an uninstructed delegation favorable to himself to the national convention. McAdoo's victory in Texas stimulated his flagging campaign, and gave it the impetus to drive on to New York City and the 103-ballot debacle in Madison Square Garden. Love was preparing to carry Texas for McAdoo in 1928 when the Californian withdrew from the race.

The control that Love and his lieutenants exercised over the state Democratic Party was challenged by a group of young, self-styled "liberal" Democrats, antiprohibitionist in sentiment, who wanted to end what they saw as an era of fanaticism that had held Texas in political thralldom. They came together under Dan Moody's "throw-the-rascals-out" banner in 1926. Although a strong dry, Moody was persuaded to join the revolt against Love, and Love was kept off the Texas delegation, which supported favorite son Jesse H. Jones at the national convention in Houston.

The Democratic Party stretched the South's loyalty to the breaking point by nominating Governor Al Smith of New York for President in 1928. Rural, Protestant, and prohibitionist Southerners were asked to support a wet, urban, Catholic with ties to New York City's Tammany Hall political machine. Cone Johnson, a dry Texas delegate, complained: "I sat by the central aisle while the parade passed following Smith's nomination and the faces I saw in that mile-long procession were not American faces. I wondered where were the Americans." Bone-dry Democrats, headed by Tom Love, organized as the "Anti-Al Smith Democrats of Texas" and arranged a fusion electoral ticket with the Republicans. This combination on behalf of Herbert Hoover put Texas into the Republican column for the first time in a presidential election. The result set up a bitter contest between the "Hoovercrats," now calling themselves "The Anti-Tammany Democrats of Texas," and party regulars (dubbed "brass-collar Democrats" by the bolters) for control of the state party. Looking beyond Texas, Love wanted the anti-Tammany forces to capture the Democratic Party in the southern states, gain control of the 1932 national convention, rescind the two-thirds rule, and nominate "clean," dry candidates.

In addition to the presidential sweepstakes, Texas witnessed a heated contest for the United States Senate. Although the Texas Klan was only a shadow of its former self, it made a half-hearted rally around the candidacy of Earle Mayfield. His defeat in the runoff by Congressman Tom Connally was the final nail driven into its coffin. Connally's impressive victory was interpreted as marking a new era in Texas politics; it was proof that the Klan was becoming as impotent in the Lone Star State as it was elsewhere. Moreover, Jim Ferguson had backed three losers in 1928; Louis Wardlaw for governor against Dan Moody; Alvin Owsley for the United States Senate in the first primary; and Mayfield in the run-off. Political analysts saw this as proof that Ferguson no longer could deliver his following to any candidate other than himself or his wife. Thus, as the 1920s drew to a close, the Klan was virtually extinct in Texas, Ferguson's political fortunes were at their lowest point in eight years, and the stage was set for a bruising fight in the "House of the Fathers," as reverential Democrats termed their party.

Suggested Reading

Alexander, Charles C. *Crusade for Conformity: The Ku Klux Klan in Texas, 1920–1930.* Houston: Texas Gulf Coast Historical Association, 1962.

Anders, Evan. *Boss Rule in South Texas: The Progressive Era.* Austin: University of Texas Press, 1982.

Barr, Alwyn. *Reconstruction to Reform: Texas Politics, 1876–1906.* Austin: University of Texas Press, 1971.

Brown, Norman D. *Hood, Bonnet, and Little Brown Jug: Texas Politics, 1921–1928.* College Station: Texas A&M University Press, 1984.

Cottrell, Debbie Mauldin. *Pioneer Woman Educator: The Progressive Spirit of Annie Webb Blanton.* College Station: Texas A&M University Press, 1993.

Gould, Lewis L. *Progressives and Prohibitionists: Texas Democrats in the Wilson Era.* Austin: University of Texas Press, 1973.

Grantham, Dewey W. *Southern Progressivism: The Reconciliation of Progress and Tradition.* Knoxville: University of Tennessee Press, 1983.

Hine, Darlene Clark. *Black Victory: The Rise and Fall of the White Primary in Texas.* Millwood: KTO Press, 1979.

McArthur, Judith N. *Creating the New Woman: The Rise of Southern Women's Progressive Culture in Texas, 1893–1918.* Urbana and Chicago: University of Illinois Press, 1998.

McCarty, Jeanne Bozzell. *The Struggle for Sobriety: Protestants and Prohibition in Texas, 1919–1935.* El Paso: Texas Western Press, 1980.

Taylor, A. Elizabeth. *Citizens at Last: The Woman Suffrage Movement in Texas,* Ruthe Winegarten and Judith N. McArthur, Consulting Eds. Austin: Ellen C. Temple, 1987.

Tindall, George B. *The Emergence of the New South, 1913–1945.* Baton Rouge: Louisiana State University Press, 1967.

Woodward, C. Vann. *The Origins of the New South, 1877–1913.* Baton Rouge: Louisiana State University Press, 1951.

James E. and Miriam A. Ferguson, circa 1925. *Courtesy of the Institute of Texan Cultures, San Antonio Light Collection, #0002-C.*

CHAPTER TEN

Texas from Depression through World War II, 1929–1945

Ben Procter

T<small>EXANS WERE OPTIMISTIC ABOUT THE FUTURE</small> in January 1929. Over the past decade the population of the state had increased to 5,824,715, representing a gain of more than 1 million people, or almost 25 percent, and by far the best ten-year growth in the state's history. Although geared to one crop—"Cotton is King"—the economy was somewhat diversified. In East Texas the Piney Woods accounted for a substantial lumber industry; in the lower Rio Grande Valley, with the introduction of irrigation, both truck farming and citrus growing had proved extremely profitable; on the Edwards Plateau and in West Texas, livestock had established the state as the nation's number-one producer of hides and wool and mohair; and in many, oftentimes isolated, areas such as Desdemona and Wink, "wildcatters" pursued the legacy of Spindletop by tapping vast amounts of oil and natural gas. In fact, Texans prided themselves in their present situation, in being the largest state— more spacious in area than any European nation—and in maintaining or inculcating American frontier traits of rugged individualism, fierce competitiveness, and unblushing patriotism.

Texans had solidified and strengthened their economic position through political action. On the state level in 1928 they had elected Dan Moody, a brilliant lawyer versed in administrative efficiency and dedicated to "wiping out debts and lowering taxes," as governor, while on the national front they had, for the first time, voted for and helped elect a Republican to the presidency. Herbert Clark Hoover of Iowa, enthusiastically promising "Two Chickens in Every Pot!" and "A Car in Every Garage!" and optimistically predicting that "poverty will be banished from this nation," had touched their wallets and had won their purse-string allegiance. But if prosperity had not been the deciding issue, Democratic nominee Alfred E. Smith surely was. Catholic, urban-born, progressive in policies, yet educated politically by boss-dominated Tammany Hall, Smith was anathema to a majority of Texans who embraced the values of the white, Protestant, agrarian South. The descendants of the Alamo could expect no less; the inheritors of San Jacinto could demand no more.

On October 29, 1929, all such optimism ended. As economist John Kenneth Galbraith phrased it, "the mightiest of Americans were, for a brief time, revealed as humans." On that day alone more than 16 million shares of stock changed hands. The *New York Times* industrial average plunged forty-three points, "canceling all gains of the twelve wonderful months preceding," thus marking the worst day in Wall Street history.

Although many economic danger signals were prevalent in 1929, the crash seemed to stun the American people, to awe and dismay them. Panic quickly set in and any thought of stabilization was illusory. First came "the slaughter . . . of the innocents"—the amateurs in the market; next, the moneyed and well-to-do appeared to receive a "leveling" treatment; then no one was safe. Over the next few weeks stocks on the New York exchange fell by 40 percent, "a loss on paper of $26 billion." The Great Bull Market was dead!

Concerned and apprehensive, President Hoover perceived the intensifying calamity rather simplistically; he viewed this twentieth-century economic debacle through nineteenth-century eyeglasses. Since the stock market was responsible for the collapse, he reasoned that the necessary additive for recovery was to correct the weaknesses within that institution. Then the panic would subside, especially if he could mold public opinion into a restoration of public confidence. Having fashioned U.S. domestic policy over the past eight and one-half years, both as secretary of commerce and as President, Hoover could not conceive, much less believe, that the economy was unsound. He therefore inundated the news media with expressions of confidence, continual testimonials by cabinet members and business leaders. For instance, on November 4, 1929, Henry Ford announced that "things are better today than they were yesterday." Less than two weeks later (November 16) the *New York Times* stated that national financiers were convinced that "the storm had blown over." And at the turn of the year multimillionaire Secretary of the Treasury Andrew W. Mellon noted, "I see nothing in the present situation that is either menacing or warrants pessimism." To keep up the prevailing tempo Hoover also resorted to numerous meetings and conferences at the White House, with accompanying press coverage, time and again predicting that the depression was at an end, that soon the lilting new tune of 1930, "Happy Days Are Here Again," would ring true.

Almost to a person, Texans agreed. For the rest of 1929, indeed through 1930, they persisted in their optimism, in their belief that the depression affected only those moneyed "gamblers" in the stock market, in their denunciation of "greedy" Easterners who had "hurt" and had tried to undermine the "sound" United States economy. They therefore readily supported "President Hoover's confidence-building crusade." After all, they relied upon the land of their fore-fathers as well as cattle and oil—and fortunately the 1929 cotton crop had been harvested already and had sold at a healthy price. Besides, New York City and financial chaos were far away; if need be, Texans could always produce enough on their farms to keep from going hungry.

Even in urban Texas this mindset prevailed, with both community leaders and news media indulging in faulty logic and provincial pride. In Fort Worth the *Record-Telegram* and *Star Telegram*, until the spring of 1931, pointed to increased construction, railroad traffic, oil production, and cattle and poultry sales as stabilizing, if not propitious influences. "As a matter of fact, in America, we don't know what hard times are," a *Star-Telegram* editorial asserted (July 30, 1930). "Certainly these times are not hard, except for the utterly improvident, the idle, and the shiftless—and all times are hard on them." In Austin both university expenditures and state government employment bolstered the economy, while the political activities of the Forty-first Texas Legislature occupied much of the newspaper space. Even though "hordes of insects" had devastated "a bumper crop" and the stock market crash had the sobering effect of sweeping away "paper profits and some cash," local merchants, fearing that "scare headlines" might have deleterious consequences on the economy, boomed the city through advertisements. Typical of their rhetoric was a paid plea to "talk Austin, write about Austin, work for Austin, and live for Austin." In Dallas, the construction business was flourishing in 1930; recent arrivals the year before had seen to that. Then the East Texas oil boom, centering around Kilgore, had tended to lessen thoughts of depression until the summer of 1931, when overproduction and falling prices affected the economy. In Houston, optimism was equally high. Although fear of depression was somewhat pervasive during the first months following the crash, the *Post-Dispatch* was a continual salve. "More and more it appears," the editor asserted on November 17, 1929, that "the changes in stock prices are purely an affair of and for stock speculators." Again in March 1930, after the mayor had dismissed a number of city employees and six hundred demonstrators had marched in protest, the *Post-Dispatch* announced that "Houston is comparatively free of discontent due to economic conditions." Besides, with proceeds from a busy port massaging the local economy, with oil refineries being constructed to meet increasing production needs, and with financier-banker Jesse H. Jones as their civic leader, Houstonians temporarily ignored harsh realities. In San Antonio, too, business leaders seemed afraid to admit depression, especially in the *Express*, even though unemployment and bleak economic conditions in the city were omnipresent. On August 31, 1930, a front-page article in the *Express* reported that San Antonio was "one of five cities . . . to which men of billions . . . [were] looking to invest money"; another on October 5 debunked the "talk of 'depression' and 'money shortage'"; and still another on September 28 noted that economists were predicting that "better times are in store for San Antonio and the rest of the United States" when, in fact, the local "newspapers any day tell the story of better times here."

But as depression worsened across the United States in 1931 and 1932, Texans had to recognize its existence, then attempt to combat its devastating effects. Since the Hoover administration seemed to have political lockjaw, incapable of meeting the people's needs, private charities shouldered the burdens of the poor and desperate until their funds were exhausted; whereupon city governments and community leaders necessarily intervened. At Temple in Bell County, after two banks folded in 1931 and cotton dropped to as low as five cents a pound, the Retail Merchants Association issued scrip—as did the San Antonio School Board—"in denominations of 25 cents, 50 cents, and $1.00." In Midland, Dallas, and Fort Worth the chambers of commerce sponsored gardening projects, either donating land or seed or encouraging people to plant vegetables. In turn, businessmen in Fort Worth and San Antonio pledged to hire laborers on a part-time or weekly basis but at the same time passed ordinances not to hire transients—the spread of hobo jungles alarmed Texans. To obtain more money for relief, to provide soup kitchens and breadlines, as well as shelter for the hapless, any number of Texas cities—Houston, Dallas, Fort Worth, Austin—sponsored plays or musicals, the proceeds of which went to charity.

In rural Texas, economic conditions during 1931–32 also deteriorated. But farmers, many of whom were "sharecroppers" and "tenants," had already "adapted to relative poverty" and therefore were not always quick to realize the higher degree of hardship. Yet, as prices plummeted, as drought exacerbated their plight, as debts rose and foreclosures mounted alarmingly, they too sought relief from a notably worsening situation.

Consequently, Texans looked for new solutions. President Hoover, whom they had supported ardently for more than two years, was now a villain of huge proportions, a betrayer of capitalism and democracy, and the man responsible for their economic calamity. With grim satisfaction they readily endorsed the debunking of their "hero" by decrying—sometimes laughingly, sometimes savagely— jack rabbits as "Hoover hogs," tent and tarpaper hobo camps as "Hoovervilles," and pants pockets turned inside out as "Hoover flags." So when Democrats nominated Governor Franklin Delano Roosevelt of New York for President and John Nance "Cactus Jack" Garner (of Uvalde) for Vice President in the summer of 1932, the election choice was evident. Texans agreed that a "New Deal for the forgotten man" required their backing; the Democratic ticket garnered 88.6 percent of the state's vote.

Hoping for immediate returns on their political decision, Texans were not disappointed. The state representation in Washington was powerful and influential, bordering on awesome, even dynastic. Besides Garner, who performed the "role as liaison man between the administration and Congress" until 1937 and who was considered by some to be "the most powerful Vice-President in history," Sam Rayburn of Bonham figured prominently in the Texas delegation. In the House, he chaired the powerful Interstate and Foreign Affairs Committee; as Garner's acknowledged protégé, he was in line for majority leader and, eventually, Speaker. Six other Texans also held House chairmanships, including James P. Buchanan of Brenham on Appropriations, Hatton Sumners of Dallas on the Judiciary, and Marvin Jones of Amarillo on Agriculture; while in the upper house Morris Sheppard, the dean of the Senate, headed the Military Affairs Committee and Tom Connally chaired Public Buildings and Grounds. Equally, if not more impressive, was the position of Jesse H. Jones. As head of the New Deal's Reconstruction Finance Corporation (RFC), he managed an economic empire within the government. By 1938 he had disbursed $10 billion in federal funds to financial institutions, agricultural concerns, railroads, and public works projects—remarkably, "nearly all was eventually paid back."

Conservative and mostly from rural areas, the Texas delegation members were, Congressman George Mahon candidly stated, "Democrats first and New Dealers second." But foremost they were

Texans interested in economic recovery for the United States, hence for their state. Philosophically most of them agreed, during Roosevelt's first term, with Jesse Jones, who bluntly told a convention of resentful bankers in 1933: "Be smart, for once. Take the government into partnership with you." They therefore figured prominently in New Deal legislation. In banking, Garner and Jones—over Roosevelt's opposition—helped incorporate the Federal Deposit Insurance Corporation (FDIC) into the Glass-Steagall Banking Act. To correct many weaknesses in the stock market, Rayburn was instrumental in passing the Truth in Securities Act and the Securities Exchange Act. He also "played a major role" in such legislation as the Emergency Railroad Transportation Act, the Federal Communications Act, the Rural Electrification Act, and the Public Utility Holding Company Act. In Agriculture, Marvin Jones helped restructure the agrarian economy in 1933 by enacting the Emergency Farm Mortgage Act, the Farm Credit Act, and the Agricultural Adjustment Act, as well as providing drought-relief funds for the Panhandle and West Texas. Then, in 1934, he aided Texas ranchers with the Jones-Connally Act, cotton farmers with the Bankhead Cotton Control Act, and sugar producers with the Jones-Costigan Sugar Act. Overall, the Texas delegation supported the National Industrial Recovery Act and emergency unemployment, ever mindful that a "large chunk" of federal aid would find its way to Texas.

Officials on the state level during FDR's first term were not nearly as effective, thus "making events in Austin seem less important." In November 1932, Miriam A. "Ma" Ferguson, a wholesome, grandmotherly-looking type, defeated incumbent governor Ross Sterling, a victim of depression politics as well as election fraud in East Texas. After her inauguration in January, Ferguson, with the help of her husband, former governor James A. "Pa" Ferguson (who had been impeached in 1917), tried to address the state's pressing economic problems. To avert a financial panic, she boldly—and with questionable constitutional authority—declared a bank moratorium on March 2; then, rather fortunately, three days later FDR sustained her decree by proclaiming a national bank holiday and promising to reopen all such institutions within a short time, but under federal guidelines. At the same time, with estimates that the state debt hovered in the $14 million range, Governor Ferguson repeatedly proposed to the legislature both sales and income taxes; she was not only rebuffed but ignored. Except for the passage of a two-cent-a-barrel tax on oil, Ferguson could only reduce deficits by cutting appropriations.

An even more important issue for the Ferguson administration had to do with unemployment and relief—and therein lay the problem, and scandal. When late in 1932 the RFC made substantial funds available to the governor who, in turn, was to dispense money to counties through three regional chambers of commerce, the Fergusons were delighted. Here was an excellent opportunity to build an even more powerful political machine with federal money. By executive order, therefore, Mrs. Ferguson established the Texas Relief Commission and selected Lawrence Westbrook as director. Immediately the governor, "Pa," and Westbrook brought local relief administrations into their organization and placed the RFC funds in "pet" banks. Then in May 1933, after Congress passed the Federal Emergency Relief Act, they had an even greater "windfall" to administer—and manipulate. And when the legislature created the Texas Rehabilitation and Relief Commission specifically to oversee and distribute federal money, Jim Ferguson, at the behest of his wife, became the commission chairman, although having "no legal basis" to do so. Together with Westbrook and several appointees, he filled county boards with constituents and "our friends."

To keep their political machine well oiled, the Fergusons needed federal money—and lots of it. Consequently they pressured the legislature to approve a $20 million relief-bond issue in the form of a constitutional amendment (upon which the electorate would vote). Then they used every possible maneuver to get it adopted. They padded the payrolls of supporters, paid poll taxes for "their voters," and financed the campaign, oftentimes with federal funds. For instance, a Senate investigating committee discovered that Bexar County had 252 people on its payroll "with an unusually high range of salaries, up to $300 a month," whereas the "normal county employed about 50," sometimes with little remuneration. Of course, the Fergusons also appealed to basic greed as well as human compassion. "We told them [social workers] if they wanted more money to give out that they had better vote with us," Bexar County Relief Administrator Tex Alsbury testified, "and we got them to get the precinct vote. The people . . . were out of work and money. They were hungry and they lined up to vote." As a final *coup de grace*, the Fergusons persuaded Federal Emergency Relief Administration (FERA) administrator Harry Hopkins to join the campaign. In a radio address three days before the election, he announced that "the federal government has no intention of continuing to pay 95 percent of the Texas relief bill after the bond election on Saturday." Hence, on August 26, 1933, Texans approved of relief for the unemployed—the Fergusons were ecstatic.

But not for long! The stench of corruption was too strong, the misappropriation of funds too blatant, the fear of the Fergusons too great. During the fall of 1933 a Senate investigating committee heard widespread and conflicting testimony. Yet the issue was soon resolved after Westbrook, who had been appointed director of the Texas Relief Commission, admitted, under oath, that "I know that in some instances outright fraud has been committed, forgeries, misapplication of funds." As a result, A. R. Johnson, the Austin City Manager, replaced Westbrook on February 12, 1934, thus destroying the Ferguson relief machine.

Still another issue during the Ferguson years had to do with law and order—or the lack thereof. A contributing factor to the situation concerned the Texas Rangers. Late in July 1932, during the Democratic primary election, the Rangers made a grave error politically: they openly supported Governor Ross Sterling, especially in the Ferguson stronghold of East Texas. In January 1933, the new governor retaliated by firing every Ranger for such partisanship—forty-four in all. But it did not end there. Besides the legislature reducing Ranger salaries, eliminating longevity pay, slashing travel budgets, and limiting force personnel to thirty-two men, Mrs. Ferguson appointed new officers, many of whom "by any standard," historian Steve Schuster candidly asserted, "were a contemptible lot." The results were disastrous. In less than a year one private was convicted of murder; several others in Company D, after having raided a gambling hall in Duval County, were found to have set up their own gaming establishment with the confiscated equipment; and still another, a captain, was arrested for theft and embezzlement. Even worse, the governor began using Special Ranger commissions, as her husband had done during World War I, as a source of political patronage. Within two years Ferguson enlarged this once elite group to 2,344 men. With the Rangers becoming a source of patronage, corruption, and ridicule, law enforcement in Texas all but unraveled. During the Ferguson years crime and violence became widespread, bank holdups and murder commonplace.

Since Mrs. Ferguson decided not to seek reelection in 1934 (she honored the two-term tradition, having first served as governor from 1925 to 1927), the Democratic primary was wide open. Into the breach stepped James "Jimmie" Allred. Brown-eyed and dark-haired, clean-cut looking and personable, the thirty-five-year-old Allred was easily the front runner in the lackluster gubernatorial campaign. As Texas's attorney general for the past four years, he had the greatest name recognition; he received powerful support from such men as Vice President Garner, Jesse Jones, and Ross Sterling. Allred also had a well-financed campaign to help him "spread the Gospel" of the New Deal as well as a stricter enforcement of the law. Nothing more was needed. He led in both Democratic primaries, eventually defeating wealthy oilman Tom Hunter of Wichita Falls by forty thousand votes.

Once elected, Allred ensured his tenure as governor for four years by attaching Texas to the New Deal money trough. He immediately sought permission to issue the remaining $3.5 million—a mere pittance—from the $20 million relief bonds passed in August 1933, hinting that the federal government might give matching funds for old-age pensions. He next decided to replace the dole to the unemployed with direct work relief: Hence, he focused on funneling more funds into the state through the New Deal's Civilian Conservation Corps (CCC), Public Works Administration (PWA), Works Progress Administration (WPA), and the National Youth Administration (NYA). Consequently, Texas received, one report stated, more than $116 million by August 31, 1936, of which Washington proffered in excess of $96 million; another source estimated the total to be $350 million by the end of the year.

What a boon these programs were to Texans! By February 1935, the CCC had enrolled more than ten thousand young men, ages seventeen to twenty-eight, in forty-two camps, providing much-needed revenue to the people in their respective areas. Moreover, since rules forbade an inductee to reside in his own state—that is, except in the South, where blacks were segregated—102,760 white Texans worked in camps across the United States by January 1938 and sent $23,388,425 to their families, usually $25 out of their $30-a-month paychecks. The NYA also greatly benefited Texans, specifically those sixteen to twenty-five years of age. Under the leadership of twenty-seven-year-old Lyndon Baines Johnson, the state program provided support for high school students in 248 of the 252 counties as well as young people in eighty-three colleges and universities. For two years, beginning in the summer of 1935, Johnson employed from ten thousand to eighteen thousand students per month "at various part-time clerical or maintenance jobs earning a maximum $6.00 per month in high school and $15.00 in college." In out-of-school work programs he hired more than twelve thousand young Texans who, in turn, constructed 250 roadside parks, graveled the shoulders of two thousand miles of highway, improved or built recreational facilities in seventy-six state parks, and refurbished playgrounds of the public schools. Unlike the CCC— and thanks to the will of Johnson—NYA programs helped approximately nineteen thousand young blacks, the primary requisite for selection being that of "need."

The emergency public employment programs of the PWA and WPA were equally, if not more, helpful to the state economy. In Fort Worth, for example, these federal agencies expended $15 million on a variety of projects. From 1935 to 1938 they "completely modernized the entire school system," historian John McClung asserted, "making it one of the best in the state." The PWA constructed thirteen school buildings and made additions to thirteen more, while rehabilitating most of the existing structures. In conjunction with these projects, the WPA "landscaped and beautified fifty-four of the existing sixty-three school grounds." These agencies also provided funds for red-brick roads (some of which are still in existence), the twelve-thousand-seat concrete high school stadium named Farrington Field, Will Rogers Memorial Coliseum and Auditorium, John Peter Smith City-County Hospital, a new city hall and jail, a new public library, and the famous Fort Worth Rose Garden. Together with the Federal Writers' Project, in which scholars were hired to index newspapers and record local history, the Federal Theatre Project and the Federal Art Project allowed money for artists, thespians, and musicians to develop their crafts.

Governor Allred proved to be the necessary conduit for these massive amounts of federal funds: as he put it, "I'm gonna grab all [the money] I can for the State of Texas." At the same time, however, he dealt with a number of problems that greatly affected his constituency. In both regular and several special sessions, legislators, at his behest, authorized a state planning board, appropriated $11 million for higher education, and set aside $10 million for rural relief. Allred also established the Department of Public Safety (DPS), which brought the famed Texas Rangers and the uniformed Highway Patrol under one aegis, thereby fulfilling one of the governor's major campaign promises—better law enforcement. After Congress passed the National Social Security Act in August 1935, the governor pushed through complementary legislation regarding old-age pensions, unemployment compensation, teacher retirement, and aid for needy children and the blind, even though increasing the state deficit to $19 million. Because he helped make such needed reforms and improve governmental service, Jimmie Allred, as the New Deal governor of Texas, ruled popularly—and reasonably well.

Yet in 1937–38, despite awesome political influence in Washington, a close tie to the federal money trough, and Allred's leadership, a number of Texans began to harbor grave reservations about the New Deal and, particularly, the power of the President. After the November elections of 1936, in which Roosevelt carried all but two states (the electoral vote was 523 to 8), Vice President Garner appeared to be increasingly alienated from the administration. With increasing frequency he openly criticized New Deal spending programs, while abhorring labor's newest tactic against management, the sit-down strike. But the arrogance of FDR disturbed him even more. On February 5, 1937, when the President attempted to reorganize the Supreme Court, Garner, together with Sam Rayburn, Hatton Sumners, Tom Connally, and most of the Texas delegation, was unalterably opposed. In fact, FDR's "court-packing" plan was, Rayburn asserted, "his big mistake"—and the four Texans were instrumental in its defeat. Then, in the midyear elections of 1938, FDR committed the ultimate political sin, as far as the Texans were concerned; he tried to "purge" the Democratic Party of those who had opposed New Deal programs. On this "hit list" were eight Texas congressmen—Martin Dies, Clyde L. Garrett, Richard Kleberg, Fritz Lanham, Joseph Mansfield, Nat Patton, Milton West, and Sumners—all of whom prevailed against Roosevelt men in the primaries, while New Deal incumbents Maury Maverick and W. D. McFarlane lost. These political events, coupled with the formation of a vitriolic group of anti-Roosevelt right wingers who called themselves Jeffersonian Democrats (led by J. Evetts Haley, Joseph Bailey, Jr., and J. M. West), nurtured dissent and unrest throughout Texas against the New Deal.

But in the spring of 1938 a political phenomenon took place in Texas that overshadowed these internecine party struggles and allowed Texans to focus upon one central figure—Wilbert Lee ("Please pass the biscuits, Pappy") O'Daniel. A Fort Worth businessman and radio personality who sold "Hillbilly Flour" with an accompanying three-man band known as the "Light Crust Doughboys," "Pappy" O'Daniel announced his candidacy for governor on May 1, 1938, after receiving more than fifty-four thousand letters in one week "begging" him to run. He then proceeded to dumbfound political analysts and stun his opponents. Using campaign techniques that resembled the old-fashioned revivalism of camp meetings, O'Daniel "stumped" the state by bus, playing traditional songs and gospel music ("Play it pretty, Leon") before passing collection plates in the form of barrels labeled "Flour—Not Pork." Texans had not seen anything like him; even "Pa" Ferguson paled by comparison. For what could opponents say about a man whose platform was the Ten Commandments and the Golden Rule, who pledged a pension of $30 a month for every Texan over sixty-five, and who recited to attentive, enraptured audiences such poems as "The Boy Who Never Got Too Old To Comb His Mother's Hair"? When journalists and political opponents pointed out that O'Daniel had not been civic-minded enough to pay a $1.75 poll tax in order to vote, he damned the "professional politicians," declaring that "no politician in Texas is worth $1.75." In a field of thirteen, which included Attorney General William McCraw of Dallas, Railroad Commissioner Ernest O. Thompson of Amarillo, and Tom Hunter of Wichita Falls, O'Daniel soon became the front runner; and in the Democratic primary in July he won by a majority of thirty thousand votes.

For almost three years the O'Daniel aura held sway in state politics, although having little legislative impact. After his inauguration in January 1939, when 100,000 people jammed into the University of Texas's Memorial Stadium, the new governor quickly demonstrated his inability to lead, his ineptness in dealing with the legislature, and his lack of understanding concerning the art of government. To support his pension plan and provide money for a state budget, O'Daniel proposed a 1.6 percent tax on "business transactions," actually a well-concealed multiple sales tax, which the legislature promptly rejected. He then campaigned for a state constitutional amendment, whereby the electorate would vote upon the merits of a state sales tax; however, a militant minority in the state House—the "immortal 56"—prevented its passage. Consequently, to cut costs as well as retaliate against, and punish legislators hostile to him, he line-item vetoed a number of appropriations that were important to the well being of Texans: new buildings for state hospitals, beds for epileptics, orphans, and the mentally handicapped; and funds for the Texas Department of Public Safety. This last economy resulted in the Texas Rangers having, at times, "to borrow ammunition from highway patrolmen." Equally inappropriate, if not laughable, were many of his appointments. For example, as state labor commissioner he selected a desk worker at Southwestern Bell Telephone who was not even an officer in his own union and whose only extant qualification was a letter written by him which praised one of O'Daniel's radio addresses. And for the state highway commission he chose oilman J. M. West of Houston, one of the acknowledged leaders of the anti–New Deal Jeffersonian Democrats; the Senate, however, fearing the possible loss of federal road funds, immediately rejected this nomination.

Despite the "carnival" in Austin and his lack of accomplishment, O'Daniel remained "strong" with the people. In the Democratic primary of 1940, he proved that his first election was not a fluke, that his vote-getting powers were real. Against a fairly strong field, including Miriam A. "Ma" Ferguson, Railroad Commissioner Jerry Sadler, State Highway Commissioner Harry Hines, and Ernest O. Thompson, O'Daniel polled a majority of a little more than 102,000 votes.

In the spring of 1941 the stalemate between the governor and the legislature therefore continued, that is, until circumstances dictated a political realignment—and an accompanying farce. On April 9, U.S. Senator Morris Sheppard died, and O'Daniel, although personally desiring the Senate seat, had to appoint a "suitable and qualified" interim replacement. So on San Jacinto Day, April 21, he selected someone who would never be a threat to his own candidacy, eighty-seven-year-old Andrew Jackson Houston, the only surviving son of Sam Houston. One veteran politician observed that Houston was already "in his dotage," or, putting it less charitably, he stated: "That old man probably couldn't tell you whether the sun was up or going down." At any rate, Houston was sworn in on June 2, filling this prestigious position until his death later in the month. In the meantime O'Daniel geared himself up for the June special election to fill Sheppard's seat. The competition was formidable. Besides Congressman Martin Dies and Attorney General Gerald Mann, the thirty-one-year-old Lyndon Baines Johnson, who received the support of FDR as well as most of the moneyed people in Texas, announced against him. But O'Daniel had certain negative factors working for him; in other words, a number of people wanted to get him out of Texas by sending him to Washington. Reputedly Jim "Pa" Ferguson, who "had been very friendly with the liquor interests for close to three decades," feared that the governor would appoint "good clean honest Christian dry citizens" to the state liquor board and thus was campaigning for his senatorial election. More important for O'Daniel was the tremendous support he received from the friends of Lieutenant Governor Coke Stevenson, who would then inherit the governorship. After a hard-fought, expensive campaign O'Daniel again proved his resiliency by receiving a plurality vote over LBJ of 175,590 to 174,279.

In August 1941, with O'Daniel's resignation, Coke Stevenson became governor, and the turbulent three-year rivalry between the executive and legislative branches subsided—and none too soon.

Within four months, on December 7, the Japanese attacked Pearl Harbor, and the United States subsequently declared war on the three Axis powers, Germany, Italy, and, Japan. In response to this "sneak" attack and threat to national security, Texans reacted with patriotic enthusiasm. During the next several weeks, many youthful volunteers stood in line outside recruiting offices. In fact, from a census-reported population of 6,414,824 in 1940, approximately 750,000 young Texans (including 12,000 women) entered the armed forces during World War II. Until August 1945, when the war ended, they fought on all fronts, with 23,022 Texans killed in action and thousands of others injured or disabled. From their number, thirty received the Congressional Medal of Honor and six the Navy Medal of Honor, the nation's highest recognitions for bravery and self-sacrifice; and two of them, U.S. Army Lieutenant Audie Murphy and U.S. Navy Commander Samuel D. Dealey, were the "most decorated" men in World War II. Texans also proudly claimed Texas-born but Kansas-reared General Dwight D. Eisenhower, the Supreme Allied Commander in Europe, as one of their own, as well as Commander-in-Chief of the Pacific Fleet Admiral Chester A. Nimitz of Fredericksburg, General Mark Clark who, with the Thirty-sixth Division, first landed in Italy at Anzio, and Colonel Oveta Culp Hobby of Houston, who headed the Women's Army Corps (WACS).

Texas also served as an important training ground for the military. Because of its typically warm weather, clear skies, and large expanses of unoccupied land, Texas was chosen by the federal government to host fifteen army posts in which to train hundreds of thousands of troops. In addition, air bases were built in or near such Texas cities as Austin, Corpus Christi, Fort Worth, Grand Prairie, Houston, Lubbock, Midland, San Angelo, San Marcos, and Wichita Falls. But of all the areas in the state, San Antonio was especially important militarily, not only as the headquarters of the Third and Fourth Armies but also as the center of aerial training in the United States at Kelly, Brooks, and Randolph Fields. As the war progressed and the Allied forces began to triumph, the U.S. military built and maintained twenty-one prisoner-of-war camps in the less-populated areas of the state.

On the home front, Texans sacrificed whatever was necessary to support "our boys overseas." Rationing became a way of life, with stamp books for meat, sugar, coffee, shoes, rubber, auto parts, and eventually gasoline. At different intervals communities held "scrap iron drives," adults bought war bonds, school children had time allotted during class periods to buy and paste savings stamps in bond books, and many a family, as in World War I, planted "Victory Gardens" to conserve food for the war effort.

Yet at the same time Texans thrived and prospered, the Great Depression becoming only a memory. Along the Gulf Coast from the Beaumont–Port Arthur area southward to Corpus Christi, the greatest petrochemical industry in the world emerged to refine fuel for the American war machine. Farmers, spurred on by inflated prices for agricultural products, cultivated the soil to its maximum, thereby helping the United States become the granary and "breadbasket" for all Allied nations. And wartime industries mushroomed throughout the state—steel mills in Houston and Daingerfield, the largest tin smelter plant in the world at Texas City, enormous aircraft factories in Garland, Grand Prairie, and Fort Worth, extensive shipyards in Houston, Port Arthur, Beaumont, Galveston, and Corpus Christi, and munitions and synthetic rubber plants scattered across the state. As a result, labor was at a premium, especially with so many men in the service, with defense contracts readily available, and with wages escalating. Texans therefore moved to job markets in nearby cities; and women, for the first time, performed such heretofore male-only occupations as punch-press operators, assembly-line workers, and riveters—hence the popular song of the day, "Rosie the Riveter."

While the state government harmoniously coordinated with federal authorities to sustain an all-out war effort, Governor Stevenson seemed to epitomize both personally and publicly a dual role: a faithful cooperator with national needs as well as a defender of Texan stances and thinking. Tall, lanky and somewhat balding, he grew up a rancher's son in sparsely settled Kimble County before becoming a banker-lawyer turned politician. Because of his relaxed demeanor—a pipe smoker with a calm expression that seldom betrayed his thoughts—this staunchly conservative man received the appellation of "Calculating Coke" from capitol correspondents. Although accepting the concept of rationing in 1942, he denounced such a deprivation for Texans in regard to gas, a resource he deemed as much a necessity as "the saddle, the rifle, the ax, and the Bible . . . for the society we have now." He also negotiated a "no-strike agreement" with labor which pleased anti-unionist Texans. And he received high approval ratings from his constituency for raising state departmental budgets, while at the same time eliminating the $42 million debt that had accrued since the depression.

Yet during the Stevenson administrations a number of trends and undercurrents surfaced that would greatly affect Texas in postwar years. After 1937, the anti–New Deal Jeffersonian Democrats gained adherents, and with each passing year their bitterness turned into unadulterated hatred. In 1940 they were appalled when President Roosevelt "broke with tradition" by running for a third term; four years later he repeated this desecration, leading the nation, they believed, toward "dictatorship." Besides, FDR was far too liberal for them, first in light of his support of and intimacy with labor unions, then by New Deal spending programs, and, most devastating of all, by "dumping" Vice President Garner for left-winger Henry A. Wallace of Iowa. And if price fixing of Texas oil was not enough, the President's "communist" wife Eleanor surely was. With her outspoken remarks for black equality under the law, together with the Supreme Court decision of *Smith* v. *Allwright* (1944) by which African Americans obtained the right to participate in white primaries, these racist Texans agreed with Coke Stevenson, who when asked to establish a Good Neighbor Commission replied: "Meskins is pretty good folk. If it was niggers, it'd be different." Consequently, in 1944 they formed a new political organization named the Texas Regulars; in the November elections they polled 135,000 votes for President, even though no one headed their ticket. Their divisiveness would cause tremendous difficulties in postwar Texas for the predominant Democratic party.

Many Texas Regulars and those of like ilk also concerned themselves with higher education as represented at The University of Texas. Under Governors O'Daniel and Stevenson a majority of their number received appointment to that institution's board of regents and attempted to rectify what they considered as the abuses and evils of academia. In the spring of 1942 the regents, by a four-to-two vote, fired four "liberal" economics instructors. Over the next two years they tried to abolish the tenure system, but University of Texas President Homer Price Rainey obstinately blocked their efforts. But after the Regulars proscribed John Dos Passos's *U.S.A.* from a supplemental reading list of the English Department, declaring the novel "obscene" and "perverted" literature, Rainey dramatically denounced them at a general faculty meeting on October 12, 1944. What a mistake! Three weeks later, on November 1, they had his "scalp." Such threats to academic freedom and the growth of higher education were of utmost concern to Texans in August 1945, especially since former U.T. president Rainey decided to "go after the board" by running for governor in 1946.

Minorities, in turn, after their experiences in and in support of World War II, began to demand equal partnership in Texas. Blacks, still suffering from segregation under the "separate but equal" clause of *Plessy* v. *Ferguson* (1896), however, saw no change in Governor Stevenson's attitude toward their plight. In Texarkana, on July 13, 1942, a mob dragged black Texan Willie Vinson from a hospital bed and hanged him after he had been identified by a white woman as the man who had victimized her; the governor, however, took no "action" on the matter, reasoning that "even a white man would have been lynched for this crime." Again on the night of June 15, 1943, when a racially motivated riot exploded in Beaumont, killing three people and injuring hundreds, Stevenson ordered the president pro tem of the Senate "to handle it," since both he and Lieutenant Governor John Lee Smith were out of the state. Then in 1944 came the *Smith* v. *Allwright* decision, and, in August 1945, the end of the war. Since many black Texans had served in the armed forces, they would return home, after being discharged, more militant in their demands for equal rights under the law.

Mexican Americans were also discriminated against, but usually in less obvious ways—although "No Mexicans" signs still hung on the walls of certain South Texas businesses. Tejanos continued to suffer low wages, the lack of good job opportunities, and difficulties with the English language, which kept a large majority of these Texans poverty stricken and in need. Nor had they been able to rectify their situation at the ballot box—through political bosses or intimidation and bribery, the white minority in South Texas retained control. In 1945, however, upon returning home from service to their country, Mexican Americans, like African Americans, would try to obtain equality under the law.

Women, too, after their many contributions to the war effort both on the home front and militarily, would begin to demand equality, especially since they were placed in the same category, one writer observed, "with minors and idiots." Although having gained the right to vote in 1921, women could not serve on juries and grand juries (until 1955). Nor could a woman sell a car or a house or stocks and bonds, make contracts, agree to promissory notes, sue if injured, or sign a bail bond without her husband's signature. In fact, a woman still could not establish a business without the court's permission and, even then, could not secure a credit rating. Women also had to endure a double standard under the law. For instance, if a wife caught her husband in bed with a lover and killed the paramour, she could be tried for murder; if the reverse were the case, the husband would not be charged. As much as anything else, however, Texas women in 1945 had to combat "tradition and custom," Judge Sarah T. Hughes insightfully pointed out, as well as being "satisfied with their role" or "too humble about their abilities."

During World War II the most obvious changes in Texas were demographic and economic. Because of wartime demands, people migrated to the state in increasing numbers, as many as 450,000 in less than four years; and since industrial jobs were plentiful in or near such cities as Houston, San Antonio, Austin, and the Dallas–Fort Worth area, Texans experienced a rapid urbanization, along with its accompanying benefits and evils. In turn, oil became the dominant resource and commodity in the state—cotton and cattle were no longer "kings"—and the petrochemical industry along the Gulf Coast boomed the economy. Texans, however, had instituted a more diversified approach in productivity during the war years. In West Texas, from El Paso to the Pecos River to the Panhandle, farmers depended more and more on irrigation and scientific agriculture; in East Texas a number of people shifted to dairying and cattle ranching, while still maintaining a prosperous lumber industry; and from Brownsville to Laredo, the Rio Grande Valley was rapidly becoming a lush truck-farming and citrus-growing country. So, together with better roads connecting all parts of the state, with rural electrification touching even the most remote and backward areas, and with more than 600,000 veterans returning home in anticipation of enjoying greater freedoms and the benefits of victory, urban Texas was, despite a frontier tradition of rugged individualism, despite a governor and legislature rooted in conservatism, being forced to inch into the twentieth century.

Suggested Reading

Caro, Robert A. *The Years of Lyndon Johnson: The Path to Power.* New York: Alfred A. Knopf, 1983.

Clark, James A. *Three Stars for the Colonel.* New York: Random House, 1954.

Connally, Tom, and Alfred Sternberg. *My Name is Tom Connally.* New York: Crowell, 1954.

Dorough, Dwight. *Mr. Sam.* New York: Random House, 1967.

Green, George Norris. *The Establishment in Texas Politics: The Primitive Years, 1938–1957.* Westport, CT: Greenwood Press, 1979.

Henderson, Richard B. *Maury Maverick: A Political Biography.* Austin: University of Texas Press, 1970.

May, Irvin M., Jr. *Marvin Jones: The Public Life of an Agrarian Advocate.* College Station: Texas A&M University Press, 1980.

McKay, Seth Sheppard. *W. Lee O'Daniel and Texas Politics, 1938–1942.* Lubbock: Texas Technical College Research Fund, 1944.

——, and Odie B. Faulk. *Texas After Spindletop, 1901–1965.* Austin: Steck Vaughn Company, 1965.

Nalle, Ouida Ferguson. *The Fergusons of Texas*. San Antonio: The Naylor Press, 1946.

Patenaude, Lionel V. *Texans, Politics and the New Deal*. New York: Garland Publishing, Inc., 1983.

Procter, Ben. *Just One Riot: Episodes of the Twentieth-Century Texas Rangers*. Austin: Eakin Press, 1991.

Timmons, Rascom. *Garner of Texas: A Personal History*. New York: Harper & Brothers Publishers, 1948.

——. *Jesse H. Jones: The Man and the Statesman*. New York: Henry Holt and Company, 1956.

Lyndon Johnson during his 1948 senatorial campaign. *Courtesy of the Jimmy A. Dodd Photograph Collection, The Center for American History, The University of Texas at Austin, #VN1187.*

CHAPTER ELEVEN

Modern Texas: The Political Scene since 1945

Kenneth E. Hendrickson, Jr.

AT THE END OF WORLD WAR II THE UNITED States and the world stood poised to enter the modern age. It would be a fast-moving age of technological development, economic growth, and changing social values. But Texans, and particularly their political leaders, were not ready. The Lone Star State was in many ways still living in the past, and comfortably so. In time, many Texans would taste the fruits of modernization and yearn for more. All the while, many others clung fervently to old ways and values. As the postwar era unfolded, this dichotomy produced severe tensions; perhaps nowhere were they more evident than in the political arena.

In the 1940s the political system in Texas was dominated by a loose coalition of ultraconservative business and industrial leaders within the Democratic Party known as "The Establishment." Rich, powerful, and comfortable, Establishment leaders wanted to maintain the status quo and were prepared to do almost anything to achieve their objectives. One of their favorite tactics, for example, was to label anyone who challenged them a "communist." Even though Texas ranked low in the nation in teachers' salaries, spending on education, spending on the poor and underprivileged, and, in fact, in spending on almost any social service, Establishment leaders were determined to resist change. Their twin battle cries were "no new taxes" and "no new social relationships."

Coke Stevenson served as governor in 1945. He had held office throughout the war, and his approach to government satisfied the Establishment. Stevenson came from a ranching family who lived in Kimble County. He was mostly self-educated and had risen from humble beginnings to become a successful banker, lawyer, and politician. He served as speaker of the Texas House of Representatives for four years (1933–1937), and in 1938 was elected lieutenant governor. His reputation as a pipe-puffing, cold-minded man of few words led journalists to dub him "Calculatin' Coke."

Stevenson had become governor in 1941 when W. Lee "Pappy" O'Daniel won election to the U.S. Senate. As a wartime governor, Stevenson was utterly reactionary and shortsighted. He opposed increased taxes and rationing as impositions upon individual freedom. At the same time, while American boys fought overseas to defend liberty, freedom, and democracy, Stevenson registered complete indifference to the outrageous treatment of minorities at home. When a Texarkana man was lynched in 1942, Stevenson responded to a complaint from Washington by observing that blacks were often themselves responsible for mob violence due to the hideous crimes they committed. Slightly less intolerant of Hispanics, or "Meskins," as he called them, Stevenson responded to complaints about the treatment of braceros by supporting the creation of a state Good Neighbor Commission, which actually functioned effectively for several years, although the living conditions of most Hispanics in the state remained substandard.

Stevenson became legendary for his penury. Although the war brought increased prosperity, he looked on impassively while state services deteriorated. He refused to call the legislature into special session to consider even vitally needed appropriations. Consequently Texas fell far behind in many important areas and did not begin to catch up for decades.

Perhaps the most unfortunate event of the Stevenson era, and one that accurately reflected the power of the reactionaries, was the firing of Dr. Homer Rainey, president of The University of Texas. Rainey was appointed in 1939 during the term of Governor Jimmy Allred when the complexion of the university's Board of Regents was somewhat liberal. However, during the O'Daniel and Stevenson administrations several new appointments gave the board a decidedly reactionary cast. Early in the 1940s this new board moved against several university faculty members, especially in the Department of Economics, whom they accused of "radicalism" and "communism." The board attempted to fire four tenured professors and successfully dismissed four untenured instructors. When Rainey protested, they fired him as well. They claimed that he had no right to oppose their judgment because a university president bore the same relationship to the regents as did a CEO to the board of directors in a private business. As these events unfolded in 1944, Governor Stevenson reacted by ignoring them. As a result, academic freedom in Texas suffered a major setback from which it did not recover for years.

When Stevenson retired in 1946, the preferred gubernatorial candidate of the reactionaries was Lieutenant Governor John Lee Smith, hailed by many as the only politician with "guts enough" to save the state from being taken over by labor, liberals, communists, and blacks. During 1945, various groups and individuals representing the most reactionary elements in the state spent a considerable amount of time and money promoting Smith's candidacy, but in his campaign he proved to be so irresponsible in denouncing his opponents as communists or communist sympathizers that he literally talked himself out of the race. On the other hand, Dr. Rainey, who also ran and was the target of much of this mud slinging, fared little better. The nomination went to Railroad Commissioner Beauford Jester who, even though a moderate, had the support of Coke Stevenson.

Jester, who was from Corsicana, had been a successful lawyer before entering public life. Conciliatory by nature, he would have preferred to avoid controversy, but this proved to be impossible. No sooner had he been installed in office than the state was wracked by an enormous controversy growing out of efforts by the nationally powerful Congress of Industrial Organizations to organize the oil, steel, auto, packing, and textile industries. Reactionaries portrayed this effort, known as Operation Dixie, as a communist plot. This bad publicity prompted the state legislature to pass a series of tough antilabor laws, which the governor reluctantly signed. These included a "right to work" law, an anti-check-off law (a check-off law requires workers to allow union dues to be deducted from their pay), an anti-mass-picketing law, and other measures that made organized labor subject to antitrust statutes.

In Democratic party politics Jester faced the unenviable task of maintaining a balance between the Texas Regulars (conservative Democrats who stood for the Establishment) and the liberal-loyalists (Democrats who followed the leadership of the national party). The former controlled the statehouse, but the latter controlled the state party machinery. The reactionary Regulars wanted to lead the state into the Dixiecrat movement in 1948, but Jester worked hard to prevent it. The governor's choice for president was General Dwight Eisenhower but he declined to run, so Jester reluctantly remained loyal to Harry Truman, who carried the state.

In 1949 the legislature overhauled the public school system by passing the controversial Gilmer-Aikin Act. Allegedly designed to streamline the educational system, this law actually initiated many problems because it was obsolete the moment it was passed. The measure mandated minimum salaries for teachers, which still left their pay absurdly low by national standards, and created a financial structure that ensured that those districts making the least effort to collect local taxes reaped the most state funding. Jester undoubtedly would have preferred to leave a more positive legacy. He clearly was a moderate, and perhaps he would have moved more in the direction of reason and rationality had he not died suddenly of a heart attack on July 11, 1949. He was succeeded by the state's forty-one-year-old lieutenant governor, Allan Shivers. A tumultuous period followed.

Before considering the Shivers era in Texas politics, we must pause to take special note of the Senate primary of 1948, which occurred during Jester's administration. In this election the forces of Lyndon B. Johnson allegedly obtained the nomination over former Governor Coke Stevenson by illegal means. Substantial evidence supports this allegation even though Johnson advocates publicly denied it. Certainly corruption was no stranger to Texas politics, but this event proved to be more significant than most because it launched Johnson on his pathway to the presidency.

Until shortly before the filing deadline for the primary in the spring of 1948, Johnson was unsure of his course. A congressman since 1937, he had something of a pro–New Deal reputation. Bored with this role, he yearned for better things but feared that defeat would end his ambitions for higher office. In conversation with friends he hinted that he might retire, but in reality he desperately wanted to be drafted into the Senate race. He wanted this in spite of the dangers implicit in the venture. In May, after much hesitation, he allowed himself to be talked into making the race for the Senate. He never looked back.

The campaign of 1948 marked a new departure in Texas politics. Johnson used the radio more extensively and effectively than any candidate before him, including "Pappy" O'Daniel, and he introduced a technological innovation—the use of the helicopter as a campaign vehicle. The craft used by Johnson, christened the "Johnson City Windmill," enabled him to move rapidly around the state and make multiple appearances on a single day. Thus, he could personally appeal to far more people than his opponent. Meanwhile, Stevenson persisted in campaigning the old-fashioned way, motoring leisurely around the state with only a driver, his nephew Bob Murphy. They simply "dropped in" on people in the county seats. Although he was a one-to-four underdog at the beginning of the campaign, Johnson's style should have enabled him to overtake his foe easily, but this did not happen. Stevenson won the first primary by more than seventy thousand votes. However, he lacked a majority, necessitating a runoff.

In the runoff campaign, Lyndon Johnson had powerful allies: money, deceit, and fraud. The money came principally from George and Herman Brown of the Brown and Root Construction Company. They had supported Johnson for some time, were satisfied with his congressional record, and fervently believed that as a U.S. Senator he would continue to serve their interests. Deceit came in the form of a lie Johnson told repeatedly: that Governor Stevenson secretly opposed the Taft-Hartley Act (a popular antiunion measure) and that, if elected, he would work to repeal it. In fact, just the opposite was true. Stevenson, a proud conservative, was a hearty supporter of Taft-Hartley. On the other hand, Johnson, supposedly a liberal, also had supported the bill and voted for it—this at the same time he was secretly accepting financial aid from the American Federation of Labor! Johnson was able to impress the lie so firmly upon the public consciousness, mainly through constant repetition in his radio broadcasts, that many began to believe him. Even some of Stevenson's oldest and truest supporters came to be unsure of him and reduced their financial support. Meanwhile, the former governor contributed to his own difficulties by failing to counterattack Johnson's claims effectively.

Fraud was injected into the campaign by the infamous George Parr, the "Duke of Duval" County, who conspired to manufacture votes and add them to Johnson's total. This was the key element because, in spite of his other advantages, Johnson did not win the election, so votes in his favor had to be "discovered." Parr was just the man to produce the desired result. On a foundation of favors, threats, and intimidation, he and his father, Archer Parr, had gained virtually complete control of a five-county area in South Texas. The younger Parr could produce any vote count he desired. In the past, Parr's people had usually "supported" Stevenson, but as governor he had refused to appoint Parr's candidate to the office of district attorney in Laredo. Parr had sworn vengeance, and now he had his chance to even the score. At a meeting in the Driskill Hotel in Austin, Parr promised Johnson that he would deliver the vote.

In spite of Johnson's aggressive campaigning, money, and powerful allies, the congressman could not be sure of victory. To ensure a positive outcome of the election, several of Johnson's campaign supporters went to Parr's headquarters in Alice, located in Duval County, and there, late at night, added two hundred names to the voter tally sheet in Precinct 13. This gave Johnson the victory by the scant margin of eighty-seven votes, statewide. Stevenson was understandably outraged by this obvious fraud and challenged the outcome of the election before the state Democratic Party's executive committee, the state party convention, and in court. Under extremely questionable circumstances, the vote was allowed to stand. Johnson became the Democratic nominee for the Senate and won easily in the November general election, while Coke Stevenson, deeply embittered, retired from politics.

Meanwhile, Governor Allan Shivers was determined to improve state services when he assumed office. During a special session of the legislature in 1950, and again in the regular session of 1951, he called for increased revenues and appropriations, especially for charitable institutions. Later, he gained moderate increases in appropriations for prisons and highways and pressured the legislature into passing the first redistricting law in thirty years. Beyond these modest gains, his administration accomplished little.

Unfortunately, the Shivers era was clouded by considerable fraud in the insurance business and in the veterans' land program, which overshadowed most of his achievements. Conspiracy and fraud in the insurance industry developed because state law and regulatory procedures had failed to keep pace with the needs of a growing state. As late as the 1950s an insurance company could be capitalized for as little as $25,000, yet it could issue unlimited stock. More than two thousand such companies operated in the state during the Shivers era, and many went bankrupt. When this happened, policyholders and stockholders alike lost millions of dollars.

When Lieutenant Governor Ben Ramsey pointed out these problems in 1955, the legislature responded by passing a number of sound, new regulatory laws, but the losses continued. When two enormous holding companies, U.S. Trust and Guarantee, and ICT Insurance Company, collapsed, it precipitated a crisis and a scandal. U.S. Trust and Guarantee, it was learned, had claims payable equal to 500 percent of its reserves, but it had bribed legislators to allow it to continue in business. Meanwhile, Ben Jack Cage, the founder of ICT, which controlled seventy-two or more insurance companies, absconded with his company's assets.

Investigation into these problems in the insurance industry led to the discovery of the veterans' land frauds, the state's greatest scandal of the 1950s and perhaps of the entire century. In 1950 the state established a $100 million fund to purchase land for resale to veterans. Administered by General Land Office Commissioner Bascom Giles, the program was intended to supplement the federal G.I. Bill of Rights by allowing veterans to purchase land with low down payments and interest on a forty-year mortgage. In addition to Giles, the governor and Attorney General John Ben Shepperd also sat on the Veterans' Land Board; unknown to both Shivers and Shepperd, Giles was a criminal. He was involved with crooked promoters who found ways to cheat the system by selling land to the state at inflated rates and passing losses on to unsuspecting veterans. Giles's misdeeds were uncovered by the work of DeWitt County Attorney Wiley L. Cheatham, Department of Public Safety auditor C. H. Caveness, and Attorney General Shepperd. Both Shivers and Shepperd were hurt politically by their close association to the scandal, although neither man was directly implicated. However, since the main perpetrator was caught and neither Shivers nor Shepperd ran for reelection in 1956, the political impact of the scandal was not as great as it might have been.

Shivers's first term as governor transpired relatively free of political turmoil. Thereafter his tenure was marred by the continual struggle between the governor and his conservative "Texas Regulars" and the more liberal national Democratic party organization. The Regulars, who represented the Establishment in Texas politics, generally were hostile to the philosophy of the New Deal and claimed to stand foursquare in favor of states' rights.

No states' rights issue generated more controversy than the tidelands question. The term *tidelands* refers to offshore land; it is a misnomer because the land in question is under water continuously and not periodically exposed by the tide, as the term implies. What made the land significant was its potential to yield large amounts of oil, which both the federal and state governments hoped to control. The problem became acute early in the 1950s when President Truman made it clear that he wanted to exert federal control over the offshore property. His claims met with strenuous objections from the Texas oil fraternity and their main political spokesman, Attorney General Price Daniel. At first Governor Shivers waffled on the issue, but, pressured by Daniel, other politicians, and the big oilmen of the state, he came out against Truman in the fall of 1951 by accusing the president of attempting to impose a federal dictatorship over fuel production. When Lyndon Johnson and Sam Rayburn pushed a bill through Congress that recognized Texas's historic claim to a ten-and-one-half-mile offshore limit, Shivers supported it vigorously. Then, when Truman vetoed the bill, Shivers was merciless in his public criticism of the President. Shortly thereafter, when Democratic presidential candidate Adlai Stevenson told Shivers that he supported Truman, the governor vowed to take Texas into the Republican camp and support the candidacy of Dwight Eisenhower in 1952. Subsequently, the national Republican ticket carried Texas for only the second time since Reconstruction. Thus began a conflict that was to last for several years.

Shivers's defection from the Democratic party infuriated Congressman Sam Rayburn, whose vow to seek revenge led to a further struggle by the conservative and liberal wings for control of the party. It began in 1954 when newcomer Ralph Yarborough challenged Shivers for the gubernatorial nomination. Yarborough lost, but only by twenty-three thousand votes, and the liberals were convinced that by 1956, with the support of the ethnic minorities, labor, and a little luck, they could seize control of the party. But they failed to consider the ambitions of Lyndon Johnson, who was running on his own personal track independent of both party factions.

Sam Rayburn persuaded Johnson to run for President as a favorite-son candidate from Texas. That would automatically make him head of the Texas delegation to the Democratic National Convention in place of Governor Shivers, a development that Rayburn most earnestly desired. With John Connally acting as their spokesman, the Johnson group asked the liberals to accept a deal. They were to support Johnson for at least one ballot in return for a seat on the executive council and a number of delegates to the national convention. Thus a temporary coalition was formed between Johnson's supporters and the real liberals in the party. This alliance went head-to-head against the conservatives, or "Shiverscrats," in a battle for power. At party precinct meetings in May 1956, scenes of some of the dirtiest politicking of modern times, the Johnson-liberal coalition won. Lyndon Johnson was the Lone Star State's favorite son. But the coalition did not last; it unraveled when Johnson demanded that the liberals support him at the convention until he released them—rather than only after the one ballot as they had agreed. Then the factions failed to agree on a choice for national committeewoman. The liberals wanted one of their leaders, Frankie Randolph, while Johnson insisted on B. A. Bentsen, wife of Congressman Lloyd Bentsen. Randolph was elected at the state convention, an apparent defeat for Johnson, but due to the skillful work of John Connally, the liberals agreed to support Johnson until he released them, and they were true to their word. However, they received nothing substantive in return. Later that year, they, not the "Shiverscrats," were forced out of party leadership. Johnson had betrayed them.

The liberals sought to cut their losses by forming the DOT (Democrats of Texas) an organization within an organization that would last until 1961. Led by Frankie Randolph and others, the DOT pursued the liberal agenda of the national Democratic party in state politics and twice helped elect Ralph Yarborough to the Senate. They followed a difficult course by trying to shape a liberal movement in a state that is not liberal. This required constant efforts to forge alliances and coalitions with more moderate elements within the party, but as time passed these groups tended to become increasingly committed to the growing ambitions of Lyndon Johnson. In the end, DOT leaders had to decide whether to join with Johnson, whom they hated, or to continue to stand against him as principled liberals. They chose the latter course and soon the organization declined, collapsing when Johnson was elected vice president in 1960.

The Shivers era in Texas was attended by additional turmoil, for it coincided with the era of Martin Dies and Joe McCarthy—the Red Scare. Martin Dies was a congressman from East Texas who had chaired the House Committee on Un-American Activities since its creation in 1938. Under his leadership, the committee began the infamous practice of compiling secret lists of the names of people suspected of having an affiliation with subversive organizations. Dies chaired the committee until 1944 and, largely through his unconscionable behavior, the impression grew that the federal government was saturated with communists and "fellow travelers." He also turned his attention toward home and, in 1941, announced that there was a communist cell in the faculty of The University of Texas. J. R. Parten, chairman of the UT Board of Regents, demanded specific proof of the assertions before acting; when Dies could produce none, the matter was dropped temporarily. It did not die, however, and it ultimately led to the Rainey affair. Dies, meanwhile, was defeated in a bid for the Senate in 1944 and again in 1948, but his public career was not over. The postwar Red Scare gave him new life, and he became a popular after-dinner speaker. In 1952, he won election to the House, his return to Washington coinciding with the rise of McCarthyism.

Senator Joseph R. McCarthy, Jr., of Wisconsin, was an ill-mannered bore who did more to damage free speech and fair play than any other American in recent times. In the atmosphere of fear and ignorance that characterized the immediate postwar period, McCarthy used the communist "boogieman" to further his own political career and personal power. Building on the foundation

192 Kenneth E. Hendrickson, Jr.

established by Dies, he charged that government agencies, particularly the Department of State, were infested with communists. He drew a portrait of a colossal communist conspiracy designed to destroy the nation. Unfortunately, just enough frightening events occurred during that period to give his exaggerated charges a ring of truth in the minds of many war-weary Americans.

McCarthy received considerable financial support from wealthy Texans such as Clint Murchison and H. L. Hunt of Dallas and Hugh Roy Cullen of Houston. Although driven by various motives, men such as these shared an almost total ignorance of human history, a complete misreading of the workings of the free enterprise system, an unreasoned fear of racial integration, and a willingness to say or do almost anything to protect their interests.

Texans in general were conservative, but in certain areas this conservatism was concentrated into a virulent paranoia that fed upon an irrational fear of communism. Nowhere was this truer than in Houston, where, encouraged by men such as Cullen, ultraright-wing extremists began to organize against the "great communist threat" in 1951. Using the American Legion, the Committee for the Preservation of Methodism, and the Minute Women of the USA as their organizational bases, they began a campaign of Red Scare activities that lasted for six years and created a living nightmare for many innocent people, especially those working in the public schools.

There were, in fact, few real communists in Houston, but the reactionaries claimed otherwise. The right-wingers vowed to protect the "American way of life," by which they meant the status quo. Thus, labor leaders, civil rights' advocates, New Dealers, educators, or anyone who promoted changes or improvements in American society became fair game. The public school system bore the brunt of their anger, largely because the influence of the educational system was so pervasive, while at the same time educators lay vulnerable. The attack, which came from within the school administration itself as well as from the organizations of the ultrareactionary activists, took the form of mandatory loyalty oaths, pressures on the exercise of First Amendment rights in the classroom, the exclusion of certain textbooks and other reading materials, and personal invective aimed at individuals. The most celebrated case involved Assistant Superintendent George W. Ebey.

In 1952 George Ebey was a talented, forty-five-year-old educator with a doctoral degree from Teachers' College, Columbia. He was a liberal and associated with various causes and organizations in favor of progress and social justice. As such, Ebey was a prime target for the reactionaries who set upon him almost immediately after Superintendent William Moreland brought him into the Houston school system. During the first—and only—year of his tenure in Houston, Ebey found himself unjustly accused of belonging to "communist front" organizations and of making "un-American utterances." He defended himself courageously, but ultimately, in the summer of 1953, he begrudgingly resigned. The reactionaries continued their crusade for several years, but as Senator McCarthy's influence gradually declined during the mid-1950s, so did their own.

Price Daniel succeeded Shivers as governor in 1957. After defeating liberal Ralph Yarborough in a hard-fought primary, Daniel went on to defeat Republican William Bryant in an easy general election. Having served as attorney general, speaker of the Texas House of Representatives, and U.S. Senator, Daniel was one of the best prepared of all Texas governors. He remained in office for three terms, until 1963, during which time he established himself as a master of the legislative game.

The main issues faced by Governor Daniel and the legislature during the Fifty-fifth Session (1957) were ethics, water-resource management and conservation, highways, law enforcement, prisons, education, welfare, and taxation. Daniel made recommendations on these and several other matters and the legislators responded to most of them. Important legislation passed during this session included laws designed to strengthen control of lobbyists, create the Texas Water Development Board, increase appropriations for prisons, and increase public school teachers' salaries. No new taxes were imposed, but some existing levies were increased.

The Fifty-sixth Legislature (1959) had one regular and four special sessions. Daniel observed that since oil revenues were down and population was increasing, there was an acute need for additional sources of income. He proposed to meet the need by adroit bookkeeping procedures and two new taxes: a 3 percent severance tax on natural gas and a tax on cigars. He also called for small increases in the vehicle sales tax and the tax on liquor. All these proposals failed in the regular session due to the activities of lobbyists representing the affected interests. Those working for pipeline companies were especially effective in blocking legislation unfavorable to them. Later, the governor achieved partial success during the special sessions when the legislature reluctantly passed severance and franchise tax bills.

During Daniel's third term, state finance continued as the major problem. There was growing interest in a sales tax, but the governor opposed it because it would be regressive. He also rejected the idea of a state income tax. However, he recognized the desirability for increased revenues to finance such major needs as education, quality roads, and planning for water-resource management. Daniel's opposition to the sales tax was countered by "Citizens for a Sales Tax," a group led by oil-industry representatives Tom Sealy of Midland and Searcy Bracewell of Houston. Not surprisingly, oilmen supported the sales tax in the hope that it would prevent the state from raising taxes on oil and natural gas. After a bitter struggle in the regular session of the legislature the sales-tax proposal failed. Then, in a subsequent special session, the sales tax went through, becoming law without the governor's signature.

During the Daniel administration the Republican party began to emerge from the shadows of Texas politics when John Tower of Wichita Falls won election to the U.S. Senate. Tower, a political science teacher at Midwestern University and the son of a Methodist preacher, grew up in East Texas and received his undergraduate college education at Southwestern University in Georgetown. During World War II he served in the Navy, and after his discharge he worked as a salesman and a disc jockey before entering graduate studies at the London School of Economics and at Southern Methodist University. He then moved to Wichita Falls where he began his teaching career.

Tower was an indefatigable worker for the Republican party. In 1954 he ran for the state legislature and lost; however, he later won a seat on the party's state committee and served as a delegate to the national convention in 1960. He also ran for the Senate against Lyndon Johnson that year. He lost, of course, but he carried 41.5 percent of the major party vote statewide as well as some of the large cities. Tower became one of the best-known leaders of the Texas Republican party, and when Johnson's resignation from the Senate in the spring of 1961 necessitated a special election, Tower easily secured the party's endorsement.

The special election attracted more than sixty candidates, but of these only six mounted serious campaigns: Tower, and the five leading Democrats. After Johnson resigned, the governor appointed conservative businessman William Blakely as interim Senator. He was opposed in the special election by Jim Wright, Henry Gonzalez, Maury Maverick, Jr., and Attorney General Will Wilson. From this melee, Tower and Blakely engaged in a runoff that Tower won by 100,00 votes, ironically because many liberals supported him. His victory was a watershed. During the next several years the Republican party experienced significant success in fund raising, recruiting candidates, and winning elective office. Although the Democrats continued to enjoy a statewide majority and domination of the legislature, Texas was on the road to becoming a two-party state.

Price Daniel tried for a fourth term in 1962, but he was defeated in the Democratic primary by former Secretary of the Navy John Connally, Johnson's old friend and protégé. In the November election Connally won over Republican candidate Jack Cox, but the results were startling. Connally received 847,038 votes to 715,025 for Cox, suggesting that the resurgent Republican party no longer could be ignored. Connally accomplished little during his first term in office, but the assassination of President John F. Kennedy in Dallas on November 22, 1963, which also resulted in the serious wounding of Governor Connally, making him a national hero. He could now do virtually anything he wished, and there was much to be done. In the twenty years since the end of World War II, the Texas political system had addressed practically none of the daunting social ills that faced its people. In 1963 Texas still ranked thirty-third in the nation in per capita income, forty-fourth in adult literacy, and fiftieth in expenditures for child welfare services. Racial attitudes were still primitive, desegregation barely had begun, and, overall, the educational system was one of the worst and least adequately supported in the nation.

Wanting to accomplish something significant as governor, Connally chose education as his special interest. In his first message to the legislature in 1963, he meticulously spelled out the problem. Then he appointed several special commissions to study education and make recommendations. Their findings, not surprisingly, called for massive spending at all levels, and the governor agreed, particularly with respect to higher education. He believed that only by improving its colleges and universities could the state improve the quality of its work force and hope to induce businesses and industries to relocate to Texas or open new plants there.

There were significant tensions in Texas politics by 1964 because Lyndon Johnson, who had assumed the presidency after the death of Kennedy, determined to support his old adversary Ralph Yarborough for the Senate over the conservative Democrat Joe Kilgore. Johnson's decision was based simply upon the fact that he knew Yarborough was more likely to support his social programs than was Kilgore, even though the latter was an old and dear friend. This created difficulties because Connally supported Kilgore, which placed the governor at odds with the President. Kilgore eventually withdrew from the race in favor of Yarborough, and Connally ran successfully for a second term, defeating Don Yarborough of Houston (no relation to Ralph Yarborough) in the Democratic primary. However, the wound to the relationship between Johnson and Connally never really healed.

At this stage of their careers, Connally was more conservative on social issues than was Johnson. Hence, the governor found it difficult to support the President's Great Society programs. Indeed, Connally sought to obstruct most of them, although he continued to work for improvements in higher education. In his second inaugural address, in 1965, he called for the reshaping of the entire educational system to make it more efficient. He called for dramatic increases in faculty salaries and for the recruitment of higher-quality personnel. He also demanded higher salaries for public school teachers. He was successful with most of these proposals, and his dream to become known as the education governor was realized. Regrettably, in later years Texas failed to keep pace with Connally's program, and again the state fell far behind most other states in its support of its educational system.

When John Connally decided not to seek reelection in 1968, Preston Smith of Lubbock took his place on the ticket. Smith, who ranks as one of the most colorless politicians in Texas history, had patiently and effectively gathered support over a period of years. He easily won the governorship. Ben Barnes, a personable young man thought by many observers to have a bright future in politics, became lieutenant governor. In the state house, Gus Mutcher became speaker. This triumvirate controlled state politics for the next three years, and this period saw some gains in the fields of higher education and water-resource management. Smith skated to reelection in 1970; shortly thereafter an infamous scandal rocked his administration.

Smith's problem derived from the "Sharpstown" affair, the discovery that Speaker Mutcher, two of his aides, Governor Smith, and others had profited from the illegal manipulation of stock-market transactions in a scheme hatched by Houston banker Frank Sharp. The plot involved legislation passed specifically to benefit the conspirators. Mutcher was convicted and removed from office for his part in the affair, but Smith, Barnes, and several others evaded prosecution. Their careers in politics, however, had ended.

Much of the pressure on the crooked politicians was brought to bear by a group of concerned legislators who styled themselves "The Dirty Thirty." Among them was the liberal Frances "Sissy" Farenthold of Houston, who attempted to become the Democratic nominee for governor in 1972. As a woman and a liberal in Texas, Farenthold had two strikes against her, and few were surprised when Dolph Briscoe, a wealthy rancher from South Texas, defeated her. Briscoe, however, was a man possessed of so little personality that he made Smith look like a zealot.

Briscoe served as governor for six years. Elected to a two-year term in 1972, he won a four-year term in 1974 after an amendment to the state constitution. The basic theme of his long administration was "no new taxes," and in this he was reminiscent of Coke Stevenson. Naturally, state services, especially higher education, suffered dramatically as a result of Briscoe's rule.

The highlight of the Briscoe era was the failed attempt to write a new constitution to replace the outmoded one framed in 1876. In January 1974, the state legislature, amid great fanfare, declared itself a constitutional convention. There followed a five-month circus of wrangling and horse-trading that resulted in the creation of a new constitution that pleased practically no one. The legislature submitted the constitution to itself for approval and defeated it. Subsequently, several of its articles were submitted individually to the voters, but these also were defeated. Thus, Texas has continued to function under an antique constitution that is so outmoded it requires constant emendation to remain operational. A new effort to replace it does not appear likely any time soon.

The resurgence of the Republican party, signaled by the election of John Tower in 1961 and sustained by his subsequent election on three occasions, entered a new phase in 1978 with the election of William Clements to the office of governor. Dolph Briscoe was candid in the expression of his desire for a third term, but many Texans were reluctant to contemplate the prospect of having the same governor for ten years, especially one as lethargic as Briscoe. Briscoe was defeated in the Democratic primary by Attorney General John Hill, who attracted the support of both moderates and liberals and appealed especially to teachers. In the Republican primary, the crude and outspoken Clements of Dallas, a successful businessman who had once served as undersecretary of defense, opposed long-time party leader Ray Hutchinson. Spending millions on his campaign, Clements not only upset Hutchinson, he defeated Hill in the general election and pulled a few more Republicans into the legislature on his coattails. The legislative session of 1979 found twenty-three members of the Republican party in the House and four in the Senate. Analysts attributed Clements's victory to a combination of factors that included light voter turnout, overconfidence by the Democrats, and some cross-over voting by ultraconservative Democrats.

Clements proved to be an aggressive and energetic governor who dominated the state legislature for the next four years while attempting to make good on his pledges to provide a favorable climate for business and reduce the cost of government. Concerning the latter, he threatened the jobs of many state employees and required every state agency to submit elaborate reports defending their work and justifying their employment needs. Few people were terminated, and, in fact, salary costs increased significantly during Clements's term.

Most observers predicted an easy Clements reelection in 1982. They were wrong. Though he spent an enormous sum on his campaign, probably in excess of $12 million, the governor lost to the Democratic candidate, Attorney General Mark White. Clements had done nothing in particular to merit this turnaround of his support, but in all likelihood his education policy, coupled with the negative image projected by his abrasive personality, contributed significantly to his defeat.

Throughout Mark White's term as governor, the major concerns of the state were education and the budget. During the campaign, White promised teachers a substantial pay raise and pledged to reform a system that was producing dreadful results. In 1982 Texas still ranked near the bottom in most educational categories, including teachers' salaries, percentage of students graduating from high school, per capita expenditures on education, test scores, and teacher-pupil ratio.

A blue-ribbon committee headed by Dallas billionaire H. Ross Perot submitted a report that resulted in the passage of the Educational Reform Act of 1984, generally known as House Bill 72. This legislation, which sincerely intended to improve the Texas educational system, has proven to be a nightmare. Among its provisions is one that imposes more structure than ever before on the classroom, thus hindering rather than assisting the teachers in the performance of their duties. Another requires that all students pass all courses each six weeks in order to participate in extracurricular activities, including sports. This provision shocked and enraged the coaching fraternity and countless supporters of high school football. Yet another provision requires regular competency testing for all students, teachers, and administrators. This generated unbridled outrage from virtually everyone in the system. Generally, most teachers found implementation of the new procedures so burdensome that they could not appreciate their higher income.

Texas experienced its worst budgetary woes in decades during Mark White's term, when long-brewing factors finally combined to produce disastrous results. For years the costs of needed state services had increased but, in relative terms, tax levies had not kept pace. Instead, Texas relied on the regressive sales tax inaugurated in the 1960s and a few additional levies such as the extraction tax on oil and excise taxes. By the early 1980s the state's financial condition was unstable, even though the treasury showed an apparent surplus in 1983. Beginning in 1986, the system practically collapsed with the precipitous decline of oil prices, from a high of near $40 per barrel to a catastrophic low of $10. Among other unfortunate consequences, deflated oil prices triggered a budget crisis when Comptroller Bob Bullock predicted a deficit of billions. Limited by the pay-as-you-go provisions of the state constitution, the government struggled in its effort to work itself out of the mess. White called a special session of the legislature, which, after interminable wrangling, approved a temporary tax increase, juggled some accounts, and froze spending in order to provide stopgap relief.

In the midst of the financial crisis, White and Clements squared off again, but this time it was White who was upset. His defeat was partly due to the unfavorable economic conditions, partly to a severe negative reaction by teachers to House Bill 72, and partly to White's admission that higher taxes were necessary. Clements swore that he would never permit a tax hike, even though all responsible observers could see that this was wishful thinking at best and deceit at worst. Predictably, Clements's second term was dominated by further budget problems and he was forced to accept a hated tax increase. However, this too amounted only to a stopgap measure. The real answer to Texas's financial difficulties, an income tax, lies somewhere in the distant future. Public opinion is still extremely hostile to this idea because many Texans still live in a dreamworld of the past where oil revenues support all essential state services. In the real world, Texans continue to suffer from the results of services that rank nationally near the bottom in terms of quality.

The Texas gubernatorial campaign of 1990 was one of the dirtiest as well as the most expensive in recent memory. It pitted Democratic State Treasurer Ann Richards against Republican candidate Clayton Williams, a successful oilman and rancher with no political experience. At first Williams's candidacy inspired snickers in all quarters. But he proved to be an effective campaigner in the primary race and overcame the opposition of Railroad Commissioner Kent Hance, Attorney General Tom Luce, and former secretary of state Jack Rains.

Unfortunately for Williams, the general election campaign was another story. He seemingly had an insurmountable lead at the outset, but as the campaign wore on he made several critical errors that precipitated his defeat. He stated publicly that the weather is like rape: "You can't do anything about it so you might as well relax and enjoy it." At a public meeting he called Ann Richards a liar and refused to shake her hand. Toward the end of the campaign he admitted that he had paid no income tax in 1986 and that he was unfamiliar with Proposition One. The only constitutional amendment on the ballot, Proposition One, dealt with the appointive powers of the governor. In the end, Ann Richards won the election with 51 percent of the vote. Williams's gaffes and errors cost him dearly, but they only partially explain the outcome. Richards did very well among female voters, and exit polls revealed that a substantial number of voters favored Richards because of her commitment to education.

At her inauguration the new governor proclaimed that she would usher in a "New Texas," meaning that she intended to make real changes. She was determined to break down the "old boy" network, which for so long had dominated state government, and bring "new people" into government, especially women and minorities. She also was determined to promote a higher degree of ethics in politics and public service. She wanted Texans truly to believe that someone was "in charge" as Texas approached the twenty-first century.

Richards's legislative agenda in 1991 called for stricter ethics laws, more effective regulation of the insurance industry, and stronger environmental regulations. She achieved them all. Her success added to her popularity and her acceptance rating soared to 60 percent, but by 1993 a change was evident. Richards seemed to be losing her enthusiasm and her zest for public life. The cause of this change is difficult to pinpoint, but it probably derived from the failure of her "New Texas" plan. Many of her appointments were disappointments, especially Railroad Commissioner Lena Guerraro, who resigned in disgrace when it was discovered that she had lied about her academic credentials. Additionally, the "old boy" network proved much harder to crush than Richards had imagined, and the burdens of office were generally becoming harder to bear. Still, Richards was not considering retirement as time rolled around for the election of 1994. She was a political warrior, and she braced herself for action. She was encouraged by the belief that her most likely opponent was a political lightweight who would be easy to defeat. This assumption proved to be a fatal error.

The Republican candidate in 1994 was George W. Bush, eldest son of the former President. Although it was true that Bush had little political experience, he had many other assets, not the least of which was his name. In 1989, long before he announced his candidacy, an informal poll placed him within eight points of the governor, the result of name recognition alone.

Neither Bush nor Richards faced a serious primary challenge, so both were able to concentrate on the general election from the outset. Bush developed a campaign based on four issues: tort reform, welfare reform, juvenile crime, and public education. He did not intend to launch a personal attack against the governor. He was determined to campaign on the issues alone and to try to take advantage of the state's conservative mood. Richards, on the other hand, seemed to believe that her personal popularity would carry her through and that she need only wait for Bush to make mistakes, as Williams had done four years earlier. Hence she did not launch a particularly aggressive campaign until it was much too late. She was soundly defeated.

Although he began with a flourish, George W. Bush actually accomplished little during his six years as governor. During the first year of his administration the legislature passed a tort reform bill allegedly designed to reduce frivolous lawsuits. As one commentator put it, this legislation so completely reversed the state's reputation as a trial lawyer's paradise that Texas had become an insurance company's paradise. People with legitimate complaints thus gained little. This was the high point of the governor's achievement.

As for welfare reform based upon the governor's policy of "compassionate conservatism," the record was dismal. In 2000, as Governor Bush pursued the U.S. presidency, Texas had a much higher percentage of poor working families with children than most other states, while Texas families living in poverty were more likely to rely on earnings for a majority of their income and less likely to receive welfare relief. Additionally, poor working families in Texas were seldom covered by health insurance, and they were less likely to receive unemployment benefits than their counterparts in other states. Moreover, the number of people in Texas living below the poverty line—one in six—was appalling.

Early in his administration Governor Bush proclaimed himself the "education governor." By this he meant that his goal was to improve the quality of education in the state, and the means that he favored to that end was to lay on more student-assessment tests. While in theory these tests prompt better teaching by indicating student achievement levels, in practice they simply mask teaching inadequacies; recent studies reveal that many of these exams are below grade level; moreover, between 1995 and 2001, all such tests routinely became easier. Meanwhile, Texas ranked forty-fourth in the nation on combined math and verbal SAT scores and forty-eighth in high school completion rate. At the same time teachers' salaries remained absurdly low, with the state ranking thirty-sixth out of fifty. Indeed, Texans are getting what they pay for.

It is now clear to most observers that Governor Bush intended to run for President from the outset of his career in politics. In his view, Austin was merely a stepping-stone to Washington. With many advisers who served his father and Ronald Reagan and the financial support of numerous deep-pocketed conservative Republicans, he approached the party primaries with confidence. Of his seven opponents, only Senator John McCain of Arizona posed a threat of any consequence, but the right wing was in control and by March 2000 it was a foregone conclusion that Bush would be the GOP nominee.

The campaign waged by Bush and his Democratic opponent, Vice President Al Gore of Tennessee, can be characterized best as dull. Gore attempted without much luck to weaken Bush by criticizing his behavior as a youth. Much more significant was the fact that in 2000 the economy was booming, but Gore's wooden stage presence reduced his ability to exploit it. Bush, on the other hand, emphasized five issues: tax cuts, education, the privatization of social security, broadening the military, and restoring civility to politics. These topics might have generated an exciting platform—unfortunately the governor's presentations were every bit as dull as Gore's.

The election of 2000 was one of the closest in U.S. history and the outcome was inconclusive. Gore won a majority of the popular vote but neither Bush nor Gore won a majority in the Electoral College because both of them claimed victory in Florida. After thirty-six days of controversy, the Supreme Court awarded Florida to Bush, thereby letting him become the nation's forty-third President. Although he faced a divided Congress, President Bush set out immediately to implement his program and was able to produce a significant tax cut. At the time the federal government enjoyed a huge surplus revenue, but the good times soon would be over. No one could have known, of course, what lay in store on September 11, 2001, and that George W. Bush would be called upon to provide leadership during one of the nation's greatest crises. How history will judge that leadership remains to be seen.

* * *

In absolute terms, the quality of life in Texas has improved considerably since the end of World War II, but measured in relative terms, these improvements were inadequate. As the population of the Lone Star State continues to increase and pressures to supply better services intensify, Texans sooner or later will be forced to decide whether they will continue to tolerate outmoded financial and governmental institutions. To compete successfully in the future, Texas needs better schools, better transportation facilities, better social services, and more effective public stewardship of natural resources, especially water. These demands can be met only at substantial cost, and it is questionable whether the state's current political system is prepared to shoulder them. Since World War II this system has been characterized primarily by intense political and personal strife, penury in government, scandal, and the rise of the two-party system that has generated even more conservatism. Far too little attention has been paid to the real needs of the people and the growing complexities of modern life. While there have been sincere attempts at reform, most of them have fallen far short of satisfactory results. Thus, as the world takes its initial steps into the twenty-first century, Texans must still decide if they are prepared to meet the demands of the twentieth century.

Suggested Reading

Carlton, Don. *Red Scare, Right Wing Hysteria, Fifties Fanaticism and their Legacy in Texas.* Austin: Texas Monthly Press, 1985.

Caro, Robert A. *Lyndon Johnson: Means of Ascent.* New York: Knopf, 1990.

Deaton, Charles. *The Year They Threw the Rascals Out.* Austin: Shoal Creek, 1973.

Green, George N. *The Establishment in Texas Politics.* Westport, CT: Greenwood Press, 1979.

Kinch, Sam, Jr., and Ben Procter. *Texas Under a Cloud.* Austin: Pemberton, 1972.

Olien, Roger. *Token to Triumph: The Texas Republicans since 1920.* Dallas: Southern Methodist University Press, 1982.

Reston, James, Jr. *The Lone Star: The Life of John Connally.* New York: Harper and Row, 1990.

Soukup, John, Clifton McCleskey, and Harry Holloway. *Party and Factional Division in Texas.* Austin: University of Texas Press, 1964.

Wolff, Nelson. *Challenge of Change.* Austin: Naylor, 1975.

Jesús De León (author's father) picking cotton in Lorenzo, Texas, 1943. De León participated in the "Big Swing," the migration of cotton pickers from South Texas to the Texas Panhandle. *Jesús De León Family Collection, Special Collections & Archives, Mary and Jeff Bell Library, Texas A&M University-Corpus Christi.*

CHAPTER TWELVE

A *People with Many Histories: Mexican Americans in Texas*

Arnoldo De León

BEFORE THE EARLY 1970s, HISTORIANS HAD given only scant attention to the lives of Mexican Americans in Texas. What literature existed depicted Texas Mexicans stereotypically: at best as an enduring population of ranch hands and field-workers, at worst as a minority lacking any importance in the saga of the Lone Star State. But thanks to dozens of academic works published during the last three decades, much more is now known about the 5 million Mexican Americans to whom Texas is home.

Contemporary literature portrays Tejanos[1] as a people with an important and richly detailed past. Modern-day scholars see the Mexican-American community as a complex entity not readily disposed to caricature. In the main, recent studies present a profile of a socially, culturally, ideologically, and generationally diverse group, the history of which has been shaped by different sets of circumstances. Economic change over time, for one, obligated Tejanos to respond as best they could to events ever in flux. Yet even as they adjusted to a dynamic Texas society, Tejanos managed to hold on to many of the cultural practices of Mexico.

From 1836 (the year Tejanos came under the sovereignty of American-based institutions) until the 1890s, the character of the Texas economy played a fundamental role in shaping the Tejano community. In the antebellum period, enslaved African Americans worked the Central Texas lands, the Trans-Nueces region developed slowly, and the frontier west of the 98th meridian remained sparsely settled. In short, not too much induced Mexicans to immi-

---

1 As used in this essay, *Tejanos* are Mexican-origin residents of Texas, whether of native- or foreign-born status. I use the term interchangeably with *Texas-Mexicans* and *Mexican Americans*, though the latter term might not be applicable until 1845, when Mexicans in Texas became citizens of the United States. All the terms imply a shared background and experience.

grate to Texas. In 1836, approximately four thousand Mexican-descent people resided in Texas; at midcentury, the number stood at about fourteen thousand.

Following the Civil War, however, new ranches and farms sprang up throughout the state, many of them in the regions bordering Mexico. Certainly the new ranches and farms needed workers, and native Mexicans living in those areas were joined by immigrants responding to the call for day laborers as well as for *vaqueros* (cowboys) and sheepherders. Demographers estimate the population of Texas Mexicans as being close to 165,000 in 1900. Compared to modern population figures, Texas Mexicans did not constitute a sizeable group or a large portion of the overall Texas population; in fact, they probably made up only about 5 percent of the total of Texas inhabitants.

Despite their relatively low number, Tejanos often clashed with Anglo-Americans. Racial prejudice underlay some of these incidents, but so did conflicting economic priorities. In 1857, for example, envious Anglo teamsters attacked Texas-Mexican *arrieros* (freight haulers) in the San Antonio–Goliad area, mainly because the Tejanos dominated the carting business between the interior of the state and the Gulf Coast. The violent episode, which resulted in the loss of several lives and damage to thousands of dollars worth of property, ended upon the intervention of Texas entrepreneurs alarmed over the interruption of trade, the Mexican foreign minister in Washington, and the U.S. secretary of state, who worried over the transparently racist attacks.

Contests over lands owned by Tejanos—received as grants from either the Spanish or the Mexican government—similarly caused bitter confrontations between the two rival groups. Anglos desired those possessions—most of them situated in the old San Antonio, Victoria, Goliad region, and in the Trans-Nueces—for full capitalist development. But Tejanos just as resolutely defended their real estate for the obvious reason that their way of life and sustenance depended on it. The earliest battles over land holdings occurred in Central Texas in the aftermath of the Texas war for independence (with much Anglo success in displacing Tejanos), then spilled over into South Texas by the 1850s.

The Tejano approach to retaining their property involved taking titles before a land claims commission (established in the early 1850s), hammering out disputes in the courts, allowing the intermarriage of the daughters of rancheros to Anglo suitors, and armed defense. No one during the nineteenth century, however, attracted more attention for protesting land dispossession than Juan

Nepomuceno "Cheno" Cortina of the Brownsville area. A some-what complicated historical personality, seen by scholars as a bandit on the one hand and as a defender of Tejano rights on the other, Cortina burst on the scene in July 1859 following a one-on-one shootout with a city marshal. In the fall of that year Cortina issued two proclamations that articulated his reasons for amassing armed followers and resisting U.S. law. Anglos, he declared, encroached on Tejano-owned lands, carried out numerous racist attacks, and even murdered Mexicans with impunity. Texas Rangers and federal troops forced Cortina to retreat into Mexico in early 1860, but an ugly campaign of retaliation against suspected Cortina sympathizers followed. Cortina himself went on to resume his political career in Mexico.

In Far West Texas, Anglos and native Mexicans clashed still again, this time over ownership of and access to salt deposits in lakes some one hundred miles from El Paso. The people of the valley had long mined the salt beds, according to the tradition that this served the common good, but in the 1860s Anglo entrepreneurs arrived in the El Paso area with designs on claiming the lakes for their personal profit. Disagreements finally culminated in violence between Anglos and Mexicans at San Elizario in December 1877, but Texas Rangers and federal troops ultimately quieted what came to be called the "Salt War," which effectively ended the Mexicans' access to the deposits.

Notwithstanding such abrasive relations between the Anglo majority and the Tejano minority, Mexican Americans attempted to find a niche within Anglo society. Nevertheless, this acculturation entailed the retention of much of what was the Tejanos' Hispanic heritage. Thus, Tejanos remained "Mexicans" in many ways. In the economic sector, merchants employed business traditions long used in Mexico or in Mexican Texas: these included offering a *pilón* (the gift of an additional item after a sale) to good customers and the selling of foods or wares in an open-air market. On the range, Tejanos earned their living by applying time-tested Spanish/Mexican ranch techniques to cattle and sheep management. More telling of the economic mindset of Tejanos was the outlook some rancheros took toward their landholdings. Many did not see their ranchos as capitalist enterprises intended to bring wealth, but as units of production in a feudal sense that bestowed respect and social standing to their owners.

But the desire to retain old ways did not mean a complete rejection of Anglo-American economic institutions and practices. In fact, Tejanos did not have too much difficulty melding their preindustrial views with the tenets of the new capitalism. All Tejanos looked for work (in whatever form) within the capitalist structure. Many sought to tap into the higher rewards offered by a predominantly ranching economy. Small business owners tried to meet Anglo society's demands for Mexican goods, services, and cuisine. Those with greater financial acumen developed ties to the Anglo buying market and successfully sold mercantile goods, real estate, or livestock to both Anglos and Tejanos. Some of the Tejano entrepreneurs' transactions for supplies and range animals extended to places as far away as the Indian Territory, Illinois, and Kentucky.

Numerous other forces socialized native-born and foreign-born Tejanos to the dominant Anglo-American ethos, among them schools, Catholic and Protestant churches, and the political system. As a result, Mexican Americans became familiar with the English language: some spoke English fluently, others did so just well enough to get by in the workplace. Tejanos also openly accepted American foods and fashions, as well as American technological innovations and selective habits of thought and behavior. The residents of many Tejano communities eagerly participated in patriotic celebrations unique to American history, such as the Fourth of July and George Washington's birthday.

Politically, Tejanos managed to insert their own traditions into the new Anglo system. Heirs to a Roman/Spanish model of governance that placed the welfare of the community over that of the individual, Tejanos were inclined to accept the authority of a local leader (*patrón*) whose position might rest on the result of a popular election or merely on his economic standing or record of service to the community. Conditioned by a pastoral life, isolation, and the need for communal self-protection, common folks entrusted their well-being to Anglo bosses (the surrogate for the old patrón), confident that he would represent the public interest.

Simultaneously, Tejanos modified traditional notions to fit new political strategies. While Anglo-American political bosses sought the manipulation of the Mexican vote for personal aggrandizement, Tejanos turned to the new system to gain social services and other benefits. As happened in other immigrant communities throughout the United States, the patrón or boss structure evolved into an unwritten arrangement whereby Tejano poor people, in return for their vote, received such amenities as employment, help in times of crisis, and even support from the boss in furthering the talents of a promising community member.

While kept from exercising the franchise fully by voting restrictions enacted by a shrewd Anglo majority—such as barring people from the polling place based on their age, level of (English) literacy, and naturalization status—Tejanos did their best to participate in the political process. Some Tejanos even became lieutenants within the boss system; others won election to city and county offices on their own, especially in South Texas. A handful even served in the state legislature, among them José Antonio Navarro (1846), G. N. García (1866), and Santos Benavides (1879). In many parts of the state, Tejanos organized local clubs designed to press for community and individual advancement.

Beginning around the 1890s, as the ranching economy collapsed, a different epoch in Mexican-American history began. Numerous singularities distinguish the two periods. For one thing, a new cohort appeared in Spanish-speaking communities in the form of immigrants from Mexico who came to constitute, at least until about 1930, the bulk of Mexican-descent people in the state.

The newcomers differed from the old Tejanos in numerous ways. Most saliently, their historical upbringing had little to do with lost lands, the American frontier, or Americanizing institutions. To the contrary, hacienda life, the events surrounding the brutal dictatorship of Porfirio Díaz (1876–1911), the Mexican Revolution of 1910, and the subsequent reconstruction of Mexico had shaped their frame of mind.

The place Mexicans occupied in the U.S. market economy of the early twentieth century also separated the histories of the old and the new group of Tejanos. While Mexican Americans in the mid to late nineteenth century had been an agrarian people, many times forced to defend their lands in order to carry on a traditional lifestyle, that no longer proved the case after the 1890s. In the twentieth century, advanced capitalism integrated Tejanos as part of a larger proletariat; now flash points between Anglos and Mexicans principally revolved around class interests. Indeed, the *Plan de San Diego* proved among the last of the rural clashes that had in part emanated from conflicting nineteenth-century economic outlooks.

In addition, the new economy took Tejano communities in different directions. About half the Tejano population lived in farms and rural towns as late as 1940, though a general trend toward urbanization was unfolding. A feature of the pre–World War II era, thus, was the tendency toward increased rural/urban diversification.

Throughout Texas, and certainly in those regions where Tejanos tended to be more highly concentrated—namely from the Austin area, to Houston, to the Rio Grande Valley, thence westward beyond the Trans-Pecos, and from El Paso back to Central Texas—a farm revolution unfolded in the period between 1900 and 1940. Ranch lands gave way to diversified farming, even in areas as far north as the Panhandle Plains. Whereas Tejanos had depended upon the paternalism of ranch owners and year-round employment in the old ranch economy, such terms became scarce in the new farm structure.

A concomitant of the age of farm commercialization was migrant field labor as a dire option for both native-born Tejanos and newly arrived immigrants who needed to work. By the 1930s, entire Tejano families had been drawn into the "Big Swing," the migratory fieldwork cycle that took laborers from the farms of South Texas into rural Panhandle towns such as Sweetwater, Lamesa, Muleshoe, and Lubbock and eventually back to their homes to await the next season's cycle.

A dramatic influx of Tejanos in the *colonias* of Texas cities,[2] the pell-mell growth of *barrios* in towns, and the appearance of temporary cotton-picker camps along the migratory route also marked the new period. The colonias (several ethnic enclaves adjacent to each other) of cities such as El Paso, Houston, and San Antonio turned into centers of the worst kind of urban blight: high unemployment, miserably substandard housing, rampant diseases, crime, and wholesale neglect from city services and officials. The luckier workers found employment on city construction crews, railroad gangs, in small manufacturing plants, and in other kinds of industrial enterprises locally—the Houston Ship Channel, for example— but the less fortunate ones could rely only upon temporary work until the start of the next year's migrant swing. Essentially, the larger cities, and even medium-sized ones such as Corpus Christi, Brownsville, and San Angelo served as bases for Mexicans answering the demands for temporary labor in the nearby cotton fields.

Rural towns in southern and western Texas, many of them surrounded by lush cotton fields, similarly saw an expansion of their

2 For purposes of this essay, *towns* are defined as municipalities of less than 20,000 residents that are dependent on surrounding farms and ranches, the local oil industry, the school system, and various sorts of small businesses. *Cities* are industrial metroplexes with a population greater than 100,000. *Medium-sized cities* include centers that combine features of the prior classifications and contain between 20,000 and 100,000 persons.

barrios (Mexican-American enclaves). Fieldworkers attracted to these towns by familial links, expectations of finding steadier jobs, or proximity to the hiring farms moved into undeveloped sections of these sites. There the workers built makeshift housing that lacked city services such as running water, electricity, and police protection. Examples of pre–World War II towns that served as temporary headquarters for Mexican-American farm workers include Weslaco, Beeville, Robstown, Falfurrias, and those of the so-called Winter Garden: Crystal City and Cotulla.

Once out in the cotton fields during the harvest season, the migrants faced even harsher conditions. Necessarily, they improvised as best they could, living primitively in old barns or chicken coups, in tents besides rural roads, or in shacks made available to them by farmers. They had the responsibility of providing their own cooking utensils and bedding, fetching their own water and wood, and administering to their own health care. To humanitarians, conditions seemed so desperate for the migrant workers and their families that during the late 1930s the federal government intervened to have labor camps built.

Expectedly, modern farming created a new set of antagonisms between Mexicans and Anglos, many of a class nature now that Tejanos had been fully integrated into the capitalist web. Both immigrants and native-born Mexican Americans sought to exact benefits from the market economy that they both admired and helped energize. But major growers and their allies had no intentions of conceding much of the economic pie, preferring to use Mexican Americans as a cheap labor source. Conflicts ensued.

Labor skirmishes reflected the contrasting expectations workers and farm owners had of the capitalist structure that both groups embraced. Tejano sharecroppers and field hands, for instance, launched campaigns to improve their working conditions during the pre–World War II era. They founded organizations, many of them short-lived, that called for concessions from landlords and farmers and for coordinated work stoppages. Invariably, recent immigrants joined native-born fieldworkers in their protests; modern scholars have determined that new arrivals participated as actively in walkout efforts as did members of the native-born population. Spinach workers in Crystal City threatened to halt work in 1930, and they successfully negotiated an agreement with local farmers for better wages and an end to child labor. In the Laredo area, *La Asociación de Jornaleros* (Association of Journeymen Workers) in 1935 likewise forced owners of irrigated farms in the area to honor certain demands in the face of a threatened strike. In 1934, some 750 sheepshearers in the West Texas area around San Angelo struck against sheepmen to dramatize their discontent with a labor arrangement they believed unfair. For the most part, however, farm and ranch strikes before World War II did not produce long-range benefits for Tejano workers.

Meanwhile, similar labor issues preoccupied the other half of the Tejano community, the urban cohort concentrated in the cities. As completely integrated into the capitalist structure as were their counterparts out on the farms, this group of Tejanos launched proletarian struggles designed to win improvements in urban living and industrial workplace conditions. The tactics they used included joining unions and engaging in strike activity. Ordinarily, Tejanos established their own, often segregated, mutualistic labor associations or independent labor unions in order to work out their problems with management; where feasible, they allied themselves with mainstream organizations such as affiliates of the American Federation of Labor (AFL).

Notwithstanding the factors that separated the histories of nineteenth- and twentieth-century Tejanos—such as the wave of new immigrants and the transformation of the economy—certain phenomena were aspects of both pasts. One element connecting the two histories was the persistence of Anglo-American racial intolerance towards those of Mexican descent. In the eyes of the majority society, Mexicans remained a biologically inferior people unworthy of equal social or economic standing. By the 1920s, views of Mexicans as unhygienic persons unfit to live with Anglos in the same sections of town or to attend the same schools perpetuated old prejudices. And racism certainly would govern Anglo-Tejano relations throughout the twentieth century.

Second, the new immigrants that inundated Tejano communities between the 1890s and 1930 did not overwhelm the older Tejano group as a social presence. The middle class of the nineteenth century, for one, showed tenacity and resilience. A number of the old rancheros, some residing as far north as the San Antonio region, managed to retain their properties, in many cases through recourse to the legal system. Even today, one finds examples, especially in the ranch counties of South Texas (Zapata, Willacy, Webb, or Duval), of families whose ranch holdings were originally grants their forbears received from Spain or Mexico. The same applies to the political elites. Many successful individuals could trace their family's political influence to the nineteenth-century lines of power that had withstood the changes in politics in the twentieth century.

J. T. Canales and Manuel Guerra may be the most prominent examples. Canales traced his political predecessors to relatives of Juan N. Cortina, and his high-profile career of involvement in Mexican-American causes continued well into the mid-twentieth century. He served in the Texas legislature from 1905 to 1910, and again from 1917 to 1920; he went on to play a leading role in the civil rights movement of the period between the 1920s and the 1950s. Guerra launched his own career in Starr County in the 1880s, and his sons maintained the Guerra family's control over county matters until World War II.

Third, culture and community remained intact even as individuals crossed watershed historical eras. Many aspects of Tejano culture, as it had been practiced since the colonial period of Texas history, endured into the twentieth century. Use of the Spanish language in the home, a strong faith in Catholicism, family relations, oral traditions such as folklore, music, and many other aspects of in-group life meshed with those of the new immigrants. Instead of supplanting the old way of life by imposing theirs upon the Mexican Texans, the immigrants actually nourished and perpetuated many of the ways of nineteenth-century Tejano cultural patterns. Culturally, therefore, Tejano communities throughout the state did not experience drastic disruption, even as everyone entered a new epoch.

Lastly, the pre–World War II immigrants did not necessarily enter Mexican-American history abruptly. To the contrary, immigration into Texas had been a constant source of population growth since 1836. Until the turn of the century, immigrants made their way into Texas for a number of reasons. They came to answer the call for more laborers on the ranches, fleeing oppressive conditions on the *haciendas*, and, in fact, for reasons not much unlike those that motivated the immigrants of the late twentieth century. In fact, between 1850 and 1930 (the 1940 federal census schedules do not provide similar information), at least 40 percent of the Texas-Mexican population claimed Mexico as their place of birth. Thus, while immigration numbers escalated before the war, cross-border migration was hardly a new event.

Therefore, even as twentieth-century corporate capitalism gave Tejano society new directions, historical continuity simultaneously acted to cushion cultural disruption. Time-honored practices persisted in a natural path of development and diversification. In-group social conventions crossed epochs very much unaltered—with immigrants reinforcing nineteenth-century Spanish/Mexican customs and traditions. At the same time, Mexican-American communities, be they farmland or town, did begin to reflect the new economic order in the years leading up to World War II.

This complex process of acculturation reveals itself in a comparison of rural and urban life. In the rural towns, mobility became routine, as entire families picked up and left to perform field labor (some of them to out-of-state farms) in the spring and did not return to their homes until late winter. The undertaking, as already noted, was fraught with hardships, but it also fostered marriage among the migrating families, which meant a recycling of similar problems for the next generation of migrants. For women, rural life entailed maintaining a mobile household and suffering numerous limitations upon personal freedoms. Traditionally, wives did not receive wages for work performed in the fields, as farmers commonly paid the whole family's earnings to the husband. Those Tejanas who worked as domestic clerks or in manufacturing plants (candy, pecan, or cigar) received pay independently, even if in the end part or all of it went directly into the family budget.

People living in the rural sector also faced particular disadvantages in gaining an education or in familiarizing themselves with mainstream institutions. Rural counties hardly earned reputations for schooling excellence, and many parents needed their children to work alongside them, though a good number did see to it that their young ones attended the classroom during two or three months of the winter season. The consequences of such a situation stand out: most rural Tejano children did not learn the English language and other skills necessary to compete effectively in the world outside their segregated communities. Isolated from other socializing institutions—the churches, government agencies, and the urban work force—entire rural families encountered great difficulty in picking up survival skills. In the towns and cities, Mexican Americans at minimum had access to schools, and, although they lived in segregated neighborhoods, had daily contact with white establishments and individuals.

Urban areas, moreover, offered a wider array of employment opportunities than did most rural towns or farms. While most Tejanos in the rural sector belonged to the lower class, the urban scene invariably featured a group of middling status. In San Antonio, Houston, Corpus Christi, Brownsville, Laredo, or El Paso, one could find a Mexican business district where retailers and professionals serviced members of the colonias, while simultaneously maintaining contact with white merchants and other distributors.

Lawyers, pharmacists, doctors, and teachers also constituted the more well-to-do of Tejano society in these urban sites.

Like education, political activity also was less evident in rural areas than in the urban centers. Naturally, political activists had trouble mobilizing laborers in transit, and, conversely, people on the move had little time to engage in political or any other abstract discourse. The urbanscape, comparatively, produced a tenable political fervor. There, Mexican Americans launched highly charged campaigns for civic improvement. An early effort occurred in Laredo in 1911 when delegates from throughout Texas came together at the *Primer Congreso Mexicanista* to highlight the need for educational parity, call for improvements in the working conditions of the laboring poor, and demand equal rights and privileges for the Texas-Mexican community at large.

During the 1920s, and particularly the 1930s, urban Mexican Americans became increasingly insistent on their right to enjoy all the privileges guaranteed them under the United States Constitution. Many of those who supported this notion hailed from the Tejano middle class, including persons more widely exposed to mainstream U.S. society.

This generation founded the *Orden de Hijos de America* (Order of Sons of America) in San Antonio in 1921. Permitting only native-born or naturalized U.S. citizens to join, the OSA dedicated itself to tearing down old barriers—such as racist practices that segregated Tejanos in public places, juries, and the schools—and winning full equality for Texas Mexicans. Unable to prosper, the OSA was subsumed by the League of United Latin American Citizens (LULAC) in 1929. The League, still the largest Hispanic civil rights organization today, became an aggressive advocate for Mexican-American equality during the pre–World War II era. On the labor front, Mexican Americans similarly sought equality and engaged in labor protest in both rural and urban areas. In San Antonio, Emma Tenayuca emerged as a determined labor leader of the pecan shellers in the late 1930s.

Along with most Texans, Mexican-descent people (both native- and foreign-born) dealt with a new set of circumstances after World War II. The postwar years featured changes of every sort: in mass culture; in infrastructural development; in manufacturing; in the process of suburbanization; and in the final decline of the old rural economy. In addition, politics became more inclusive of disadvantaged groups.

The rapid industrialization of Texas derived in part from the influx of federal dollars into state defense plants built in response to the Cold War threat of communism. The process accelerated as Texas became a major player in the international oil-petrochemical business. Thousands of other enterprises unrelated to the defense and oil industries also grew out of the postwar prosperity. Today, high-tech corporations, real estate developers, chain stores, and even universities continue to find Texas an appealing place to turn a profit.

Now, farming largely became "agribusiness," as corporations moved in, gobbled up large tracts of land, streamlined production, and introduced innovative management techniques. The mechanization of work, accomplished by the new mechanical cotton pickers and other machines, began to replace manual laborers, who turned to the city to find employment. While 45 percent of all Texans lived in urban areas in 1940, in excess of 80 percent of the total Texas population made the city their home by the last decade of the twentieth century.

Despite its urbanized character, Texas still has an economy that combines industrial and agricultural elements. Texans, regardless of nationality or race, have all had to derive their livelihood from such a mixed system. In the work crews of the rural areas, however, African Americans and Mexican Americans have been disproportionately represented: African Americans in East Texas, and Mexican Americans in South and West Texas. Moreover, for many in both these minority groups, temporary farm labor remained a way of life until mechanization finally displaced them during the late 1950s and early 1960s.

Mexican-American farm life in the postwar period meant twelve-to-fourteen-hour days in the fields performing strenuous hand labor such as el desaije (hoeing) or la pisca (cotton picking). Urban dwellers from the lower Rio Grande Valley and the Coastal Bend accompanied hands living on local ranches and farms to hit the fields in early spring to weed out the plants. Those having no choice but to enter the stream of migrant labor pushed northward to follow the harvest, joined by others in the smaller rural towns of Central Texas (but also from folks living in San Antonio and Austin), and from there pushing farther north into West Texas towns such as Lamesa and, ultimately, into the Panhandle farms around Tahoka, Levelland, and Littlefield.

Tejanos on the migrant trail relived the annual experience traceable to the 1920s. Some of them stayed in the aforementioned labor camps built during the 1940s: besides meager bathroom facilities, these shelters offered little more than privacy. The majority of migrant families still were forced to improvise on the road, and besides the lack of proper housing they faced dire conditions, including low wages, improper medical attention, constant exposure to diseases, and discrimination in the towns they visited. By the 1960s, such experiences abated for farm hands somewhat, as improved educational opportunities afforded a number of them better career choices, and, in some cases, steadier employment in the urban centers. To this day, however, those having to resort to farm work (usually the poorest of the poor) face a grim future as farms further modernize and agribusiness seeks new farmlands in foreign countries with lower pay scales.

Nonetheless, one should not assume that Tejanos were purely passive figures within the capitalist farm structure. Historians have identified several ways in which field hands expressed their discontent and exerted some control over work schedules, among them, deliberate slowdowns on the job, the destroying of crops and the breaking of tools, refusal to work for particularly oppressive farm owners, and union organizing. Formal union activity on Texas farms does not seem to have gained much momentum, however, until the mid-1960s. After César Chávez, the California farm organizer, sent lieutenants to South Texas, wildcat strikes occurred there in 1966 and 1967. A chapter of Chávez's California United Farm Workers Union took the lead in trying to reorganize the stoop laborers in that region during the 1970s, with no more success than Chávez's lieutenants had enjoyed a decade earlier. Since then, the United Farm Workers (or UFW, now an AFL-CIO affiliate) has maintained lobbying efforts for farm workers' rights in the state legislature. During the 1980s and since, the farm workers made several gains. These included the passage of labor laws that granted them numerous benefits (among them a guaranteed minimum wage and unemployment compensation) and governmental regulation of sanitary facilities for workers in the fields. Nevertheless, the UFW membership simultaneously struggled with new political attitudes in the mainstream society that minimized the needs of farm workers, many of whom were Mexico-born.

In the towns and the large cities, Tejanos did better materially than their rural counterparts, although the record of aggregate achievement in the urban setting is mixed. Like the majority of Texans, Mexican Americans made the move to the urban scene after World War II. There they found a wider range of available employment, but their general lack of necessary industrial skills and the lingering presence of racism in the workplace limited their prospects for good-paying jobs. The majority accepted positions as unskilled or semiskilled laborers. Some joined construction, railroad, or city maintenance crews, others found work in industrial plants, in nearby oilfields, and even in local defense establishments such as naval or air force bases. Still others became janitors or cafeteria workers on school campuses. Women primarily turned to employment as waitresses, house, hotel, or hospital cleaners, or as seamstresses in the garment factories of the medium-sized and larger cities (wherein at least some engaged in strike activity—a bold undertaking in an anti-union state). Less fortunate urban residents did odd jobs while awaiting the next harvest cycle on the farms. The urban cohort of Tejano society generally clustered in blue-collar neighborhoods that featured homes ranging from the comfortable to the substandard—shacks with outside privies, no running water, electricity or gas, and little attention from municipal governments. While residents of Mexican-American enclaves today hardly endure the primitive conditions faced by old working-class urbanites, they continue to support themselves by filling the same kinds of jobs that their predecessors had during the rural to urban migration that occurred at midcentury.

Not all urban Mexican Americans belong in the blue-collar category, however. Certainly, a Tejano middle class exists today, just as one has since before the Texas war for independence. College-educated Mexican Americans have in part realized the American Dream in the large cities; this group includes educators, doctors, attorneys, real estate agents, architects, media personalities, journalists, and numerous other professionals. Houston, Dallas–Fort Worth, Lubbock, San Antonio, El Paso, Corpus Christi, and the cities of the lower Rio Grande Valley all can point to a circle of very successful Hispanic businesses, Hispanic Chambers of Commerce, Hispanic Business and Professional Women's Clubs, and Tejano residents who live in affluent suburbs and drive status-symbol automobiles.

Several factors contributed to such success stories; one was the continued incorporation of Tejanos into the U.S. capitalist system. While such a process entailed the exploitation of a good segment of Mexican-American laborers, it also allowed some Tejanos to reach new heights. The decline in racial intolerance since World War II, and certainly since the 1960s, further explains the pace of achievement. Helping to ease the climb to middle- and upper-class status has been the ability of a larger number of Mexican Americans to acquire the type of education essential to hold white-collar jobs. The migratory waves from Mexico—which had characterized Tejano history from the 1890s to about 1930—decreased in magnitude after World War II; by the year 2000 only around 20 percent of those comprising the Mexican-American community were born in Mexico. As Tejanos carved a niche in the expanding economy, as white society conceded more rights to minorities, and as the exposure to mainstream life gave an increasing number of native-born Tejanos the necessary skills to compete effectively, upward mobility followed.

Interestingly, the overall achievements made both by the Tejano middle and lower classes have come without the complete assimilation social scientists once believed essential to immigrants' success. For the most part, Tejanos have retained their in-group lifestyle, while synthesizing elements of both American and Mexican culture. But even while undergoing Americanization, Mexican Americans in Texas have not become monolithic. The state's size and, in part, distinct economic regions contributed to diverse identities amongst Tejanos today.

Throughout Texas, one will find some regions highly influenced by a metroplex, some that contain a combination of rural towns and country areas, and still others that consist of generally isolated town sites. Regional diversity, consequently, has played a large part in molding different Tejano histories since the late 1940s.

One who travels throughout the Lone Star State immediately senses a certain distinctiveness upon entering South Texas. The reasons for the contrasts are obvious. In this region the origins of European exploration and settlement go back to the early Spanish *entradas* of the eighteenth century and the later efforts of José de Escandón, the pioneer credited with colonizing settlements along the Rio Grande. Mexico's proximity to South Texas and continued immigration have strengthened cultural accouterments implanted in the region by the first *pobladores* (settlers), and life maintains a traditional cadence that serves to blunt disruptive modernizing influences. A more traditional farming economy, coupled with a heavy presence of Mexicans and Mexican Americans, allows a "Mexican" milieu to persevere along the border and to overlap from there into San Antonio.

As a cohort, Tejanos in South Texas remain more faithful to their Mexican heritage than their counterparts in other parts of the state. Manifestations of this loyalty include the facile use of both Spanish and English by almost everyone in the region, the continued faith some segments of the population have in *curanderismo* (folk healing), the tenacity of folkloric stories, such as those of *chupacabras* (mysterious and deadly phantoms said to kill goats) or of the devil attending dances, and the attachment they maintain to traditional Mexican foods and music. Indeed, the Tejanos of South Texas have been quite successful in contributing to U.S. culture. Homemade delicacies such as *fajitas, burritos,* and *migas* have found their way onto restaurant menus across the state and the nation while Tejano music, the Spanish-language songs that mix traditional Latin and contemporary sounds, has slowly earned a foothold on the pop and country-western charts.

South Texas Mexicans have also been in the forefront of political activism, and, in fact, much Tejano political history has its roots in South Texas. Figures such as Juan Cortina, Santos Benavides, Catarino Garza, Manuel Guerra, J. T. Canales, and Sara Estela Ramírez made their political impact in South Texas during the nineteenth and early twentieth centuries, most of them speaking out, in their own way, in behalf of the working poor. The G.I. Forum, founded in Corpus Christi in 1948 by Dr. Hector P. García in an effort to expedite federal benefits for Mexican-American veterans, soon united with LULAC to become the most vocal advocate of Mexican-American rights. The Forum came to national prominence in 1949 when it exposed the racist practices of a funeral home in Three Rivers, Texas, that refused to handle services for the slain war hero Félix Longoria. With LULAC, the Forum took several cases of educational inequality into litigation: during the 1950s they targeted school districts in Del Rio, Carrizo Springs, Kingsville, Mathis, and Driscoll. During the 1960s and 1970s, the Chicano Movement, a grass-roots populist outpouring that also addressed class issues, held its greatest appeal throughout the farm communities and rural towns of South Texas. Presently, the region can boast of two U.S. representatives (Solomón Ortíz and Rubén Hinojosa) and some of the most successful legislators in Austin.

The triangular region from San Antonio to the Dallas–Fort Worth metroplex and then to Houston, continues as the economic heart of Texas. Its industry, for example, does not consist solely of traditional manufacturing; to the contrary, large corporations engaged in the production of the most advanced technology have found this region the ideal setting for some of their offices and industrial plants. Such an economic climate creates and supports many well-paying positions in the white-collar sector. In this so-called Golden Triangle, the work force includes thousands of people who earn their living in downtown skyscrapers, huge law offices, massive hospital complexes, and the most prestigious universities in the state. However, the region also includes towns such as El Campo, Gonzales, Huntsville, Rockdale, and others where life depends (as it does in South Texas) on a combination of agriculture, oil-related commerce, state or federal institutions (such as prisons), and local manufacturing plants.

The geo-economic setting of this part of Texas obviously stands in marked contrast to that of South Texas. In the densely populated region, one finds the coexistence of several heritages: mainstream American, European ethnic, African American, and Hispanic. The eastern half of the state north of the San Antonio/Houston line historically has retained the closest ties to the Upper and Lower South. Today, it remains home to the greatest number of Texas's African Americans, many of them descendants of Deep South migrants. At the same time, several European-heritage communities, namely German American, dot the region. To diversify things further, "the South meets the West" somewhere along I-35.

The industrial/urban atmosphere of the region thus tends to shape the cultural identity of its Tejano inhabitants in different ways. While many Mexican Americans in this section of the state continue to live on farms and in small rural towns, Houston and San Antonio each have larger concentrations of Mexican Americans than any other U.S. city (in fact, only Los Angeles and Chicago have greater numbers of Hispanics).

Political involvement may be one measure of how an urban/industrial setting stimulates Tejano communities. Excepting San Antonio, Mexican Americans did not penetrate the urban sites of this largely industrial section until the twentieth century, yet the region as a whole has been the center of important Tejano political activity. This was home to some of the most venerable names in twentieth-century Tejano history—Alonso Perales and M. C. Gonzales of San Antonio, Carlos E. Castañeda and George I. Sánchez of Austin, Félix Tijerina of Houston—as well as the crucible of many struggles for equal rights. Expectedly, many in the larger cities contributed to the politics of the Chicano Movement, but, at the same time, life in the urban centers deflected the more militant strain of the rebellion. The heterogeneity along class and economic lines of the Tejano urban population made it difficult for young militant Chicanos to supplant the leadership of the already entrenched, and generally more content, middle class.

West Texas (including the Panhandle), is a spacious place where one finds numerous cattle and sheep ranches, irrigated farms, small rural towns (at times situated miles from one another), and medium-sized cities. Big Lake, Fort Stockton, Plainview, Muleshoe, and many other towns depend on the oil industry, farming, livestock sales, educational institutions, tourism, and, of course, the employment opportunities offered by fast-food restaurants, supermarkets, and department stores. From the small towns, residents commute into the medium-sized cities such as San Angelo, Abilene, Midland-Odessa, or Wichita Falls to work or to shop for a greater variety of merchandise.

In West Texas, yet another set of historical forces shaped the Texas-Mexican persona. Texas west of the ninety-eighth meridian, the last section of the state settled by Anglos, has always lacked, save for El Paso in Far West Texas, the Hispanic aura traceable to the colonial era. Instead, West Texans seem to associate with the history of the Texas Rangers, the cattle wars, and the Indian battles of the 1870s. The region's continued reliance on sheep and cattle raising naturally fosters a mythic "West" mentality. In West Texas, "kicker" culture seems most pervasive, an expected manifestation given the region's landscape and economic orientation.

Except in a few counties just west of the Pecos River, Tejanos hardly constitute a majority of the region's population. Here Tejano identity derives from the tenacity of an in-group Mexican culture influenced by a minority status, the landscape, and the regional economy. The vast expanse that is West Texas features countless small farm and ranch communities that often see their best and brightest head for the cities in search of upward mobility. This exodus, or "brain drain," saps the fledgling Tejano middle class (a problem that plagues even the moderate size towns of West Texas) and widens the cultural gap between those who leave and those who remain to work in the oilfields, ranches, farms, and small businesses. Tejanos of West Texas are no less "Mexican" than their counterparts in other regions of the state, but the factors that have shaped their identity work to weaken the passion some have for their Hispanic heritage.

This disposition also seems to explain the lukewarm political commitment West Texas Tejanos have to the cause of *la raza* (the Mexican-American people). The Chicano Movement, for instance, never caught on in West Texas as it did in South Texas or in the large urban areas. Though as politically ambitious as any others, Tejanos in western Texas have yet to register the accomplishments of communities elsewhere in the states.

***

Clearly, Tejanos are a people with many histories. Different stages of a broad economic change, beginning in 1836 and continuing until the present, spawned an array of different experiences for the people's several subgroups. In the nineteenth century, Tejanos and the white majority came into conflict due to disparate economic outlooks; whereas disputes in the twentieth century increasingly centered on class issues. By this time Mexican Americans had been fully absorbed into the U.S. capitalist system. The ranch economy that prevailed for much of the period after the Texas war for independence fostered a way of life different from that of the new farm economy before 1940, which in turn, was different from that forged by a renewed industrialization after World War II.

Up until 1940 cultural homogeneity characterized the Tejano population in a predominantly rural state, but the regional economic diversification that occurred in Texas after World War II affected subgroup culture and identity, differentiating city-reared Tejanos from those living in rural areas, and the Mexican Americans of West Texas from those living in South Texas. Lastly, the new economy brought the prospect for upward mobility. Ranch capitalism had not allowed the majority of Mexican Americans much space for achievement, nor for that matter had the rural farm economy of the pre–World War II years. But the greatly diversified postwar economy did, and the result has been the expansion of the Tejano middle class since 1945 (currently placed as high as 40 percent of the Tejano population). Certainly, Tejanos have encountered numerous barriers in their quest to obtain a place in Texas society, but no one can dispute their integral place in the Texas heritage.

Suggested Reading

De León, Arnoldo. *Mexican Americans in Texas: A Brief History*, Second Edition. Wheeling, IL: Harlan Davidson, Inc., 1999.

García, Richard A. *Rise of the Mexican American Middle Class: San Antonio, 1929–1941*. College Station: Texas A&M University Press, 1991.

González, Gilbert G., and Raúl Fernández. "Chicano History: Transcending Cultural Models." *Pacific Historical Review* LXIII, November 1994.

Montejano, David. *Anglos and Mexicans in the Making of Texas, 1836–1986*. Austin: University of Texas Press, 1987.

Orozco, Cynthia E. "The Origins of the League of United Latin American Citizens (LULAC) and the Mexican American Civil Rights Movement in Texas with an Analysis of Women's Political Participation in a Gendered Context, 1910–1929." Ph.D. diss., University of California at Los Angeles, 1992.

Zamora, Emilio. *The World of the Mexican Worker in Texas*. College Station: Texas A&M University Press, 1993.

Ron Kirk, a Democrat, who in 2002 waged a hard fought but unsuccessful race to represent Texas in the United States Senate. *Courtesy of Ron Kirk for U.S. Senate.*

CHAPTER THIRTEEN

The Civil Rights Movement in Texas

Robert A. Calvert

SHORTLY BEFORE WORLD WAR II ENDED, Walter Winchell, the well-known newspaper columnist and radio commentator, asked a young black woman how Adolf Hitler should be punished. "Paint him black and bring him over here," she answered. Her ironic comment revealed much about U.S. society. American troops fought for other nations' freedoms, while at home black citizens attended separate and unequal schools, lived largely in substandard housing in segregated neighborhoods, and existed in a society that sanctioned Jim Crow laws. These state statutes denied black people access to public accommodations and to political processes. Legally prescribed and fiercely enforced segregation rules thus closed for black citizens the traditional avenues for attacking inequality: politics and education. Furthermore, Jim Crow laws were psychologically debilitating. They negated for many blacks the concept of self-help: Why should one try if laws deemed the basest white to be socially better than the most moral black?

The contradiction between democratic promises and actual injustices that prompted the young black woman to make her suggestion to Winchell also infuriated some black Texans. The tensions of war increased the rage felt at home. Protests of white newspaper editors and government officials against the stationing of black soldiers in Texas led both to the removal of some troops and to clashes between them and white citizens in El Paso and Galveston. Black enlisted men, moreover, left basic-training sites to serve in segregated outfits commanded by white officers, or went to duty posts where they found that the military assigned black personnel to marginal and menial tasks. Perhaps, a black poet best captured the anger:

> On a train in Texas, German prisoners eat
> With white American soldiers, seat by seat
> While black American soldiers sit apart,
> The white men eating meat, the black men heart.

The war created other situations that heightened racial tensions. Defense industries turned Fort Worth and Dallas into boom towns. The Gulf Coast, from Houston to Lake Charles, Louisiana, sprouted new factories as the petrochemical industry expanded to meet the demands of war. Texans left the rural countryside for jobs in these and other urban areas. For example, in 1939, 55 percent of all Texans lived in rural areas; in 1950, 60 percent of the population resided in cities. Black people joined this migration. Although they mostly took jobs that demanded unskilled labor, worked under segregated conditions, and made less pay in the same jobs than did whites, African Americans became, nevertheless, more visible and seemingly more of an economic threat to white workers. Some white Texans also feared that wartime rhetoric and military service might be refined into black Texans' demands for social and economic equality. In 1943, Beaumont witnessed an unruly white mob destroying and looting property in the black ghetto, allegedly beating and killing two black people. It took state and local law enforcement agencies twenty hours to restore order. Similar occurrences, although on a lesser scale, struck Houston and Port Arthur that year. Once again black aspirations met with white resistance and violence.

Long before World War II the black community had chafed under whites' charges of racial inferiority and the barriers of segregation. Black Texans, such as Antonio Maceo Smith of Dallas, organized African-American professional societies to encourage black pride and to fight for first-class citizenship. Many of these people, usually members of the black middle class, looked to the newly formed Progressive Voters League and the older National Association for the Advancement of Colored People (NAACP) as vehicles for advancing the cause of civil rights. African Americans in Texas, along with a few white, liberal allies, drew up a plan at the 1940 state NAACP convention to attack discrimination. Their ten-year goals aimed at ending the all-white primary, acquiring equal educational opportunities, and eradicating Jim Crow laws. The organization chose the courts as their battleground. Clearly the NAACP could expect little aid from local and state politicians. Moreover, black resistance through active confrontation provoked white violence—frequently condoned by law enforcement agencies—that destroyed the property of African Americans and threatened their lives. The riots during World War II reaffirmed the NAACP's convictions concerning the dire need for action.

The NAACP sought plaintiffs to challenge both the segregation of schools and the voting-discrimination laws. Individuals were not anxious to come forward. Such a volunteer would lose time, incur expenses, and risk the retaliation of whites. Indeed, if an African American became a civil rights plaintiff, whites identified that person as a troublemaker, an "uppity nigger," who faced possible loss of job, harassment of family and friends, and bodily harm from racial extremists. Of the two, voting rights and educational lawsuits, the NAACP could secure plaintiffs more easily for cases involving the former. White Texans seemingly resented social integration more than black political participation. For example, a poll of white Texans in 1946 stated that 44 percent believed that blacks should be allowed to vote in the Democratic primary. Furthermore, a volunteer for a voting-rights lawsuit could fade into anonymity after spending a relatively short amount of time in court; whereas a black who challenged educational segregation appeared in court and then had to face hostile whites when he or she attended the institution that had been sued for refusing to admit minorities. Rather than becoming invisible, the minority applicant became a target for expressions of prejudice.

Lonnie Smith, a black dentist in Houston and an active spokesman for civil rights, came forward in 1942 to challenge the all-white primary. The NAACP furnished him financial and legal aid. Their team included the African-American attorney W. J. Durham of Sherman, Carter Wesley, the publisher of the *Houston Informer* and a well-known civil rights activist, and Thurgood Marshall, a brilliant lawyer who would become the first black U.S. Supreme Court justice. The brief stated that white primaries disfranchised black Texans since, in Texas at the time, being barred from participation in Democratic party elections—the winner of which almost always won the general election—was tantamount to being barred from voting for state and federal officials. Therefore, all-white primaries violated the U.S. Constitution.

In *Smith* v. *Allwright* (1944) the Supreme Court agreed with the NAACP. The majority of white politicians and Texas newspapers responded by proposing defiance. Expediency dictated otherwise; astute Democrats in Texas realized that the rise of urban liberalism had changed their party. The Great Depression began the exodus of northern black voters from the party of Lincoln to the party of

Roosevelt. White liberal politicians, moreover, recognized the potential voting strength of black citizens. Thus decency and opportunism combined to produce northern statesmen such as Robert Wagner of New York, who proposed federal antilynching laws, endorsed black people's aims, and won elections. If the Democratic party in the North recognized the potential of black support, could southern politicians stray far behind? Both the liberal candidate for governor of Texas, Homer Rainey, and the conservative candidate, Beauford Jester, campaigned for black votes in the 1946 Democratic primary. Approximately 85 percent of the black voters supported Rainey, who lost the election.

Black Texans realized that the number of African-American voters needed to increase before they could wield political influence. With political clout would come white support for racial equality, or so black Texans supposed. Several obstacles stood between them and their goals: the poll tax still disfranchised the poor; African Americans had little experience in discerning political issues or the process of voting; and rural whites, particularly in East Texas, feared black political participation and used economic pressure and legal subterfuges to maintain the status quo.

Organizations to combat difficulties that potential African-American voters encountered grew in number and in size. The Progressive Voters League and the Texas Club of Democratic Voters disseminated information concerning voter registration and issues of major concern to black Texans. These coalitions conducted voter registration drives and endorsed liberal candidates and causes. In urban areas black leaders created councils or committees that could define political goals for the separate ghettos. These organizations worked toward increasing voter registration, approving candidates, and influencing locally elected officials. The federal courts aided the organizations in 1951 and 1953, when rulings eliminated local white citizens primaries in Harrison and Fort Bend Counties.

After 1953 the poll tax stood alone as the legal barrier to black voting. Polls showed that 71 percent of black Texans opposed the tax and that the majority of whites supported it. Most newspapers, representative of conservative white opinion, used a subtle argument to defend the poll tax: the money it garnered went to the public schools. Thus, the rationalization continued, poll taxes supported education for blacks as well as whites. But despite the wishes of most white Texans, the poll tax was doomed. Northern voters demanded its end as a requirement for federal elections. In 1964 the Twenty-fourth Amendment to the U.S. Constitution outlawed the poll tax as a qualification to vote for national officeholders. Texas kept the poll tax as a provision for voting in state elections until the Supreme Court ruled in 1966 that the restriction was unconstitutional.

Senate Bill 1 of the special session of the Texas legislature of 1966 established a very restrictive voter-registration law. The Supreme Court struck down this law in 1971. In addition, the federal Voting Rights Act of 1965 required the government to monitor and supervise registration of voters in the southern states. The Department of Justice had to approve of any changes in state election procedures where the percentage of minority voters seemed inordinately low. Congress extended the act twice in the 1970s, including the monitoring of Hispanic voters under the act's mandate, and ruled in 1982 that Texas should remain under special scrutiny. The registration of black voters in Texas increased from 35 percent of those eligible in 1960 to 56.8 percent in 1970 and to 68 percent (875,000)—or roughly 11 percent of the state's registered voters in 1988. In short, federal intervention has made black voters a force that office seekers must acknowledge in state politics.

The Supreme Court decisions of *Baker* v. *Carr* (1962) and *Reynolds* v. *Simms* (1964) asserted that the state legislatures must redistrict to conform to the principle of "one man, one vote." The decisions were the beginning of the switch of political power from the rural countryside and small cities to large urban areas. The change in voting patterns therefore combined with changes in registration laws to increase the number of black election officials. Barbara Jordan was elected to the state senate from Harris County in 1966. Jordan, who held a law degree from Boston University, became the first black state senator since 1881. Later, as the first black U.S. congresswoman, she earned national fame with her eloquent performance during the Watergate hearings. Two other African Americans, Curtis M. Graves, a graduate of Texas Southern University, and J. E. Lockridge, an attorney from Dallas, also won seats in the legislature in 1966. Lockridge received the endorsement of the conservative Democratic Committee for Responsible Government, an arm of the Dallas business community. The number of black elected officials in Texas in 1987 was 282, including a congressman and fourteen legislators.

The black population of Texas in 1990 comprised about 12.5 percent of the state's inhabitants. Obviously, if political power were to lead to equality, black voters needed to turn out voters and forge political coalitions with the more numerous white liberals and

Mexican Americans. In national elections about 90 percent of black voters supported Democratic candidates, aiding John F. Kennedy, Hubert H. Humphrey, Lyndon B. Johnson, and Jimmy Carter to win Texas's electoral votes. State elections elicited the same response from blacks: they voted for liberal candidates and then tended to support whichever Democrat won the primary.

Yet the political coalition of blacks, Hispanics, and liberal Anglos may never have coalesced. Blacks doubted that blue-collar workers and Mexican Americans would vote for an African American. Some black leaders expressed dismay that liberal Democrats voted for one of their own and then turned to a Republican, such as Paul Eggers, in 1968, when the conservative Preston Smith defeated the liberal Don Yarborough for the Democratic gubernatorial nomination, or when liberal Anglos deserted the party in 1972 to vote for La Raza rather than Dolph Briscoe. Furthermore, Mexican Americans and blacks competed for the same, usually substandard, jobs and experienced the same economic and racial tensions that have affected relations between all ethnic groups locked into poverty. The Vietnam War, moreover, strained political coalitions. Minorities were ambivalent about peace movements that protected middle-class (mostly white) college students even as thousands of blacks and Mexican Americans died in combat overseas.

The broadened franchise did, however, bring blacks more public political respect. Politicians, conservative and liberal, campaigned at black barbecues, spoke to African-American organizations, and avoided the racist tirades of hate that had marked too many pre–World War II speeches. The Texas Democratic party moderated its stands to accommodate the bloc of black voters. Potential African-American voting strength could defeat the rabid segregationist, but could it be mobilized to swing the election to moderates and liberals who endorsed black aspirations?

Throughout the 1970s and 1980s the question remained moot. Unlikely combinations of urban Republicans and minority groups fought rural legislators for a more equitable drawing of legislative and congressional districts, one that gave more representation to urban areas. Nevertheless there still existed in 1990, by which time the state's population was 80.5 percent urban, district boundaries drawn in such a way as to award a token seat to a ghetto, throw minority votes into majority white suburbs, or gerrymander legislative districts to protect certain rural legislators. Although the urban areas had responded more rapidly to the rights of black citizens, Dallas was still embroiled in a controversy about at-large council elections, which diluted minority voting strength in 1990. Some rural blacks feared that their actively campaigning or even voting encouraged white economic retaliation. Poverty ridden and often landless, they needed credit, jobs, medical care, welfare, and public services: white folks dispensed these "favors."

Moreover, to register to vote did not mean to cast a ballot. As the apathy of the 1970s set in, blacks as well as whites discovered fewer issues that pulled them to the polls. In the 1988 elections Texas's per capita turnout of registered voters ranked in the bottom 10 percent of all the states. Black voting was consistently (in terms of percentage of ballots cast by registered voters) lower than that of whites. In Texas, several commentators attributed Governor Bill Clements's victory in 1978 to the failure of urban blacks to vote. Some local candidates ran uncontested races that year, and no state controversies demanded affirmation or rejection. Black leaders could not muster their troops just to support a Democrat, John Hill. Pundits suggested that low voter turnout among minorities might also be attributable to the years of suffrage denial: these groups simply had no history of voting. Political scientists asserted that a likely indicator for voting behavior might well be one's parents' level of political participation. And in the case of Texas and other southern states, which led the nation in low voter turnout, a history of poverty and disfranchisement has long discouraged black voters.

The struggle for educational equality went hand-in-hand with the demand for the vote. Integration of the public schools met more white opposition than did black enfranchisement. Americans looked always to the public schools as an institution of social advancement, and in the minds of many whites, the prospect of racially mixed classrooms conjured up specters of collapsing morals, interracial marriages, and falling academic standards. Integration also implied racial equality, a concept most white Texans disputed. A poll taken in 1954 demonstrated that 80 percent of the state's Anglos opposed school integration.

The 1940 NAACP convention, which outlined a ten-year plan to eliminate segregation, recognized white attitudes. Consequently the strategy was first to challenge in court the state's election laws and then the constitutionality of separate schools. Thurgood Marshall believed that lawsuits that forced enrollment of blacks into professional and graduate schools would least antagonize whites. Therefore, after the *Smith* victory, Marshall, Maceo Smith, Wesley, and John J. Jones, president of the Texas State Conference of the NAACP, decided to begin litigation against a previously designated target, The University of Texas Law School. The executive committee of the NAACP instructed W. J. Durham to prepare a case and started a fund-raising drive to finance it. Then they began the next step—the search for a plaintiff.

It took from June until October 1945 to find the right person. He must possess special academic qualifications, a college degree, and a willingness to confront harsh prejudices that would disrupt his life. Talented black Texans could, of course, attend better, out-of-state law schools. And many chose that route rather than suffer a martyr's pain. The committee therefore needed a man who would pursue the cause to its end; he must not abandon the suit or fail to attend the university should that right be won. To the keen disappointment of the NAACP, plaintiffs in similar cases elsewhere had sometimes faltered. That autumn the committee announced its candidate, Heman Marion Sweatt, a Houston post-office employee.

A short, slight man who wore glasses, Sweatt was not physically imposing. Friends and fellow employees described him as introspective, calm, and intellectual. James L. Sweatt, Heman's father, taught school in Beaumont before moving to Houston to take a more lucrative job as a railway mail clerk. An early activist, the elder Sweatt organized the national Alliance of Postal Employees to fight discrimination against blacks in postal appointments, and he helped charter the first NAACP branch in Houston. He located his family in an isolated region that grew into a neighborhood dominated by whites. As a child, Heman Sweatt walked past all-white schools and parks to attend and play in segregated facilities. He grew up in a Jim Crow Texas that proscribed him to back seats on public transportation and to economic discrimination, first as a teacher and then as a postal employee. Witnessing prejudice firsthand and knowing people such as his father, who fought it, instilled in Sweatt a fierce idealism and a determination that his demeanor disguised.

After Sweatt volunteered to sue, the NAACP outlined its strategy. Durham and Smith agreed that the organization should finance the suit and Sweatt's educational expenses. For several reasons the lawyers were optimistic that the NAACP's national officers would agree to help fund and support Sweatt's case. Texas lacked professional school facilities for African Americans, and out-of-state scholarships were not a perfect alternative, as they did not eliminate the cost of travel or the hardships of homesickness. Moreover, blacks in Texas opposed segregation in education more vehemently than did those in other NAACP states. Thus the organization anticipated a measure of public and financial support. The leaders decided to file the suit after February 1946, assuming that the university would turn Sweatt away from Spring registration. Sweatt pretended that his enrollment request had nothing to do with the NAACP; rather, he wanted an education, and the organization, somewhat surprised at his petition, offered aid. Evidently, the plaintiff hoped that the subterfuge would focus attention on the merits of the suit and not on the NAACP.

The state, however, had expected that some such suit was imminent. As early as 1938 white newspapers pointed out the lack of graduate and professional courses for African Americans. By 1945 editorials warned that civil rights advocates contemplated law suits to create adequate educational opportunities for blacks. The legislature reacted in March by changing the name of Prairie View State Normal and Industrial College to Prairie View University. The bill authorized the university to offer professional courses to qualified black Texans. The legislature, however, did not appropriate funds for the new degree programs. Moreover, the university would not initiate the courses; a student specifically had to request that they do so. Black leaders considered the victory a hollow one and continued their drive for admission of black Texans to the state's white schools.

Sweatt filed his suit on May 16, 1946, in Judge Roy C. Archer's 126th District Court, Travis County. The plaintiff asked Archer to issue a writ of mandamus instructing University of Texas officials to allow Sweatt to enroll in the law school. The judge refused, but in effect told the state to establish a law school for black Texans. In response to the ruling, white politicians scurried around, hunting for potential black law schools. The Board of Regents of Texas A&M passed a resolution authorizing legal training for blacks in Houston. Two African-American attorneys agreed to teach the new curriculum in their law offices. No one applied. In March 1947, the legislature created Texas State University for Negroes, later to be called Texas Southern University, in Houston. The new university would offer a law degree. Pending the opening of the university, the state established a temporary law school in Austin: three University of Texas law professors composed the entire faculty; the library of the Texas Supreme Court became the law library; and the basement of a building on East 13th Street served as classrooms.

The deadline for registration was March 10, 1947. Again, no one applied. Yet, technically, the state had met Archer's instructions: a law school existed for black Texans.

Now the NAACP altered its strategy. The first legal brief, based on *Plessy* v. *Ferguson* (1896), demanded equal educational opportunities. The new brief asserted that segregation guaranteed inequality of the state's black citizens. The lawyers for Sweatt compared the difference in facilities between the two schools, pointing out that they were not equal, and introduced sociological evidence on the inequality created by segregation. The NAACP's legal team asserted that segregation limited the potential growth of an individual, damaged the potential of the black community, and branded black Texans as inferior. Furthermore the reputation of The University of Texas Law School ensured a prestigious law degree, thereby increasing its graduates' chances for success over those of degree holders from a segregated (and lesser) institution. Attorney General Price Daniel defended the educational facilities of the basement law school and charged that Sweatt wanted integration, not a law degree. Marshall and Durham felt that their case was the stronger for addressing the issue of Jim Crow rather than simply arguing that a segregated law school was inferior to the state university. They expressed no disappointment when Archer denied the petition. All along they assumed that the U.S. Supreme Court ultimately would decide the case. Three years later, on June 5, 1950, in a unanimous decision, the highest court in the nation concluded that to deny Sweatt entrance to The University of Texas Law School violated the Fourteenth Amendment.

State officials expressed no alarm. Three black Texans enrolled in graduate courses at The University of Texas that summer. African-American undergraduates entered Del Mar College in 1952. By 1955 The University of Texas and Southern Methodist University had followed a similar course. Most of the other all-white colleges were integrated by the end of the decade. The black students met limited hostility. A picket line in Beaumont in 1956, for example, tried to bar black freshmen from entering Lamar University. The tactic failed.

The failure of African Americans and other minorities to attend the state's major universities in numbers proportional to their population created political and social tensions that continue to exist. As more minority legislators and their supporters went to Austin and voted on appropriation bills, the universities became more concerned about recruiting minority students and faculty.

The federal government applied pressure upon state universities, too, since government grants depended partially upon equal hiring and educational opportunities. In 1983 the state submitted the Texas Equal Opportunity Plan for Higher Education, which pledged to increase minority enrollment, to the U.S. Department of Education.

Minorities expressed particular discontent with the two largest state universities, Texas A&M and The University of Texas, where they perceived that subtle forms of discrimination remained. The University of Texas, for example, maintained segregated dormitories until 1965, abolished dormitory requirements for freshmen rather than face the issue of integration, and fielded the last all-white national championship football team in 1969. The university hired its first black professor in 1964, but in 1990 the former all-white colleges still lacked a substantial number of African-American teachers and administrators. Citing these and other examples of discrimination, a Mexican-American legislator, with support of black allies, threatened to sue the state if the universities did not undertake extensive programs of recruitment and retention of minority students and faculty. The universities had not met the desired quotas in 1990. Overall, Texas senior institutions enrolled about 55 percent of the state's mandated goal for blacks and 66 percent for Hispanics. The Bureau of Census reported, moreover, that in 1988, 23 percent of white high school graduates, as compared to 10.8 percent of black graduates, and 19 percent of Mexican-American graduates intended to enroll in college.

Certainly college administrators and faculties have worked hard to increase the recruitment and retention of minorities on Texas campuses. However, many universities throughout the state and the nation were still reporting ugly incidents of racial intolerance late in the 1980s. Particularly disappointing has been The University of Texas, where charges of racial slurs and lack of sensitivity to issues of race led to an investigation of fraternities and demands from student demonstrators that the administration undertake a more active role to root out racism. Although that was the most obvious example on a college campus in Texas, at other schools, including Texas A&M University, there have been incidents of anti–African American feelings on the part of some members of the white student body.

Nonetheless, the *Sweatt* case did open more educational opportunities for black Texans. Heman Sweatt intended it to do so. He thought of himself as heading a cause for all members of his race, but the resulting pressure on him was great. During the years he waited for the Supreme Court decision, he developed ulcers and could no longer work at the post office. Publicity from the suit spurred racists to engage in acts of vandalism against him and to harass him with obscene telephone calls. The resulting tensions disrupted his marriage, and eventually his wife filed for a divorce. By the time he entered law school, at age thirty-seven, he was drained emotionally and physically. Most students and professors either befriended or ignored him, but instances of on-campus racial hostility did occur—someone slashed the tires of his car and a few students made abusive comments—which added to his discontent. Like many fellow students, he did poorly his first year. In 1952 he returned to Houston, having failed to complete law school. Later, after the sense of failure waned, Sweatt moved to Atlanta and earned a degree in social work. He remained proud of his efforts to confront segregation.

The *Sweatt* case also challenged more than segregation in universities. After the Supreme Court's definition of "separate but equal" overturned the *Plessy* decision, Marshall urged that the NAACP attack all Jim Crow education. To the most casual observer it should have been clear that southern education was separate but a long way from equal. In Texas as late as 1960 some black teachers received less pay than their white counterparts. Black students attended schools deficient in the ranges of courses offered and which frequently lacked gymnasiums, laboratories, up-to-date textbooks, counselors, and health facilities. Library holdings in white schools doubled those in black schools. School districts spent less money on the construction and maintenance of black schools, which deteriorated faster because of poor building materials and lack of funds for routine repairs. The Court considered these and other facts when it issued a unanimous decision on May 17, 1954, "that in the field of public education the doctrine of 'separate but equal' has no place. Separate educational facilities are inherently unequal." Thus, *Brown* v. *Topeka Board of Education* affected seventeen states.

The reaction of state officials to Brown varied. Some governors in the Deep South immediately proposed resistance. Most officials in the Border South took a more moderate stand. Governor Allan Shivers of Texas counseled against racial demagoguery but promised to resist integration by all legal means. In November 1954, the Court announced that it would open hearings on methods for carrying out and enforcing racial integration. The NAACP asked for total desegregation by 1956; southern states, including Texas, filed briefs seeking an indefinite stay of execution. In April 1955, the Court ruled that desegregation must begin with "all deliberate speed." This vague, long-delayed decision met with howls of protest from the South. Thus began the campaign of massive resistance.

Massive resistance, the rallying cry against integration, entailed passing legislative acts that delayed or defeated school desegregation in the eleven ex-Confederate states. Some districts, as in Prince Edwards County, Virginia, went so far as to abolish their public school systems. Texans flirted with interposition. Governor Shivers and Attorney General John Ben Shepperd vigorously supported interposition in public speeches. The governor even recommended that the South force the Democratic party to include an endorsement of interposition legislation in its 1956 platform.

A majority of white Texans agreed with Shivers's efforts. A public opinion poll taken after the *Brown* decision demonstrated that 80 percent of the white population opposed public school integration. Hoping to capitalize on this attitude, local groups organized White Citizens' Councils. Dr. B. E. Masters, president emeritus of Kilgore Junior College, founded the first chapter in Kilgore during the summer of 1955. The organization grew spasmodically, primarily in East Texas. During the spring of 1956 the councils, claiming twenty thousand members, combined with the Texas Referendum Committee to collect signatures on a petition to force the Democratic party to include three segregation propositions on its ballot. Texas voters overwhelmingly endorsed the measures in the primary in July 1956, and they became part of the state Democratic party platform.

Segregationists, however, were losing their influence in the executive branch. The Shivers forces made segregation and interposition the key issues in the fight for control of the state Democratic party in 1956. An opposition moderate-loyalist-liberal coalition emerged. Led by Lyndon Johnson, then majority leader of the U.S. Senate, and Speaker of the House Sam Rayburn, this disparate group had in common only loyalty to the Democratic party and opposition to Shiverscrats—Democratic supporters of Shivers who had followed his lead to support Republican Dwight David Eisenhower for president in 1952 and 1956, but who had endorsed conservative Democrats rather than Republicans for state offices. In the Texas Democratic convention in May, the moderates routed the governor's forces. Shivers did not seek reelection, and Johnson-Rayburn moderates allied with Price Daniel, a conservative but not a Shiverscrat, and barred true liberals from positions of power in the party. Consensus politics had won, and little had changed. Daniel, who became governor, negated any possibility that the state would either endorse interposition or comply with the desegregation decision.

The election of Daniel did not eliminate the previously heavy vote for segregation. In addition Shivers, while governor, had created an Advisory Committee on Segregation in the Public Schools. He loaded the committee with ultraconservatives and instructed it to report on methods to prevent "forced integration." Late in 1956 the committee recommended twenty-one profoundly racist and conservative proposals. For example, one advocated a return to complete segregation of public education. Among the proposals, two passed the legislature. One required local voter approval for integration of public schools, authorizing the withholding of state funds if such an action were not taken. The other, concerning pupil placement, allowed local officials to assign students to specific schools. Other bills died in committee, and Daniel unenthusiastically signed the two that the legislature passed, which later were declared unconstitutional. Nevertheless, one authority maintained that the two new laws stopped progress toward integration for the remainder of the decade.

Even if they did not halt forever the demand for integration, the laws certainly signified that state officials did not intend to encourage desegregation. Local officials, hence, with the state's blessings, could evade the *Brown* decision. Some eighty-four districts, all in the western part of the state, desegregated in 1955. In the fall of 1956, Shivers dispatched Rangers to Texarkana Junior College and Mansfield High School to prevent violence during attempts at integration. When questioned about his actions, the governor suggested that the Supreme Court might try to enforce its decisions.

Thus began the pattern: state officials did nothing to comply with the constitutional demand that civil rights be accorded to black Texans; the federal courts ruled time and time again that local districts would have to integrate. The judiciary increased pressures on school districts that continued to evade the law, first by stair-step integration, then through busing orders. Spokespersons for white Texans condemned the courts. Newspapers charged that the Fourteenth Amendment, ratified while the southern states were undergoing Reconstruction, was somehow illegal. White publications excoriated the Warren Court for liberally deviating from the law by using sociological data rather than legal precedents, and for allegedly usurping legislative prerogative by interfering with states' rights. As the Court's activism grew—"one man, one vote" and the *Miranda* decisions, for example—criticism of the judges increased as well. Finally, it became popular to say that federal courts, not elected officials, governed the nation. Indeed, Richard Nixon won the presidency in 1968 with a campaign that included a promise to appoint men of conservative philosophy to the Supreme Court. Yet much of the controversy surrounding the judiciary would have abated if state legislatures had enacted laws to desegregate with all due speed.

Statistics refute contentions that Texas willingly integrated public schools. Five years after the *Brown* decision, Houston, Dallas, and most East Texas school districts continued segregation. In 1964 only 5 percent of black Texans attended formerly all-white schools. That year Congress passed a Civil Rights Act that allowed the withdrawing of federal funds from segregated schools, and local districts finally began to comply with the law. In 1967, 47 percent of black pupils were enrolled in integrated institutions. Still, fifteen years after the Brown decision, 65 percent of black pupils went to predominantly black schools. In large metropolitan areas the figure topped 90 percent. District courts issued decisions designed to modify segregation patterns. They paired schools, evaluated magnet-school concepts, issued desegregation orders, and after 1971 approved busing as a way to achieve racial balance. For the rest of the decade political battles were waged over the issue of busing children to schools outside their home district.

Its promises to prevent such actions and to curb the powers of the Supreme Court encouraged the growth of the Republican Party in Texas. By the Reagan years, 1981–1989, most white males in the state endorsed the Republicans. Since most African Americans remained Democrats, Republicans could simply back away from demands that public schools continue to push for integration. In general, smaller communities have had to comply with the newer court rulings; large metropolitan areas, where wide-scale busing would have been needed to integrate the schools, have not always done so. Dallas challenged the Fifth U.S. Circuit Court's decision in 1976 to eliminate the fifty single-race city schools on the grounds that compliance with the order required too much busing. The case remained in the courts throughout the next decade.

The leadership of Dallas and other large Texas cities expressed more interest in accommodating minorities after the inner cities had majority populations. Nationally the Republican party, with its strength in the suburbs, has shown little interest in integrating single-race schools. In addition, the cut in federal monies targeted for education has left many of the inner-city schools bereft of resources to improve their current facilities. A recent list of the twenty most highly segregated school systems in the country includes Dallas, Houston, and Fort Worth, as well as other large southern metropolises and northern cities such as Cleveland, New York, and Detroit. Rather than busing, city leaders cited the need for more school funds and searched for ways to reduce the dropout rate among minority students. It is estimated that more than one-third of Texas students will not graduate from high school. Moreover, the state was under court order (as of 1990) to equalize funding for local school districts, an act that entailed both considerable expense and much political debate. Segregation, by law, ended, but segregation by race and class continues, and conflicts over this condition will intensify in the future.

In general Texans adapted to court-ordered integration better than did most of the other ex-Confederate states. For a time, school boards continued to represent their white constituency, and the threat of integration encouraged "white flight" to the suburbs, rumors of boycotts of the public schools, and threats of public funding of private academies. Some acts of violence to prevent integration did occur, particularly in East Texas, but the schools remained open. One reason may have been that conservative Texas wanted no incidents such as had occurred in Little Rock in 1957 or New Orleans in 1960 to harm its positive business climate. The struggle for civil rights in the 1970s took a more subtle twist, manifested in dress codes, exclusivity of student offices and organizations, teacher transfers, and administrative decisions aimed at excluding black participation both in official and extracurricular school activities. Honors courses were instituted, consequently segregating classrooms in integrated schools. Fights and verbal confrontations broke out between black and white students. Some white parents identified busing and integration as the cause of a wide range of new ills in the school systems—a decline in SAT scores, drug use, an increase in discipline cases, and a rise in educational expenses. Moderates urged African Americans to temper their demands.

Martin Luther King, Jr., said in 1962, "I have almost reached the regrettable conclusion that the Negroes' greatest stumbling block in the stride toward freedom is not the White-Citizens' Council or the Ku Klux Klan, but the white moderate who is more devoted to order than to justice." For many black Texans and other African Americans, to speak of voucher systems for schools or for Republican appointments to the courts to rule against civil rights legislation and integration orders is simply to abandon earlier commitments to civil rights.

King spoke of more than integration of education. By the 1960s the civil rights crusade had entered a new period of direct confrontation. On December 1, 1955, Rosa Parks refused to move to the back of a bus in Montgomery, Alabama. The age of peaceful resistance was born. Five years later, in Greensboro, North Carolina, four black students from North Carolina Agricultural and Technical College sat down at the lunch counter in Woolworth's and, after the waitress refused to serve them, remained in their seats, initiating the "sit-in." That summer black and white students began the Freedom Rides, moving into the Deep South to register voters and challenge segregated accommodations. Their efforts called forth, once again, violent reactions, and they were jailed, beaten, murdered, and portrayed on television as martyrs. The apex of this phase came with the March on Washington in 1963, the assassination of President John F. Kennedy, and the passage of the Civil Rights Act of 1964 and the Voting Rights Act of 1965.

Black and white Texans participated in the sit-ins. Beginning in college communities, civil rights demonstrators forced the integration of local establishments. In 1960 black students at Wiley and Bishop Colleges participated in nonviolent demonstrations. The next year students picketed establishments in Denton and Austin. Sit-ins occurred throughout the state in 1962. Local and state politicians, now that blacks voted, mostly kept quiet concerning sit-ins. However hostile they might have been, local authorities avoided the violence that shook the Deep South. Some professors and students encountered administrative pressures in the form of expulsion or economic reprisals as a means of limiting their civil rights activities. Most restaurants, hotels, and other private facilities had desegregated early in the 1960s. The Civil Rights Act of 1964 and five state acts in 1969 ended legal segregation in Texas. The civil rights movement had eliminated de jure segregation, and moderate and liberal whites congratulated themselves.

But by 1966 the civil rights movement took a new turn. Young blacks adopted the cry of black power, turned away from nonviolence, and demanded an end to de facto segregation. They wanted a larger share of America's opportunities, more respect, and a termination of racism in the North. New organizations such as the Black Panthers and the Muslims claimed their allegiance. The Student Nonviolent Coordinating Committee (SNCC) and the Congress of Racial Equality (CORE) abandoned black-white coalitions as being unproductive. Whites, they said, had a Tarzan complex; that is, they wanted to fill only leadership roles in the movement. On August 12, 1965, after a series of clashes between police officers and blacks, fire bombings began in the Watts ghetto of Los Angeles. More police officers and, later, National Guardsmen moved in. Thirty-four people died, all of whom were black. The "long hot" summers from 1965 to 1968 dominated the media, as ghetto after ghetto erupted into flames and violence. White moderates and liberals charged that the movement had gone too far. Property destruction, they said, could not be condoned.

No ghettos burned in Texas, but riots did occur there. In 1967, at Texas Southern University, students gathered on the campus to debate mounting grievances over public school discipline and police harassment in the ghettos. When police arrived on the scene, they were met with flying bottles and stones. Later that evening a shot was fired. The police responded by opening fire on the dorm from which they assumed the shot had come. The gunfire continued all night. At 2:00 P.M. the next day the officers charged the dorms and arrested 448 students, doing considerable damage to property and roughing up innocent bystanders. A Houston grand jury no-billed the police department and indicted five student activists for murder for having incited a riot that killed Policeman Louis Kuba (who may have died from a police bullet). For lack of evidence, the case never came to trial.

Relations between the African-American community and the Houston Police Department worsened. Blacks charged the police with brutality and illegal searches of citizens and homes in 1969 and 1970. A group similar to the Black Panthers, Peoples Party II, was organized in the summer of 1970. Members raised money for free-breakfast programs, distributed used clothing to the impoverished, and monitored reports of police brutality. The police considered them a revolutionary group. A confrontation occurred in July 1970, after the arrest of two party members in front of the organization's headquarters. Plainclothesmen on a nearby roof, claiming that they were fired upon, killed Carl Hampton, the party's chairman. African Americans reported that the police fired first. The media and white opinion, however, backed the Houston Police Department.

Black people's negative impressions of law enforcement agencies were reinforced in other areas. Ernie McMillan and Matthew Johnson, SNCC leaders, led boycotts against grocery stores in the

Dallas ghetto. A local court sentenced them to ten years for doing $211 worth of damage to one store. Riots protesting the clearly unfair sentencing erupted in Lubbock, Midland, and Denton, but the protesters were treated unsympathetically by local citizens and the police. Lee Otis Johnson, a black activist at Texas Southern University, was sentenced to thirty years for allegedly passing an undercover police officer a marijuana cigarette. Blacks believed that these and other examples demonstrated a continued white opposition to black aspirations. Whites believed that outside agitators unnecessarily increased black discontent. White Texans joined the national consensus, which argued that the federal government had gone too far in support of black demands for social and economic equality. By 1971 the so-called Second Reconstruction ended, and white opposition to the civil rights movement intensified.

What had the Second Reconstruction accomplished? De jure segregation ended, but schools were not completely integrated. The Black Power movement had made administrators more aware of black pride, colleges offered black studies programs, and black athletes and cheerleaders now appeared on college and high school campuses. It still was not clear, however, that whites appreciated African-American culture or that any voluntary integration would have occurred without governmental pressure. Facilities, thus, were no longer segregated, nor were they integrated either. Furthermore, in the most important of all attainments, income, blacks lagged behind.

The economic status of black Texans improved somewhat from 1965 to 1975, when many black families joined the middle class. Since the mid-1970s, however, the income level of African Americans in Texas has not advanced much, and by 1992 the number of blacks unemployed, the number of blacks living below the poverty line, and the percentage of black teenagers unemployed more than doubled that of whites in each category. Economic competition among the unskilled and undereducated for meager jobs has been complicated by the continued immigration of Latinos into the state. Since 1965 the Tejano population has grown. In 1994 it was estimated that people with Hispanic surnames comprised roughly 23 percent of the total number of Texans (18.4 million), and the percentage increase of Latinos is expected to rise. African Americans comprised 11.8 percent of the Texas population. Rather than the emergence of a so-called Rainbow Coalition to shape Texas politics, tensions between black Texans and Tejanos have heightened. Although both groups tend to vote for Democratic candidates, on the local level, particularly in larger cities, their respective candidates contest each other for positions on school boards, city councils, and other elective bodies. Leaders of both groups argued that such competition must end if minorities were to realize the full potential of their political leverage. The number of black officeholders in the state increased from 45 in 1971 to 472 in 1993, and in larger cities some minorities began to wield citywide power. In 1995 Ron Kirk won the race for mayor in Dallas, a city with a 51 percent minority population, and became the first African-American mayor of a major Texas metropolis. Nevertheless, political competition among minorities reflected the competition for marginal jobs and made interethnic coalitions precarious.

The efforts to respond to limitations on educational equality for minorities continued as some educators argued that the holding of low-paying jobs represented poor education rather than race and ethnicity. The problems with desegregating and decreasing the high school drop-out rates among black Texans were complicated by the migration of so many whites to the suburbs, leaving inner cities both poor and with a declining tax base. Tri-ethnic committees to assist urban school boards in desegregating began to appear in the 1980s. School boards attempted to address minority problems by offering special classes and services to retain at-risk (of dropping out) children. Many educators argued that more minority teachers were needed, but in 1995 nearly one-half of Texas schools had no African-American instructors and only 7 percent of the recently certified teachers that year were black. For whatever reason the drop-out rate of black Texans (23 percent) almost doubled the rate of whites in 1990.

That same year closed with a presidential veto of a civil rights act intended to restore some of the rights that had eroded due to unfavorable court decisions. The Fifth U.S. Circuit Court dealt the most recent setback to affirmative action. Three judges, all Republican appointees, ruled in the 1996 *Hopwood* case that Texas and Mississippi public institutions of higher education cannot consider the race or ethnicity of an applicant for either admission or financial aid. University administrators complained that race was only one of a myriad of factors that influenced admission policies—along with grades, test scores, and athletic ability, for example. Nevertheless Attorney General Dan Morales ruled that the court's decision had the force of law and that Texas institutions must comply with it. On the other hand, Mississippi held that its public colleges did not have to enforce the ruling until all legal appeals had failed. In startling contrast to the post–*Brown* decision climate in Texas, all forces within the state have decided rapidly to obey a court mandate concerning public education.

The dawn of the new century poses a strange double vision for African Americans in Texas. On one hand, black Texans have achieved a new level of acceptance. A mere forty years ago blacks could not travel, stay, eat, work, live, vote, or attend school where they chose to in Texas or in many other states. Now African Americans legally can do all of those things. On the other hand, racial prejudice continues; and black Texans are losing in the race for income and face a growing hostility in educational institutions that supposedly were the key to ending prejudice in our society. Everything changes, and nothing changes at all. Is that not what author Kurt Vonnegut said? Or did he say, "To read history is to weep"?

Suggested Reading

Barr, Alwyn. *Black Texans*. Austin: Pemberton Press, 1973.

Bartley, Numan V. *The Rise of Massive Resistance*. Baton Rouge: Louisiana State University Press, 1970.

Gillette, Michael L. "Heman Marion Sweatt: Civil Rights Plaintiff" in *Black Leaders: Texans for their Times*. Edited by Alwyn Barr and Robert A. Calvert. Austin: Texas State Historical Association, 1987.

Green, George N. *The Establishment in Texas Politics*. Westport, CT: Greenwood Press, Inc., 1979.

Hodgson, Godfrey, and Douglas T. Miller. *America in Our Time*. New York: Doubleday, 1976.

Jordan, Barbara, and Shelby Heron. *Barbara Jordan: A Self Portrait*. Garden City, NY: Doubleday, 1979.

Nowak, Marion. *The Fifties*. New York: Doubleday, 1977.

Sapper, Neil G. "A Survey of the History of the Black People of Texas, 1930–1954." Ph.D. diss., Texas Tech University, 1972.

Weeks, O. Douglas. *Texas One-Party Politics in 1956*. Austin: University of Texas Press, 1957.

———. *Texas in the 1960 Presidential Election*. Austin: University of Texas Press, 1961.

———. *Texas in 1964: A One-Party State Again*. Austin: University of Texas Press, 1965.

Katherine Stinson being sworn in as an airmail pilot by Postmaster George D. Armistad in front of a Wright model "B" airplane, San Antonio, Texas, May 14, 1915. *Courtesy of the Institute of Texan Cultures,* San Antonio Light Collection, *#85-27.*

CHAPTER FOURTEEN

Women in Texas: A Pioneer Spirit

Linda S. Hudson

AS DIVERSE AS THE LANDSCAPE AND AS UN-
predictable as the weather, Texas women are depicted in songs,
novels, and folktales as being strong and unconventional. Some
have suggested that features of Spanish law gave women in Texas
more freedoms and opportunities than their counterparts in states
under English common law. Some point out that the cultural and
ethnic mosaic that developed early in Texas history exposed women
to different lifestyles and ideas. Still others assert that the dangers
and challenges posed by the state's frontier heritage galvanized in
generations of Texas women a "can-do-anything" spirit.

Indeed, in each phase of Texas colonial history—the French,
Spanish, Mexican, and Anglo eras—during the years of the Republic, and into early statehood, Texas women not only performed traditional female roles but shared with men in the protection of family and property. Whenever men left home to go to war, confront
intruders or political enemies, hunt wild game, or obtain supplies
or conduct business, wives, mothers, daughters, and other female
members of household shouldered the responsibility of maintaining and defending the homestead—be it a sod house in a sea of
prairie grass or a sprawling rancho comprising several buildings.
Regardless of race or economic class, women worked hard to ensure the survival of their families, homes, and enterprises.

This pattern of leadership survived the close of the frontier in
the nineteenth century and blossomed in the reforms of the Progressive Era (1900–1917), when certain groups of women enlarged
their prescribed sphere of influence. While many men resisted this
new interpretation of women's domain, others accepted it, electing female candidates to public office even before women had
gained the right to vote. With the adoption of the Nineteenth Amendment in 1920, American women realized the potential for full po-

litical participation. Texas women not only exercised their right to vote but obtained city, state, and national offices.

* * *

The story of Texas women begins long before they started to break societal restraints and join men as reformers, educators, politicians, and professionals. Indeed, the story predates even the arrival of the first Europeans in Texas. Hundreds of names identify the tribes, clans, and family groups of Indian peoples—each with a different culture and lifestyle shaped by their food supply—that once occupied Texas. Much of what we know about their lifestyles in the sixteenth and seventeenth centuries comes from accounts of European explorers and missionaries.

The first Native group that Spaniards encountered in Texas was the Karankawa, a nomadic people who migrated between the barrier islands and the Gulf Coastal Plains between present-day Galveston and Corpus Christi. These Indians ate fish, turtles, and other food they carried in baskets and earthen pots. Their shelters were crude animal-skin lean-tos, their bedding, rush mats. According to the journal of Alvar Núñez Cabeza de Vaca—a Spaniard shipwrecked along with a handful of companions on the Texas coast in 1528 who lived among the Indians for six years before making it to New Spain—Karankawa women had few rights and a lowly status. He reported that these women wore two-piece dresses fashioned from deerskins. In the winter, they waded into the bays to dig up the roots of water plants, which they cooked for the family meal. They supplemented this fare with wild fruits, nuts, and berries.

Next, Cabeza de Vaca met the Coahuiltecans, with whom he lived for eighteen months as he and his companions wandered across Texas and the Southwest. He noted that several related clans of these hunter-gatherers, ranging the South Texas Plains between the Rio Grande and the Edwards Plateau in search of food, shared a common language. While the men generally wore no clothes, the women wore animal-skin skirts. According to Cabeza de Vaca, the Coahuiltecan sometimes practiced female infanticide by throwing baby girls out to hungry dogs or alligators. Among the Coahuiltecan, men customarily purchased their wives from members of other bands, usually for useful items such as bows and arrows or fishing nets. When traveling from camp to camp, women bore most of the burden of lugging along the family belongings. The band might leave behind those women who fell ill or grew too old to carry their load. Nevertheless, Cabeza de Vaca also noted that among the

Coahuiltecan, women acted as peacemakers and universal traders between tribes, even in times of war.

Another Spanish explorer, Francisco Vásquez de Coronado, made mention of Indian women of *El Llano Estacado* (the Staked Plains) in his report to King Charles I of Spain in 1541. Coronado wrote that the *Querecho* (Comanche) followed the buffalo, using every part of the animals for food, clothes, shelter, and tools. After men killed the beasts, it fell to the women and children to skin, dress, and tan the hides, which they fashioned into clothes or tee-pees. Like their counterparts in other Texas tribes, Comanche women moved most of the family belongings by hand, sometimes dragging items behind them. Women also did the cooking. They fueled cooking and heating fires in their teepees with dried buffalo dung. Any leftover scraps of food they fed to the dogs. Coronado recorded that Comanche women were much like the Moorish women of North Africa, presumably referring to the relative level of freedom Comanche women enjoyed.

The Caddo of the East Texas woodlands consisted of some twenty-five or thirty groups with a common language and culture. Considered by some as the most culturally advanced of the Texas Indians, the Caddo were an agricultural people with stable villages. Caddo women enjoyed a higher status than their counterparts in other Texas tribes. One Caddo subgroup, the Tejas, from which Texas derives its name, initially welcomed Spanish missionaries. In the 1760s, Spanish priests wrote an account of a female chief, Santa Adiva, whom they encountered in Tejas country. While the account is not highly detailed, it states that Santa Adiva had several hus-bands and ruled over many tribal members.

More than a century after Spanish explorers first visited Texas, Europeans began to settle on the far northern frontier of New Spain. Whether French, Spanish, Mexican, or Anglo, women in this un-forgiving environment faced similar hardships and difficulties in making a home and caring for a family. Throughout each cultural era of Texas history, pioneer women performed many tasks. House were typically crude, made of logs, adobe, or stones; "dugout" homes were carved into hillsides. Settlers consumed whatever family members could hunt or gather locally or grow in small plots. Women typically grew corn—the most productive food crop—in family gar-dens and prepared it in many different ways, ground, boiled, roasted, baked, or fried. It remained a staple of the diets of Texans for many generations. Clothing consisted of whatever articles women could construct from available materials, whether buckskin, locally raised wool or cotton—both of which had to be spun into thread before being placed in looms and woven into cloth—or manufactured cloth imported at great expense. In remote settings, professional medical care was nonexistent, so women relied on home remedies and what few medicines they had managed to bring along to the frontier.

The first European women to arrive in Texas were members, along with men and children, of a French colony led by the explorer René Robert Cavelier, Sieur de La Salle. With a group of 150 persons, La Salle established Fort Saint Louis near Lavaca Bay in 1685. The colonists found life on the Texas coast extremely difficult. La Salle left the fort with several men in search of help for the struggling colony. He never returned. Those who remained behind suffered repeated Indian attacks. In 1688 Gabriel Minime gave birth to the first European child born in Texas. Soon thereafter Karankawa raiders smashed her newborn's head against a tree before killing her. The Indians killed everyone at the fort with the exception of four boys and one girl, the Talon siblings, whom they took into their tribe temporarily. The young girl, Marie-Madeleine Talon, related the ordeal suffered by the colonists. In the meantime, Spanish officials had dispatched a military contingent led by Alonzo De León to investigate rumors of a French colony in Texas. But by the time the expedition arrived from Mexico, the colony had been destroyed by the Karankawas. De León found the French children living with the Indians and took them back with him to Mexico.

This intrusion by the French alarmed officials in New Spain, prompting them to promote Spanish settlement in Texas. In 1718, Franciscan priests established the Mission San Antonio de Valero on the San Antonio River. Three years later the Spanish secured control of the Bay of Espíritu Santo, on which they built a fort and, in the next year, a mission known as La Bahía. Later they moved the mission La Bahía farther inland, near present-day Goliad. Seven Indian families, bringing with them sheep, goats, chickens, mules, and horses, founded the tiny village known as San Antonio near the mission. In 1722, fifty more families relocated in San Antonio from the Rio Grande area. By 1730, Texas had three cities, Los Adaes, La Bahía, and San Antonio, but the province produced few trade goods. Families had to make all of the tools, clothes, and furnishings they needed—tasks in which women shared equally with men.

With titles of nobility as enticement, fifteen families relocated from the Spanish-controlled Canary Islands (off the coast of Africa) to San Antonio in the spring of 1731. María Rosa Padrón was the first child born to these settlers in Texas. Eventually, some of the Spanish settlers in Texas grew prosperous as ranchers, and several women assumed leadership roles in the Rio Grande Valley. One such figure was Rosa María Hinojosa de Ballí, the first cattle queen of Texas, who lived with her husband near present-day Harlingen. After her husband died, she increased her land holdings. By 1803, Rosa María, hailed by family and community members as "La Patrona," owned more than 1 million acres. Her ranching domain stretched across five present-day Texas counties from Padre Island westward.

Under Spanish law, Texas women enjoyed a greater measure of freedom and opportunity than women in the United States. For example, English common law gave men control over women from birth to death. In Texas, tenets of Spanish law carried over and merged with the laws of the state in 1846. Single women had control of their property, and married women retained, as separate property, inheritances received before or during marriage. Any increase in the joint wealth of husband and wife acquired during the marriage was shared equally. Texas women also could make contracts, sue or be sued in court, and make wills.

A census taken in the 1790s listed only about three thousand persons (including mission Indians) living in Texas. Persons of mixed Indian, Spanish, and African ancestry composed some 15 percent of this population. All of those who had settled in Texas by the turn of the nineteenth century faced hardships. Homesteads along the western line of settlement suffered raids and attacks from Comanche and Apache warriors. In 1812, rebels of the Gutiérrez-Magee expedition attempted unsuccessfully to liberate Texas from Spain. In 1813, some Texas settlers joined the invaders in their revolt. One such group was the Arocha family, who were prominent among the Canary Islanders in San Antonio. At the Battle of Medina, the army of General José Joaquín Arredondo defeated the insurgents. For their role in the revolt, the Arocha men faced execution, while Arredondo put the Arocha women, along with their counterparts in the community, to work as a punishment for their role in the insurgency. Reportedly, the general forced the women of San Antonio to produce thirty-five thousand tortillas each day to feed his troops. Angry over having been made a slave of the Mexican forces, Josepha de Arocha issued a reward of 500 pesos for the paunch of Arredondo, out of which, she declared, she would make a drum. When the general got wind of this audacious decree, he had Josepha arrested and jailed.

Citing the activities of La Salle, some Americans contended that Texas should have been included in the territory sold to the United States by France in 1803. After the Adams-Onís Treaty of 1819 set the international border between the United States and Spain at the Sabine River, James Long of Natchez, Mississippi, tried to liberate Texas from Spain. With three hundred men and his wife Jane, Long set up headquarters in Nacogdoches. Long and his fellow filibusters were driven back into Louisiana. James and Jane Long returned to Texas in 1820, this time landing at Point Bolivar in Galveston Bay, where James left the pregnant Jane while he attempted another insurgent operation. Later Jane learned of his arrest and death. In the meantime Jane, alone on Bolivar except for her little daughter Ann and a black servant girl named Kian, struggled to survive the winter. Jane and Kian managed to fend off attacks by Indians and forage along the frigid shores for food. In December, Jane, with Kian attending her, gave birth to a girl. After returning to Mississippi, Jane Long arrived in Texas yet again—this time with Stephen F. Austin as one of the first legal Anglo settlers in Mexican Texas.

Other women who came to Texas in the 1820s generally adopted the lifestyles of the Spanish, Mexican, and Indian women already living there. One successful immigrant couple was Martín De León and his wife Patrícia, who led a group of settlers to Texas from Mexico and established the only permanent Mexican colony in Texas. The De Leóns founded Victoria, the colony's principal settlement. Although the De León home was built of rough-hewn logs, it contained fine furniture and fixtures and served as a community center of art and culture. Patrícia also directed the construction of church and school buildings. After Martín died of cholera in 1833, Patrícia carried on the family ranching business. She later supported Texas Independence by smuggling guns and supplies from New Orleans for Texan forces.

Another of Austin's "Old Three Hundred" settlers was Jesse Burnam, who gained fame as an Indian fighter and Texas patriot. In 1824, he established Burnam's Ferry on the bank of the Colorado River near present-day La Grange. Burnam arrived in Texas with several daughters. The Burnam girls wore deerskin dresses and learned to grow white Mexican corn, which they made into bread. Generally, Anglo women fed their families milk and poultry raised in their own pastures and vegetables from small garden plots.

A few Anglo families settled near friendly Indians, and some of these whites recorded their impressions of Native peoples. Annie

Fisher Harris, daughter of Republic of Texas Navy Secretary Samuel Rhodes Fisher, recalled in her memoirs that Karankawa women who lived near Matagorda in 1833 had Spanish names and spoke Spanish, but that they wore only deerskin skirts and large leaf wreaths around their necks. Annie and her brother played with the Indian children when their mothers came to trade at Grasmeyer's, the local general store. At night, the Anglo residents of Matagorda could hear the beat of drums as Indians sang and danced in the moonlight in nearby encampments.

The Texas frontier was a multicultural society on the eve of the Texas Revolution. Contrary to the American statutes, Spanish law did not prohibit mixed-race marriages in Texas. Consequently, Texas attracted some racially mixed couples from the United States. For example, William Goyens of Nacogdoches, a black man with a white wife, migrated to Texas from Louisiana, and John Webber of Massachusetts, a white man with a black wife, settled near Austin. The data also reveal the formation of racially mixed marriages made in Jefferson, Wharton, Hill, and other counties during the years of the Texas Republic. Many of the migrant Indians who arrived in Texas after 1790 were of mixed Anglo and Indian heritage, including the Blount, Chisolm, Hawkins, Ridge, Conner, Shaw, and Bowles families.

Immigrants of many different ethnic backgrounds made their way to Texas. In addition to being the destination of nonindigenous American Indians, Texas became home to Spanish, Mexican, French, Irish, English, American, African-American, and German settlers. Frederich Ernst and his wife Louise founded one of the first German settlements in Texas at Industry. Their daughter Caroline wrote in her *Life of German Pioneers in Early Texas* that the family's first Texas home had walls made of sticks and Spanish moss. When their shoes wore out, Caroline and her sister went barefoot. When they first arrived in Texas in 1831, the Ernst girls were unprepared for life on the frontier. Unlike the American women in the community, they did not know how to spin cotton or weave wool. Nonetheless, the Ernst girls learned quickly and soon attended a boarding school run by Miss Frances Trask at Cole's Settlement, later renamed Independence.

During the fighting of the Texas Revolution, some Texas women found themselves caught up in the general panic known as the "Runaway Scrape." After Antonio López de Santa Anna marched across the Rio Grande at the head of an army of five thousand men, he intended to drive every Anglo from Texas. While many of the men were away preparing to fight the dictator, the women loaded up their families and what belongings they could carry and fled to the safety of Louisiana. Creed Taylor, a soldier who helped his family to safety before rejoining the army in time to fight at San Jacinto, recalled the bond created among the fleeing women. There were no strangers; no one rode alone whose horse could carry double. Jeff Parsons, a slave of the Sutherland family, recalled the confusion of the moment—children crying, women praying, and men cursing. Stephen Sparks, president of the Texas Veterans Association, wrote that it was impossible to overstate the courage and fortitude of the women. He extolled, "God bless the women of Texas!"

One Texas woman, Dilue Rose Harris, recounted the trauma her family experienced during the "Scrape." Hearing of the fall of the Alamo, Dilue's father, Dr. Pleasant W. Rose, left to join the Texas army. On their own and confused, the Rose women decided to join the throng of settlers fleeing the region. Before they left, young Dilue was instructed to melt lead for bullets while her mother, Margaret, packed bedding and provisions. As they departed it began to rain. When they reached the banks of the rising San Jacinto River, they found a crowd of five thousand other desperate and frightened people waiting to board the ferry. After waiting three long days in the rain, the Rose family boarded the ferry and made it across the San Jacinto. By the time they reached the Trinity River, water overflowed the banks. Children, some with measles, sore eyes, or whooping cough, were carried along by their relatives. Dilue's own sister went into convulsions from a fever. Because of the large number of refugees seeking passage over the floodwater, the Rose family waited five days to cross the Trinity—and still it rained. Once on the far bank, they lingered there a day: Dilue's sister had succumbed to the fever, and her weary mother needed to rest in order to nurse her four-month-old baby.

From their encampment the Rose family heard cannon fire. Then they learned of the Texan victory at the Battle of San Jacinto. Exhausted but relieved, the Roses and the other refugee families began the difficult trip home. The Rose women were reunited with Dr. Rose at the San Jancinto ford. He took them to view the battlefield, where Dilue saw the bodies of dead Mexican soldiers. When the Roses made it back to their home, they worked all through Sunday, something they had never before done. Rose remembered it well—it was two days before her eleventh birthday.

While many students of Texas history consider the story of the lovely young mulatto Emily West distracting Santa Anna at San

Jacinto a fabrication, recent scholarship shows that the story may be true. The Texan army, composed of Anglos and Tejanos, attacked the Mexican encampment at siesta time and startled the entire Mexican army, especially General Santa Anna, who fled wearing little more than silk drawers. Sam Houston told historian William Bollaert that Emily West (sometimes cited as Emily "Morgan") had detained Santa Anna in his tent on the afternoon of the battle. Emily was a member of the New Washington Association organized by New York investors to colonize free blacks and Europeans in Mexican Texas. She had arrived in Texas as a free woman and worked as a housekeeper for the association's general manager, James Morgan. When Mexican soldiers raided the warehouses of the abandoned association at New Washington, they found Emily left behind to fend for herself. The troops took her to the general. After the revolution, she returned to New York.

After the Battle of San Jacinto, families in the new Republic of Texas hardly led safe or comfortable lives. Many returned to burned-out or ravaged homes to begin anew with nothing more than determination and grit. Others faced disputes over land claims. The greatest threat facing Texans during the years of the Republic was attacks by Indians. Apache, Comanche, Kiowa, and Wichita raiders at times took women and children settlers captive and forced some female captives to serve as concubines or become wives. Z. N. Morrell, a pioneer Baptist preacher who settled near the falls of the Brazos River in Limestone County, wrote that townsfolk dreaded hearing that Indians had killed or captured a child. Some of the abducted children were held for ransom or sold to traders; still others were adopted into their captors' tribes.

A notable kidnapping victim in 1838 was Matilda Lockhart, who was abducted by Comanches along with four Mitchell Putnam children. In March 1840, a meeting convened in San Antonio to arrange for Lockhart's ransom. Mary Maverick witnessed the so-called Council House fight, which broke out after a Comanche band rode into San Antonio with the then fifteen-year-old Matilda Lockhart and a few Mexican children—but without other captives left behind at the main camp. When the Texans discovered that the Indians had not, as promised, brought in white captives other than Lockhart, they decided to hold the band of Comanches as captives. When the Indians tried to escape, Texan troops attacked. Most of the sixty Indians and some Texans were killed. Mrs. Maverick ran to her house during the melee to check on her family. She arrived there in time to see her cook, Jinny Andrews, standing in front of the children huddled in the back yard. Facing them was an Indian warrior. Threatening him with a rock, Jinny told the man, "If you don't go 'way from here I'll smash your head in with this rock!"

Perhaps the most famous Texas Indian captive was Cynthia Ann Parker, who lived with the Comanches for twenty-four years after most of her family died in a massacre in 1836 in Limestone County. Although returned against her will to white society some twenty-four years later, Parker, the wife of Chief Peta Nacona, never relinquished Indian ways. Her son Quanah became a prominent Comanche leader.

The annexation of Texas by the United States in 1846 brought little change to the roles and lives of Texas women. Those living on the frontier faced many of the same conditions as women of an earlier generation—physical hardships, loneliness, and Indian raids. In the more settled regions, however, Texas women lived much like their counterparts in the southern United States. This era included a mass migration of slaveholders and their black slaves to the fertile bottomlands of the Colorado, Brazos, Trinity, Neches, Sabine, and Red Rivers. German families arrived by ship and settled in the Hill Country. Some immigrant women enjoyed life on the frontier, finding a sense of liberation from the restraints of a proscriptive lifestyle there. After the War with Mexico ended in 1848, Mexican women living along the Texas bank of the Rio Grande also received American citizenship—but often in name only.

The annexation of Texas to the United States was achieved partly because of the efforts of a talented New York woman, Jane McManus Storm, who wrote extensively on Texas in newspapers, magazines, and books. After a failed attempt to establish a colony of Europeans and free blacks near Waco, Storm returned to New York City, where she anonymously wrote proannexation columns for the New York *Sun* and expansionist magazine articles for the *United States Magazine and Democratic Review,* edited by John L. O'Sullivan. One of these articles, "Annexation," contained the term *manifest destiny* to justify the U.S. foreign policy of continental expansion. A recent comparison of grammatical errors in Storm's and O'Sullivan's signed works indicates that Storm actually wrote the famous and oft-cited "manifest destiny" materials long attributed to O'Sullivan. Rival editors and Texas politicians recognized Storm's contribution to the successful public relations campaign for Texas annexation. She earned a by-line in the *Sun*, became the first Washington correspondent for the Associated Press, and received a 1,000-acre tract in appreciation by Texas land dealer Adolphus Sterne. In 1850 Storm married Texan William Leslie Cazneau. The couple moved to a dugout on the Rio Grande, where Storm wrote *Eagle Pass: or Life on the Border* (1852), a borderland classic that promoted the southern (stage and rail) transcontinental route and featured the life stories of women who had escaped from peonage in Mexico and lived along the Rio Grande.

Texas women have long valued education. The first schools in Texas were run by Spanish missionaries in the 1690s. The first known Hasinai Indian convert to Catholicism, Angelina, had a river named for her by the missionaries. San Antonio had private schools during the Spanish and Mexican eras. The first school for Anglo girls was at Cole's Settlement, where Miss Frances Trask established a boarding school in 1834. Born in Boston and educated in New York, Trask arrived in Texas from Michigan. She continued to teach until 1860. Texas legislators awarded her a section of land for her services as a pioneer teacher. The Female Academy of San Augustine and the Female Department of Rutersville College were founded in 1840. Six years later, women attended class with men at Baylor University, the first institution in the state to offer coeducational instruction. At this time several communities still featured schools exclusively for women. Rebecca Red, born in Pennsylvania and educated in Ohio, moved to Texas in 1852. She opened Live Oak Female Seminary and served as its principal from 1853 to 1875 despite bearing and raising five children during the period. Red, the first woman with a college degree to teach college-level classes in Texas, was honored by Delta Kappa Gamma, an international society for outstanding women in education.

Louise Wigfall, a Southern belle whose family moved to Marshall, Texas, in 1848 from Charleston, South Carolina, led a lifestyle shared by only a small number of elite women. Her father, Louis T. Wigfall, won election to the U.S. Senate in 1858. Accompanying her father on a trip to Washington, D.C., Louise remembered wearing a special dress of gray merino pelisse together with a black beaver-fur hat. She recalled sitting on the porch of their house and watching a comet streak across the night sky. Crepe myrtle and roses lined the quiet streets of the town, and the night air was fragrant with honeysuckle. Gender as well as race segregated Texas society of that day. For example, at the Methodist Church the Wigfalls attended, women sat on one side of the center aisle and the men sat on the other.

In adjoining Marion County, Rebecca McIntosh Hagerty, a mixed-blood Creek Indian, was the only woman planter in Texas to own more than one hundred slaves. An excellent manager, Hagerty routinely shipped 500 to 600 bales of cotton a year to New Orleans. Rebecca did not suffer disloyalty gladly; she once had her husband publicly horsewhipped for infidelity.

The western half of Texas remained a frontier in the 1850s. Many of those who had lived in West Texas during the mid-nineteenth century were interviewed in the 1930s by federal employees of the Works Progress Administration (WPA). Miss Mattie Mather, whose parents had moved from Louisiana to Gabriel Mills in Williamson County in the 1850s, said that her father operated a gristmill, blacksmith shop, post office, and general store. Fort Croghan, at nearby Burnet, served as an Indian trading post. Mather recalled that Indians often stopped at her father's blacksmith shop and that her father frequently went hunting with Indian companions. After Indians ambushed the Skagg boys from nearby Lampasas, Mattie grew afraid for her father's well-being. When she asked him not to hunt with the Indians, he assured her that there was no chance of his being scalped, because he was bald!

During the Civil War, Texas women, like their counterparts in other states of the Confederacy, cheered fathers, husbands, brothers, sons, and sweethearts who went to war. Texas women were long accustomed to carrying on in the absence of their male relatives. But during the Civil War, conditions were different. It was a time of great uncertainty, as Indians increased raiding activity on the frontier. Union sympathizers along the Red River gave sanctuary to deserters, some of whom became criminals. In addition, Union troops attempted to invade Texas from the east and along the Gulf coast. Finally, planters from other states brought their slaves to Texas, swelling the black population.

With so many men gone, life on the Texas home front grew uncertain. For instance, the young women of the Tyler Masonic Female Institute practiced with pikes to defend themselves if necessary. Mary Davenport, a resident of the Sabinal River country west of San Antonio, recorded that during those years renegades, on their way to Mexico in order to avoid military service, were every bit as threatening as marauding Indians. Such men ransacked homes, raided gardens, and stole horses. Expressing what may have been a widespread frustration, Elizabeth Scott Neblett of Grimes County wrote, "I can never gain worldly honor. Fame can never be mine. I am a *woman!* A Woman! I can hardly teach my heart to be content with my lot." True to the pattern during the Civil War, women carried on ably, addressing the needs of their families, nursing the sick and wounded, and overseeing the day-to-day operations of family farms, ranches, and businesses. They continued their work after the war, although the upper-class among them no longer had slaves to do their bidding.

The end of the Civil War brought a new wave of pioneers to Texas. Women ran boarding houses, taught school, and generally continued to do what pioneer women before them had done for the last two centuries. Some helped move their families farther west in the hope of making a fresh start. For instance, after her father died, Annie Heckman Hightower followed her brother John from Virginia to the Little River country west of Belton, where John worked as a ranch hand. Once in Texas, Annie worked the range beside her brother, a six-gun on her hip. Because she could play the fiddle, Annie often provided music for local dances, sometimes riding as many as thirty miles to do so. In 1880, Annie married a farmer named Albert Hightower. Because Albert had gone to seek the help of their nearest neighbor, Annie gave birth to her first child alone in their frontier house.

Cynthia Elizabeth Fletcher Roe was born in Azle during the days when Indians still raided the community. "Lizzy" Roe learned to shoot as soon as she was old enough to hold a gun. She married Montgomery Roe, a Texas Ranger. The couple took up residence in a one-room log home. Being a Ranger entailed the duty of tracking and arresting cattle rustlers and desperados, as well as breaking up fights between cattlemen in disputes known as the "range wars." Naturally, Lizzy feared for the safety of her husband.

Miss Gula Foote arrived in the San Angelo area with her parents in 1876. Departing from Michigan, the Foote family rode the train as far as Round Rock, then took the stage to San Angelo. The stage driver let Gula drive the team to the corral after the other passengers had disembarked. Gula soon proved that she was no tenderfoot; she grew up to become a rugged Texas woman. She rode bucking broncos in rodeos and bred both saddle and harness horses. Never married, she remarked, that once a shiftless widower had sidled up to her and asked if she ever had the need for a man about the place. "Yes," Gula replied, "but when I do, I hire one."

Mexican women came north into Texas seeking relief from the violent political strife and desperate poverty of their homeland. Juanita Hernandez García migrated with her family to San Angelo from Mexico in the 1870s. On their way north, the Garcías were frightened when they encountered a band of Indians, but they did the emigrants no harm. In fact, according to Juanita, the Indians liked her because she looked Indian. They gave her a gift of a pair of beaded moccasins. Years later, Juanita married the Mexican foreman of a cattle ranch on which she served as a cook.

A remarkable person of the era was Miss Joanna July, a woman of mixed Seminole, Creek, and African-American heritage. July and her family went from Indian Territory (Oklahoma) to the Rio Grande borderland in 1850 under the leadership of Wild Cat, a Seminole chief. July's father scouted for the U.S. Army in the 1870s. After he died, she continued to work for the army, breaking horses for the troopers. Wearing long gold earrings and a bright dress, this barefoot young woman cut a colorful figure as she rode bareback, with only a rope looped around the horse's nose. To break the horses, she rode them out into the Rio Grande, making the animals swim until bending to her will. At the age of eighteen, July married a scout who assumed she would cook and clean house, expectations that led to a stormy and ultimately broken marriage.

Not all women enjoyed frontier life. Susan Bartholomew, who lived along the Cap Rock on the High Plains, wrote that it was the last place on earth where a woman would want to live. The Staked Plains near Lubbock was one of the last areas settled. As a consequence, Allie Blankenship, like other settlers, lived in a dugout and spent many hours grubbing mesquite roots to clear the land. Nevertheless, she mused, "We had plenty of time to be still and know God. He was our nearest neighbor." She saw gasoline pumps come to the region in the 1920s, innovations that brought irrigation to the plains. In her old age she looked forward to rejoining her husband, telling the WPA interviewer, "We again shall have the thrill of pioneering another life together."

Amanda Maxey Lockered of McLennan Country also spoke movingly of the times, "And so the past as it rises up before me looks as if it were a dream, times are so changed . . . to us who have been through the turn of the century." Indians were no longer a threat by the 1890s, but hard financial times challenged Texas women. An example is Mrs. Ben Miskimon, who kept her ranch out of debt with profits from her clothing store in San Angelo. Her clientele included the women of the Red Light District.

The women of Texas exercised power in the 1890s as never before through the leading prohibition women's club in the nation. Some women were compelled to act after an amendment to the state constitution failed in 1887. Thereafter, the Texas Women's Christian Temperance Union added equal franchise (the right of women to vote) to their agenda. A number of Texas women became social activists. Black, white, and Hispanic women formed groups dedicated to civic action, became pioneers in occupations and professions outside the home, and ran for political office—becoming among the "firsts" in the nation.

Between 1870 and 1890, approximately 1.5 million farm families migrated to Texas expecting to find fertile land and good prices for crops. But prices for farm commodities fell, even as the basic costs of living and farming rose. In Texas and elsewhere, discontented farmers, who felt that they lay at the mercy of greedy middlemen and monopolistic railroads, joined local chapters of the Patrons of Husbandry, commonly known as the Grange. The Grange offered member farmers social and economic benefits. In 1877, disgruntled Grangers met in Lampasas to initiate a new agrarian organization, a grass-roots and overtly political body known as the Farmer's Alliance. During the next decade farmers formed cooperatives that allowed them to buy and sell as a unified force able to command better prices for their products and better rates from railroads and wholesalers. The Alliance admitted females to membership, and females enjoyed the same rights and privileges as male members. In Texas, women composed 43 percent of the membership, and the Texas branch was the only one to permit female officials.

Bettie Gay of Columbus represented Texas at the National Alliance Convention in 1892, where the Peoples or Populist party was formed. While many Alliance members were sharecroppers and tenant farmers, Mrs. Gay owned her own farm of more than one thousand acres. In the *Southern Mercury,* the state Alliance newspaper, she urged women to boycott certain goods, keep family gardens, wear homemade clothes, and agitate for the vote. "Like John the Baptist, the women of Texas have been in the wilderness too long," she stated. In another letter, she demanded, "Women! are you a power in the land? I say you are. You have the power, if you will properly exercise it."

In 1892 women used their new power to effect the preservation of historical documents, buildings, and artifacts through the Daughters of the Republic of Texas. Shocked that owners of the Alamo intended to sell the historic building to developers who wanted to erect a hotel on the site, Adina De Zavala, a San Antonio teacher and the granddaughter of Lorenzo De Zavala, a signer of the Texas Declaration of Independence, launched the "Second battle of the Alamo." Adina and Clara Driscoll, a wealthy South Texan, organized and oversaw an effective public relations campaign that saved the Alamo from destruction despite charges of "misguided patriotism" by the developers. De Zavala later located Spanish Missions in East Texas and helped preserve the Spanish Governor's Palace in San Antonio.

During the Progressive Era, Texas women asserted themselves in a variety of ways. In 1893, the Texas Women's Press Association organized in Dallas to encourage women to apply for admission to schools of journalism. In 1894 Frances Allen became the first woman to graduate from a Texas medical school. When the Texas State Historical Association formed in 1897, Julia Sinks became its vice president. Two years later, Mollie Armstrong of Brownwood became the second woman optometrist in the United States while, in Mason, Anna Martin became the nation's first female bank president.

In *Women and the Creation of Urban Life, Dallas, Texas, 1843–1920* (1998), historian Elizabeth Enstam illustrates that Texas women exerted a political force long before they could vote. Women owned, operated, and managed businesses, provided social services, and worked outside the home for pay and as volunteers. Women were responsible for maintaining their homes as well as the schools, churches, and libraries of their communities. Women's literary clubs spawned the formation of the Texas Federation of Women's Clubs (1897) and the Texas Association of (Colored) Women's Clubs (1905). In Laredo, Jovita Idar formed *Liga Femenil Mexicanista* (1911), a social, cultural, political, and charitable organization for Mexican-American women. Some women's clubs went beyond their original charters and organized for political action on the local, state, and national level. In 1912, Texas clubwoman and lay historian Anna Pennybacker became the national president of the General Federation of Women's Clubs in America, after having served as president of the Texas Federation of Women's Clubs.

Through their clubs, Texas women sought improvement and reform in public health, education, and the prison system. They created awareness and brought political action to the local and state level through 132 Texas clubs organized into districts. They supported projects regarding pasteurized milk, water-treatment plants, and facilities for juvenile offenders. Male voters responded by electing women to school boards throughout the state. Alarmed over the use of child labor, women lobbied the legislature for changes in school-attendance laws. In 1915 state leaders increased the compulsory age of school attendance from eight to fourteen years. That same year, Houston women organized the Texas Woman's Fair, the first of its kind in the world, which featured demonstrations on housekeeping, childcare, and sanitation.

It appeared that Texas women could accomplish nearly anything they set out to do. In San Antonio, Katherine Stinson, the fourth licensed pilot in the United States, trained U.S. Army pilots at Fort Sam Houston. In 1917 residents of Marble Falls elected Birdie Harwood the first woman mayor in the United States. The next year proved even more auspicious: Annie Webb Blanton became the first woman to win statewide office when she was elected state superintendent of public instruction; Coleman County officials appointed Emma Bannister as sheriff, the first female sheriff in the United States; and Eleanor Brackenridge became the first woman to sit on the board of directors of a bank. Later, Brackenridge was the first woman to register to vote in Bexar County. The first female registered voter in Harris County was Hortense Sparks Ward, who in 1910 became the first woman to pass the Texas Bar Exam. In 1918 Governor William P. Hobby signed legislation allowing women to vote in primary elections. The next year, Texas became the ninth state to ratify the Nineteenth Amendment to the U.S. Constitution.

After the turn of nineteenth century, African-American women in Texas began to assert themselves through participation in women's clubs, through attempts to improve educational opportunities for children in their communities, and through public displays of courage. In 1909, Ollie Louise Bryan of Dallas became the first black woman dentist in the South. In the 1920s, Bessie Coleman, the first licensed black female pilot in the world, made Houston her Texas home and performed her first Texas air show. Born in Atlanta, Texas, and educated in Waxahachie, Coleman received pilot's training in France before going on to give flying exhibitions throughout the South, at which she urged young blacks to learn to fly. The 1920s also saw the Texas Association of Colored Women's Clubs successfully petition the legislature to create a reform school for black female offenders. As the 1920s closed, Mary Elizabeth Branch became the first African-American woman president of a university as chief executive of Tillotson College in Austin.

As artists, Texas women entered the public sphere with zest. Gordon Conway of Cleburne set New York and Paris ablaze with her images of the Jazz Age. A graphic artist as well as a set composer for stage and screen, Conway first designed the image of the "flapper": a "New Woman," independent and optimistic, as featured in *Vogue, Harper's Bazaar,* and *Vanity Fair* magazines. This image was contrasted by that of the tragic character in Dorothy Scarborough's novel *The Wind* (1925) in which the female protagonist is driven insane by the relentless wind of the Texas plains.

Many women aspired to political office. In 1922, women's organizations, white and colored women's clubs, mothers' clubs, and PTA groups joined forces as the Joint Legislative Council, derided as the "Petticoat Lobby" by critics. In 1922, Edith Wilmans of Dallas became the first woman elected to the state legislature. Especially concerned with child support and childcare, she helped create Domestic Relations (family) courts—the first such institutions in the nation to deal exclusively with family matters. In 1924, Governor Pat Neff appointed a special all-woman Supreme Court to hear a case involving the all-male Woodmen of the World, of which most male judges were members. That same year Miriam A. Ferguson won election as governor of Texas, becoming the first female governor of the state and only the second in the nation: Ferguson assumed the high office only fifteen days after Nellie Ross began her tenure as governor of Wyoming. Although not much more than a proxy for her impeached husband James E. Ferguson, Miriam Ferguson garnered more votes than did her Ku Klux Klan-backed opponent, Felix Robertson. Two years later, Margie Neal, the first woman to register to vote in Panola County, won election as the first woman state senator. While serving four terms in the legislature, Neal was instrumental in establishing the State Board of Education, physical education classes in public schools, and state rehabilitation services. In 1928, Austin Democrat Minnie Fisher Cunningham, who had helped organize the National League of Women Voters, became the first woman in Texas to campaign for the U.S. Senate.

During the Great Depression beginning in October 1929 women of all levels of the social scale were active in public life. Sarah T. Hughes of Dallas won election as a state representative in 1931, but the constitutional amendment she drafted to allow women to sit on Texas juries did not pass until 1953. In 1933, the League of United Latin American Citizens (LULAC) formed its first women's auxiliaries. Concerned with helping children, the elderly, and the poor, the women's auxiliary continued until merging with the main organization in the 1950s. Among the most prominent women to serve LULAC in the Depression era were Mrs. J. C. Machuca of El Paso and Alice Dickerson Montemayor of Laredo. In 1938 activist Emma Tenayuca helped organize a strike of some twelve thousand San Antoniopecan shellers that received national attention; these workers, most of them women, had endured deplorable working conditions for $2 a week. Yet not all Tejanas of the day were poor. For example, Herlinda Morales Rodríguez ran a bottling company in San Antonio and became one of the most prosperous Mexican Americans in the state.

Many Texas women made national headlines in the 1930s. "Ma" Ferguson secured reelection as governor in 1932. Meanwhile, the notorious criminals Bonnie Parker and Clyde Barrow went on a two-year rampage of robbery and murder before law enforcement officers shot "Bonnie and Clyde" to death in 1934. Other Texas women took a far different road to fame by becoming Hollywood movie stars during a time when Americans looked to screen icons to take their minds off the hard times of the Great Depression. Joan Crawford usually portrayed a strong, independent-minded woman, while Ginger Rogers danced and sang with Fred Astaire. Other Texans who landed starring film roles included Ann Sheridan, Linda Darnell, and Gene Tierney. Mary Martin made the switch from Hollywood movies to the Broadway stage and played lead roles in musicals for three decades.

During World War II, Texas women served in every branch of the armed forces. Women also took jobs in factories and defense plants. With so many men in the military, jobs normally filled by men fell to women, who rolled up their sleeves and drove trucks and tractors, flew planes, and built ships. After the war, some women returned to home and family, while others, no longer content to stay within the traditional female roles, remained in the workforce. Some embarked upon political careers.

One notable Texan of the World War II era served as the highest-ranking women in the American armed services. In 1942, Oveta Culp Hobby, wife of former Texas governor William Hobby, became the first director of the newly formed Women's Army Auxiliary Corps (WAAC). She had not wanted the job, but her husband encouraged her, asserting that taking on the monumental chore was her duty to the nation. Once Hobby made up her mind to serve, she did so admirably. In recognition of her efforts, she received the Distinguished Service Medal, the first female recipient of that high honor. Hobby continued in public service after the war. In 1953, she became the first secretary of the Department of Health, Education, and Welfare and only the second female cabinet member in American history. In 1955, she became the editor of the *Houston Post.* When asked how she had overcome gender discrimination over the course of her successful career, she replied, "All you have to do is be equal. And don't go into whatever you're doing with a chip on your shoulder."

After World War II, some women of color, especially those who had served in the military or helped staff wartime production plants, decided that they deserved more than a second-class status and became political activists. The Women's Auxiliary of LULAC now worked to end segregation in public facilities, register voters, and provide college scholarships to outstanding students in the Mexican-American community. Together with their male counterparts, lady LULACers brought about the end of school segregation for Mexican Americans in 1948. Since then two Texas women, Delores Guerrero and Rosa Rosales, have served as president of the Texas State branch of LULAC. In 1991, women composed one-half of the membership of LULAC.

Simultaneously with LULACs' efforts, the National Association for the Advancement of Colored People (NAACP) stepped up its activities throughout Texas. Instrumental in the work of that organization was civil rights leader Juanita Craft, a remarkable person whose legacy of activism spanned fifty years. Beginning her work in the 1930s as a field organizer for the NAACP, Craft helped found 182 local chapters. In 1946, she became the first black woman in Dallas County to vote as well as the first black woman elected to the Dallas City Council. Craft was instrumental in publicizing desegregation at the University of North Texas. In Houston, Lulu Belle White was also a dynamic civil rights leader. Like Craft, she had been active since the 1930s in organizing NAACP chapters. As secretary of the South's largest NAACP chapter, White helped pursue civil suits that led to the end of Texas's all-white Democratic primary (*Smith* v. *Allwright*) and effected the integration of the University of Texas (*Sweatt* v. *Painter*). She served on the Houston school board and became the first African American elected to state political office since Reconstruction. From 1949 to her death in 1957, she served as state director of the NAACP.

In the 1960s Texas women continued their roles as political activists. In 1963, Sarah T. Hughes, who in 1961 became the first woman federal judge in Texas, made history again when she administered the oath of office to Lyndon Baines Johnson as President following the assassination of John Kennedy. While President Johnson oversaw the most sweeping Civil Rights legislation in American history, his wife, Claudia "Lady Bird" Johnson, began a publicity campaign to protect the nation's scenery and preserve its wildflowers. Legal equality came to Texas women when Louise Raggio of Dallas introduced legislation that resulted in the first phase of the Texas Family Code (1974). This measure, the first such legislation in the nation, made sex-based discrimination illegal and granted a woman the right to own and manage property separately from her husband. Janis Joplin of Beaumont personified another type of Texas woman—that of the 1960s "hippie" culture of drugs, alcohol, rock and roll, and rebelliousness against authority. A famous singer with a powerful voice, she died from an overdose of alcohol and heroin in 1970.

In the 1970s Texas women won mayoral elections in Austin, Houston, Dallas, San Antonio, El Paso, Galveston, and Nacogdoches. In 1972, Democrat Frances "Sissy" Farenthold of Houston became the first woman in American history nominated at a national party convention for Vice President. The same year Barbara Jordan of Houston became the first woman from Texas and the first African-American woman from the South elected to Congress. In 1974 she gained national recognition during the Watergate scandal investigation as a knowledgeable and eloquent member of the Judicial Committee that conducted hearings into the actions of the administration of President Richard M. Nixon. In 1976, the Democratic party selected Jordan as keynote speaker at its national convention, the first time the honor had fallen to a woman. Another legal expert, Dallas attorney Sarah Weddington, challenged the Texas 1854 abortion law, taking her client's case all the way to the Supreme Court, where she won a landmark victory in *Roe* v. *Wade* (1972). The high court affirmed the right of a woman to have an abortion legally performed by a medical doctor during the first trimester of pregnancy. In 1974, Lorene Rogers became president of The University of Texas, the first woman president of a state university in the nation. That same year saw Irma Rangel become the first Mexican-American woman to serve in the Texas Legislature.

In 1982 Ann Richards was elected the first woman treasurer of Texas. In her first year in the office, Richards increased state funds by an additional $141 million. Her keynote speech at the Democratic National Convention in 1988 challenged the party to look at its roots, "The men and women who go to work everyday." Richards was elected governor of Texas in 1990. She appointed an unprecedented number of women, Latinos, and African Americans to state offices. Richards remained chief executive of the state until George W. Bush defeated her in the election of 1994.

In 1993, Kay Bailey Hutchison became the first woman U.S. Senator elected from Texas. She is a descendent of Charles S. Taylor of Nacogdoches, a signer of the Texas Declaration of Independence and the law partner of Texas's first U.S. Senator, Thomas J.

Rusk, whose linear Senate seat Hutchison now occupies. Senator Hutchison first became involved in politics as a reporter for a Houston television station. She gained election as the first Republican woman to the Texas House of Representatives, and then as state treasurer. Since assuming national office, she has maintained a concern with issues important to women such as homemakers' rights, stalking, education, and crime. In 1999, the Texas Women's Chamber of Commerce named her as one of the one hundred most influential Texas women of the twentieth century.

***

From pre-Columbian times to the present, Texas women have been active participants in providing food and shelter for their loved ones and protecting the home. Whether on the frontier, in an urban setting, in the private sphere of the home or the public workplace, women of every race and social status have sought improved conditions for their families and the greater community. The lines separating the roles society prescribed for males and females often blurred as Spanish law extended Texas women special rights and necessity provided them with experience and leadership opportunities not extended to their counterparts in other states. The Populist and Progressive Eras changed conditions for women in the workplace, in professional status, and in full participation in politics. Texas women were leaders in historic preservation, the professions, education, business, arts and entertainment, the military, and civil rights. Today Texas women are well equipped to carry on this pioneer spirit as private citizens and public leaders in a rapidly changing world.

Suggested Reading

Barthelme, Marion K., ed. *Women in the Texas Populist Movement: Letters to the Southern Mercury.* College Station: Texas A&M University Press, 1997.

Brown, John Henry. *Indian Wars and Pioneers of Texas.* Austin: L. E. Daniel, 1880. Reprint, Greenville: Southern Historical Press, 1978.

Cabeza de Vaca, Alvar Núñez. *The Journey of Alvar Núñez Cabeza De Vaca* (1542). Translated by Fanny Bandeleir (1905). Albuquerque: University of New Mexico Press, 1983.

Chipman, Donald E. *Spanish Texas, 1519–1821.* Austin: University of Texas Press, 1992.

Crawford, Ann Fears, and Crystal Sasse Ragsdale. *Women in Texas.* Austin: State House Press, 1992.

Downs, Fane, and Nancy Baker Jones, eds. *Women and Texas History.* Austin: Texas State Historical Association, 1993.

Drago, Gail, and Ann Ruff. *Outlaws in Petticoats: And Other Notorious Texas Women.* Plano: Republic of Texas Press, 1995.

Enstam, Elizabeth York. *Women and the Creation of Urban Life: Dallas, Texas, 1843–1920.* College Station: Texas A&M University Press, 2001.

——, ed. *Texas Tears and Texas Sunshine: Voices of Frontier Women.* College Station: Texas A&M University Press, 1985.

Flynn, Jean. *Texas Women Who Dared to Be First.* Austin: Eakin Press, 1999.

Holley, Mary Austin. *Texas.* Reprint, Austin: The Texas State Historical Association, 1985.

Hudson, Linda S. *Mistress of Manifest Destiny: A Biography of Jane McManus Storm Cazeneau, 1807–1878.* Austin: Texas State Historical Association, 2001.

Lutzweiler, James. "Emily D. West and the Yellow Prose of Texas: A Primer on Some Primary Documents and their Doctoring," in Francis Edward Abernathy, ed. *2001: A Texas Folklore Odyssey.* Denton: University of North Texas Press, 2001.

Marcy, Randolph Barnes. *Thirty Years of Army Life on the Border. . . .* New York: Harpers Brothers, 1866.

Maverick, Mary, A. *Memoirs of Mary A. Maverick.* Edite by Rena Maverick Green. San Antonio: n. p., 1921.

Morrell, Z. N. *Flowers and Fruits from the Wilderness, or Thirty-six Years in Texas and Two Winters in Houduras.* Boston: Gould & Lincoln, 1872.

Olmstead, Frederick Law. *Journey through Texas or a Saddle-Trip on the Southern Frontier.* New York: Dix, Edward, 1857. Reprint, Austin: University of Texas Press, 1978.

Rogers, Mary Beth, et al. *We Can Fly: Stories of Katherine Stinson and Other Gutsy Texas Women.* Austin: Ellen C. Temple, 1983.

Smithwick, Noah. *The Evolution of a State, or Recollections of Old Texas Days.* Austin" Steck-Vaughin, 1968.

Thompson, Joyce, ed. *Texas Women: The Myth, The Reality.* Denton: Texas Women's University Press, 1984.

Tyler, Ron, Douglas E. Barnett, Roy R. Barkley, Penelope C. Anderson, and Mark F. Odintz, eds. *The New Handbook of Texas.* 6 vols. Austin: Texas State Historical Association, 1996.

Wright, Louise Wigfall. *A Southern Girl in '61: The War-time Memories of a Confederate Senator's Daughter.* New York: Doubleday, Page & Co., 1905.

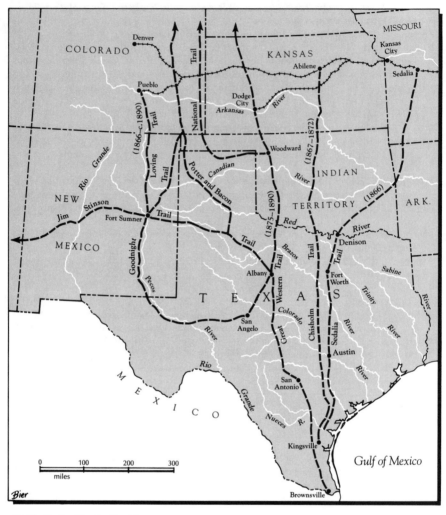

Cattle Trails. *Map by Jim Bier.*

CHAPTER FIFTEEN

The Cattle Frontier in Texas

Eddie Weller

IN 1990 WHEN PRESIDENT GEORGE BUSH, an adopted Texan, hosted the G7 Economic Summit at Rice University in Houston, the attention of the world focused on Texas. Members of the international press corps, who had inundated the city, complained that they wanted to see the "real" Texas. Some wondered where everyone tied up their horses downtown. Others asked about the dust and blowing shrubs (tumbleweed). Still others wanted to know why they had not seen any cattle in the streets. Apparently, even supposedly well-informed journalists had major misconceptions about Texas and America's fourth largest city. In this capacity, however, they were not exceptional.

Indeed, Texans traveling in the northeastern part of the United States or abroad often are surprised by questions people typically ask one from the Lone Star State: "When do they drive the cows through your town?" "Where's your hat and boots?" "How many horses do you own," or even "How big is your cattle ranch?" Often, when the perplexed Texan replies that he or she does not own a ranch, the local looks down in an apologetic way and says something like "Oh, I'm sorry," not meaning to have embarrassed the presumably impoverished Texan. So ingrained in the minds of many the world over is the mystique of the Texas cowboy and the cattle culture that they cannot imagine even present-day Texas without them.

The Hollywood film industry undoubtedly helped plant the romantic image of the Texas cowboy in the modern consciousness, but, like much that is Texan, the cattle industry and the attendant cowboy culture started centuries earlier with the Spanish. Neither longhorns nor horses, so central to the image, are native to the land we know as Texas or, for the matter, the Western Hemisphere; both were first brought across the Atlantic Ocean by the early Spanish explorer-adventurers. When those *conquistadores* trekked north-ward out of New Spain in the sixteenth century, they often drove herds of cattle and horses along with them. Inevitably some of the livestock strayed from the herd and were not recovered; others were lost during raids by Indians; still others may have been lost when left out too long to forage. Many years later, from the time the padres assumed their posts at the first Texas missions in the 1690s until the close of the mission era, Spanish priests, soldiers, and settlers continually brought livestock into Texas. As before, many cows and horses went free. Over the years, the ownerless livestock began to spread and multiply in the wild.

Even before Texas became a province of an independent Mexico in 1821, Spanish settlers sought to profit from the vast herds of wild horses and cattle, known as *mesteños* (from which the term *mus-tang* derives) by taking up ranching. Therefore, it was the *vaquero*, the original Spanish cowboy, who brought the utilitarian trappings of the cattle industry to Texas long before Anglo-Americans ap-peared in the region. The vaquero's wide-brimmed, high-crowned sombrero protected him from the sun and sheltered him from the rain. The *bandana* that hung around his neck could be placed over his nose and mouth to filter dust out of the air. Hard leather chaps protected his legs from the sharp sticks of the prickly pear cactus or mesquite thorns, and high leather boots safeguarded his ankles and legs from snakebite. Finally, a wide leather belt supported his back while astride a horse for hours each day.

At the heart of the cowboy's life lay the wiry and durable long-horn, its ancestry a mixture both of Spanish and English—probably the Bakewell Longhorn—cattle. This new, Texas hybrid could ap-parently survive on little grass and water. In South Texas, also called the "brush country" because of its lack of tall trees and preponder-ance of low bushes and shrubs such as mesquite, the Texas long-horn thrived, even on land that appeared barren. Its tough hide protected it from cactus and mesquite thorns. Over time, it had even developed immunity to Tick Fever, also known as "Texas Fe-ver," a bovine disease which could quickly kill cattle with no such immunity. Its hard hoofs could equally withstand near desert-like conditions and long treks. Finally, its namesake long horns, which often spanned five feet or more, proved excellent in self-defense against coyotes and most other predators.

Over the years the cattle that had escaped from the Spanish and later the Anglo-Americans had intermingled and reproduced rapidly, making the wandering longhorns one of Texas's biggest economic assets when it became a state in 1846. The cattle were so plentiful that their price plummeted in Texas, but elsewhere people were willing to pay handsomely for longhorn beef. Since most of the longhorns were unbranded, they were free for the taking. Some Texans rounded up herds and tried shipping them by water to New Orleans, but the animals arrived in port skinny or ill from the trip, having refused to eat aboard ship. This, of course, greatly reduced the price buyers offered for the stock, making the costly shipment unprofitable. Therefore, the remaining problem was how to get healthy longhorns, nearly worthless in Texas, to a market where they were valuable.

The solution was the cross-country trail drive, in which a few Texans on horseback led a herd of wild longhorns to a distant purchasing center. Ideally, the animals would feed along the way on the grass of the open range, and arrive at the market in good enough condition to bring a fair price. Although many people think of the Texas cattle drives as a late-nineteenth-century phenomenon, during the years of the Republic of Texas, James Taylor White of Liberty County drove cattle to New Orleans for sale. In 1846, Edward Piper drove approximately 1,000 head of cattle to market in Ohio. Others drove herds northward to Indiana, Illinois, and Missouri. Some even tried driving their cattle to the gold-mining regions of California. While some of these early long-drives were profitable, many of them did not make enough money to justify the effort: the longhorns arriving skinny and worn out, reducing their owners' expected return considerably. Perhaps the biggest problem, however, was the disease left in the wake of the Texas cattle.

Indeed, shortly after the longhorns passed through an area, Texas Fever began to kill the local cattle. The disease baffled farmers and ranchers across the Midwest; all they knew was that their herds were dying. Today we know why. The longhorns were carriers of the protozoan *Babesia*, a microorganism that destroys red blood cells, to which Texas cattle had developed immunity. *Babesia* is actually transmitted by cow ticks. After these parasites sucked the blood of a host cow and digested the protozoan, they dropped off to lay their eggs; each of which produced a newborn tick carrying the protozoan. When the young ticks attached to a healthy animal with no immunity to the protozoan, the death of the new host cow came swiftly.

Unconcerned about the exact diagnosis, local farmers and ranchers worked together to stop the Texas trail drives—or at least divert them from their regions. Armed and angry, they succeeded in closing off the Midwest to Texas cattle by the mid-1850s. Without a real market for its beef, the Texas cattle industry stagnated. Only some hide-and-tallow works along the Gulf coast kept the industry viable.

Then came the Civil War, which from its start in 1861 affected the cattle industry greatly. With men off at war, few people even tried to round up their cattle; fewer still had the ability to drive them to market, especially as the war progressed and the Confederate cause faltered. With little oversight, the herds multiplied quickly. Because Texas remained an open range state, the cattle roamed and spread freely. The longhorns not only ranged throughout the brush country of South Texas to the Rio Grande, but also in the Hill Country north of San Antonio and along the coastal plain as far north as Lavaca Bay and even Victoria. Their territory continued to increase throughout the war, and by 1865, according to some experts, the wild or "maverick" herd numbered between 3 and 6 million head—easily one of the greatest resources of post–Civil War Texas.

At the same time, Northerners were clamoring for fresh beef. With many northern and midwestern cattle herds decimated during the war by army quartermasters trying to feed Union armies, the beef supply was low. Accordingly, prices rose steeply. But, with their success in the war complete and their manufacturing economy growing, Northerners could now afford beef, even at inflated prices.

Nevertheless, when Confederate Texans returned from the war, they had hard work ahead of them if they were going to make the shattered cattle-ranching business profitable. All across South Texas and into the Hill Country, ranchers organized "cow-hunts" (roundups) of all cattle in the area. Teams of men from local ranches formed to gather cattle together for branding. Cattle bearing a brand were returned to their owner, as were the calves that resembled or followed them closely. Those participating in the cow-hunt divided all other unbranded cattle. With the cattle divvied up and newly branded, the next question facing the ranchers was what to do with the cattle they had acquired, how they might profit from Northerners' hunger for beef.

Entrepreneurial Texans moved quickly to fill the void at Northern meat markets. In 1866 they again organized trail drives. With most of the herds living in South Texas, the coastal plain, or the Hill Country, the cattle were pushed northward along what is often called the Shawnee Trail or Sedalia Trail. At first they were driven north through Austin and Fort Worth, then on into the Indian Territory (Oklahoma). After the herds crossed the Arkansas

River, they either traveled through the low valleys of the Ozark Mountains or skirted just west of that range before finally arriving at the newly completed railhead at Sedalia, Missouri. Some herds were pressed a little farther northwest to the main line at Kansas City. From either railroad depot, the live cattle soon reached eastern markets, where they brought good prices. Their herds delivered, the Texas cowboys headed home with a healthy profit.

The drive north was not an easy undertaking. Along the trail in Arkansas, local farmers complained that the herds trampled their pastures. In the Ozarks of Arkansas and Missouri, mountain folks might stampede herds into hidden canyons—then offer to help the cowboys find their "lost" cattle for a fee. Sometimes herds would have to be "found" two or three times on the trip! More bothersome were the Missouri farmers and ranchers who barred the way following outbreaks in their region of Texas Fever. After the drive in 1866, Missourians and Kansans quarantined by law much of their states to Texas cattle, making the Sedalia Trail all but unusable.

As the drive season in 1867 approached, ranchers again planned to drive cattle to northern rail lines, but the outlook seemed bleak since Sedalia and Kansas City were now closed off to the drovers. It appeared a deep divide separated Texas cattle and northern buyers. Then twenty-six-year-old Joseph McCoy of Illinois provided a bridge. He convinced a syndicate of Chicago businessmen to establish a new railhead especially for the shipment of cattle far out on the Great Plains, at Abilene, Kansas. From there, the Kansas-Pacific Railroad would take the cattle to the Missouri River, where the Hannibal and St. Joe Railroad would carry it to the Mississippi River. Finally, via more rail connections, the Texas longhorns would arrive in Chicago for processing. The railroad even built pens in Abilene in anticipation of holding as many as one thousand cattle at a time, as well as chutes for loading the animals onto the trains.

Everything was ready; all the enterprise lacked was cattle, and McCoy next tackled that obstacle. He sent stockman W. W. Sugg south to Texas to convince the trail drivers to abandon the route to Sedalia that had been so successful the previous year. Instead, he asserted, they would make greater profits with less difficulty if they drove the beef to Abilene. Many cowmen, however, still regarded that area as a part of the "great American desert." Some of them had never heard of Abilene and were not convinced that a railroad line ran to any such town so far west of "civilization."

That same year saw the first cattle drive up the trail from Texas to Abilene, one undertaken unintentionally. In 1867 Colonel O. W. Wheeler bought 2,400 head of cattle in the San Antonio region with plans of driving them north to Kansas and then west to California. With fifty-four well-armed drovers, Wheeler headed north from Luling, passing near Fort Worth on his way to the Red River. In the Indian Territory they discovered wagon ruts and decided to follow them north. The tracks, originally made by Scots-Cherokee trader Jesse Chisholm, thus became the main thoroughfare for cattle through the Indian Territory to Kansas. When Wheeler arrived in Kansas he heard about the new town being set up for the trail drivers due north of him and decided to take the easier trek and sell his cattle in Abilene. Thus, without any detailed planning, use of the Chisholm Trail began.

Abilene soon prospered as a livestock railhead. Once there, each trail boss would sell his herd to a representative of an Eastern meat-processing company, which would then ship the cattle to Chicago, St. Louis, or farther east. With gold for his livestock, the trail boss paid off his hired hands and then headed back to Texas—often carrying a small fortune for the ranch owner. Before the end of 1867, approximately thirty-five thousand head of cattle rolled out of Abilene in boxcars. By 1871, the railhead freighted out more than six hundred thousand cattle in a single year.

Abilene also did its best to cater to the cowboys at the end of the trail. McCoy and his backers built a three-story hotel that accommodated as many as eighty guests. Across the street from the hotel they built a bank, guaranteeing quick cash payments for the cattle. Nearby saloons, gaming parlors, and houses of prostitution sprang up to provide "entertainment" for the cowboy in town after his long journey. After losing part or nearly all of the pay he had received upon arriving in Abilene, and perhaps after having shot up the town a bit while drunk, the cowboy headed back to Texas, eager to return to Abilene for the money as well as the good times.

Thus began the major years of the great Texas trail drives, which lasted until 1885. Only occasionally did the ranchers actually accompany their herd; instead most commissioned the job to experienced trail bosses who received part of the profits as well as about $100 a month. The trailing contractor business made numerous men famous and sufficiently wealthy to start large ranches of their own. Captain John Lytle, who blazed the Western Trail, led more than 450,000 head northward before settling down on a large ranch located approximately twenty-five miles south of San Antonio. One of his partners, Captain Charles Schreiner, invested his earnings in banking and ranching, becoming the leading citizen of Kerrville, Texas. The three Blocker brothers, Bill, J.R., and Ab, drove cattle for twenty years. Their last drive was to Deadwood, South Dakota, in 1893; all three bought ranches with their proceeds. Others such as Abel H. "Shanghai" Pierce acquired land, raised cattle, and acted as trail boss themselves. Pierce led thousands of his animals northwards under his own direction. Eventually he owned more than 250,000 acres of grazing land on the Gulf Coast Plain.

Although Hollywood romanticized the trail drives, they were anything but glamorous. Mostly they were boring and mundane, with the trip lasting up to four months, depending on where the herd started. For the cowboys, who earned little except at roundup and branding time, the money was good, even if the work was routine. Typically, a crew of less than fifteen persons would take two to three thousand cattle north at a pace of roughly ten miles a day. Leading the entourage was the chuck wagon, driven by the cook, and the wrangler with the *remuda* (a string of horses). These two hundred or more horses were necessary additional mounts, for the cowboys had to change horses several times throughout the day. Then came the cattle. Usually two experienced men rode in front of the herd on "point," while others rode on each side or "flank," placing themselves about one-third and two-thirds of the way back. At the rear came two more young men riding "drag," the dustiest, most hated position on the drive. Most of the cowboys, except the trail boss, cook, and wrangler, were young; many, if not most, were between the ages of thirteen and eighteen. The rest of the men, including the trail boss, often were only in their twenties.

This dull, boring lifestyle could become exciting on a moment's notice, but rarely in a positive manner. A thunderstorm could bring blinding rain, punishing hail, rising water, and dangerous lightening, which might strike cowboys or cattle or spook the herd, perhaps causing a few cattle to stray—perhaps causing a stampede of the entire herd. In the spring, crossing swollen rivers threatened the safety of the cattle; in the fall, drought might cause a shortage of forage or water en route, weakening some cattle and killing others. The trail bosses also had to worry about Indians raiding their herds as they crossed Indian Territory. But even allowing the trail hands to carry guns might prove to be dangerous: an untimely misfire could start a stampede and cost the lives of cattle and men.

From 1866 until 1885, the main years of the cattle drives, many people of all types and backgrounds made the journey. According to George Saunders, longtime head of the Old Time Trail Drivers Association, at least 35,000 people made at least one drive, with many going repeatedly. While nearly two-thirds of the cowboys were white, probably one-quarter of them (8,750) were African American; the rest were Hispanic. Often given the worst jobs as well as extra duties, men of color proved themselves capable and usually won the respect of the white trail bosses. Some women made the trek as well. One young woman, wanting to follow in her father's footsteps, went up the Goodnight-Loving Trail disguised as a boy and only revealed her gender after she reached the railroad and booked passage on the next train home. Occasionally women accompanied their husbands on the trip. They spent months riding in a wagon or carriage over rough terrain and faced the same obstacles of hail, prairie fire, stampede, or drought as the men. The trails showed no favorites.

Although the trail drives, as mentioned, continued until 1885, they changed in important ways during the era. At Abilene, citizens tired of reckless cowboys who would trash part of the town while drunk. Therefore, in 1872 local residents called for the enforcement of a quarantine on Texas cattle, forcing the drovers to take their herds sixty miles westward to the railhead of Ellsworth, Kansas. Later that year, the Atchison, Topeka, and Santa Fe Railroad, having advanced southwestward across Kansas, opened a more southerly site at Wichita, the new railhead attracting the herds until, once more, local citizens demanded the enforcement of a quarantine on Texas cattle. The cattlemen then abandoned the Chisholm Trail and moved even farther west to Dodge City, Kansas.

Located 150 miles west of Wichita on the Arkansas River, Dodge City first gained attention as the center of the buffalo-hide trade. Catering to buffalo hunters, it developed into a "wide-open" town with more saloons, gaming parlors, and houses of prostitution than Abilene. Close to the frontier, Dodge City commonly hosted gunfights, the losers of which found their final resting-place in the Boot Hill Cemetery located on the outskirts of town.

With Abilene closed to them, Texans abandoned the Chisholm Trail and looked west. Foremost of this group was John Lytle, a contract drover and trail boss who blazed a route to Dodge City in 1874. The Western Trail—some called it the Dodge City Trail or, after an extension to the Ogallala, Nebraska, depot of the Union Pacific Railroad, the Ogallala Trail—started at Kerrville, Texas, seventy miles northwest of San Antonio, the junction of several smaller feeder routes. From there, it extended north past Brady, Coleman, Albany, Throckmorton, Seymour, and finally Vernon before crossing the Red River into the Indian Territory. Because the Western Trail was farther west, traversing a more sparsely populated region, taking the new route allowed the drovers to avoid the complaints that trail cattle destroyed crops. In times of little rain, however, the Western Trail often dried up, leaving both cattle and cowboys parched. And before the end of the Red River Campaign in 1876, the Comanche, Kiowa, Cheyenne, and Arapaho could make the trek dangerous for the crew and herd.

Even so, the Western Trail supplanted the Chisholm Trail as the primary route, with well over 3 million, perhaps as many as 5 million, cattle driven over it by 1885. Other trails of importance to Texas stockmen also existed. As early as 1866, Oliver Loving and Charles Goodnight contracted to provide beef for the federal troops stationed at Fort Sumner, New Mexico. They left the upper Brazos River area with a herd heading southwest. After reaching the Pecos River, which provided plenty of water for the cattle for much of the trail, they changed directions, followed the river north into New Mexico, and finally up to Denver, Colorado. A few years later, Goodnight extended the trail to Cheyenne, Wyoming, where he put his cattle on a Union Pacific train bound for Chicago. Other trails saw use only for a short time. For example, the Potter-Blocker Trail, also known as the Potter-Bacon Trail, left the Western Trail in Texas and veered northwestward to Cheyenne; because it lacked a dependable water supply, it never gained popularity with the drovers. Another, the Adobe Walls Trail, served as a short cut from the western Panhandle to Dodge City. Again, because of the uncertainty of water, it only survived a few years before the drovers abandoned it in the mid-1880s.

One outcome of the trail drives was the opening of many ranches in the Panhandle of Texas and farther north on the Great Plains. With most of the Indians on reservations and the buffalo nearly exterminated, cattle ranches could survive there. Some of the new ranches were tiny concerns; some of them grew into huge enterprises. In some cases, a small farmer might purchase and manage a small herd of cattle with the hope of selling the animals to commission agents buying for the Chicago meat-packing interests. In others, large syndicates, some of them backed by European investors, bought or leased the grazing rights to hundreds of thousands of acres. These large-scale, nonresident owners contracted with Texans for a cattle herd to start their enterprises. In time, the herd would increase and fatten on the rich grass of the plains. By the mid-1880s, the "Great American Desert" had been transformed into a profitable livestock-raising region by the arrival of the Texas longhorn.

Soon thereafter the era of the long trail drives north as the primary method of getting cattle to market ended. As more and more settlers moved west and began to farm near the trails, they petitioned their state legislatures to ban Texas cattle—out of fear of Texas Fever and to protect their crops. Kansas and Colorado enacted the ban in 1885, making it much harder to trail cattle north to the railheads. Then, two successive, incredibly harsh winters, 1885–86 and 1886–87, caused the "Big Die-Up," which killed hundreds of thousands of cattle from the Great Plains of Texas northward. Finally, the introduction of barbed-wire fencing tolled the death knell of the open range.

Only through widespread use could that little ribbon of steel make such difference. And only because of one of the greatest marketers and businesspersons of all time, John W. "Bet-a-million" Gates, did barbed wire change the landscape of Texas. Gates, a salesman for the Washburn-Moen Company, sold Joseph Glidden's recently patented fencing material. In 1878 Gates rented the Military Plaza in San Antonio and constructed a pen of barbed wire in which he placed a small herd of longhorns. Workers then tried to stampede the cattle through the fence. Although some of the posts broke, the fence held the herd. Many people witnessed the demonstration or heard about it from others, and the orders from Texas inundated the company. Requests quickly totaled more barbed wire than the company could manufacture in the course of an entire year.

Barbed wire changed Texas in numerous ways. On the plains it was first used to make "drift fences," intended to prevent cattle from drifting too far south (and too far away from the owner's property) during severe blizzards. In this capacity, it worked too well: unable to continue walking, cattle tended to stack up against the fencing, sometimes suffocating one another or freezing to death under piles of snow. Many people cited these barbed-wire drift fences as a principal factor in the Big Die-Up. Then farmers and ranchers began to surround their fields with the wire, cutting off the paths trail drivers had used. Some illegally encircled water holes they did not own to keep out the herds. In general, the fences destroyed the mobility and open range in much of Texas.

Many Texans did not approve of barbed wire and tried to halt its introduction into Texas, resulting in the fence-cutting fights of 1883. Because of a prolonged drought that year, good pasturage was difficult to find. Many who had good land, either owned or leased, began fencing the perimeter in order to protect the grass for their cattle alone. Others, accustomed to the traditional open-range system, fought back, trying to save their way of life. They began cutting down fences at night. A few unscrupulous ranchers exacerbated the problem by fencing in more than their property, restricting public access to roads, water holes, and creeks. At night, small-time herders would secretly cut the wire and leave warning notes not to repair the fence. Sometimes these men would start brush fires in the fenced pastures. Throughout the course of the year, at least three people were killed trying to protect their fences. Finally, Governor John Ireland called a special session of the legislature to make fence cutting, as well as the fencing of someone else's property, illegal.

Although the fence-cutting fights evoked selfishness, greed, even violence, barbed wire also helped the cattle industry adapt and change in the 1880s and 1890s. As Americans became tired of the tough, stringy meat the free-range longhorns rendered and began to demand, and get, better beef from animals raised in feedlots, Texans fenced their pastures with barbed wire to control breeding. This in turn allowed ranchers to mix in British breeds, such as the Angus, Hereford, and Shorthorn, which had more pounds per cow and yielded more tender beef. When longhorns were part of the breed, calves often were significantly smaller at birth, often twenty or more pounds lighter, which made calving easier. But as the cattle matured, they reached the larger size of the English stock. A major concern about these pastures was the lack of water. By damming creeks or digging out low spots to catch and hold rain water (known as stock tanks), ranchers partially solved the problem. With the advent and widespread use of the windmill, they could find water for almost any pasture. The windmill continually pumped the subterranean water to the surface where it flowed into a trough easily accessible to the livestock, except in the severest of droughts.

With the advent of barbed-wire fencing, more large ranches and cattle syndicates were established in Texas. While some large ranches existed before the Civil War, such as the King Ranch in South Texas and the Allen Ranch in Harris County southeast of Houston, most of Texas's large spreads were either begun or experienced growth as the open range ended. For example, Perry McFaddin added to his family's land holdings near Beaumont until they reached a zenith of more than 150,000 acres in the 1890s. Rachel McKenzie Hudgins accumulated more ranch land after her husband's death in 1873, gaining more than 10,000 acres in Wharton County. Still others, such as brothers John and Lee Kokernot, opened new cattle territory in the Trans-Pecos region and eventually owned more than 300,000 acres. And in 1878 cattleman Hank Campbell and banker A. M. Britton started what would become the largest combined holding in North America, the Matador Land and Cattle Company. To expand their holdings, they attracted European investors, especially a group of merchants from Dundee, Scotland. Under the leadership of Murdo Mackenzie, the Matador was expanded to more than 1 million acres of grazing land in Texas and eventually included more than 1 million additional acres in Colorado, Montana, South Dakota, and Saskatchewan, Canada.

Perhaps the most famous and largest ranch in Texas was the XIT. When the Texas capitol in Austin burned in 1881, the legislature quickly proceeded with some earlier plans to build a new home. Because Texas was cash poor, but had ample land, the legislature "appropriated" 3 million acres in the Panhandle to be exchanged for a completed new capitol building. In 1882 the Capitol Syndicate of Chicago entered such an agreement with the State of Texas, and an enormous ranch was born. The syndicate planned to sell the land in small plots to farmers and ranchers at a profit, running the ranch themselves in the meantime. Situated in all or part of ten counties, the XIT bought its first cattle, just 2,500 head driven up from the Fort Concho area, in 1885. Within two years the herd had expanded to more than 110,000 cattle, which were enclosed by 781 miles of barbed wire. At its peak near the end of the decade, the XIT had more than 150 cowboys and one thousand horses working in seven divisions—an eighth was added in 1898—with more than 150,000 cows. The ranch even had its own trail drive, sending more than ten thousand steers north to Montana or South Dakota for fattening each year. By 1900 the ranch had more than one hundred dams and three hundred windmills to provide water.

Even with these impressive efforts, the XIT usually lost money, for several reasons. First, the beef industry struggled as prices declined because of an ever-increasing supply and a weakening economy. In addition, every year wolves attacked the herds—especially at calving time—cutting into the syndicate's profits; to combat these predators, the owners paid large bounties for wolf hides. Another problem was the abominable weather. Droughts caused water holes to dry up, especially in the early years before windmills were operating. Then the winters of 1885–86 and 1886–87 brought enormous blizzards that caused the deaths of many XIT cattle in Texas. Indeed, the immensity of the spread made it difficult to administer; outlaws, fence cutters, and cattle rustlers wreaked havoc and escape without being detected. After the turn of the century the syndicate began selling off land and cattle, and by 1910 it had turned an overall profit on the venture, although the last of the lands were not sold until 1963.

With the closing of the range and the growth of the big ranches, the trail drives and the cattle frontier ended. Nevertheless, the era gave much to Texas and its heritage. Perhaps foremost was the financial impact on the state. As other southern states struggled to survive after the Civil War and became virtual economic colonies of the Northeast, Texas received a large and fresh influx of "Yankee" money for its beef. While many unemployed southerners found themselves eventually forced into sharecropping, in Texas many jobless Confederate veterans, Mexican Americans, and newly freed African Americans found work on the trail drives north as well as on the ranches—avoiding, at least for the period, the kind of agricultural serfdom that appeared in other southern states.

Other differences developed in Texas during this time. Women earned a reputation of toughness and strength in an era when soft gentility and feigned helplessness was often expected by society. With women coming to the cattle frontier and surviving there, men had to recognize their contributions. Besides the arduous tasks of rearing children, sewing and mending clothes, cooking and cleaning, and raising vegetables and chickens, many women spent time in the saddle, working cattle alongside the men. The only difference was that women faced many additional "chores" once back at the ranch house after a long day of cow punching. And since some women founded successful ranches and others managed them after their husbands' deaths, men also had to recognize their business sense and acumen. Women handled even the tough, months-long trail drive. In Texas, women had proven that they had the physical ability to perform any job a man could do long before they realized such freedom in other sections of the country.

The Texas cattle industry also served as catalyst for significant changes in the United States. Texas cattle, starting with the original, tough, stringy longhorn, made the United States a beef-eating nation; without the longhorn, the country would not have been able to supply the demand for meat. Texas, like much of the West, served as an outlet for surplus workers from the East, whether new immigrants, freedmen, or displaced farmers. All felt that in Texas they had the chance to start over. And the long trail drives opened much of the Great Plains to settlement, as towns sprang up to ship beef eastward. People also began setting up their own ranches on the plains, often originally stocked by cattle driven north from Texas. Colorado, Kansas, Montana, North and South Dakota, Nebraska, and Wyoming all benefited from the Texas connection.

The job of the cowboy has changed dramatically. Moving cattle long distances involves a pick-up truck and a gooseneck trailer, not mounted riders and a chuck wagon. Today a cattle rancher is more likely to drive an old Ford or Chevy truck than ride a horse. Records are kept on computer, rather than by hand. The siring of calves is probably directed by a geneticist: gone are the days when the cattle-man merely sized up a huge bull by eye. As for the rancher's fare, it is more likely to be a fast food burger than a bowl of beans or stew. While the work is different, the vision has remained the same.

Perhaps the most enduring feature of the cattle frontier has been the image of the Texas cowboy. Tough, resourceful, and inde-pendent, the cowboy, as long as he had a horse and gun, still had a chance to survive, even thrive. Americans who can not fathom working in a factory or office—and even some who do so daily—still look to the cowboy as their model, their hope. Even in the state's largest cities, whenever the rodeo comes to town, Texans young and old dust off their Stetsons and break out their cowboy boots, eager to try to relive that most romanticized portion of their heritage. Why else would the fourth largest city in the United States, with one of the most cosmopolitan populations in the country, in-vest so much time and energy in the Houston Livestock Show and Rodeo? Each year the event draws more people to its performances than do any of the professional sports teams in the city. In short, all Texans look to the days of the cattle frontier with pride and hope that the future will mold people of the same character.

Years ago the cowboy lassoed the Texas dream and hitched it to the back of the chuck wagon, where it still proudly trots along to-day.

Suggested Reading

Atherton, Lewis. *The Cattle Kings.* Bloomington: Indiana University Press,1961.

Dary, David. *Cowboy Culture: A Saga of Five Centuries.* New York: Alfred A. Knopf, 1981.

Emmett, Chris. *Shanghai Pierce: A Fair Likeness.* Norman: University of Oklahoma Press, 1953.

Gard, Wayne. *The Chisholm Trail.* Norman: University of Oklahoma Press, 1954.

Haley, J. Evetts. *Charles Goodnight: Cowman and Plainsman.* Norman: University of Okla-homa Press, 1949.

Hunter, J. Marvin, ed. *The Trail Drivers of Texas: Interesting Sketches of Early Cowboys and Their experiences on the Range and on the Trail during the Days That Tried Men's Souls— True Narratives Related by Real Cowpunchers and Men Who Fathered the Cattle Industry in Texas.* Austin: University of Texas Press, 2000.

Lea, Tom. *The King Ranch.* Two volumes. Boston: Little, Brown, and Company, 1957.

Massey, Sarah R., ed. *Black Cowboys of Texas.* College Station: Texas A&M University Press, 2000.

Mora, Jo. *Trail Dust and Saddle Leather.* Lincoln: University of Nebraska Press, 1946.

Shaw, James C. *North from Texas: Incidents in the Early Life of a Range Cowman in Texas, Dakota, & Wyoming, 1852–1883.* College Station: Texas A&M University Press, 1996.

Skaggs, Jimmy M. *The Cattle Trailing Industry: Between Supply and Demand 1866–1890.* Lawrence: University of Kansas Press, 1973.

Worcester, Don. *The Chisholm Trail: High Road of the Cattle Kingdom.* Lincoln: University of Nebraska Press, 1980.

One of several oil derricks in downtown Breckenridge, Texas, 1922. *Courtesy of the Basil Clemons Photograph Collection, Special Collections Division, The University of Texas at Arlington Libraries, #AR317.*

CHAPTER SIXTEEN

The Oil and Gas Industry in Texas

George N. Green

Oil seeps were familiar to Indians in Texas as well as to Spanish and French explorers. Some Texans may have dug small oil wells or pits long before Edwin L. Drake, regarded as the father of the modern petroleum industry, successfully drilled for oil in Titusville, Pennsylvania, in 1859. Shortly thereafter, in 1866, Lyne Barret drilled the first-known producing well in Texas in Nacogdoches County. Using an eight-foot-long auger powered by a steam engine, Barret struck oil at 106 feet, but his efforts were abortive because of lack of capital, a declining demand for petroleum, and the uncertainties of the post–Civil War years. The 1870s and 1880s saw additional oil discoveries, but the oil found only local markets as patent medicines or as a lubricant for saddles and wagon axles. Then the accidental discovery of a huge deposit of oil at Corsicana in 1894 triggered a boom. There, J. S. Cullinan established the first major oil refinery in Texas—which helped supply the first oil-burning locomotive—and experimented with oiling streets to prevent dust from blowing. Output from the Corsicana field boosted the state's annual production of oil from 50 barrels in 1895 to 65,955 barrels in 1897. By 1899, the Corsicana field was so littered with abandoned wells and the oilmen so careless in their drilling practices—maintaining highly dangerous work sites and letting untold gallons of oil spill to the ground—that the State of Texas adopted its first law attempting to regulate aspects of the oil industry. Thus began what proved to be a pattern.

Early in the 1890s amateur geologist Patillo Higgins startled the other members of his Beaumont community by proclaiming the presence of oil in the area known as Spindletop, located three miles south of town. After three shallow drilling attempts failed, Higgins ran out of working capital and advertised for financial backers in a New York newspaper. Answering the call was A. F. "Cap"

Lucas, a mining engineer and prospector. Lucas believed that Gulf Coast salt domes such as Spindletop were natural reservoirs for petroleum. But, since no producing oil fields supported his theory, Lucas too had trouble generating necessary funds for further exploration in the Spindletop area. Finally he persuaded two Pennsylvania oilmen, J. M. Guffey and J. H. Galey of Pittsburgh, to finance his effort. Guffey and Galey too a ⁷/₈ interest, Lucas was granted an 1/8 interest, and Higgins was cut out, although he did retain a lease in the area that proved to be very profitable. Now the new investors sent into Spindletop an experienced drilling team from Coriscana, Al and Curt Hamill.

Lucas and the Hamill brothers deployed a newly devised, heavy, rotary drill bit to penetrate the treacherous rock and quicksand, hitting pay dirt at 1,139 feet. The lamp-and-lubrication era ended dramatically when the gusher at Spindletop blew in on January 10, 1901. The eruption spewed six tons of casing and other equipment. Then, according to historian C. C. Rister:

> Without warning a large volume of heavy mud shot out of the well with the sound of a cannon shot, followed by a sustained, deafening roar. First came a strong flow of gas, then oil by head flows. The flows increased in force so that within a short time rocks shot upwards for hundreds of feet. Then black oil in a powerful stream, increasing in volume, gushed skyward for more than twice the height of the derrick, crested, and settled back to earth in a greasy shower.

Some farmers and field hands prayed, believing it the end of the world. Cattle and chickens fled before the roaring, evil-smelling, two-hundred-foot black plume. Within minutes local spectators arrived, and within hours many more crowded trains leaving cities as far away as Dallas and San Antonio to see the spectacular gusher spew upwards of seventy-five thousand barrels of oil a day.

Beaumont boomed. In three months its population leaped from ten thousand to thirty thousand, many of the newcomers residing in tents or lean-tos. Fortunetellers, promoters of phony oil-company stock, gamblers, and speculators were on hand to witness unprecedented land deals. A local garbage collector sold her pig pasture for $35,000. In 1902 the Spindletop field produced 17 million barrels of oil, almost one-fourth of the total national output, and was valued at $500,000 an acre; two years earlier the same land could have been purchased for $10 an acre. The rate of crime soared right along with the newfound wealth, the sheriff advising townspeople to "tote your guns" in the open "so everybody can see you're loaded."

Hundreds of wells were drilled and dozens of companies were formed in and around Beaumont, including the forerunners of Gulf (originally Guffey Oil) and Texaco. At least one company, the Hogg-Swayne Syndicate, specialized in selling drilling sites just large enough to support a single derrick. This practice spread oil money and a measure of experience among innumerable independent operators, but it also led to innumerable well fires and the early exhaustion of the fields. Under Texas capitalism's "law of capture," every leaseholder knew that he had better drill as soon as he signed, lest his neighbor begin draining the oil out from under his lot. At one point, oil sold for as little as three cents a barrel, while the going rate for drinking water was five cents a cup. Nonetheless, Beaumont blossomed with sawmills, oil-tank factories, the largest ironworks in the South, and an array of other industries. Bank deposits in the city increased three and one-half times during the first seven months of 1901.

Spindletop launched the fuel-oil era. A Houston brewery and a Galveston flour-milling company switched from coal to oil-burning equipment early in 1901, and they were soon followed by a spreading wave of oil-burning factories. Railroads and steamships also hastened to make the conversion. The Southern Pacific Railroad explained that 915 pounds of oil would generate as much boiler steam power as 2,000 pounds of Indian Territory coal. In the 1910s the industry entered the gasoline-for-motor-fuel stage and developed symbiotically with the automobile.

Other salt-dome fields along the coast soon were discovered. The more famous ones—Sour Lake (1902), Batson (1903), Humble (1905), and Goose Creek (1908)—peaked at 9 million barrels or more and produced more than 1 million barrels a year each for an average of twenty-five years. A dozen other million-barrel fields brought in elsewhere in the state included fabulous booms in Burkburnett and Mexia.

The gaudiest boom occurred in Ranger, 1917–1920, where thousands flocked to town. When men left their hotel rooms in the morning to go to the oil fields, managers rented out their beds to others without a change of linen. When a crippling drought finally broke in the autumn of 1917, heavy rains and the deep ruts left by trains of wagons loaded down with heavy oil-field equipment combined to turn the streets into a quagmire. Men wearing hip boots did a brisk business, charging up to a quarter each to carry passengers across the street or to pull them across on sleds or boats. Two horses actually drowned at a low place in the main street. Boomtown justice was tenuous. One man found guilty of murder was fined $100 and ordered to leave town. Murder, thievery, gambling, and prostitution became so rampant that the Texas Rangers intervened in 1920, while Rotary members and the honest faction of the local police raided liquor joints and poured spirits valued at $16,000 into the streets. As was the case with many other boom towns, the Ranger field played out quickly, sending the town into a swift decline. Banks and businesses failed, leaving the city with a bonded indebtedness. Ranger became a virtual ghost town.

Mail-order stock promotion became a huge and corrupt racket, with perhaps one-fifth of those soliciting investors actually engaged in a search for oil. Fort Worth, especially the lobby of the Texas Hotel, became a hub for the bogus stock promoters. The racket was so intricate that on one occasion federal agents obtained an indictment against M. P. "Pat" Murphey, a nonexistent officer in the Agua Dulce Oil Company. Despite warnings from the Texas governor and the Federal Reserve System against buying oil stock, the con artists duped more than 1 million Americans out of more than $1 billion.

Some fields were depleted largely because of the wastefulness of the producers. At Desdemona, active from 1918 to 1920, operators allowed natural gas wells to flow for weeks in the hope that they might blow into oil wells. They also purposely left oil gushers uncapped, hoping the sight of them would promote stock sales. Perhaps as much as half the field's potential output was lost because of the operators' ignorance of conservation methods. Before the end of the 1920s, however, improvements in oilfield procedures and methods became important considerations. For instance, treating wells in Breckenridge in 1925 with hydrochloric acid, which dissolved calcareous blockages, practically doubled the life of that field.

Despite the fate of a number of boom towns, the oil industry gave impetus to the economic development of Texas. Not only did the oil itself generate wealth, but the manufacture and sale of oilfield equipment and supplies became a major industry. Until the mid-1930s most of the derricks were constructed from East Texas lumber. Railroad traffic increased markedly with the shipment of oil in tank cars. And Houston became a center for the manufacture of oilfield equipment, a crossroads for pipelines, and the locale for numerous refineries.

The 1920s saw the sensational West Texas and Panhandle discoveries. For example, the Santa Rita #1, wildcatted in 1923 against great odds in the desolate flatlands of Reagan County, poured wealth into Midland, Odessa, and the University of Texas (UT), which owned much of the land. Indeed, royalties received on the oil extracted from its land allowed the university—which at the time of the discovery held classes in unheated wooden shacks—to construct the sprawling Austin campus that exists today. By 1990, UT and its sister institutions had earned close to $2.5 billion.

The colossus of the oil industry, John D. Rockefeller's Standard Oil of New Jersey, missed out on much of this development, both because its executives had not believed there was much oil in Texas and because the company had been driven from the state in the 1890s for violating antitrust law. In 1918 Standard Oil insinuated its way back into the state by purchasing half the stock in the Humble Oil Company; it bought the remainder in 1926.

In 1913, Congress passed the first "depletion allowance" for oil and other extractive minerals, a tax formula providing an incentive for exploration and drilling and compensation for the loss of an irreplaceable asset. But not until 1926 could oilmen deduct 27.5 percent of their gross income from producing wells before calculating their income taxes. This arbitrary new formula, whose cost to the U.S. treasury was mostly underestimated, constituted massive federal aid, the first of many tax breaks for the oil industry. It wrecked the theory and system of a graduated income tax for all Americans. It also accelerated the search for new oil fields and allowed a few of the luckiest and shrewdest Texas wildcatters, such as Clint Murchison, Sid Richardson, and H. L. Hunt (originally from Arkansas), to parlay their new wealth into big-time oil operations. The government finally eliminated the allowance for major energy companies in 1975.

As noted, oil seekers also discovered pockets of natural gas. In 1918 geologist Charles Gould inspired the discovery in the Panhandle of the world's largest gas field. Soon thereafter, nine major pipeline companies, which supplied natural gas to residential and industrial customers locally and in far-flung cities, monopolized the field's pipeline runs to their own advantage. They crushed independent producers and bypassed many nearby gas wells, leaving those who owned them without a market. In the 1930s state laws attempted to empower the Texas Railroad Commission to enforce equal marketing opportunities for all gas producers, but federal courts tossed out the proposed mandates at the request of the pipeline companies. The Stripper Act of 1934 allowed massive pumping and induced incredible wastage of natural gas. A billion cubic feet of gas blew into the air every day. Finally a law passed in 1937 authorized the Railroad Commission to determine the market demand for residue gas (a lower-grade product with impurities) and to allocate reasonable production levels among all producers. The gas and pipeline companies challenged even this limited interference in their oligopoly, but this time they lost in the courts. Even in the late 1930s, after the distribution of market demand was established, estimates indicate that the amount of natural gas wasted almost equaled the volume of production. Federal regulation ensued for interstate natural gas lines in 1938 with the establishment of the Federal Power Commission.

The oil and gas industry was one of the few in the nation that spawned its own legendary hero, a mythical figure who became part of the frontier heritage of tall tales. Gib Morgan allegedly operated as a prospector, rig builder, and drilling crew all by himself. He could build a derrick in the matter of a few hours, once building one so high that it took a man fourteen days to climb to the top of it. To maintain the giant derrick and keep a man on duty at the top at all times, Gib brought in a crew of thirty men. At any given time, fourteen were going up and fourteen were coming down, one was on duty at the top, and one was off duty on the ground. Bunkhouses built a day's climb apart gave the men places in which to sleep on their way up and down.

The stuff of legends notwithstanding, the work week in the oil industry was long and dangerous. In 1920 the hours worked per week by those in the field averaged about seventy-nine, in pipelines about sixty-two, and in refining nearly sixty. Field work was especially hazardous. Roustabouts (semi-skilled workers) roughnecks (skilled workers) and drillers (well borers) ran the risk of death or serious injury every day. They might be struck by a spinning chain, cat line, or cable or entangled in a belt drive or a gearbox. They also stood the chance of being gassed, electrocuted, or crushed under a load of pipe. Fires presented a constant danger, as did trying to extinguish them. Joe Cullinan, the founder of Texaco, once accepted command of a fire-fighting crew only on condition that he be allowed to discipline those who tried to run away by shooting them.

The most spectacular development in the 1930s was the discovery of the East Texas field, where a wildcat operator named C. M. "Dad" Joiner completed the drilling of the Daisy Bradford #3 near Kilgore on October 3, 1930. As a crowd of eight thousand onlookers cheered, the East Texas boom began. It was apparent by the spring of 1931 that the "Eastex" field was enormous. In fact, it lay over the largest known concentration of oil in the world at the time, covering some ninety-two thousand square miles. By the end of 1931, the field supported approximately 3,400 wells, which peaked the next year at more than 200 million barrels, more than all the rest of the state produced that year. Unlike other fields, Eastex was developed almost entirely by small independent operators and promoters. The major companies had refused to believe there was sufficient oil in the area to warrant development, so they obtained few leases there, even after three discovery wells outlining the area brought in gushers. Joiner himself sold his land holdings to H. L. Hunt before realizing that he had hit a massive field.

As early as 1931 overproduction had become a problem. Many lease, land, and royalty owners, as well as small operators, feared that the state government would allocate production (a measure known as prorationing), which they considered a menace to their newfound source of income. Perhaps a majority, however, did favor some curtailment of production, noting that overproduction threatened the early flooding of many wells and also had lowered the price of oil in nine months from $1 a barrel to ten cents. Refineries operated by the majors refused to purchase the East Texas oil, hoping to squeeze the independents into selling their leases. In June 1931, engineers and geologists informed the Texas Railroad Commission that East Texas was capable of producing 400,000 barrels of oil a day without causing physical waste, but that trying to produce anything beyond that amount would likely result in premature flooding. The Railroad Commission promptly fixed 400,000 barrels as the maximum withdrawal, but the order was challenged in a federal district court, which ruled that the Railroad Commission's quota had no reasonable relation to physical waste.

An increasing number of East Texas operators became convinced that an excessive number of oil wells and overproduction would shorten the life of the field, and some of them turned violently against the most prolific producers. Threats of setting wells on fire and dynamiting pipelines supposedly prompted Governor Ross Sterling, a former president of Humble Oil, to declare martial law in the region and shut down all gas and oil wells in Upshur, Gregg, Rusk, and Smith Counties. In August 1931 a unit of the National Guard under the command of General Jake Wolters, a lobbyist and chief counsel for Texaco, was dispatched to suppress the runaway free enterprise. One of Wolters's aides was a Gulf official. Now the orders of the Railroad Commission were enforced, and the price of oil rose dramatically.

By June of 1932, allowable production in the Eastex was fixed at 325,000 barrels a day, although "hot-oil" operators such as Clint Murchison sometimes produced half again that much and sold the excess on the market illegally. The independent hot-oil runners resented the production "allowables" seemingly imposed—albeit through the Railroad Commission—by the major oil companies. To skirt the mandates, the hot-oil runners employed many techniques, including sticking hundred-dollar bills on wells to bribe Railroad Commission inspectors, using lockstops that flowed when apparently closed, and installing secret pipelines and bypasses. Sometimes they literally turned away Railroad Commission investigators from refineries with raised shotguns and violent threats. Between 1932 and 1934, Texas adopted three laws that squeezed the hot-oil runners, while Texans in Congress put through the Connally Hot Oil Act of 1935, which outlawed the interstate shipment of oil in violation of state quotas.

The new state and federal laws ensured that the Texas Railroad Commission could "stabilize" the oil industry. While prorationing indeed allowed the majors to drive the independents out of the processing aspect of the business, it also protected Texas independents from the price-cutting practices of the major companies, none of which were based in Texas. But because the Railroad Commission continually set the allowable output at whatever level the majors and independents requested, or compromised on, the agency soon became the creature of the industry it purported to regulate.

Meanwhile, Texas oilmen began testing their lobbying power before the legislature. In 1936 Texas lawmakers raised the tax on well-head production to 2.75 percent of the market value of the oil produced. The oil lobby denounced the new measure as confiscatory, even though prorationing—deliberate price fixing established by the state and federal government—had recently boosted the income of the oil industry by $500 million a year. Oklahoma already had in place a 5 percent well-head levy, while that of Louisiana hovered near 8 percent. One keen witness observed that Louisiana oil taxation "is being kept remarkably quiet in Texas, as certain influential interests prefer that the people of this state do not learn about the situation." Only once in the fifteen years following 1936 did the Texas legislature raise the percentage.

In the gubernatorial election of 1938, most oilmen supported W. Lee O'Daniel, the singing salesman who stormed into the governor's mansion. While the new governor and his well-heeled supporters wanted to raise revenue by adopting a state sales tax, many legislators preferred taxing oil and other natural resources. The two forces deadlocked during the legislative session of 1939, after which there went up a general demand for O'Daniel to call a special session of the legislature to settle the issue, especially after mid-August when the majors posted drastic price reductions for Texas crude. This was probably the last time when an action of the majors drew a barrage of criticism in Texas. The price cuts threatened to end drilling and eventually to wipe out the independent operators. At the instigation of the Texas Railroad Commission, especially Chairman Ernest Thompson, Texas and the other oil-producing states agreed to shut down all production for fifteen days. Thompson, looking ahead to his own candidacy in the next gubernatorial election, proposed that O'Daniel call the legislature into special session to adopt a five-cents-a-barrel tax on oil to fund the state's old-age pensions. Thompson asserted that it was "the opportunity of the age" to levy a "nickel for grandma" tax. He observed that Texas oil could not last forever and reminded statewide audiences of the much higher oil taxes in neighboring states. But O'Daniel still did not intend to tax the oil industry, or any industry for that matter, and he flatly refused to call a special session. Moreover, he easily defeated Thompson in the Democratic primary in 1940. In 1941, however, O'Daniel was forced to sign an omnibus tax bill that did raise the levies on natural resources.

Meanwhile, the usual corporate resistance to organized labor hindered the unionization of oil workers, as did the relatively high pay scales and enlightened seniority policies adopted by the major companies. Yet as early as 1905, Guffey Oil cut wages from $3 to $2.5 for a twelve-hour day, which triggered the first big oil worker strike and the creation of the first American Federation of Labor oil workers' local union. The strike secured the maintenance of the $3 scale, but it was to remain constant for more than a decade, during which time the union collapsed and the price of oil increased one-hundred fold. In 1917, ten thousand field hands and refinery workers across the Southwest walked off the job after the operators refused even to meet with their representatives. In California the oil workers won the eight-hour and $4 day, but in Texas the majors utilized martial law and armed guards to break the strike, ensuring that $3 and twelve hours still prevailed. Standard Oil companies, such as the Humble plant in Baytown and the Magnolia refinery in Beaumont, were particularly adept in maintaining company-directed unions, even after the passage of the Wagner Act in 1935 legitimized collective bargaining, forbade company domination of unions, and established the National Labor Relations Board.

During World War II unions finally succeeded in organizing most Texas refineries. Perhaps the crucial union triumph came at Port Arthur's Texaco refinery during the winter of 1941–42. In this struggle the Oil Workers' International Union (OWIU) overcame an antilabor local police force and citizenry—both of which made fierce denunciations of the union as an allegedly communist organ—vigorous company efforts to play off white workers against black workers, and a major campaign waged by a rival union to win the bargaining rights. Then, led by Standard, the oil companies tried but failed to smash the OWIU in 1945 during a relatively successful nationwide strike led by the Texas locals. Eventually oil workers became the best-paid segment of the nation's industrial work force.

Texans created an oil and gas infrastructure that was more dangerous than they knew. The greatest prewar tragedy occurred in New London, Texas, where the high school got its gas supply by tapping into a company line. The gas company winked at the common but dangerous practice of using odorless residue or waste gas, which saved the school district $3,000 a year. Then a leak developed somewhere along the school's tap line, filling the basement and hollow walls of the building with the undetectable gas. On March 18, 1937, a spark from a light switch or a shop machine ignited the pent-up gas and the school building exploded like a bomb. Some three hundred persons, most of them schoolchildren, were killed. The tragedy was so horrible that no memorial or anniversary services were held for three decades thereafter. The incident prompted new state laws, one of which required that all gas sold to the public be injected with Mercapton to give it a readily identifiable odor. A decade later, on April 16, 1947, the worst industrial accident in United States history occurred in Texas City, where a docked cargo vessel loaded with ammonium nitrate fertilizer exploded, igniting the nearby refinery tanks and creating a doomsday inferno that killed more than 570 persons. At least four thousand others suffered injuries, and the accident left more than three thousand persons homeless, as Texas City was virtually leveled. Again, safety awareness increased, but new laws and work practices were far from sufficient to safeguard the welfare of refinery workers and the local environment or to prevent future accidents.

Meanwhile with daring, expertise, and luck, hundreds of independent operators made quick fortunes in the oil business. They apparently believed that boundless opportunity awaited anyone willing to reach out for it. This simplistic image of rags-to-riches success became entrenched in the Texas mystique because the independents, many of whom had little formal education, made money without having to deal with stockholders, unions, masses of employed or unemployed persons, and the responsibility of maintaining good public relations. These men bitterly resented any governmental interference or regulation, particularly given the atmosphere during the nation's second red scare in the 1940s and 1950s. Indeed, a number of oilmen actually believed that the United States was disintegrating and that the communists were about to take control of the nation.

In 1944 and 1948 political activists among the newly rich Texas oilmen, including Hugh Roy Cullen, Arch Rowan, and E. E. Townes, spearheaded energetic third-party efforts to defeat the incumbent Democratic Presidents. They fervently believed that the federal government was overrun with communists, blacks, Jews, and bureaucrats who opposed their interests. In the election of 1944 these anti-New Dealers, posing as Democrats, almost succeeded in removing the Franklin D. Roosevelt presidential ticket from the Texas ballot. When FDR's successor, President Harry Truman, faced election in 1948, the Texas oilmen threw up the tidelands issue against him. They protested the recent United States Supreme Court ruling (1947) that California did not own its offshore lands, which, like those of Texas, were rich in oil.

In 1952 the oilmen joined the political mainstream and supported the Republican nominee, Dwight Eisenhower, who endorsed Texas's claim to its tidelands. Texas oilmen naturally preferred state to federal jurisdiction over the tidelands because state taxes were so much lower, which also helps explain the oilmen's decades-long embrace of states' rights issues. Eisenhower won Texas and the nation, and he soon signed federal legislation that delivered to Texas control of the submerged lands extending ten and one-half miles out to sea.

In the 1950s Texas oilmen such as Cullen, H. L. Hunt, and Clint Murchison attempted to control elections in other states. Rather than confining their donations to party campaign funds, usually Republican, they contributed to favored candidates in state primaries from coast to coast. Primaries customarily were envisioned as the exclusive concern of the voters of each state. Indeed, Texans would have been enraged if Pennsylvania steel money had been used to influence their choices in the Texas Democratic primary.

Yet Texas oil money contributed to the demise of senatorial candidates in several states who had the temerity to oppose, in some fashion, Wisconsin senator Joe McCarthy and his red scare.

Ever since the O'Daniel gubernatorial years, Texas oilmen have comprised a crucial element in the rise and maintenance of the establishment in Texas politics, a loosely knit, white plutocracy that has dominated the state. One of its major goals has been to keep corporate taxes low, and in this effort the oil lobby has been especially effective. After the omnibus tax of 1941, the level of oil taxation did not change until 1951, and despite repeated attempts by moderates and liberals, has not increased since 1951. The regulation pipeline portion of the tax has remained unaltered since 1935. If wellhead or refinery taxes matched those of neighboring states, Texas need not have lagged so woefully behind other industrial states in vital state services such as education.

Another goal of oilmen was to maintain continuous production. Although one reason for granting the Railroad Commission the power of prorationing was to conserve oil, according to one geologist in the 1940s, Texas "has permitted a depletion of her natural resources at a rate unequaled in the world's history." Until the 1970s Texans seemed unaware that this irreplaceable resource (and tax base) would dry up in a few decades. The stance adopted by the Railroad Commission and the oil industry, especially the independents who were so strong in the state, was to drain Texas first and furiously resist the importation of foreign oil. They also assured the citizenry that more oil could always be discovered. Genuine considerations of national defense pricked the consciences of a few Texas oilmen, who thought it might be wise to import oil from Arabia before the Russians seized it, but such thinking rarely surfaced because Arabian oil cut down on the Texans' profits. Ironically, "national security" was the very pretext used by the oil lobby in Washington, ably assisted by Senator Lyndon B. Johnson, to persuade the Eisenhower administration to restrict oil imports in 1957. The argument was that the importation of inexpensive foreign oil depressed domestic oil prices and sapped drilling incentives: while this may have been true, it was irrelevant to national defense.

In retrospect, the policy that should have been pursued—for the greater good of American society as well as of the national defense—was the establishment of national oil preserves, perhaps with some entire fields shut down and others leased to private companies. The United States, its allies, and the major oil companies controlled oil production in all of the nations of the Middle East from the late

1930s through the 1960s, and that was clearly the time to import all the oil possible from that area and conserve domestic oil for a later time. Secretary of the Interior Harold Ickes had attempted to implement such a plan during World War II, but the industry blocked him. Royalty owners and independent operators could have been compensated, though doubtless some would have had to join unemployment lines just like average Americans.

Texas stepped up its oil production in the 1960s and basked in the limelight of Lyndon Johnson's presidency. Both oil and gas production reached their all-time peaks in 1972. Three and one-half million barrels of oil per day were produced, but even that failed to meet the insatiable American demand. The import controls became irrelevant in 1973, when the Organization of Petroleum Exporting Countries (OPEC), a cartel of oil-producing nations dominated by the Muslim member-nations of the Middle East, temporarily refused to ship oil to the United States because of its support of Israel in the Yom Kippur War. With so much oil suddenly off the market, the price of U.S. oil doubled in a few months, and the continually rising prices sustained a booming decade for the Texas economy from 1973 to 1982. Texans began to take note of regional tensions and policy differences; a popular bumper sticker of the day called upon fellow Texans to "Cut off the gas and freeze a Yankee." The price of oil reached a peak of $40 a barrel in 1981, but the worldwide recession took hold the next year. Prices fell below $10 a barrel in 1986, and the oil industry and the state's economy never fully recovered. Prices fell because of low-cost drilling and the building of new, efficient refineries in OPEC nations, a decline in petroleum demand, and OPEC's inability to regulate the annual output of all its member nations. Texas oil prosperity also eroded because of the failure of many of the state's banks and savings-and-loan institutions as well as mergers and consolidations among large oil companies that left many Texans out of work.

During the boom of the 1970s, as in the 1950s, Texas oilmen tended to project an image of irresponsible power and hypocrisy. The industry became so outraged over Houston congressman Bob Eckhardt's votes for controls on oil prices and windfall profits that it spent an estimated $1 million in three elections to defeat him, finally succeeding in 1980. Eckhardt had been rated as one of the most scholarly and independent legislators in Washington. In total, the industry spent about $6 million in the elections of 1980, contributing greatly to the defeats of Senators George McGovern, Birch Bayh, and Frank Church.

Specific examples of outspoken oilmen include Eddie Chiles of Fort Worth, who in 1979 estimated that his Western Company spent more than $200,000 annually on radio advertisements decrying the dangers of big government. Chiles was continually "mad," demanding the government do only three things: "defend our shores, deliver our mail, and leave us the hell alone." He successfully wrote off the cost of the commercials as legitimate business expenses on the theory that his company would go to the dogs unless government intervention was curtailed. Meanwhile the press revealed that during the previous six years the federal government had granted Chiles $115 million in guaranteed loans to finance more than half the drilling rigs in his company fleet. This massive aid notwithstanding, Chiles's company went bankrupt during the bust of the 1980s. Another standout was Bill Clements of Dallas, who took office as governor in 1979 and claimed to be a model example of the free enterprise system. Interestingly, Commerce Department documents showed that during the previous six years Clements's Sedco Company had received $152 million in government-guaranteed loans to finance six of his rigs. Finally, a cousin of Chiles, Midland oilman Clayton Williams, attempted to succeed Clements as governor in the 1990 election. The oil and gas industry was his largest contributor in a campaign that turned into a runaway spending spree. But even with so much money in his campaign coffers, Williams, a political novice, managed to blow a fifteen-point lead over the Democratic challenger Ann Richards, self-destructing in a series of embarrassing gaffes.

The industry has also established itself as a polluter and a dangerous neighbor. In 1971 a Texas legislative committee investigated oil spills and concluded these recurring accidents introduced long-lasting toxins into the marine environment and food chain. The committee declared that the Railroad Commission has displayed a "callous disregard for the environmental damage" and that the Water Quality Board had been "conspicuously derelict in its duty" to enforce pollution laws. In the 1970s and 1980s in large sections of West Texas the industry's sloppy secondary recovery practices allowed salt water tainted with oil to seep from illegal unlined pits and faulty injection wells into the water table. Both the companies and the Railroad Commission were unresponsive to complaints. In 1988 the Railroad Commission adopted a program designed to help producers weather economic cycles by keeping inactive wells open during dips in the price of oil. In theory, such wells would be ready for reactivation as soon as oil prices returned to higher levels. In practice, however, operators who went bankrupt or left the business during the lean years simply abandoned the open wells, which posed a continual contamination hazard to groundwater supplies. In the summer of 2000 some six thousand wells had apparently been abandoned, even after eighteen months of strong prices for oil. In response, the railroad commissioners, dependent on industry money for re-election, voted two to one to do nothing about the problem.

In 1980 the *Dallas Morning News* published a series of stories that detailed the failure of the Lone Star Gas Company to maintain properly its pipeline system in the Dallas–Fort Worth area. Lone Star continually ignored gas leaks, simply recovering the cost of most of its lost gas by raising the prices it charged consumers. From 1978 to 1981 at least fifteen gas explosions ripped through area homes and businesses, killing seven residents and injuring eight. The hideously bad publicity forced the Railroad Commission to take initial steps to enforce the federal pipeline safety act in Texas— more than a decade after it was charged with doing so. The Railroad Commission soon gratefully yielded jurisdiction over pipelines to the federal Office of Pipeline Safety.

With 250,000 miles of pipelines, Texas has far more than any other state. Texas's known total of 1,654 pipeline accidents between 1985 and 2000 is more than three times greater than that of California, the state with the second worst record. Chevron compiled the worst record among the nineteen companies that reported leaks during a seventeen-month period. One aging Chevron line broke four times in eight months. On the fourth occasion in 1987 it leaked seventeen thousand gallons of gasoline and tainted the water supply of Mineral Wells with carcinogenic benzene. The company responded by distributing free bottled water to city residents and spent millions of dollars on pipeline replacements, but the problem is ongoing. One Explorer Company pipeline split open in March 2000 and released more than 500,000 gallons of gasoline and other poisons into Lake Tawakoni, one of Dallas's drinking-water reservoirs. Clearly, the industry influences, and in fact funds, the Office of Pipeline Safety, whose inspections may best be described as casual.

As for the possibility of oil spills in the Gulf of Mexico, the state's "policy" is that private industry should control them. Yet the Texas oil industry has done nothing to prepare for these potentially catastrophic events, and the Texas Gulf Coast may be the most vulnerable area in the nation for an oil spill of any type. The 1994 rupture of a forty-seven-year-old pipeline sent more than ninety thousand gallons of oil into a creek, creating a twelve-mile-long slick that contaminated ecologically sensitive wetlands along Nueces and Corpus Christi Bays. It was merely one of hundreds of leaks in pipelines operated by Koch Industries, from which the Environmental Protection Agency collected $35 million in penalties in 2000, half of which was turned over to the State of Texas for clean-up purposes.

Also notorious is the Phillips Petroleum Company. Before 1989 there were eighteen known deaths and 130 injuries at Phillips plants in the southwestern United States. A 1980 explosion caused millions of dollars worth of damage and triggered the virtual abandonment of the entire town of Phillips, Texas. Then, a 1989 explosion in another Phillips plant near Pasadena, Texas, killed twenty-three persons and cost the company a fine of $4 million for willful and serious safety violations. Two more employees lost their lives there in 1999, after which the Occupational Safety and Heath Administration fined the company $204,000 for thirteen health and safety violations. In 2000, in the same K-resin (clear plastic) unit of the same plant, a supervisor was killed and sixty-nine others were injured, some of them very badly.

Since late in the 1960s the OWIU's successor, the Oil, Chemical, and Atomic Workers Union (OCAW), has designated workplace health and safety as a premier issue. The union called a landmark strike in 1973 against Shell, allegedly the first environmental work stoppage in U.S. history. The union wanted a say in monitoring the workplace environment, calling for mandatory periodic medical examinations of employees exposed to dangerous substances and access to employee mortality statistics. This strike brought the oil workers into alliance with environmental groups also concerned about the effects of toxic wastes on the environment. But after four long months, the 1,800 members of the OCAW local in Deer Park, Texas, grudgingly accepted a severely watered-down monitoring system. This capitulation set the pattern for the 2,200 other strikers across the Southwest.

Most of the forty workers killed in the explosion in the Phillips plant near Pasadena in 1989 and a blast at Arco in Channelview in 1990 were contract laborers. Given the downturn in the industry during the 1980s, the companies hired as many nonunion employees as possible. Their wages and benefits were less expensive, but many of the newly hired workers were inexperienced. Worse yet, they often were assigned the most dangerous jobs in the plants.

Indeed, the largest single factor in the safety of the workplace has been the human element rather than technology. But the OCAW, a small union with a small national staff, has been put on the defensive in hard times and seemingly overwhelmed by trying to oversee the health and safety problems in hundreds of plants scattered around the nation. In 2000 the oil workers union merged with the larger Paperworkers union.

Oil industry spokespersons delighted in the election of one of their own, George W. Bush of the West Texas oil patch, as governor of Texas. Bush was the younger son of former president George Bush, whose administration had been unable to do much for the industry due to a massive savings-and-loan debacle and massive federal deficits. During the turbulent 1980s, the younger Bush had lost millions of investors' dollars at his company, Arbusto, but twice engineered merger deals with better-financed companies, rescuing Bush from financial ruin. He was named a general partner among other new owners of the Texas Rangers baseball team in 1988, though his contribution of $600,000 of borrowed money meant that he owned less than 2 percent of the franchise. One of Bush's oil, real estate, and baseball partners was Richard Rainwater, who contributed $100,000 to Bush's winning 1994 gubernatorial campaign against incumbent Ann Richards. Five years later, the state faced dire educational and public health problems, but Governor Bush first pressed lawmakers for an emergency $45 million tax break to help small operators continue production amid sagging oil prices. The biggest break of $1 million in savings went to Richard Rainwater's company, followed by Chevron, Texaco, and Exxon. Small operators were indeed hurting during the 1997–1999 slump in oil prices, when at times a barrel of oil cost seven times less than a barrel of Coca-Cola, and the tax break did keep many marginal wells in production.

Meanwhile, the glaring loophole in the Texas Clean Air Act of 1971 began to attract attention. The law grandfathered industrial facilities operating in 1971—many of them petrochemical concerns—to exempt them from having to install pollution-control devices required in all other plants. The solons were told that virtually all of the older plants would be decommissioned within a decade anyway. But in 1997—with Texas leading the nation in poor air quality—it was revealed that the grandfathered plants were contributing more than one-third of the state's massive amount of industrial air pollution. Confronted by a serious effort in 1997 to close the loophole allowing the dirty plants to operate, Governor Bush

pushed through a program that invited polluters to reduce voluntarily the amount of harmful emissions generated by their plants—
but with no mandated target levels, deadlines, or meaningful penalties for those who did not cooperate. In 1999, the same year a
Bush spokesperson claimed the voluntary initiatives were effective, Houston overtook Los Angeles as the smog capital of the nation. By 2000, more than 60 percent of Texans lived in areas where
the air is unhealthy to breathe.

Two Texas oilmen on one presidential ticket would seem possible only in the fantasies of the CEOs of oil and gas companies,
but Governor Bush and Dick Cheney, the latter of whom had resided and voted in Dallas for eight years, captured the Republican
party's highest nominations in 2000 (Cheney hustled back to Wyoming that summer in order to re-establish residency there). Not
surprisingly, the oil and gas industry contributed upwards of $2
million to the victory of the Bush-Cheney ticket. After barely winning the election, the results of which lay in dispute for months,
the George W. Bush administration put forth its first budget plan,
which proposed to slash funding for renewable energy programs
by 36 percent—this from a piddling appropriation in the first place!
At the same time the administration moved to encourage drilling
for oil on federal wildlife preserves and in sensitive coastal waters
then off-limits to development. Vice President Cheney specifically
denounced conservation as a major part of the solution to the current energy crisis. Even the traditionally Republican newspapers
believed that Cheney had "squandered an opportunity," with his
"narrowly drawn policy" (*Fort Worth Star-Telegram*) and was guilty
of a "cavalier treatment of conservation" (*Dallas Morning News*).
The administration soon backed down, but its orientation was obvious.

In 2001, officers in the Houston energy giant Enron Corporation, partially an oil and gas company, misrepresented it earnings
on financial statements dispatched to the government and investors. While lower-level employees and investors thought the company was actually going strong, certain CEOs dumped their holdings of Enron stock as well as awarded themselves huge bonuses.
As the news of the scandal began to emerge, these same people
barred all other employees from selling their Enron stock, much of
which constituted their retirement plans. In the fall of that year,
Enron collapsed, constituting the greatest and one of the most rapid
corporate bankruptcies in history. The whole affair was so shame-

ful that a few politicians from both major parties actually returned Enron campaign contributions. In the case of the President, this would have meant shelling out some $600,000 he had garnered over the years. In the case of Bush's successor as Texas governor, Rick Perry, the amount totaled $187,000. Perry eventually returned a fractional amount, while Bush gave nothing back.

***

Spindletop was a defining moment in Texas history, but so were the oil busts of the 1980s. The oil crashes of 1982 and especially 1986 forced the state to rely less on volatile oil and develop other means of making a living, including high-technology industries. Oil, gas, and petroleum-related products composed one-fourth of the state's gross domestic product in 1981 but less than half that amount twenty years later. At the close of 2001, the 384 drilling rigs in the state represented one-fourth of the total in 1981. Texas oil production in 2000—399 million barrels—was the lowest since 1935. The trend, if not the specific events, was inevitable. Indeed, the trajectory of the oil industry worldwide is following the pattern observed in Texas, if with a few decades' lag time. Moreover, before oil is actually tapped out sometime in the twenty-first century, much of it may simply be left in the ground, which is exactly what happened to much of the world's coal in the twentieth century. In time, oil will be replaced by other energy sources such as natural gas, wind and solar power, and fuel cells. Major energy companies currently are investing in the development of alternative fuels. Perhaps a sign of things to come, one of the world's largest windfarms is located seventy miles south of Odessa.

Texas has been the leading oil-producing state since 1928, except for 1988, when Alaska surpassed it, but perhaps three-fourths of the oil discovered in Texas remains underground. The Permian Basin, for instance, has produced 25 billion barrels of oil, but an estimated 75 billion still lies in place. Some Texas oil is being retrieved through the use of enhanced-recovery techniques, such as horizontal drilling, which allows a single drill to pierce though several oil-bearing formations as far as five miles apart. Other techniques include the injection of liquids into wells to force out more oil and the deployment of measurement-while-drilling instruments. Finally, the gathering of three-dimensional seismic data allows geologists to determine the precise holdings of any given field. These practices may stretch out the life of the industry in Texas for decades.

It would help if industry-wide unitization were adopted, mandating that deposits be drilled and developed efficiently and the maximum quantity of oil and gas obtained. Texas is the only major oil-producing state that does not provide for some form of compulsory unitization. Stripper wells, those that produce less than ten barrels per day, constituted 83 percent of the wells in Texas in 2000, and those who owned them believe that only big companies profit from unitization. Meanwhile, the majors largely are abandoning Texas for such areas as the Gulf of Mexico, the Middle East, and Russia.

The oil industry takes pride in its production, and nearly 900,000 oil and gas wells have been drilled in almost 30,000 fields in all but 37 of the state's 254 counties since 1889. Texas and U.S. oil production saved the world as we know it, since oil propelled allied military machines to victory in World War II. Production has declined every year since 1972, but even in its twilight years, the oil and gas industry (especially petrochemicals) is in no danger of fading away just yet. Certainly its political power stretches from the court house to the White House. The monument at Spindletop bears an inscription that reads, in part: "Petroleum has revolutionized industry and transportation; it has created untold wealth, built cities, furnished employment for hundreds of thousands and contributed billions in taxes to support institutions of government."

The oil industry also generated enormous waste in its early and middle years, saddled Texas with a one-industry mindset, spawned political corruption and political reaction, deliberately destroyed the development of mass-transit systems, polluted the air, water, and soil with impunity, offered unsafe working environments, dodged taxes and lobbied for regressive taxes, concealed oil and gas holdings from the federal and state governments, and engaged in monopolistic price fixing. Texas has, in a sense, paid a high price for being so rich in oil and gas.

Suggested Reading

Clark, James, and Michael Halbouty. *The Last Boom.* New York: Random House, 1972.
——. *Spindletop.* New York: Random House, 1952.
Engler, Robert. *The Politics of Oil.* Chicago: University of Chicago Press, 1961.
Forbes, Gerald. *Flush Production.* Norman: University of Oklahoma Press, 1942.
Goodwyn, Lawrence. *Texas Oil, American Dream.* Austin: The Center for American History, The University of Texas at Austin, 1996.
King, John. *The Early History of the Houston Oil Company.* Houston: Texas Gulf Coast Historical Association, 1959.

Larson, Henrietta, and Kenneth Porter. *History of the Humble Oil and Refining Company*. New York: Harper, 1959.

Lynch, Gerald. *Roughnecks, Drillers, and Tool Pushers*. Austin: University of Texas Press, 1987.

Malavis, Nicholas. *Bless the Pure and Humble*. College Station: Texas A&M University Press, 1996.

Moore, Richard. *West Texas after the Discovery of Oil*. Austin: Jenkins Publishing Company, 1971.

O'Connor, Harvey. *History of the Oil Workers International Union*. Denver: Monthly Review Press, 1950.

Olien, Roger, and Diana Olien. *Oil Booms*. Lincoln: University of Nebraska Press, 1982.

——. *Wildcatters*. Austin: Texas Monthly Press, 1984.

Presley, James. *A Saga of Wealth*. New York: Putnam, 1978.

Rister, C. C. *Oil*. Norman: University of Oklahoma Press, 1949.

Tait, Samuel. *The Wildcatters*. Princeton: Princeton University Press, 1945.

One Riot–One Ranger. Photo from the Texan House, Inc. *Courtesy of the Collection of Mr. and Mrs. Robert Summers.*

CHAPTER SEVENTEEN

The Texas Rangers: An Overview

Ben Procter

THE LAND FROM WHICH THE TEXAS RANGERS arose was a primitive frontier, fraught with danger and a disquieting struggle with nature. The Anglos who settled in Texas early in the 1820s found themselves in an abundant, yet inhospitable, country. In certain areas the soil was rich, capable of producing bountiful crops of cotton and corn; but fearsome and unpredictable climatic conditions—northers, tornadoes, sleet and hail, torrential rain, and blistering heat—were also rampant. Partly because of the Spanish influence many Indian tribes were not a threat to the newcomers, but in August and September a "full Comanche moon," signifying the most propitious time for brutal raids, ominously arose, spreading terror throughout lonely frontier settlements and outposts. For that matter, simply to live beyond the pale of organized society, in an area far from the dictates of the government in Mexico City, was challenge enough—perhaps romantic, at times foolhardy, and definitely unhealthy.

So in this raw land the Rangers pooled past knowledge and experience. Out of necessity they used whatever means they had at hand to survive. From the Mexicans they learned horsemanship, the importance of a good mount on the open prairies, the spirit of the *vaquero*. From the Indians they acquired an understanding of plainscraft, of tracking and relentless pursuit, and of ferocity in fighting. And from their own background they inherited a rugged stubbornness for frontier living and an ability to adapt to new environments. Through this combination of cultures the Rangers were, in fact, an awesome force of men, prompting John S. "Rip" Ford to remark admiringly: "They ride like Mexicans; trail like Indians, shoot like Tennesseans; and fight like the devil."

In looks and manner the Rangers were quite distinguishable from such fighting units as the militia or regular army. Recruited at first from the craftiest frontier fighters, and later from leather-faced cowboys and hard-bitten lawmen, they were not concerned with clothes and personal appearance but rather with performance. During the War with Mexico—and for that matter during most of the nineteenth century—they had a "ferocious and outlaw look" about them, usually "dressed in every variety of garment" and armed to the teeth with knives, rifles, and a brace of pistols. In fact, the only well-groomed "critters" among them were their horses, magnificent animals which the Rangers cared for meticulously. Nowhere was there evidence of military organization—no flags or pennants, no insignias or evidences of rank, no government-issued equipment or medical supplies, no formality between officers and enlisted men.

Yet no one could fail to identify a Ranger captain. He had a charismatic quality that set him apart from his men. Although not necessarily large or powerful physically, he exuded a quiet confidence. In a time of crisis he knew, almost instinctively, what to do, possessing that rare combination of boldness and judgment which allowed him, as historian Walter Prescott Webb observed, "to lead rather than direct his men." For him, retreat was unpardonable, defeat unbearable; his reputation and prestige demanded success, because in any given situation he still had to prove himself capable of leadership before his men.

So for a century, beginning informally as early as 1823 and officially in 1835, the Rangers protected Anglo settlers in a personalized manner. Along the Rio Grande or on the northern and western frontiers, they conducted investigations in man-to-man confrontations, relentless in their performance of duty and oftentimes pitiless in their administration of the law. After all, there was nothing complex about frontier justice; the only criteria for law enforcement officers being affirmative answers to the following questions: Could they ride? Could they shoot? Did they have the guts and skills to enforce Anglo-Saxon law?

Because of their special aptitude for survival, the Rangers achieved an awesome reputation as frontier fighters. In the War with Mexico (1846–1848), with captains John Coffee "Jack" Hays, Ben McCulloch, and Samuel Walker as leaders, the Rangers were "the eyes and ears" for General Zachary Taylor as well as "the cutting edge" for the American army that conquered Mexico City. During the late 1850s under Senior Captain "Rip" Ford the Rangers fought the formidable Comanches to a standstill, then confronted Juan Cortina, the "Red Robber of the Rio Grande," routing his forces in a series of encounters. After the Civil War and Reconstruction they again became the scourge of the outlaw population, with the brutally efficient Captain Leander McNelly administering primitive six-gun protection to Anglos along the Rio Grande and Captain John B. Jones effectively directing the Frontier Battalion on the northern frontier. And during the late nineteenth and early twentieth centuries Captains J. W. "Bill" McDonald, J. H. Brooks, John H. Rogers, John R. Hughes, Will Wright, Tom Hickman, and Frank Hamer upheld Ranger traditions through their forceful, unrelenting application of the law.

Because of their incredible deeds, these captains fashioned traditions that affected all future Rangers. For each new member they created an aura of invincibility, a course of action requiring dedication and perseverance, toughness and endurance. No Ranger could escape their exploits—Jack Hays in 1841 single-handedly fighting off a hundred Indian braves at Enchanted Rock (in Gillespie County); Ben McCulloch in 1847 risking torture and death at Encarnacion to obtain accurate information for General Taylor; Lee McNelly in the 1870s instructing his men that "you can't lick a man who just keeps on coming on"; Bill McDonald in 1906 successfully backing down twenty armed black soldiers at Fort Brown and then disdainfully telling an angry mob that demanded he turn over to them a black prisoner in his custody that they (the lynch mob) "looked like fifteen cents in Mexican money"; and Frank Hamer in 1934 doggedly pursuing "mad-dog killers" Clyde Barrow and Bonnie Parker for 102 days.

Yet these captains also fixed an image of personal toughness, indifference to cruelty, and six-gun justice (a reputation most helpful to them in frontier Texas) that would cause considerable difficulties for the force in modern times. In Mexico during 1846–47 Hays, McCulloch, and other Rangers slaughtered people with such cold-blooded hatred that they soon became known among the populace as *los Tejanos Sangrientos* (the bloody Texans). On one occasion in 1875, McNelly stacked the bodies of fifteen Mexican cattle rustlers like cordwood in the Brownsville town square, pointedly demonstrating Ranger efficiency and warning all wrongdoers to cease and desist. Then along the Rio Grande during World War I, because of suspected German intrigue and sabotage, because of growing numbers of Mexican nationalists and their growing hatred for the gringo, and because of the need to round up draft dodgers attempting to escape across the border, the Rangers—particularly the Special Rangers appointed by Governors James E. Ferguson and William P.

Hobby—created a veritable bloodbath along the Rio Grande, killing as many as five thousand Mexicans in five years. Webb described this reign of terror by saying: "Lead . . . [sank] more men in the Rio Grande in a year than gold . . . [did] in a decade." And finally in the 1920s Frank Hamer, who was utterly fearless, who "didn't give a damn whether he lived or died," and who therefore personified Ranger tradition, continued in much the same manner. In that brutal land along the Rio Bravo or in the rowdy oil-boom towns or even in the violent young cities of Texas where the law was as unsophisticated as the people, Hamer often used the hard toe of his boot to intimidate an unruly mob or a cantankerous opponent. At the same time he despaired of modern technology in apprehending bank robbers, cattle rustlers, and desperadoes, commenting on more than one occasion to his Ranger company that "nothing was as effective as a .45 slug in the gut."

By the early 1930s, however, neither leadership nor tradition could sustain the Rangers sufficiently. With the state legislature slashing departmental budgets because of the Great Depression, the force, which at full complement could number seventy-five men, usually employed only thirty-five to forty-five men. Besides being undermanned, they had also become antiquated by modern science and urbanization. While criminals in high-powered cars "shuttled between distant cities like commuters," the Rangers relied on free railroad passes or their own cars—with a monthly allotment of $50 per company for "repairs or upkeep"—to traverse the state. And as for weapons, although receiving "one improved carbine [usually a lever-action Winchester .30-30 or a .30/06 rifle] and a pistol [a single-action Colt .45] at cost" from the state, the Rangers were hard-pressed to compete with gangsters who used Thompson submachine guns and Browning automatic rifles acquired at no cost.

Then, late in July 1932, the Rangers almost destroyed themselves by becoming involved in politics. Their grave mistake was openly supporting Governor Ross Sterling against Miriam A. "Ma" Ferguson in the Democratic primary. Sterling lost. So in January 1933, upon assuming office, the new governor fired every Ranger for his partisanship—forty-four in all. Then matters grew worse. The state legislature reduced Ranger salaries, eliminated longevity pay, slashed travel budgets, and limited force personnel to thirty-two men. Governor Ferguson added to the chaos by appointing new officers, many of whom "by any standard," historian Steve Schuster candidly asserted, "were a contemptible lot." In less than a year one private was convicted of murder; several others in Company D, after having raided a gambling hall in Duval County, were found to have set up their own gaming establishment with the confiscated equipment; and still another, a captain, was arrested for theft and embezzlement. Worst of all, the governor began using Special Ranger commissions, as her husband had done during World War I, as a means of political patronage. Within two years she enlarged this once elite force to 2,344 men, prompting the *Austin American* to comment that "about all the requirements a person needed . . . to be a Special Ranger was to be a human being."

The deterioration of the Rangers into a source of patronage, corruption, and ridicule brought catastrophic effects upon state law enforcement. During the second Ferguson administration crime and violence became widespread, bank holdups and murder commonplace. Soon few states could boast of a more vicious assortment of gangsters or provide a safer sanctuary for the outlaw element. For instance, criminal residents in the Dallas–Fort Worth area alone included George "Machine-Gun" Kelly, Raymond Hamilton, Clyde Barrow, and Bonnie Parker. And who besides "Ma" Ferguson was responsible for this breakdown in the public defense? To most Texans the answer was obvious. As one newspaper editor sarcastically remarked, "A Ranger commission and a nickel can get . . . a cup of coffee anywhere in Texas."

In January 1935, however, Governor James V. Allred soon obviated the causes of such derision. Having campaigned the previous year to "overhaul" the state law enforcement machinery, he pushed through the legislature a bill creating the Texas Department of Public Safety (DPS). To formulate and supervise administrative policies and procedures, he appointed a three-man Public Safety Commission, which in turn selected a director and an assistant director. In organizational structure the new state agency had three basic units—the Texas Rangers, the Highway Patrol, and a newly created Headquarters Division at Austin, which served as a modern scientific crime laboratory and detection center. Thus on August 10, 1935, with the official initiation of the DPS, the Rangers became an important part of a much larger law enforcement team. And although Walter Prescott Webb sadly predicted the demise of the Rangers as a separate entity, fearing that they would lose their identity and be absorbed by the more sizeable Highway Patrol, it did not happen. Through reorganization came much-needed reform and state support; hence the modernization of the Ranger force began.

Yet, to a certain extent, Webb's fears were not unfounded, for this reorganization did mark the end of a law enforcement era, of certain procedural methods and techniques, of the frontier-marshal type of confrontation. Under the new system Rangers had to meet certain physical requirements, write reports detailing their actions, and were eligible for advancement through a merit system that emphasized knowledge and skill. No longer would they be subject to the caprice or whim of a governor's appointment, to individual economic threats of the legislature—the DPS would see to that. And no longer would they have to combat criminals with outmoded, obsolete law enforcement machinery. In other words, they received scientific training and the latest equipment. Organizationally the three DPS commissioners and director divided the state into five parts—in 1937 into six—and assigned a Ranger captain and his company to a specific area. In turn, privates received duty stations in key towns throughout each district; under no circumstances could they leave their home territory without orders.

In spite of such reforms, the Rangers remained in a precarious position for the next three years, one problem after another undermining leadership and lowering morale. Late in September 1938, however, the commissioners appointed Homer Garrison, Jr., as director, and thereafter all segments of the DPS were in safe hands. But for the Rangers especially, this six-foot, two-inch, square-jawed, and bespectacled new leader proved to be an ideal choice. A former deputy sheriff in Angelina County who had joined the Highway Patrol at its inception, Garrison understood these rugged, individualistic men; therefore, he was able to integrate them into a well-organized structure without blunting their initiative and pride. They considered the "Colonel," in fact, as one of their own; he was a man of unquestionable integrity who demanded loyalty and discipline and pride, traits of character which they identified as those of a Ranger. Increasingly over the years they came to appreciate his tact and diplomacy, his strong support, and his ability to "handle legislators." Thus the Garrison legend began to build, growing to gigantic proportions during the next thirty years.

From the beginning Garrison worked adroitly and patiently to build the force. Whenever a major criminal case occurred in the state, he immediately sent Rangers to investigate, thereby enhancing their prestige as well as giving them back the freedom of movement so ingrained in their character and tradition. Against new Governor W. Lee "Pappy" O'Daniel and legislators on an "economy jag," he struggled to maintain appropriations. In 1939, before Garrison's "educational approach" began to have the desired effects upon state leaders, the Rangers lost two captains and five investigators to a cut in funds. And throughout 1939 and 1940 Garrison ignored gubernatorial entreaties to place the Rangers in the Adjutant General's Department, refusing to let the Rangers fall once again under political domination. But most important, during the next few years, Garrison surrounded himself with men who had the ability, courage, and dedication to uphold the world-renowned reputation of the force. Thus he encouraged A. Y. Allee, Hardy Purvis, Leo Bishop, Manny Gault, and Zeno Smith to continue their service, while luring into the organization such outstanding lawmen as future Captains M. T. "Lone Wolf" Gonzaullas, Bob Crowder, John Klevenhagen, Raymond Waters, Eddie Oliver, J. C. Paulk, and Clint Peoples.

In September 1941, because of Garrison's persuasive counseling, the legislature increased the Ranger force to forty-five men—and just in time. After the Japanese attack on Pearl Harbor many additional duties were thrust upon them. Together with the Highway Patrol and the FBI, the Rangers immediately rounded up suspected enemy aliens and placed them in detention camps near Kenedy, Crystal City, and Seagoville. In turn, they kept close surveillance over the thousands of German Americans in Central Texas and the few Japanese Americans in the Lower Valley, although they found little reason to suspect the loyalty of these U.S. citizens. Then, when Garrison accepted the chairmanship of defense police mobilization in Texas and soon thereafter of other important home-front duties, the Rangers were repeatedly called upon to show films on the training of air-raid wardens, to take a statewide inventory of the guns, armament, and ammunition of all law enforcement agencies, and to instruct civilians and local police in the latest techniques of defending factories, refineries, generating plants, dams, and other vital industries from sabotage. At the same time, because of their experience along the border, Rangers tracked down escaped prisoners-of-war trying to reach Mexico. Despite these diverse responsibilities, however, they still carried out equally time-consuming and often dangerous regular police work. In June 1943, for instance, Rangers Johnny Klevenhagen and Eddie Oliver apprehended two criminals in downtown Houston after a running gunfight. While in Beaumont, Captain Hardy Purvis and several of his company helped maintain order after a bloody race riot near the shipyards.

Nor did Ranger duties decrease in post–World War II America because, with demobilization, a serious crime wave enveloped the nation. Under these circumstances Colonel Garrison succeeded in impressing state legislators with the need for more efficient law enforcement; therefore, the DPS budget rose from $1,549,831 in

1944 to $4,717,400 in 1950. With such encouragement Garrison strove to improve the DPS, the Rangers specifically reflecting his demand for greater excellence. In 1947 he increased their number from forty-five to fifty-one men, equipped them and the Highway Patrol with seventy-five state-owned automobiles with three-way radios, and required the Bureau of Education to instruct Rangers annually in the latest crime-fighting techniques. By the next year Garrison further aided investigative methods by providing Rangers with additional mobile receivers and transmitters as well as the newest AM and FM power equipment. And in 1949 he broke ground on new buildings in Austin that by 1953 would house a modern crime-detection center.

The Rangers responded accordingly, making headlines continually during the 1950s by acts of daring and heroism. But in spite of their excellent performance, a personnel increase to sixty-two men in 1961, better training, able leadership, and more comprehensive service, the Rangers came under heavy political fire in the 1960s. Charged with being "*pistoleros*" (hired gunmen) of the governor, "strike-breakers" against labor unions, and "the Mexican Americans' Ku Klux Klan," the Rangers found themselves in an impossible situation—and to a man they did not like it. Because of Supreme Court rulings after 1954 regarding a defendant's civil rights, they felt "handcuffed" by the judges—their previous methods of police procedure under question, their attempts at law enforcement stymied by legal technicalities. Nor did the Civil Rights Act of 1964 and subsequent amendments improve their disposition or position, especially with Mexican Americans charging them with violations at every turn. But more than anything else, their involvement in 1966 with "la Huelga"—a strike involving stoop farm laborers at the 1,600-acre, well-irrigated La Casita Farms near Rio Grande City—proved a source of irritation, a bewildering, unpleasant assignment which brought into question their methods of law enforcement, indeed an excuse for the dissolution of their organization. In trying to keep peace between management and labor, to protect property, and to uphold the law, they were ineffective in the eyes of a generation facing the riots and violence of a Newark or a Detroit. As one DPS commissioner observed, they tried "to cope with current problems by using yesterday's tools." They became, therefore, a political football that Texas liberals could kick at conservatives, a club that U.S. Senator Ralph Yarborough could swing at his inveterate enemy Governor John Connally, a straw man that organized labor could attack to strengthen the cause of farm unionism in Texas, even a symbol of oppression which Mexican Americans could use to help stir a social revolution in the lower Rio Grande Valley. Captain A. Y. Allee, a crusty veteran of thirty-five years on the border, probably reflected Ranger feelings best in stating to State Senator Don Kennard of Fort Worth: "Son, this is the goddamdest thing I've ever been in."

Taken aback by such charges levied against the force, as well as by the death of Colonel Garrison in May 1968, DPS commissioners took a "hard look" at the Rangers—and after a lot of investigation and some "soul-searching," as in the past, came new guidelines to meet present and future needs. Under the leadership of Colonel Wilson E. "Pat" Speir, the new director of the DPS who had worked his way up through the ranks since entering the department in 1939, and his assistant, Lieutenant Colonel Leo Gossett, the Rangers regrouped and reorganized. By November 1969, after the legislature had enlarged the force to seventy-three men—then to eighty-two in 1971, eighty-eight in 1973, and ninety-four in 1974—Speir and the commissioners established a Criminal Law Enforcement Division (Narcotics, Intelligence, and the Rangers) under Chief James M. "Jim" Ray. In turn, they elevated veteran Ranger Clint Peoples to senior captain and soon thereafter (in 1971) Captain Bill Wilson as his assistant. When Peoples retired in April 1974, Wilson assumed command with Captain J. L. "Skippy" Rundell as his assistant.

As a result of such reorganization the Rangers became more efficient, better-trained law enforcement officers. Under this regime applicants for enlistment had to be between the ages of thirty and fifty, had to have eight years of on-the-job police experience, and had to have an intermediate certificate, which entailed from four hundred to six hundred hours of classroom instruction. After 1974 they were required also to have sixty hours of college work. In an intensive training program Rangers received special courses running the gamut of law enforcement experience—including detection and apprehension, gathering of evidence, criminal law, and courtroom presentation of facts. At the same time they became proficient in using their equipment as well as learning how to cultivate good public relations. While on the job, they attended monthly company meetings where their captain kept them abreast of the latest procedures in criminal investigation and department policies. Unlike those Rangers of the Republic and frontier days, or even of the 1920s and 1930s, they now rode in high-powered, state-furnished automobiles equipped with multi-frequency radios as well as riot guns and a rifle, tear gas, transport gear, and a scientific investigative kit. They also had standardized weapons provided by the state, including a .357 combat magnum sidearm and a Remington .30/06 and .30/30 rifle with a telescopic sight. Yet they still maintained an individual style of dress, which usually consisted of western-style pants and coat, black boots, black tie, white shirt, and Stetson hat.

The modern Texas Rangers, most of whom are stationed in strategic rural counties that often lack sufficient law enforcement manpower and criminal investigative facilities, are therefore walking police laboratories—highly mobile, well-armed, and well-trained. Yet they have retained the traits and qualities of character that in 1935 Webb lamented were being lost; indeed, in many ways they appear to be shaped in the same rough mold as their predecessors. Basically they are uncomplicated men—direct, straightforward, and not especially concerned about social amenities. They use the English language as a tool for direct communication, not as a device to trick or deceive; hence their difficulty at times with newspeople or reporters who tend toward sensationalism. Grammatically they are an English teacher's nightmare; yet they clearly express themselves, sometimes punctuating their sentences with colorful if not downright earthy expressions. Although outwardly friendly and easy-going, they are suspicious of strangers and hesitant to talk, "You might have been one of those damn New York magazine writers." Once a person wins their trust, however, they will go out of their way to be helpful.

But make no mistake about these men. The Rangers have been, and are, the scourge of those outside the law, obviously feared, sometimes hated, always respected. They are proud men—proud of their traditions and their fellow officers' accomplishments. They have an intangible, almost unexplainable quality of toughness about them: possibly it is the way they handle themselves. Some are no longer lean and trim, a few are wrinkled and graying, yet all exude a certain poise and strong self-confidence. Perhaps it is the realization that these men have confronted the toughest criminals in the state, that their tradition of "One riot, One Ranger" has steeled them toward danger and death. Whatever the reason, these men do have the reputation of toughness and bravery, of dedication to law enforcement, of being the elite of Texas lawmen. Their esprit de corps is almost unbelievable; they will admit, in fact, that becoming a Texas Ranger has transformed their lives completely. "You feel lucky to get the Ranger badge. So many want it," Captain Jim Riddles candidly stated in 1966. "So you take an eternal vow that whatever happens you won't break your oath to uphold the law." Colonel Pat Speir, in viewing the history of the force and assessing the modern-day Rangers, probably put it best: "The Rangers . . . still exhibit the same alertness and dedication to duty and courage and a willingness to stand up and be counted that they did from 1823 on."

Suggested Reading

Conger, Roger, et al. *The Texas Rangers*. Waco: Texian Press, 1969.

Gillett, James B. *Six Years with the Texas Rangers, 1875 to 1881*. Edited by M. M. Quaife. New Haven: Yale University Press, 1925.

Greer, James Kimmins. *Colonel Jack Hays: Texas Frontier Leader and California Builder*. New York: E. P. Dutton & Company, Inc., 1952.

Martin, Jack. *Border Boss: Captain John R. Hughes—Texas Ranger*. Austin: State House Press, 1990.

Paine, Albert Bigelow. *Captain Bill McDonald, Texas Ranger: A Story of Frontier Reform*. New York: J. J. Little & Ives Co., 1909.

Procter, Ben. *Just One Riot: Episodes of The Twentieth Century Texas Rangers*. Austin: Eakin Press, 1991.

Reid, Samuel C., Jr. *The Scouting Expeditions of McCulloch's Texas Rangers*. Philadelphia: G. B. Zieber and Company, 1847.

Sowell, A. J. *Life of "Big Foot" Wallace*. Bandera: Frontier Times, 1934.

Sterling, William W. *Trails and Trials of a Texas Ranger*. Norman: University of Oklahoma Press, 1968.

Vestal, Stanley. *Bigfoot Wallace, A Biography*. Boston: Houghton Mifflin Company, 1942.

Webb, Walter Prescott. *The Texas Rangers: A Century of Frontier Defense*, 2nd ed. Austin: University of Texas Press, 1965.

Nolan Ryan. *Courtesy of the Office of Nolan Ryan.*

CHAPTER EIGHTEEN

Sports in Texas

James W. Pohl

TEXAS LONG HAS BEEN IDENTIFIED AS A
sports center in America. Although many Texans regard football as
the sport, ironically the game was a bit slow in coming to the Southwest. Football had been played in the East since the 1870s, but the
first recorded college game in Texas took place in Austin in 1894.
On that day The University of Texas (UT) defeated Texas A&M 38-
0. The Southwest Conference was organized in 1914 with eight charter members—Arkansas, Oklahoma, Oklahoma A&M, Baylor, Rice,
Southwestern, UT, and Texas A&M. Oklahoma was the first conference champion, but by 1919 it had moved on to midwestern football. After eighty years, it would return to play in a new conference, the Big-Twelve.

Perhaps the best-known Texas player during the early years
was the slightly built Alvin "Bo" McMillin, quarterback for the Praying Colonels of Centre College, Kentucky. McMillin and his team-
mate, fellow Texan James "Red" Weaver, were the first All-Americans from a southern team. In 1919 Centre accomplished what many
eastern sportswriters regarded as an impossibility, beating Harvard
6-0 on the Crimson's home field. This same Centre team, with seven
Texans on its roster, stopped off in Dallas to play what was regarded
as an outclassed Texas A&M team coached by Dana X. Bible. When
time ran out, the Aggies had stunned Centre with a 22-14 victory.
The celebrated sportswriter Walter Camp, who along with Caspar
Whitney named the All-American "teams" and conducted national
rankings, observed that "now we have reached a situation when a
first-class and winning team might be developed in any section of
the country." In 1923 Texas had its first All-American, W. D. Johnson,
a guard from Texas A&M who made Camp's third team.

By 1934 the Southwest Conference had come of age. In that
year Rice beat a good team from Purdue; Southern Methodist (SMU)

defeated Fordham before a huge New York crowd; and UT, in a supreme effort, overcame Notre Dame. Although a few players made relatively minor All-American Lists, the conference achieved its first bona fide, first-team All-Americans with Darrell Lester, a center from Texas Christian (TCU), and Bill Wallace, a running back from Rice. In 1934, the football was made slimmer to make it easier to throw, and soon the forward pass was dramatically altering the game. Two teams closely identified with passing were TCU, coached by L. D. "Dutch" Meyer, and SMU, coached by Matty Bell. In a thrilling game in Fort Worth in 1935, the SMU Mustangs, led by its versatile All-American halfback Bobby Wilson, defeated TCU, led by quarterback Sammy Baugh, 20-14. The victory earned the Mustangs a number-one ranking and a trip to the Rose Bowl, where they were upset 7-0 by an inspired Stanford team. That same year TCU defeated Louisiana State University in a tight game in the Sugar Bowl. In addition to Wilson, Lester repeated his All-American honors, and Baugh made the second team. In 1936 and 1937 Baugh was first-string All-American, and TCU established itself as a team with a passing quarterback. In 1938 a 5' 8", 150-pound Davey O'Brien out of Woodrow Wilson High School in Dallas led the Horned Frogs through an eleven-game, undefeated season, which included another Sugar Bowl victory. O'Brien was named All-American, and TCU won the national championship. In 1940, A&M fullback "Jarrin' John" Kimbrough became an All-American. The University of Texas also developed a potent team with Bobby Layne, another passing All-American quarterback of the 1940s.

But it was in 1947, 1948, and 1949 that the Southwest Conference produced a young man who is generally regarded as the most remarkable football player to come from Texas. Doak Walker, a quarterback in the single wing at Southern Methodist, did everything: he ran, passed, kicked extra points after touchdowns, returned punts and kick-offs, blocked, defended against the pass, and kicked field goals (his specialty in the pros). He made the All-American team three years in a row. Furthermore, Walker won the Maxwell Trophy as a sophomore, the Heisman Trophy as a junior, and the Sportsman of the Year Award as a senior. The legendary sports writer Grantland Rice, who inherited the responsibility of selecting the All-American teams after Camp's death, called Walker "the most authentic all-around player in football history." In time, Walker's following became so great that SMU moved its home games to the Cotton Bowl, which had to be expanded to hold the crowds. It was truly "the house that Doak built." Walker remains the only SMU player to have his jersey retired.

Counting Walker, the Southwest Conference has produced seven Heisman Trophy winners: Davey O'Brien, TCU; John Kimbrough, Texas A&M; John David Crow, Texas A&M; Earl Campbell, Texas; and Andre Ware, Houston. One Texas high school, Woodrow Wilson in Dallas, has produced two Heisman Trophy winners, O'Brien and Tim Brown, the magnificent punt returner and running back of Notre Dame and the Oakland Raiders. In addition, six Southwest Conference players have come in second in the balloting for the coveted prize. The Heisman Trophy, granted by the New York Athletic Club, is named after Rice's John Heisman, one of football's great pioneers. It was Heisman who had the idea in 1893 of centering the ball off the ground rather than rolling it. He also began the use of the words "hep" and "hike," and urged the legalization of the forward pass. Another Heisman winner from The University of Texas was Ricky Williams, who played in the newly formed Big-Twelve Conference.

There have been many exciting games involving Texas varsity football teams. Perhaps the greatest one was played in 1949—SMU versus Notre Dame. Ironically, it was a game in which an injured Walker did not play. That year Notre Dame had one of the best teams in the entire history of college football. Loaded with superstars, it had crushed all opposition and was unanimously voted the number-one team in America. SMU, on the other hand, was injury-riddled and had been beaten several times. What very few football fans could have predicted was the dazzling performance of SMU's Kyle Rote, a young back out of San Antonio's Thomas Jefferson High School. Rote ran and passed for 261 yards and averaged forty-eight yards per punt. Notre Dame won the game 27-20, but the Fighting Irish had been forced to play very hard indeed. The next year Rote became an All-American.

The Southwest Conference's next great period was the 1960s and 1970s. During this time Darrell Royal, UT's coach, led his Longhorns to eleven conference games and three national championships, together with sixteen bowl games. A list of exciting Longhorn games must include the victories over Navy in 1964 in the Cotton Bowl, over Arkansas in 1969, and over Notre Dame in 1970. In 1968 an assistant coach at UT and former Southwest Texas player, Emory Bellard, invented the Wishbone-T, which improved the triple option that was so much a part of Royal's success. The triple option itself came from Bill Yeoman, who used it with his Houston Cougars in 1966. During these years Texas Tech and Houston entered the Southwest Conference, the latter with early success, the former with later success.

The Houston-TCU game in 1990 proved thrilling. Houston's All-American David Klingler quarterbacked the unbeaten Cougars to a victory, but the star of the show was a TCU second-string quarterback, Matt Vogler, who came off the bench because starter Leon Clay suffered a broken thumb. Vogler not only set a new Southwest Conference passing record but also a new National Collegiate Athletic Association (NCAA) record by passing for an amazing 690 yards in a single game. Curiously, in that same game, Klingler threw for 563 yards. Two weeks later Klingler threw for 572 yards on his way to setting an NCAA record of eleven touchdown passes. Unfortunately, the record came against Eastern Washington, a school hardly known as a football power. Amazingly, it was not long before Klingler went on to break Vogler's record by passing for more than 700 yards.

But Texas football is not merely the Southwest Conference. From the old Texas Intercollegiate Athletic Conference came the excellent Lone Star Conference, which continually amazed spectators from other parts of the country who heard little of that league. The teams of the Lone Star Conference were little short of sensational. Sam Houston in 1964, Southwest Texas in 1967 and 1971, East Texas in 1972, Abilene Christian in 1977, and Angelo State in 1978 played first-class football and were often NAIA champions. The most phenomenal performance, however, was that of Texas A&I (now Texas A&M, Kingville), which under coach Gil Steinke had one of the best records in American varsity football (182-61-4). A&I won six NAIA championships between 1959 and 1976 and was ranked number-one in thirty-six consecutive polls between 1974 and 1977. Another good small-college team has been Texas Lutheran, of the Big State League, which won NAIA Division II championships in 1974 and 1975. In 1980 and 1981, Southwest Texas State University won two national championships in a row, blowing out a highly regarded and previously undefeated Northern Michigan in the process.

The University of North Texas (UNT), formerly a member of the TIAA, the Gulf Coast Conference, the Missouri Valley Conference, and the Southland Conference, has consistently fielded solid teams with top athletes such as Ray Renfro and All-Americans Abner Haynes (1959) and Joe Greene (1968). Steve Ramsay set ten NCAA records including one for sixty-nine touchdown passes, and Cedric Hardman was a first-round pro draft choice in 1969. Over the years UNT has beaten solid teams such as the University of Houston and Texas Tech, and in the 1980s and 1990s UNT defeated Tennessee, Rice, SMU, and TCU, while narrowly losing to UT by a margin of two hotly contested decisions by the officials, one of whom later admitted having made bad calls.

In the 1980s, collegiate football in Texas faced some of its greatest challenges, and the Southwest Conference dropped in strength and reputation. Just a few years earlier, Eric Dickerson and Craig James had formed the splendid running tandem known as "the Pony Express" at SMU, while Texas and Texas A&M were unchallenged as national powerhouses. But by the late 1980s, SMU received the NCAA "death penalty" for major violations, and for two more seasons it was not even allowed to field a team. Meanwhile in College Station the A&M Board of Regents, led by "Bum" Bright, hired Jackie Sherrill, a successful coach from the University of Pittsburgh, at the then incredible salary of more than $400,000. Amazingly, university president Frank Vandiver was not even consulted on the matter. A&M had developed a reputation for dumping coaches, and the selection of Sherrill was supposed to put an end to that practice. Although A&M's football improved, its program came under scrutiny, and NCAA sanctions followed. In the midst of controversy, Sherrill felt compelled to resign. He was replaced by R. C. Slocum, who has managed a lengthy tenure with the Aggies and, despite some setbacks, has fielded very good teams. In 1989, A&M went so far as to hire a Compliance Officer to see that the Athletic Department understood and abided by NCAA rules. Matters went from bad to worse for the conference in 1990, when, also because of recruiting violations, the NCAA prohibited a solid University of Houston team from participating in any bowl games at the end of the season. Unfortunately, more scandals followed. In 1989 Associated Press ran a story entitled "Scandals hurt SWC's recruiting" and quoted a Pacific Ten (PAC-Ten) recruiting coordinator who predicted that "the SWC will be lucky to keep a third of the top players in the state." Simultaneously, an Atlantic Coast Conference coach opined even that figure was too optimistic.

As the reputation of the Southwest Conference declined, so did the quality of its football. Thus, in the midst of its seventy-fifth anniversary as a conference, Arkansas dropped a bombshell by announcing that the Razorbacks were leaving the SWC for the Southeastern Conference (SEC). Although the reasons seemed apparent, the SWC spent $100,000 on a study to examine the cause of its decline. When published, the report confirmed the obvious. Among other things, the SWC ranked seventh among the nation's seven major conferences in game attendance. On any given Saturday, stadiums held a mere 68 percent of capacity. Even worse than the low gate receipts was the loss of television revenue. In the age of sports video, the SWC was ranked only sixth in national television marketing, fifth in revenue gained from televised bowl appearances, and fifth in athletic department budgets.

Trouble really followed when Notre Dame, convinced that it could make more money elsewhere, stopped its home games from being televised through the traditional auspices of the College Football Association (CFA). That decision meant that each CFA school (including those in the Southwest Conference) would lose about $150,000 each in the regular season alone. Though Notre Dame was shaken by the outraged reaction of the other CFA members, in the end "money talked" and money won. As one leading Texas sportswriter wrote, "Notre Dame officials traded a large slice of precious integrity for $30 million." It was a far cry indeed from that November day in 1920 when the first football game was given play-by-play coverage on radio. It was a Southwest Conference game, Texas versus Texas A&M, broadcast by KTAW College Station, and neither university received any money from the station. By contrast, in 1991, nineteen bowl games paid out approximately $60 million to various colleges. If the athletics remained "amateur," the universities themselves became "professional."

In any event, when Notre Dame bolted, other colleges followed suit, and the obvious unsavory question was asked: "What is tradition compared to money?" At this point Arkansas fled the SWC for the more lucrative SEC. Before long, Texas and Texas A&M also considered leaving the SWC; and, in fact, they put out feelers to the Big-Eight, the SEC, and the PAC-Ten. Those two Texas universities, which have international reputations as major research institutions and also usually rank third or fourth in the nation in obtaining National Merit Scholars, worried about the rather poor academic standing of the SEC, but the PAC-Ten was another matter. Naturally, there followed hurt feelings, even rancor. The smaller SWC colleges, such as Baylor and SMU, with enrollments of about twelve thousand each, were concerned about the survival of their athletic programs, as were universities such as Rice and TCU that also had particularly rigorous academic standards and kept their enrollments down to about three thousand and five thousand undergraduates respectively. Before long, even the Texas legislature became involved. House Speaker Gib Lewis, Democrat from Fort Worth and a graduate of TCU, along with the support of Chet Edwards, a Democrat from Waco and a Baylor booster, threatened to convene a special meeting of the House State Affairs and Higher Education Committees to thwart such a move. Lewis warned that tradition was being sacrificed for money. Paradoxically, the state legislature appropriated $233 million to The University of Texas and $183 million to A&M for 1991, none of which funds were for athletics. And just as paradoxically, although Lewis also attended Sam Houston State, he did not choose to protect the Lone Star Conference when that college and two other Texas universities leaped to the Southland Conference. One observer sardonically noted that the leadership of the Texas legislature, despite its protestations, also seemed to be motivated more by money than by tradition. Nonetheless, tradition won a temporary victory when Texas and Texas A&M agreed to remain in the SWC a while longer.

No sooner did the SWC schools breathe a sigh of relief than another controversy arose; again it involved money. Because TCU, Rice, and Baylor got off to good season starts, Cotton Bowl officials stated that the Cotton Bowl might not invite the SWC winner as it traditionally had done. They reasoned that if one of the smaller universities made it to the Bowl, television revenues might decline. In a time of generally outrageous and insensitive comments, that cold-blooded, dollar-driven statement ranked among the worst. Its ill-advised timing simply demoralized the private universities. The suggestion also drew an immediate and angry response from Jim Wacker, the TCU coach, who shortly thereafter left to become the head coach at Minnesota in the Big-Ten. Where the matter might end was anyone's guess. By 1990, the school that started the conference's problem, Arkansas, was smashed on the football field by every SWC team except SMU. Meanwhile the private universities improved their play considerably, and Texas and Houston both produced winning seasons.

In the end, however, love of money won out over love of tradition, and the Southwest Conference was destroyed. Texas and Texas A&M moved to the Big-Eight and were joined there by Texas Tech and Baylor. The new conference, the Big-Twelve, formed into two divisions, the southern, with the former SWC teams plus Oklahoma and Oklahoma State, and the northern, composed of Nebraska, Colorado, Missouri, Kansas, Kansas State, and Iowa State. Texas won the Big-Twelve football championship in its first year of membership, defeating Nebraska in the process. At that point TCU, SMU, and Rice transferred into the Western Athletic Conference, which held an incredible sixteen teams. Houston, now but a shadow of its former self, drifted until it dropped into the six-team Conference USA. TCU would join Conference USA shortly thereafter.

An example of the unfortunate but dominant influence of money also may be seen in the Baylor program. Baylor consistently fielded one of the weaker teams in the Big-Twelve; however, as a sportscaster sardonically observed, Baylor could make more money losing its games to Big-Twelve opponents than it could by winning games in a lesser conference that would more nearly match its talent.

The trend hit other schools. By 1995, UNT felt ready to join the big boys, and after a major push by the university's administration it reentered the elite Division 1-A category with a will. Its first year held a killer schedule that included Oklahoma, Texas A&M, LSU, Missouri, and Alabama and produced only two victories; but with the dedicated backing of its governing body and alumni, its future was promising. It might have erred, however, in its second season when it joined the little regarded Big West Conference. One inducement was possible postseason play in the glitzy Las Vegas Bowl.

The influence of money, unfortunately, was not restricted to the larger universities. Smaller Texas conferences were under similar pressures, and nowhere could the problems better be seen than in the Lone Star Conference (LSC). The LSC had come to be known as one of the best, if not the best, of the small-college conferences in America. Its teams consistently won national football championships, and the conference was prominently featured in national sports publications such as *Sports Illustrated*. But this excellent conference broke up, becoming a shell of its former greatness. Again, money, not tradition, was at the helm.

Other problems rocked Texas football. If the image problems at SMU, Texas A&M, and Houston were not enough, a minor gambling problem was discovered at The University of Texas. Then Stephen F. Austin, a small college powerhouse, after an investigation by the SLC, was cited for seven alleged NCAA infractions in 1990. In one specific allegation, a football player who had completed four years of eligibility had been allowed to play again on a Lumberjack team that went 12-2-1 in 1989 (the first runner-up in the national championship).

Even in the much reduced Lone Star Conference, two Texas A&I players were convicted of felonies. One of them won the Harlon Hill Award, the NAIA's equivalent to the NCAA's Heisman Trophy, and held the national rushing record. The other served a probationary sentence for vehicular burglary. Obviously, Texas football was in trouble.

And this trouble trickled down to the high school level. In Dallas, players on the Carter High School team were convicted of crimes and sentenced to jail. It was not the only problem for that school, as the University Interscholastic League (UIL) and the Third Court of Appeals stripped Carter of its state championship title in 1988 for using ineligible players. Furthermore, the UIL banned the Odessa-Permian Panthers from postseason play and placed the team on probation for unauthorized practices.

As if all these difficulties were not enough, the UIL discerned a growing lack of sportsmanship in high school athletics. In one incident an athlete struck an official; in another an umpire and a baseball coach came to blows. And in yet another a basketball coach physically threatened a game official. The Director General of the UIL said that 1990 gave "more problems . . . from crowds, players, coaches, student bodies . . . than we have ever had." Unless the situation were to improve, decay in Texas state athletics was inevitable. Then the UIL had to come to grips with another matter. In the mid-1990s, the NCAA established stricter academic standards. If Texas high school athletes did not do well in the classroom, Division 1-A athletic scholarships would go to athletes in other states. One sportswriter offered the dismal advice to potential Texas high school players to "take the S.A.T. early, and take it often." There is little doubt that Texas high school football players are among the very best in the nation, but their academic skills must rise to a correspondingly high level with their athletic skills.

Not only are high school and college football games important to Texans, but professional football is vastly popular. Until Doak Walker went to play for the Detroit Lions, Texans had not been particularly enthusiastic about professional football. Signed by "Bo" McMillin, Walker found himself on the same team with Bobby Layne, his old backfield mate at Highland Park High School (outside Dallas). Despite his relatively slight stature (5' 10", 170 pounds), the "Doaker" proved his worth immediately. In his first year Walker led the National Football League (NFL) in scoring with 128 points, only 10 short of the record. This was before televised live games, but films of the Lions' games were shown every week on Dallas television. In 1950, Kyle Rote was drafted by the New York Giants. Suddenly Texans realized that their heroes were still playing.

In 1952 more than fifty-six fans attended a professional exhibition game in the Cotton Bowl. When the local patrons saw Walker score eighteen points, six of them on a ninety-five-yard run, pro football fever was upon Dallas. A pro franchise was available, and the Dallas Texans were born in 1952. The team was poorly supported: on opening day only seventeen thousand fans showed up. The Texans posted a dismal record, losing eleven straight before being drummed out of Dallas. The city's franchise was purchased and transferred to Baltimore, where the appellation changed to the Colts. Today the Colts reside in Indianapolis.

Of those who still wanted pro football in Dallas, none was more persistent than Lamar Hunt, a multimillionaire who had played behind Raymond Berry at SMU. Unable to attain another NFL franchise, in 1960 Hunt and fellow millionaire K. S. "Bud" Adams of Houston started their own American Football League (AFL) and their own clubs, the Dallas Texans and the Houston Oilers. Free from the shackles of the NFL, the AFL held its own draft and competed with the senior league by offering "fat" contracts. In this fashion AFL teams picked up players of considerable talent, some of whom talked with a Texas accent. To the Texans went Abner Haynes of UNT, Jack Spikes of TCU, and E. J. Holub of Texas Tech. The local flavor satisfied, the Texans then recruited two exceptional outlanders, Len Dawson of Purdue and Curtis McClinton of Kansas. The Oilers picked up the Heisman Trophy winner from LSU, Billy Cannon, and the redoubtable passer and field-goal kicker George Blanda, who had "retired" from pro ball and the Chicago Bears the year before. Over the next two years, the Oilers signed Scott Appleton, the All-American tackle from Texas, and Don Trull, the fine Baylor quarterback. As might be expected, the Texas clubs dominated the AFL in the league's early years; Houston won the first two AFL championships and Dallas the third. That third championship game, Dallas versus Houston, was the longest game on record, going seventeen minutes and fifty-four seconds into sudden death before Tommy Brooker kicked a field goal to win the game 20-17.

But trouble lay ahead for the Dallas Texans. Clint Murchison, Jr., and Bedford Wynne, also wealthy men, received an NFL franchise for Dallas in 1960. The new club was called the Cowboys, and two alumni from The University of Texas, Tex Schramm, formerly with the Los Angeles Rams, and Tom Landry, of the New York Giants, became general manager and head coach respectively. The new franchise also mixed Texans and non-Texans. It picked up Don Meredith, a fine quarterback from SMU, and Bob Lilly, a solid lineman from TCU, but it also gave up a first-round draft choice to

Washington in order to get the veteran University of the Pacific quarterback Eddie LeBaron. The impact of the NFL was irresistible to fans and players, so Hunt decided to leave Dallas for Kansas City, where his Texans became the Chiefs.

The Cowboys remained a solid but unimpressive loser until 1965, when they gathered in a brace of fine rookies: tackles Ralph Neely and Jethro Pugh and wide receiver "Bullet Bob" Hayes, who lived up to his billing as "the fastest man alive." That year Dallas made the playoffs. The next year Dallas played Green Bay for the championship of the NFL but lost. The following year was a repeat—a loss to Green Bay on the latter's home field in minus-thirteen-degree weather. But afterwards the Cowboys made numerous playoffs, and they have since gone on to play in an impressive eight Super Bowls—five of which they won. Much of the reason for Dallas's success in the 1970s lies in a shrewd choice of quarterback. Roger Staubach, a Heisman Trophy winner from Navy, was ignored by some clubs because of his impending active-duty obligation. Selected in 1964, he did not report to the Cowboys until 1969, a date that coincided with Meredith's retirement. Ultimately the Cowboys abandoned the Cotton Bowl for a newly constructed stadium with exceptional seating facilities in the nearby suburb of Irving. In time, the Cowboys gained national popularity and even were given the sobriquet "America's Team." When the Cowboys played the Pittsburgh Steelers and the Washington Redskins, two other traditional powerhouses, tickets were sold out months in advance and all over the nation television sets hummed as more than 40 percent of all viewers tuned in to watch.

The Cowboys made pro football work—and pay. They had what appeared to be the perfect winning combination. Clint Murchison, the conservative and staid owner, provided the money, gained the profits, and gave the team's management a clear hand to do what it needed to do. Tex Schramm, the intelligent and innovative president, forged an enviable organization that consistently produced both money and fans. And Gil Brandt, the gifted general manager, turned player selection into a science. In NFL drafts, the Cowboys always seemed to pick able athletes, such as defensive tackle Randy White, cornerback Everson Walls, wide receiver Drew Pearson, running backs Walt Garrison, Calvin Hill, and Tony Dorsett, and linebackers Lee Roy Jordan and Bill Bates. Finally, there was the team's ornament, head coach Tom Landry, whose very name became synonym for coaching excellence. *Newsweek* magazine called the whole charismatic concept "Cowboy Cool" as the team continued its winning tradition well into the mid-1980s, playing in an incredible thirty-six playoff games. But in 1986, the team went 7-9 and then slid to 3-13 in 1988. Landry was in the midst of a massive rebuilding program when tragedy struck. In ill health and financial difficulty, Murchison sold the team to a consortium headed by none other than "Bum" Bright, who in 1989 resold the team to a group headed by Arkansas businessman Jerry Jones. A blustery personality, Jones made sweeping changes. In a matter of days Schramm, Brandt, and Landry were gone.

Of course by this time, Landry had become a Texas legend, and few fans were happy to see him ousted. To add to Jones's problem, his method of firing had all the grace of a clumsy left hook. Later in the same year Landry was inducted into the Pro Football Hall of Fame, his luster untarnished, and, if anything, made brighter by his martyrdom. Jones's old college roommate at Arkansas was Jimmy Johnson, coach of the successful college team the Miami Hurricanes. Immediately Johnson was installed as the new head coach of the Cowboys, prompting some rumbling among the players. All-Pro tackle Randy White was public in his comments and quit the club shortly thereafter. Predictably, the fans responded with outrage as Jones attempted, without much success, to explain his actions. It appeared that not only Dallasites but all Texans were angry; they were angry not only with Jones but also with Bright, who appeared to have dumped the team for money. Their anger spilled over to include Johnson, who in his first year posted a miserable 1-15 record. Johnson's second year was better, and some fans returned.

Then, in rather short order, Dallas acquired excellent players by both judicious drafts and shrewd trades. Landry already had signed the able safety Bill Bates, and before his firing he also signed the exceptional UCLA quarterback Troy Aikman. Emmitt Smith (who in October 2002 broke the NFL's all-time rushing record), Leon Lett, Erik Williams, Charles Haley, Nate Newton, "Moose" Johnson, Jay Novacek, and Ken Norton, Jr., among others, soon followed. It was at this point that the salary cap, a plan designed by the league to equalize talent among the teams and to keep down costs, hurt the Cowboys, as Ken Norton, Larry Brown, Alvin Harper, Russell Maryland, as well as other stalwarts left for other clubs that offered better pay. Nevertheless, the Cowboys never seem to run out of quality players; Deion Sanders, the league's only bona fide two-way player signed, and the 1996 *Sporting News Pro Football Yearbook* described Larry Allen as "the best lineman in the league." Between 1993 and 1996, Dallas won three Super Bowls.

Yet all was not well with the Cowboys, and Jones and Johnson had a falling out that resulted in Johnson tendering his resignation. He was replaced by Barry Switzer, a former Oklahoma Sooner coach who had no pro experience. Although the Cowboys under Switzer failed to make the Super Bowl in 1995, they returned to the championship game and won it in 1996. Then new problems began to appear, the most serious of which was the indictment of Michael Irvin, perhaps Dallas's most talented receiver, on drug charges. Although he was arrested in a hotel room with cocaine and two young "models," Irvin pleaded no contest and was given a rather lenient sentence. Switzer also lost some of his better coaches, as Norv Turner and Dave Wannstedt landed head coaching jobs in the NFL and Butch Davis left to coach a prestigious college team. Still, the Cowboys seemed to be a winning team. By the late 1990s and early 2000s, however, the Cowboys bore little resemblance to past teams. The drop was characterized by numerous coaching changes and questionable player selections.

Houston also had its share of problems. Unlike the Texans, who had hired Hank Stram and kept him, or the Cowboys, who kept Landry even longer, the Oilers ran through ten coaches in fifteen years. Then there were stadium problems. In the beginning, Dallas had the ready-made Cotton Bowl, but, unable to use the seventy-thousand-seat Rice Stadium, the Oilers were forced into a renovated high school field. The team finally did get into Rice Stadium, but it was not until 1968 that it found a permanent home in the Astrodome. By 1969 the legitimacy of the Oilers was assured by a merger of the AFL into the NFL, but that year also began a slide for Houston that included the 1972–73 seasons, in which the team went 1-13 during both years. By 1974, however, they were 10-4, and by 1978 and 1979 the Oilers were again in the champion class. In 1975 the Oilers hired O. A. "Bum" Philips, whose coaching services they retained for a while at least. In addition, the Oilers began to acquire such impressive players as linebacker Robert Brazile. Their greatest coup was the acquisition in 1978 of Earl Campbell, a Tyler native and Heisman Trophy winner at The University of Texas. With the Oilers, Campbell set running records and established himself as first-class star of the game. He seemed to remain unimpressed by it all and appeared to be a soft-spoken and mild-mannered man to whom the youth of the state could look as an example. He seemed, also, to symbolize for Texans what was finest in Texas varsity and professional football.

But, again, the firing tradition prevailed in Houston, and this time the axe fell on Philips. Another round of musical chairs with a complete set of coaches occurred when head coach Jerry Glanville arrived. Although the team had its moments under his command, Glanville proved to be something of a lightning rod, his battles with players and other coaches legendary. He was fired in 1989, and the highly successful Houston Cougars coach, Jack Pardee, took over a talented Oilers team led by star quarterback Warren Moon and excellent running backs. Houston had good receivers as well in Ernest Givins, Tony Jones, and Curtis Duncan, all of whom were necessary components of Pardee's "Run and Shoot" offense. Two other quality players were Ray Childress and Anthony Cook. For all its many years in the NFL, however, the Houston Oilers never went to a Super Bowl, and many believed that the franchise's proclivity for coaching changes had something to do with that fact. The top coaching spot at Houston remained a Kamikaze job. In turn, Pardee was sacked, and Buddy Ryan, late of the Philadelphia Eagles, appeared to be in control. Then, in 1994, Jeff Fisher took over. The next year proved disastrous for the Oilers, who went 2-14 in 1995, but the club improved to 7-9 in 1996. In that year, however, Adams again stumbled upon the scene and announced that the franchise would move to Nashville, seemingly forgetting that he still had two years remaining on his lease at the Astrodome. Houston had become a lame duck team if there ever was one, yet it was required to continue to play in the city that Adams had renounced. The soap opera ended when the move was made, and the team was renamed the Tennessee Titans. In the year 2001, however, Houston gained another NFL franchise, which took the name the Texans, the same name as the two previous Dallas teams. The team took the field for the first time at the start of the 2002–03 season.

Another major sport in Texas is baseball. Minor league baseball, developed in 1877, came to Texas in 1888 in the form of the Texas League, whose charter members included Austin, Fort Worth, Galveston, Houston, San Antonio, and Dallas. Dallas won the pennant the first year. Many other towns later joined the league. Minor leagues are classified from Class AAA to Class D, depending on the size of the cities involved and the players' salary level. The Texas League was—and remains—AA. Largely because of its pitching, it was regarded as a particularly good circuit. Older pitchers normally were sent down to keep their arms warm in the Texas sun, and younger pitchers were brought up in order to learn from the veterans. Furthermore, the small size of most Texas ball parks required pitching skill. Some of the league's outstanding pitchers included: Carl Hubbell and Dizzy Trout (Beaumont); Red Murff, Joe Kotrany, Hank Oana, and Dave Hoskins (Dallas); Mort Cooper, Dizzy Dean, Murray Dickson, Harry "the Cat" Brecheen, Wilmer "Vinegar Bend" Mizell, and Howie Pollett (Houston); Carl Erskine (Fort Worth); Gaylord Perry (Rio Grande Valley); Rinold Duren, Carl Scheib, "Bullet Bob" Turley, and Fernando Valenzuela (San Antonio).

The state has had many other minor leagues, some of which were the Mexican National League (B), which had only one U.S.-based team in it, El Paso; the East Texas League (C); the West Texas–New Mexico League (C); the Big State League (C); and the Gulf Coast League, whose class was undetermined. By 1958 Houston and Dallas, mainstays of the Texas League, joined the AAA American Association in which Houston, in both 1959 and 1961, went to the playoffs.

Houston wanted major-league status, and in 1962, when it became the first southern city to join the big leagues, the Colt 45s were born. In 1964 the multimillion-dollar Astrodome was completed, and the next year it became the home park for the rechristened Astros. Houston's major-league baseball history has been mixed. Although the Astros enjoyed good seasons in 1972, 1979, 1980, 1986, and 1996, they developed an early reputation for trading some of their better players. Both Rusty Staub and Joe Morgan, among others, were both dealt away. The latter, an All-Star, was voted Most Valuable Player and remained a mainstay of the pennant-winning Cincinnati Reds before he was voted into baseball's Hall of Fame in Cooperstown, New York. After that, the Astros lost the enormous box-office attraction of pitcher Nolan Ryan, a free agent who was picked up by the Texas Rangers. In 1990, Ryan's appearance on the mound attracted huge numbers of fans to the Texas Ranger stadium, where television cameras recorded his every twitch, smile, and pitch for eager baseball buffs. In that year he became one of only twenty 300-game winners in the history of baseball and pitched his sixth career no-hitter (he pitched his seventh no-hitter early in the 1991 season). He also took over sole claim to the record of five thousand strikeouts. Even in his forties, Ryan could hurl a fast ball nearly one hundred miles per hour.

Yet the Astro trades continued; another to go was Billy Hatcher. Once aboard his new team, the Cincinnati Reds, Hatcher rose to stardom in the 1990 World Series, setting a new Series record by getting seven consecutive hits. (He actually reached base eight times in a row because the opposing Oakland A's pitcher, fearing another hit, walked him.) In addition, free agency lost Houston Dave Scott, Danny Darwin (later reclaimed), and the excellent firstbaseman Glenn Davis. Over the years, however, Houston has had its stars, such as Cesar Cendeno, Ken Johnson, Mile Cuellar, Larry Dierker, Doug Rader, Jim Wynn, Joe Niekro, and J. R. Richard. In 1990, pitcher Danny Darwin had the lowest earned-run average in the National League.

Then there were other problems. A salary dispute between players and owners led to a players strike that ground major league baseball to a halt. Play stopped on August 11, 1994, and was tardy resuming in 1995. It was the first time in baseball history that the World Series was not held, and for that period every record was marked by an asterisk. Even World War II had not closed down the game that greed brought to its knees in 1994. An unanticipated fallout of the strike was that exasperated fans across the country responded in kind and stayed away from the ball parks in droves when play finally resumed. They had been pushed too far—especially in light of the fact that the cost of attending a game has skyrocketed. So in 1995, even with a winning season led by excellent players such as Craig Biggio and Jeff Bagwell, the Astros could not draw; and although the ownership changed and the statement was made that the team would stay in Houston, there was serious talk that the team would move. Of course, such speculation did nothing to encourage fan enthusiasm or support. Even the move in 2000 into a new stadium, Enron Field, a beautiful setting but with very short fences, that has since been renamed Minute Maid Park, did not seem to help, for another good Astros team collapsed and died in the stretch in the 2001 season.

Dallas and Fort Worth achieved major league status later. In 1972 the metroplex acquired the American League's Washington franchise. The team was renamed the Texas Rangers, and it stayed in a park in Arlington, located between the two big cities. Plagued by coaching problems, the Rangers had nine managers in just seven years, three in the 1975 season alone. Over the relatively few years of their existence, the Rangers have had such noteworthy players as Gaylord Perry, Ferguson Jenkins, Bert Campaneris, Jim Kern, Al Oliver, and the able catcher Jim Sundberg. Between 1972 and 1976, Jeff Burroughs was on the roster, and in 1974 he received the American League's Most Valuable Player Award. The Ranger team also benefited from the acquisition in the 1980s of Rueben Sierra, a consistently high percentage hitter, and Pete Incaviglia the rotund, mustachioed, clutch hitter and crowd pleaser. But the chief source of Ranger pride was the aforementioned Nolan Ryan, who just happened to be a native Texan.

By the 1990s, however, things had changed. Sierra and Incaviglia were gone, again because of disputes over money, but the Rangers did not move to the verge of collapse, as did the Astros. Club ownership, that included George W. Bush, later governor of Texas and President of the United States, labored hard to bring the club around. The revamping included a new fan-friendly stadium, christened "The Ball Park at Arlington," and at least an attempt to keep ticket costs affordable for the average person. To be sure, the strike of 1994 had hurt the Rangers as well, but by 1996 they too had become a pennant contender behind the solid play of Juan Gonzales, who had a career-long hitting streak, and Juan Rodriguez and Rusty Greer. More recently it acquired Alex Rodriguez, a considerable talent, who became the highest paid player in baseball. Indeed, the cost of keeping "A-Rod" was so high that there was little money left over for other position players. Pitching in particular suffered greatly in the 2001 season.

Many ballplayers who did not play in Texas but who hailed from the state should not be forgotten. Tris Speaker, "the Grey Eagle" of the Cleveland Indians came from Hubbard, near Waco. Rogers Hornsby of the St. Louis Cardinals, one of only two triple-crown winners in the game and the only one in the National League, lies buried at Pilot Knob, just outside of Austin. Monty Stratton, a pitcher for the Chicago White Sox, was a Texan, as were Mike "Pinky" Higgins of the Boston Red Sox and the great Ernie Banks of the Chicago Cubs.

Baseball in Texas is not confined to the professionals. Southwestern colleges have fielded excellent clubs and players, with The University of Texas and Texas A&M being the most prominent powers. The University of Texas has been the dominant force, however, with an incredible forty-six outright titles and seven more shared ones. At least one reason for UT's impressive showing lies in its coaching staff, which has consisted of Billy Disch (1911–39), Bill Faulk (1940–42), and Cliff Gustafson (1968–96) who compiled more than a thousand victories as a manager. Texas beat A&M in Austin before 6,649 fans in Gustafson's last game as coach. Fittingly, it was the last SWC event held in Austin. One of Gustafson's pitchers, Roger Clemens, who later played for the Boston Red Sox and then the Torono Blue Jays, won the Cy Young Award—given each season to the best pitcher in major league baseball—in 1986, 1987, 1991, 1997, and 1998, and he came in a close second in the balloting in 1990. In 1999 he was traded to the New York Yankees, where, in his "twilight years," he won an amazing sixth Cy Young award in 2001. The Longhorns have sent many good pitchers to the major leagues: including Burt Hooten, Greg Swindell, Eric Stone, and Kirk Dressendorefer. In addition to the large universities, Texas Lutheran College has produced excellent baseball teams.

Until recently, basketball in Texas might have been aptly described as the game one fooled around with between the football and baseball seasons. Yet as the only major sport of purely American origin, basketball deserves a better fate. An early figure in Texas basketball was E. O. "Doc" Hayes, from Krum. At UNT, early in the 1920s, he was a three-time All-Texas player. He later coached at Crozier Tech High School in Dallas, where his teams won eleven championships in seventeen years, including the 1946 state championship. In 1947 he moved to SMU, where his teams continued to win. While the Mustangs never won a national championship, they often went to the NCAA playoffs.

The University of Texas also has produced good basketball teams, such as the one in the late 1940s led by the 5' 10" guard from El Mina, Slater Martin. His height proved no handicap, and in one game against TCU he scored forty-nine points. Although many believed that he could not compete in the pros, he became a standout. His tenacious defensive struggles against Bob Cousy still evoke strong memories for the aficionados of the game. Martin once held Bob Davies, an all-pro, scoreless for an entire game. Under Coach A. E. "Abe" Lemons, the Longhorns won the National Invitational Tournament in 1978.

Over the years, the University of Houston and the University of North Texas also added to the development of Texas basketball. At one time, both were in the Missouri Valley Conference (MVC), then the hottest college basketball league in America, with such traditional powerhouses as Cincinnati, Bradley, Drake, Louisville, St. Louis, and Wichita State. Houston served its apprenticeship and became a major independent before joining the Southwest Conference. Like Houston, UNT also left the MVC and began to establish itself as a powerful independent. Newcomer West Texas was left as the sole Texas representative in the MVC. It was no accident that Houston's and UNT's basketball stars rose accordingly. In the 1950s and the 1960s, Houston had developed to the point that it went to the NCAA playoffs with considerable consistency. In only thirteen seasons it had ten All-Americans. While overwhelming in basketball, the MVC was weak in football, and in Texas, football is king; so both Texas colleges left the league.

Other good basketball teams and players have surfaced occasionally in Texas. Southwest Texas won the NAIA title in 1960, as did Prairie View in 1962 and East Texas in 1965. Stephen F. Austin came close in 1970. Each one of SFA's championship seniors was drafted by the NBA, and one of them, George Johnson, went in the first round. Texas Western (now The University of Texas at El Paso) won the NCAA title in 1966. Nate Archibald, a former UTEP player, was the first guard in the NBA to score one thousand field goals and was the NBA player of the year in 1973. Pan American University won the NAIA in 1963, and one of its players, Lucious Jackson, became a first-round draft pick for Philadelphia. At that time, the outstanding basketball players from the region included Jay Arnette and Jim Krivacs (Texas), "Big Daddy" Lattin (UTEP), Otis Birdsong and Elvin Hayes (Houston), Jim Mudd (UNT), and Gene Phillips and Jim Krebs (SMU). Another Texas-born player, Dave Stallworth, left the state, but he was twice an All-American at Wichita State.

But for all the early efforts, it was really the 1980s when Southwest Conference basketball came of age. The University of Houston's famous fast-breaking, slam-dunking Phi Slamma Jamma, composed of teammates Hakeem Olajuwon, Clyde Drexler, Michael Young, and Larry Micheaux, went to the NCAA championship game for two successive years and was runner-up both times. The inevitable question was raised: Was Houston's success an aberration? Was the Southwest really ready for a leap into the "real" game, the game as it was played by such traditional powerhouses as UCLA, St. John's, Georgetown, Villanova, Bradley, Duke, North Carolina, and the University of Nevada at Las Vegas? The answer came in 1990 at the NCAA tournament, where both UT, coached by Tom Penders, and Arkansas, coached by Nolan Richardson, the first African American head coach in the Southwest Conference, made the "Great Eight." Arkansas then made the "Final Four." Texas has since returned to the playoffs under Coach Rick Barnes.

Furthermore, recent roundball players from the state increasingly made it in the professional ranks. They include Houston's Hakeem Olajuwon, Arkansas's Sidney Moncrief, and Texas's Johnny Moore and Lance Blanks. Another excellent player, UT's Travis Mays, the Southwest Conference's all-time leading scorer, compiled more than a thousand collegiate points, twenty-seven of them when he set another conference record with nine in a single game from the three-point line. As the new century arrived, Texas Tech, in a desperate bid to attain major status in men's collegiate basketball, hired Bobby Knight, a contentious, volatile, and unpredictable coach only recently fired by Indiana University. Texas Tech's faculty voiced considerable and open regret over Knight's hiring. How the Red Raiders will fare under Knight's leadership remains a question at the time of this writing.

Perhaps the greatest gains in college basketball in Texas were made by women. Jody Conradt, the amazing coach of the Lady Longhorns, led her team to numerous conference championships and a national championship. In 1986 her team posted a perfect season. For a time, more people attended her team's regular season games than attended men's basketball in any college in the state. An amiable woman, Conradt set a winning record that may never be equaled, an incredible 304-36 in the 1980s. Included among her players were greats such as All-American Clarissa Davis, Kaime Ethridge, Annette Smith, Fran Harris, and Susan Anderson. Dominant forces in women's basketball in the state and nation have been the Flying Queens of Wayland Baptist College, the Ladyjacks of Stephen F. Austin, and the Lady Bobcats of Southwest Texas. In 1995, the Ladyjacks won eighty-seven consecutive home games and were a contender for the national championship. In 1992, led by the All-American superstar Sheryl Swoopes—perhaps the best woman ever to play the game—Texas Tech won the NCAA Women's Basketball Championship.

Professional basketball reached Texas in 1967 with the Dallas Chaparrals of the old American Basketball Association. Plagued by poor attendance, the Chaps eventually were leased with an option to buy to a San Antonio organization headed by Angelo Drossos and B. J. "Red" McCombs. Thus the San Antonio Spurs came into being. In their first year (1973–74) the Spurs obtained superstar George "the Iceman" Gervin from Virginia and went to the playoffs. They went the next year too. In 1976 the ABA was dissolved, and San Antonio entered an expanded NBA. Again it reached the playoffs, under a new coach, Doug Moe. In 1977 the Spurs were in an expanded facility, the Arena, and won their divisional title. In 1978, San Antonio won another divisional title and came within a whisker of going to the NBA finals.

In the 1980s, the Spurs slipped, and it was not long before Larry Brown, coach of the University of Kansas's NCAA championship team, was brought to San Antonio. When he had a poor season, impatient wolves howled for his firing, but the calls died out during the 1989–90 season. In one of the most remarkable turnarounds in professional basketball history, the Spurs won the Midwest championship before suffering a heartbreaking 108-105 overtime loss to Portland in the seventh and final game of the Western Conference finals. After owner-Coach problems led to Brown's dismissal, in walked James Lucas, whom, after some small success, also was released. But the next coach, Bob Hill, seemed to have the touch, as the Spurs moved from the Arena to the enormous Alamodome, which seats more than twenty thousand fans. Then came a clash of personalities between the coach and the very able but erratic rebounder Dennis Rodman, who was traded to Chicago. By the 1995–96 season, the Spurs won fifty-nine games and lost only twenty-three. They had talent galore—David Robinson, Avery Johnson, and Sean Elliott.

Much of the credit for the success the Spurs have enjoyed must go to first-round draft pick David Robinson, a 7' 1" center from the Naval Academy. As a Spur, Robinson averaged more than twenty points a game, was named the NBA Rookie of the Year, and was selected to the All-Star Team. In 1995, he was named the league's Most Valuable Player. Twice a member of the U.S. Olympic "Dream Team," he also was named that team's MVP in 1996 as well. Robinson remained not only a magnificent player but also a complete gentleman, setting an example for the entire NBA. The Spur's high mark was winning the NBA championship in 1999. The acquisition of Tim Duncan, an enormously talented player, had much to do with the Spurs' success.

Another of the state's three NBA franchises was the Rockets, who played in San Diego for four years before Houston acquired them in 1971. In subsequent years they won their division five times. In the mid-1980s, led by former University of Houston All-American Hakeem Olajuwon, a Nigerian who averaged more than twenty points per game in his rookie season (1985–86), the team developed rapidly. Olajuwon was a magnificent rebounder and shot-blocker with great physical strength. He too played on numerous All-Star teams, and he was named the league's Most Valuable Player in 1994 and led the Rockets to back-to-back NBA championships in 1994 and 1995.

Dallas finally regained an NBA team with the birth of the Mavericks. It has been an often brilliant but just as often troubled franchise. Despite their difficulties, the Mavs have some positive aspects. Their court, the Reunion Arena, ranks among the best in the NBA, and North Texans enjoy the games and have confidence in the future of their team, especially in view of the acquisition of Jason Kidd in the 1994 draft. (Kidd was later traded.) Other good

Dallas players included Dennis Harper and Rolando Blackman. Finally, mention must be made of another Texas player from San Antonio, Shaquille O'Neal. "Shaq" attended LSU and was drafted by the Orlando Magic. In 1996 he was drafted as a free agent by the Los Angeles Lakers, whom he led to back-to-back-to-back NBA championships in 2000, 2001, and 2002, receiving the Most Valuable Player award each time.

Mention varsity golf and three schools come to mind: UNT, Houston, and Texas. *Golf Digest* once called UNT "the Notre Dame of Golf" and described coach Fred Cobb as "the Knute Rockne of Collegiate Golf." The accolade came after the school won four consecutive NCAA national championships between 1949 and 1952. Upon Cobb's death, Herb Ferrill assumed the coaching duties and guided the team to forty-one more tournament championships. Houston, under able coach David Williams, claimed twelve NCAA championships between 1956 and 1970 and won more than 250 other titles. UT, too, has produced NCAA golfing champions; and TCU also has had its golfing moments.

Many of the golfers from these schools became seasoned amateurs and professionals. From UNT, for example, came Joe Conrad, the first American to win the British Amateur, and Don January, winner of the Texas Open, the Tournament of Champions, and the Professional Golfer's Association (PGA) in 1967. Other professionals from UNT include Billy Maxwell and William Garrett. From the University of Houston came Mark Hopkins, who won the Texas Open as an amateur; others are Red Baxter, Homero Blancas, Martin Fleckman, John Mahaffey, Tom Jenkins, Ed Couples, Ed Fiori, and Keith Fergus. From UT came Ben Crenshaw, winner of the Texas Open and the Crosby; UT also produced Tom Kite (the game's top money winner), Rik Massengale, and Wesley Ellis. Charles Coody, who won the Masters in 1971, came out of TCU, as did Don Massengale. Texas Tech produced Jeff Mitchell. Payne Stewart of SMU won over $7 million on the pro tour.

Other great golfers from Texas include the formidable Ralph Guldahl of Dallas, who in the 1930s won the United States Golfer's Association (USGA) Open two years in a row, the Western Open four years in a row, and the Masters Tournament. Another was Byron Nelson of Fort Worth, who won forty-nine PGA tournaments in the 1930s and 1940s, including the PGA championship in 1940 and 1945 as well as two Masters. In the 1940s and 1950s Jimmy Demaret of Houston won the Masters three times, and Lloyd Mangrum, a dapper East Texan, picked up thirty-four PGA victories. Other prominent Texas golfers are: Jack Burke, Jr., another Masters winner; Lee Trevino, a PGA champion; Lee Elder of Dallas, the first African American to play in the Masters; PGA champion Dave Marr; Henry Ransom; Jackie Cupit; and Don Cherry. But probably the greatest Texas golfer was the diminutive Ben Hogan, from Dublin. In 1946 and 1948 he won the PGA. In 1949, after nearly dying in an automobile accident, he achieved even greater heights, winning four USGA Opens, two Masters, two PGAs, and the British Open.

Texas women also have been prominent in golf. Chief among them are Betty Johnson, winner of the USGA Amateur two years in a row; Polly Ann Riley, who won more than a hundred tournaments; Sandra Haynie, two-time winner of the Ladies Professional Golfers' Association (LPGA); and Mary Lou Dill and Mary McAllister. The greatest of them all, however, was Mildred "Babe" Didrikson Zaharias, the Beaumont–Port Arthur woman who set three Olympic records and was a major American athlete. She won her first attempt at the Women's Amateur USGA in 1946, and the following year she won the British Women's Amateur. Turning professional, she overpowered the LPGA. One of the most promising players currently on the professional tour is Shirley Furlong, who attended A&M.

While Texans have always had an interest in boxing, this sport has not been consistently developed in the state—it was not even legal in Texas until late in the 1930s. In the 1940s Dallas had a strong high school league, which thrived principally because of a large ROTC program. Boxing never caught on in colleges, except through the inane and dangerous "Fite Nites," at which throngs of spectators, ignorant of the sport, come out solely for the purpose of seeing blood. Those who understand and enjoy the sport wisely avoid these sleazy spectacles. Serious amateur boxing in Texas, consequently, has remained within the province of the Golden Gloves.

The boxing that takes place in the state is largely the function of the pros. Probably two of the most important bouts took place in Houston. In the Astrodome in 1966 and 1967 Muhammad Ali (formerly Cassius Clay) successfully defended his title with the knockout of Cleveland Williams and a decision over Ernie Terrell. Later in 1967 Ali knocked out a promising Dallas heavyweight, Zora Folley, in New York City's Madison Square Garden.

As late as 1955, Texas law forbade a black man and a white man to fight each other in the ring. In 1958, however, I. H. "Sporty" Harvey, a black preliminary fighter from San Antonio, challenged the law; he won the case and signed for a ten-round bout against a white man, which Harvey lost. The first national television exposure to a Texas fight came when middleweight Bobby Dykes of San Antonio lost to France's Pierre Langlois in Dallas on May 3, 1953. Although a solid contender, Dykes never won the title.

Another Texas fighter was Curtis Cokes, a Dallas welterweight who won the vacated title against Jean Josselin in a fifteen-round decision in New Orleans in 1966. Cokes also made a successful defense of his crown in Dallas by knocking out Francois Pavilla in ten. He held the title for two and a half years before losing it to Jose Napoles in Los Angeles. Another Texas champion was Lew Jenkins, a lightweight billed as "the Sweetwater Sweet Swatter." (His real name was Verlin Jenks, and his real home was Milburn.) Jenkins won the title with a knockout of Lou Ambers in New York in 1940 but lost it a year and a half later to Sammy Ingot in fifteen (also in New York). Other Lone Star champions include Orlando Canizales, the bantamweight champion from Laredo, junior bantamweight Robert Quiroga, and Raymond Medel, a featherweight from San Antonio who fought in a title match in Fort Worth in 1990 with Ricardo Cepeda, the WBC Continental American champion. A rising ring figure is San Antonio's Jesse James Leija, the WBC superfeatherweight champion. Another is Mike "Night Train" Trejo of San Marcos, a world champion flyweight with middleweight knockout power.

Texas is best remembered for three other figures in ring history. George Foreman, of Marshall, won the gold medal as a heavyweight in the 1968 Olympics. An impressive puncher, he put away "Smokin' Joe" Frazier in the second round of a title fight in 1973, but he lost the title to Ali in 1974. After his years as a boxer seemed to be over, Foreman, an active Christian, became a minister of a church in Houston. Then, many years older and many pounds heavier, he began a long road back to a title fight. On April 19, 1991, in Atlantic City, New Jersey, the forty-two-year-old, 257-pound Foreman surprised most people by lasting twelve rounds with the heavyweight champion Evander Holyfield before losing by unanimous decision. Then, to the world's astonishment, on November 5, 1994, Foreman knocked out twenty-six-year-old Michael Moorer to reclaim the heavyweight title belt.

Another Texan and heavyweight was Jack Johnson of Galveston. He was the first-rate fighter who captured the title in fourteen rounds against Tommy Burns in Sidney, Australia, in 1908. He knocked out the great Stanley Ketchel in the defense of his crown in 1909, and the following year he did the same to James J. Jeffries. After holding the title for seven years, he lost it to Jess Willard, who knocked him out in the twenty-sixth round in Havana. Johnson was the first black man to win the crown, but he was plagued by two misfortunes: racial prejudice and his own bad judgment. The third, and most colorful, figure to come out of Texas and into the fight game was not a boxer at all but the dazzling promoter George "Tex" Rickard, born in Sherman in 1890. He managed the great Jack Dempsey and brought Madison Square Garden into existence.

Soccer, or as the rest of the world calls it, football, is the most popular sport in the world, but it is a relative newcomer to the United States and to Texas. A spectator's game, if successful, must be one in which people have participated. In this regard soccer has caught on across Texas, which has major-league soccer clubs. Many towns and cities have soccer leagues reminiscent of the growing popularity of baseball in the nineteenth century. In 1976 in Dallas, for example, 65,000 youngsters participated in that city's youth soccer program. By 1990 the number had grown to 150,000. In fact, Dallas was so attached to the game that the city became the site for the Dallas Cup Games (determining the championship of youth soccer). The nearby suburb of Richardson held the under-12 Soccer America National Indoor Championship.

In 1984 Major Soccer League (the MSL) reorganized itself. It held eight teams, Dallas being the only one from Texas. In 1987, the Dallas Sidekicks won the championship, and they finished strongly in 1989. By 1990 the team set a club record of thirty-one victories in its fifty-four-game season and won its division. Soccer has been somewhat slower in developing at the college level. Because of low budgets, the program remained, essentially, an intramural and later a college club sport. In recent years, however, it has found NCAA status with some universities. In this growth, SMU has led the way in the 1980s. Perhaps it is only natural that it should, for SMU is located in soccer-mad Dallas. During that period, SMU produced many All-Americans and repeatedly went to the NCAA playoffs.

Perhaps the most impressive of all the Texas soccer stories is that of Mia Hamm, who learned the game while growing up in Wichita Falls and San Antonio. At the University of North Carolina, her team won four NCAA titles; but that was only the beginning. Hamm helped the American women's team capture Olympic gold in 1996 in Atlanta, and she starred on the team that won the Women's World Cup championship in 1999.

Curiously, ice hockey has been played in Texas for many years. As early as the 1940s, Dallas, Fort Worth, and Houston were in the United States Hockey League. Houston, in the 1970s, skated the Aeros of the World Hockey Association (WHA), but that club disbanded in 1977 when the National Hockey League (NHL), the arbiter of the game, absorbed four WHA clubs. The most famous Texas hockey player was probably Gordie Howe, the all-time NHL great. He and his sons, Marty and Mark, played for a while with the Aeros.

The National Hockey League arrived in Texas with the expansion of franchises, and the decision to transfer the Minnesota North Stars to Dallas. The team—now known merely as the Stars in commemoration of the Lone Star—did very well, despite the dire predictions of many northern hockey fans. From the start the Stars had an excellent rink and a determined management. Attendance was not a problem. The team, however, needed more work. Early in 1996, Bob Gainey stepped down as coach and took the reins as General Manager. It remained to be seen if the new coach, Ken Hitchcock, could produce an offense. Dallas's goal production was second worst in the league in the 1995–96 season, but hope was generated by the excellent play of Mike Modano, who had eighty-one points that year, and the acquisition of free agent Pat Verbeek, a forty-one-point producer with the New York Rangers. That hope and the team's hard work have paid good dividends: at the time of this writing, the Stars are enjoying an explosive success in Dallas, even having won the Stanley Cup, the ultimate achievement in professional hockey, in 1999.

There are other sports in Texas. Track and field come readily to mind with the great Texas Relays, one of the premier sporting events in America. The Texas Relays were founded by Clyde Littlefield, legendary coach at The University of Texas, where his teams won twenty conference crowns in twenty-six years. Texas A&M remains the only university in the country to produce three athletes who have put the shot more than seventy feet. In 1965 Randy Matson broke the world's record by a full three feet on his way to three NCAA crowns and an Olympic gold medal. Randy Barnes hit the seventy-plus mark in 1986, as did Mike Stulce in 1990.

In the summer of 1990, two Southwest Texas Bobcats established their names in the NCAA record books: Charles Austin cleared seven feet, seven and three-fourths inches in the high jump; and Charles Fucci took the NCAA decathlon with 7,922 points. Charles Austin's greatest achievement, however, came in the 1996 Olympic Games, where he took a Gold Medal. In those same games, Waco's Charles

Johnson became the first man to win gold medals in both the 200 and 400 meter races, and Carl Lewis of Houston capped his brilliant career by winning his ninth gold medal, tying an Olympic record.

Other sports in Texas include swimming, tennis, horse racing (with Willie Shoemaker), auto racing (with A. J. Foyt, Johnny Rutherford, and Terry LaBonte), fencing (the championship teams of Southwest Texas) and rodeo (featuring the college competition at Tarleton and such legendary pros as Bill Pickett, the great black star credited with inventing bulldogging, and Tuff Hedeman of Bowie, the three-time world champion bull rider). And the list goes on.

In order to preserve the rich heritage of sports in the state, the Texas Sports Hall of Fame has been established. Considering the enormous contribution that Texans have made to sports, that organization will remain busy for many years to come.

Suggested Reading

Cozens, Frederick W., and Florence S. Stumpf. *Sports in American Life.* Chicago: University of Chicago Press, 1953.

Danzig, Allison, and Peter Brandwein, eds. *The Greatest Sports Stories from the New York Times.* New York: A. S. Barnes, 1951.

Dulles, Foster Rhea. *America Learns to Play.* New York: Peter Smith, 1952.

Higgs, Robert J. *Sports: A Reference Guide.* Westport, CT: Greenwood Press, 1982.

Kieran, John. *The American Sporting Scene.* New York: MacMillan, 1941.

Manchester, Herbert. *Four Centuries of Sport in America, 1490–1890.* New York: Derrydale Press, 1931.

Newcombe, Jack. *The Fireside Book of Football.* New York: Random House, 1964.

Oxford Companion to World Sports and Games, The. London: Oxford University Press, 1975.

Ratliff, Harold V. *Towering Texans: Sports Sagas of the Lone Star State.* San Antonio: Naylor Company, 1950.

Spivey, Donald, ed. *Sport in America: New Historical Perspectives.* Westport, CT: Greenwood Press, 1985.

Sports Illustrated 1994 Sports Almanac, The. Boston: Little Brown, 1994.

Yee, Min S., ed. *The Sports Book.* New York: Holt, Rinehart, and Winston, 1975.

Appendix

Provincial Governors of Texas

Antonio Martínez, 1817–22
José Félix Trespalacios, 1822–23
Luciano García, 1823

Governors of Coahuila y Texas

Rafael González, 1824–26
José Ignacio de Arizpe, 1826
Victor Blanco, 1826–27
José Ignacio de Arizpe, 1827
José María Viesca (provisional)
Victor Blanco, 1827
José María Viesca, 1827–30
Rafael Eca y Músquiz, 1830–31
José María Viesca, 1831
José María de Letona, 1831–32
Rafael Eca y Músquiz, 1832–33
Juan Martín de Veramendi, 1833
Francisco Vidaurri y Villaseñor,
  1833–34
Juan José Elguezábal, 1834–35
José María Cantú, 1835
Marciel Borrego, 1835
Agustín Viesca, 1835

Miguel Falcón, 1835
Bartolomé de Cárdenas, 1835
Rafael Eca y Músquiz 1835
Henry Smith, Nov. 14, 1835–
March 1, 1836 (Provisional
during Texas War for Indepen-
dence)

Presidents of Texas

David G. Burnet	March 17, 1836–Oct. 22, 1836
Sam Houston	Oct. 22, 1836–Dec. 10, 1838
Mirabeau B. Lamar	Dec. 10, 1838–Dec. 13, 1841
Sam Houston	Dec. 13, 1841–Dec. 9, 1844
Anson Jones	Dec. 9, 1844–Feb. 19, 1846

Governors of Texas

J. Pinckney Henderson	Feb. 19, 1846–Dec. 21, 1847
George T. Wood	Dec. 21, 1847–Dec. 21, 1849
P. Hansborough Bell	Dec. 21, 1849–Nov. 23, 1853
J. W. Henderson	Nov. 23, 1853–Dec. 21, 1853
Elisha M. Pease	Dec. 21, 1853–Dec. 21, 1857
Hardin R. Runnels	Dec. 21, 1857–Dec. 21, 1859
Sam Houston	Dec. 21, 1859–March 16, 1861
Edward Clark	March 16, 1861–Nov. 7, 1861
Francis R. Lubbock	Nov. 7, 1861–Nov. 5, 1863
Pendleton Murrah	Nov. 5, 1863–June 17, 1865
Andrew J. Hamilton	June 17, 1865–Aug. 9, 1866 Provisional
James W. Throckmorton	Aug. 9, 1866—Aug. 8, 1867
Elisha M. Pease	Aug. 8, 1867–Sept. 30, 1869 Provisional
Edmund J. Davis	Jan. 8, 1870–April 28, 1870 Provisional
Edmund J. Davis	April 28, 1870–Jan. 15, 1874
Richard Coke	Jan. 15, 1874–Dec. 1, 1876
Richard B. Hubbard	Dec. 1, 1876–Jan. 21, 1879
Oran M. Roberts	Jan. 21, 1879–Jan 16, 1883
John Ireland	Jan. 16, 1883–Jan. 18 1887
Lawrence Sullivan Ross	Jan. 18, 1887–Jan. 20, 1891
James Stephen Hogg	Jan. 20, 1891–Jan. 15, 1895
Charles A. Culberson	Jan. 15, 1895–Jan. 17, 1899
Joseph D. Sayers	Jan. 17, 1899–Jan. 20, 1903
S. W. T. Lanham	Jan. 20, 1903–Jan. 15, 1907
Thomas M. Campbell	Jan. 15, 1907–Jan. 17, 1911
Oscar Branch Colquitt	Jan. 17, 1911–Jan. 19, 1915
James E. Ferguson	Jan. 19, 1915–Sept. 25, 1917
William Pettus Hobby	Sept. 25, 1917–Jan. 18, 1921
Pat Morris Neff	Jan. 18, 1921–Jan. 20, 1925
Miriam A. Ferguson	Jan. 20, 1925–Jan. 18, 1927

Dan Moody	Jan. 18, 1927–Jan. 20, 1931
Ross S. Sterling	Jan. 20, 1931–Jan. 17, 1933
Miriam A. Ferguson	Jan. 17, 1933–Jan. 15, 1935
James V. Allred	Jan. 15, 1935–Jan. 15, 1939
W. Lee O'Daniel	Jan. 15, 1939–Aug. 4, 1941
Coke R. Stevenson	Aug. 4, 1941–Jan. 21, 1947
Beauford H. Jester	Jan. 21, 1947–July 11, 1949
Allan Shivers	July 11, 1949–Jan. 15, 1957
Price Daniel	Jan. 15, 1957–Jan. 15, 1963
John Connally	Jan. 15, 1963–Jan. 21, 1969
Preston Smith	Jan. 21, 1969–Jan. 16, 1973
Dolph Briscoe	Jan. 16, 1973–Jan. 16, 1979
William Clements	Jan. 16, 1979–Jan. 18, 1983
Mark White	Jan. 18, 1983–Jan. 20, 1987
William P. Clements, Jr.	Jan. 20, 1987–Jan. 15, 1991
Ann Richards	Jan. 15, 1991–Jan. 17, 1995
George W. Bush	Jan. 17, 1995–Jan. 17, 2000
Rick Perry	Jan. 17, 2000–

United States Senators

Sam Houston	Feb. 21, 1846–March 4, 1859
Thomas J. Rusk	Feb. 21, 1846–July 29, 1857
J. Pinckney Henderson	Nov. 9, 1857–June 4, 1858
Matthias Ward	Sept. 29, 1858–Dec. 5, 1859
John Hemphill	March 4, 1859–July 11, 1861
Louis T. Wigfall	1859–1861 (Went to Confederate Senate)
Morgan C. Hamilton	Feb. 22, 1870–March 3, 1877
James W. Flanagan	Feb. 22, 1870–March 3, 1875
Samuel B. Maxey	March 3, 1875–March 3, 1887
Richard Coke	March 3, 1877–March 3, 1895
John H. Reagan	March 3, 1887–June 10, 1891
Horace Chilton	Dec. 7, 1891–March 30, 1892
Roger Q. Mills	March 30, 1892–March 3, 1899
Horace Chilton	March 3, 1895–March 3, 1901
Charles A. Culberson	March 3, 1899–March 4, 1923
Joseph W. Bailey	March 3, 1901–Jan. 8, 1913
R. M. Johnson	Jan. 8, 1913–Feb. 3, 1913
Morris Sheppard	Feb. 13, 1913–April 9, 1941
Earle B. Mayfield	March 4, 1923–March 4, 1929
Tom Connally	March 4, 1929–Jan. 3, 1953
Andrew Jackson Houston	April 21, 1941–June 26, 1941

W. Lee O'Daniel	Aug. 4, 1941–Jan. 3, 1949
Lyndon B. Johnson	Jan. 3, 1949–Jan. 20, 1961
Price Daniel	Jan. 3, 1953–Jan. 15, 1957
William A. Blakley	Jan. 13, 1957–April 19, 1957
Ralph W. Yarborough	April 19, 1957–Jan. 12, 1971
William A. Blakley	Jan. 20, 1961–June 15, 1961
John G. Tower	June 15, 1961–Jan. 21, 1985
Lloyd Bentsen	Jan. 12, 1971–Jan. 20, 1993
Phil Gramm	Jan. 21, 1985–Nov. 30, 2002
Robert Krueger	Jan. 20, 1993–June 14, 1993
Kay Bailey Hutchison	June 14, 1993–
John Cornyn	Dec. 1, 2002–

Index

industry and, 283; Civil War and, 106, 109; oil industry and, 199, 290, 305; post-Reconstruction, 122; Reconstruction and, 114–15; Tejanos and, 205–06, 209
Edey, George W., 192–93
education: Briscoe and, 197; Bush and, 202, 303; during Civil War, 113; in colonial Texas, 56; Connally and, 195–96; desegregation of, 231–40, 244–45; in early statehood, 90, 98; financing of, 146; funding for, 137, 186; Lamar and, 77–78; politics and, 184; post-Reconstruction, 134–36; Reconstruction and, 115; Red Scare and, 192–93; reforms in, 148, 153, 198–99, 262; teacher salaries, 185–86, 193, 196; Tejanos and, 208, 214; for Texas Rangers, 316; women and, 257; WPA and, 172
Education Bill of 1839, 77
Education Reform Act (1984), 198–99
Edwards, Benjamin, 61–62
Edwards, Haden, 54, 61–62
Eisenhower, Dwight D., 176, 185, 190, 237, 297
Elizondo, Ignacia, 47
Elliot, Charles, 83
El Paso, TX, 25, 210, 214, 218
England, 83
Enron Corporation scandal, 304–05
Enstam, Elizabeth, 262
environment, 200, 300–304
Ernst family, 253
Escandón, José de, 30, 219
Estevanico, 3, 9, 23, 24

Fannin, James, 68, 69
Farenthold, Frances, 196–97, 267
Farias, Gómez, 66
Farmers' Alliance, 124, 125–26, 136, 261
Federal Art Project, 172
Federal Emergency Relief Act, 169
Federal Power Commission, 292
Federal Theatre Project, 172
Federal Writers' Project, 172
Ferguson, James E.: governorship of, 147–50; "Ma" Ferguson and, 154–55, 161, 168–69; O'Daniel and, 175; progressivism and, 157; Texas Rangers and, 311
Ferguson, Miriam A.: Depression and, 168–70; first term, 151, 154–55, 157, 264; race for third term, 175; second term, 265; Texas Rangers and, 312–13
filibusters, 33–34, 43–50, 252
Fisher, William, 79–80
flag, of State of Texas, 87–88
Folsom culture, 3–4
football, 321–34
Ford, John Salmon, 17, 46–48, 89, 96, 309, 310
Foreman, George, 344
Forsyth, John, 74

forts, 17, 25, 94, 96–97, 250
Fort Worth, TX, 94, 172, 176, 177, 240
France: Indians and, 13; possessions of, 31, 41, 42, 252; Spain and, 29, 251; Texas and, 10, 28, 83; trade with, 80
Franciscan missionaries, 26–33, 250, 257
Fredonia Republic, 54, 61–62
Freedman's Bureau, 114, 115, 116
Freedom Rides, 241
French and Indian War, 31, 41
Fucci, Charles, 346

Gainey, Bob, 346
Galbraith, John Kenneth, 164
Galey, J. H., 288
Galveston, TX: Civil War and, 108, 109, 112, 116; filibusters and, 49–50; shipwreck, 3, 23, 248; trade, 100; World War II and, 177
Galveston Bay and Texas Land Company, 54
Gálvez, José de, 42
Garay, Francisco de, 23
Garner, John Nance, 167, 168, 171, 173, 178
Garrison, Homer, Jr., 314–17
Gates, John W., 280
Gay, Bettie, 261
General Colonization Laws, 52, 53
geography, 6, 35, 219–22, 248
Gib Morgan (legend), 292
G.I. Forum, 220
Giles, Bascom, 188–89
Gilmer-Aikin Act, 185
Glanville, Jerry, 334
Glidden, Joseph, 280
Golden Triangle, 220–22
golf, 342–43
Goliad, TX, 69, 88
Good Neighbor Commission, 179, 184
Goodnight, Charles, 279
Gore, Al, 202
Goree, Thomas J., 131–34
Gossett, Leo, 317
Gould, Charles, 291
Gould, Jay, 131
Goyen, William, 253
Grange, the, 117, 124–25, 261
Grantham, Dewey W., 141
Grant, Ulysses S., 18
Grayson, Peter, 66, 74, 75
Great Depression, 159, 164–75, 264, 312
Greenback movement, 124, 125
Green, Tom, 108
Gregory, Thomas Watt, 147
Groce, Jared E., 52, 55
Guerra, Manuel, 213, 220
Guerraro, Lena, 200
Guerrero, Delores, 266
Guerrero, Vicente, 50, 62, 63
Guffey, J. M., 288

oil industry and, 298–99; tidelands question and, 189–90
Johnson, Matthew, 242–43
Johnston, Albert Sidney, 97, 108
Joiner, C. M., 292–93
Jones, Anson, 81, 83
Jones, Jerry, 332, 333
Jones, Jesse H., 160, 165, 167, 168, 171
Jones, John B., 311
Jones, John J., 231–32
Jones, Marvin, 167, 168
Joplin, Janis, 267
Jordan, Barbara, 229, 267
July, Joanna, 260
Jumanos Indians, 7–8, 10–11, 12

Karankawa Indians, 6–7, 11, 14, 248, 250, 253
Kelly, George "Machine-Gun," 313
Kemper, Samuel, 47
Kendall, George Wilkins, 77
Kennard, Don, 317
Key, V. O., Jr., 155
Kickapoo Indians, 14, 15, 20, 76
King, Martin Luther, Jr., 240–41
Kiowa Indians, 11, 13, 17–20, 255
Kirby, John Henry, 129
Kirk, Ron, 244
Klevenhagen, John, 315
Knight, Bobby, 340
Knights of Labor, 117, 130–31
Knights of the Golden Circle, 106–07
Knights of the Rising Sun, 116
Kokernot brothers, 281–82
Kuba, Louis, 242
Ku Klux Klan, 150–51, 154–55, 159–61

La Bahía del Espíritu Santo, 33, 47, 48, 250
labor: laws, 185; legal reforms, 146; migrant workers, 210–11, 214, 216–17; in oil industry, 292, 295–96, 302–03; railroad unions, 130–31, 152–53; Tejanos, 210–12, 215; Texas Rangers and, 316; women, 264; World War II and, 177
La Branche, Alcee, 74
Lafitte, Jean, 49–50
Lamar, Mirabeau B., 14, 15, 74, 75–76
land grants: empresarial system, 43, 51, 53–55, 61; Law of April 6,1830 and, 53, 54, 62–64; to railroads, 127; Spaniards and, 35; Tejanos and, 206–07, 212
Landry, Tom, 330, 331–32
Langlois, Pierre, 344
Lanham, S. W. T., 145
La Salle , René Robert, Cavalier Sieur de, 10, 28, 40, 250
Law of April 6, 1830, 53, 54, 62–64
Layne, Bobby, 329

League of United Latin American Citizens (LULAC), 215, 220, 264, 266
Lee, Robert E., 97
Lewis, Carl, 347
lifestyles, 55, 89–93, 113–14, 219–20, 249–50
Linn, John, 87
Lipan (Apache) Indians, 11, 12, 13
Littlefield, Clyde, 346
Lively (schooner), 52
livestock. See ranching
Llano culture, 3–4
Lockhart, Matilda, 255
Lockridge, J. E., 229
Lone Star Conference, 324, 327, 328
Long, James, 43, 49, 252
Long, Jane, 49–50, 252
longhorns. See ranching
Louisiana Purchase, 33, 41, 60
Love, Thomas B., 150, 157, 159–60
Loving, Oliver, 279
Lubbock, Francis R., 107
Lucas, A. F., 287–88
lumber industry, 128–29, 163, 290
Lutcher, Henry J., 129
lynchings, 102, 108, 179, 184
Lytle, John, 276, 278

Machuca, Mrs. J. C., 264
Mackenzie, Murdo, 282
MacKenzie, Ranald S., 20
Magee, Augustus, 43, 46–48, 251
Magruder, John Bankhead, 107
Mahon, George, 167
Major Soccer League (MSL), 345
Manifest Destiny, 39–41, 81, 88, 256
manufacturing, 107, 109–10, 114, 117
March on Washington (1963), 241
Marshall, Thurgood, 227, 231–34, 236–37
Martin, Anna, 262
Martínez, Antonio María, 34, 51, 52
Martin, Slater, 338
Masters, B. E., 237
Matador Land and Cattle Company, 282
Matson, Randy, 346
Maverick, Mary, 255–56
Mayfield, Earle B., 151, 160–61
McAddo, William Gibbs, 159–60
McCarthy, Joseph, 298
McCarthy, Joseph R., Jr., 191–93
McClellan, George, 94
McClung, John, 172
McCoy, Joseph, 275
McCulloch, Ben, 16, 89, 310, 311
McFaddin, Perry, 281
McLeod, Hugh, 77
McMahon, Samuel Doak, 55
McMillan, Ernie, 242–43
McNelly, Leander, 311

Medina River, Battle of, 34, 251
Mellon, Andrew W., 164
Mendoza, Antonio de, 24
Mesta system, 30–31
Mexia, José Antonio, 65
Mexican Americans: African Americans and, 243–44; business of, 207–08, 214–15; employment, 217–18; higher education, 235; history of, 205–23; new vs. old, 209–13; politics and, 208–09, 212–15, 221, 267; progressivism and, 156; racism and, 179, 184, 209; in ranching, 206, 278; strikes, 211–12, 316–17; Texas Rangers and, 316; voting rights, 229; women, 215, 220, 259–60, 264–65, 266
Mexican Texas, 59–60
Mexican War, 88–89, 256, 310
Mexico: Anglos and, 39–40; independence, 14, 34, 41, 50; Lamar and, 77; Texan independence, 23
Mier expedition, 79–80
migrant farm workers, 210–11, 214, 216–17, 316–17
Milam, Ben, 68
Miles, Nelson A., 20
military: Civil War and, 106–08, 111–12; customs collections, 64; women in, 263, 265; World War II and, 176
Mina, Francisco Xavier, 50
Minime, Gabriel, 250
Miró, Esteban, 43
missions, 8–9, 10, 12–13, 25–34, 249, 250
Mississippian culture, 5–6, 8–9, 12–13
Missouri Compromise, 82–83
Moe, Doug, 340
Molyneaux, Peter, 158
Monroe, James, 48
Montemayor, Alice Dickerson, 264
Moody, Dan, 151, 155–58, 160, 161, 163
Moore, G. Bedell, 129
Moore, John, 67
Morales, Dan, 244
Morelos, José María, 44, 50
Morgan, James, 255
Morgan, William, 43
Morrill Act, 135
Moscoso de Alvarado, Luis de, 9–10, 11
Muldoon, Father Michael, 55
Murchison, Clint, 192, 291, 294, 297, 331, 332
Murphy, Audie, 176
Murrah, Pendleton, 107
Mutcher, Gus, 196

Nacogdoches, TX: education in, 56; filibusters and, 46–48, 252; independence proclamation, 47; revolution and, 61, 64–65; settlement of, 32, 44–45

Narváez, Pánfilo de, 3, 23, 248
National Association for the Advancement of Colored People (NAACP), 226–37, 266
National Labor Relations Board, 296
National Social Security Act, 172
National Youth Administration (NYA), 171–72
Native Americans. *See* American Indians
natural gas, 291–92, 296, 301
Neal, Margie, 264
Neblett, Elizabeth Scott, 258
Neches, Battle of, 15
Neff, Pat M., 151–54, 160, 264
Neighbors, Robert S., 17–18, 95–96
Neill, James C., 68
Nelson, Byron, 342
Neutral Ground agreement, 33, 45
Newcomb, W. W., Jr., 6
New Deal, 167, 168–70, 171–73, 178, 189
New Laws of 1543, 25
New Washington Association, 255
Nimitz, Chester A., 176
Nixon, Richard M., 229
Nixon v. *Herndon*, 156
Niza, Fray Marcos de, 24
Nolan, Philip, 43–44
Norris, Samuel, 61
Nuestra Señora de Guadalupe de Zacatecas, 26–32
Nuevo León, 25
Nuevo Santander, 30

O'Daniel, Wilbert Lee, 173–75, 294–95, 314
O'Donoju, Juan, 50
oil and gas industry: in 1929, 163; in 1980s, 199; conservation, 290; current trends, 305–06; discovery, 122, 138; economy and, 290–91; environment and, 300–304; history of, 287–306; laws regulating, 291; overproduction, 293, 298–99; politics and, 303–04, 306, 297300; prorationing, 291–94, 298; stock market crash, 165, 166; taxes and, 193–94, 198–99, 280, 291, 294–95, 298; tidelands question, 189, 297; universities and, 78, 135; wells, 288–94; World War II and, 177, 180
Olajuwon, Hakeem, 339, 341
Oldham, W. S., 111
Olivares, Fray Antonio, 29
Oliver, Eddie, 315
Olmstead, Frederick Law, 90–91, 92, 100
Oñate, Juan de, 25
O'Neal, Shaquille, 342
Onís, Luis de, 48
Operation Dixie, 185
Order of the Sons of America (OAS), 215
Organic Law, 67
Organization of Petroleum Exporting Countries (OPEC), 299

Ortiz Parrilla, Diego, 13
O'Sullivan, John L., 256
Otey, Martha Anne, 123
Owsley, Alvin, 161

Padrón, María Rosa, 251
Paleo Indians, 3–4
Panic of 1819, 51
Panic of 1837, 74, 78
Pardee, Jack, 334
Paredes, Mariano, 88
Parilla, Diego Ortiz, 11
Parker, Bonnie, 265, 311, 313
Parker, Cynthia Ann, 14, 18, 97–98, 256
Parker, Quanah, 18–19, 20, 98, 256
Parks, Rosa, 241
Parr, George, 187–88
Parsons, Jeff, 254
Peace of Paris, 31, 41, 42
Pease, Elisha M., 96, 99
Pedraza, Gómez, 63
Pennybacker, Anna, 262
Peoples, Clint, 315, 317
People's party, 124, 126, 141–42, 261
Peoples Party II, 242
Permian Basin, 305
Perot, H. Ross, 198
Perpetuities and Corporations Land Law
    (1993), 137
Perry, Henry, 47
Perry, Rick, 305
Peta Nocona, 18, 97, 256
petroleum industry. *See* oil and gas industry
Petticoat Lobby, 150, 264
Philips, O. A., 333–34
Pickett, Bill, 347
Piedras, José de las, 64–65
Pierce, Abel H., 277
Pierce, Henry Clay, 143
Pike, Zebulon, 45
Pilgrim, Thomas J., 55–56
Piney Woods, 28, 31, 163
pipeline safety act, 301
Piper, Edward, 273
Plan of Iguala, 50
Plessy v. *Ferguson*, 179, 234, 236
Plum Creek battle, 76
Plummer, Rachel, 14
Poinsett, Joel, 62
politics: in 1928, 163–64; in 1932, 167; African
    Americans and, 227–31, 243–44, 267; Anglo
    settlers and, 40, 60, 63; Baileyism and, 143–
    44; business and, 151; of Caddos, 8;
    corruption in, 156, 160, 168–70, 186–88, 196;
    in early statehood, 93; Grangers and, 124–
    25; military and, 111; oilmen and, 297–300,
    303–04, 306; post-Reconstruction, 131–38;
    post–World War II, 183–203; progressivism,

141–61; prohibition and, 144; Reconstruction
    and, 116, 121; reforms, 145–46, 203;
    Sharpstown affair, 196; Tejanos and, 208–09,
    212–13, 215, 220, 221, 243–44; Texas Rangers
    and, 312; two-party system, 194–95; women
    in, 149–50, 229, 247–48, 260–61, 263, 264,
    265, 267–68
Polk, James K., 81–82, 83, 88
poll tax, 142, 228–30
Ponton, Andrew, 67
population: in 1850s, 98–99; in 1929, 163;
    Indians, 21; in Mexican Texas, 62; post-
    Reconstruction, 123; recent, 203; Recon-
    struction and, 115; Tejanos, 206, 213, 243;
    during World War II, 180
Populism, 124, 126, 141–42, 261
Potter-Blocker Trail (Potter-Bacon), 279
Prairie View A&M University, 135, 233, 339
Prairie View Normal and Industrial College.
    See Prairie View A&M University
Preemption Act, 99
presidios, 11, 13, 25, 26, 29–30
Primer Congreso Mexicanista, 215
prison system, 131–33, 137, 146, 153, 155, 156,
    193
Progressive Era, 247
Progressive Voters League, 226, 228
progressivism, 141–61, 262
prohibition, 141, 145, 147, 149, 152, 159–60,
    260–61
Provisional Government, 68
Public Works Administration (PWA), 171, 172
Pueblo peoples, 5, 6, 7–8, 12
Purvis, Hardy, 315

Quakers, 18
Quick, Edward, 45

racism, 59, 150–51, 206, 212, 218–19, 225–45
Raggio, Louise, 266–67
Railroad Commission, 137, 291–92, 293–95,
    298, 300–301
railroads: Civil War/Reconstruction and, 107,
    114; development, 99, 127–28; Grange and,
    124; labor unions and, 130; lumber industry
    and, 128–29; oil industry and, 289, 290;
    ranching and, 127, 275, 278; urban
    development and, 129–30
Rainey, Homer Price, 178, 184–85, 191, 228
Rainwater, Richard, 303
Ramírez, Sara Estela, 220
Ramsey, Ben, 188
ranching: colonialism and, 30–31, 32; history
    of, 273–84; legislation for, 168; post-
    Reconstruction, 126–27; Reconstruction
    and, 114; Tejanos and, 206, 207, 210, 223; in
    West Texas, 222; women in, 251, 259, 281;
    World War II and, 180

The Texas Heritage, Fourth Edition
Developmental editor and copy editior: Andrew J. Davidson
Production editor: Lucy Herz
Proofreader: Claudia Siler
Cartographers: Jane Domier and James Bier
Indexer: Pat Rimmer
Cover designer: DePinto Graphic Design
Printer: McNaughton & Gunn, Inc.